This pose of a Roman senator addressing the Senate is based on that of the famous life-sized bronze statue called the Arringhatore ("Haranguer") discovered at Lake Trasimene in 1566. Dating from the late second or early third century B.C., it represents a magistrate making a speech. Even in the twentieth century, strongly nationalistic leaders copied this pose when addressing the people.
BBC Copyright Photograph

ALLYN AND BACON, INC.
Newton, Massachusetts

Jenney's

FIRST YEAR
LATIN

Charles Jenney, Jr.
Belmont Hill School
Belmont, Massachusetts

Rogers V. Scudder
Groton School
Groton, Massachusetts

Eric C. Baade
Brooks School
North Andover, Massachusetts

Illustration: Roman general
reporting to the Senate
BBC Copyright Photograph

Cover: Chariot Race
From the MGM release *Ben Hur*
© 1959 Loew's Incorporated

KEY FEATURES OF *FIRST YEAR LATIN*

(Page references are given for selected examples of each feature.)

- Presentation of the language in an orderly, systematic fashion

  Forms: clear presentation, often in chart form, of new structures (*pp. 9, 156, 309*)

  Syntax: simple explanation of how forms are used (*pp. 10, 156, 309*)

  Vocabulary: traditional Latin-English word lists in alphabetical order, according to parts of speech (*pp. 11, 157, 310*)

  Exercises: numerous practice materials involving the manipulation of English into Latin and Latin into English (*pp. 12–13, 157–159, 311–312*)

  Readings: brief readings using new words and structures (*pp. 13, 159, 312*)

  Review: cumulative review lessons for reinforcement of vocabulary, forms and syntax (*pp. 24, 185, 357*)

- Influence of Latin on English and other languages

  Word Studies: additional background material on selected vocabulary (*pp. 62–63, 171, 343*)

  Word Formation: use of prefixes and suffixes to change word meaning (*pp. 467–468*)

- Roman Civilization

  Photographic presentation: arrangement of photos in special categories to present a comprehensive view of Roman culture (*pp. 17, 288–289, 332–333*)

  Literary presentation: special background material about the various art categories (*pp. 379–424*)

- Enrichment features

  Supplementary reading selections (*pp. 365–378*)

  Latin expressions encountered in English (*pp. 425–429*)

  Comprehensive Appendix (*pp. 431–522*)

- Supplementary Aids

  Teacher's Resource Guide with Testing Program

  Workbook

ISBN 0-205-08723-0

Printed in the United States of America

8 9 94

WHY STUDY LATIN?

We realize that it is very important to today's students to select school subjects that will have relevance and meaning for their future. Therefore, we wish to compliment you on your choice of Latin. It is a choice that you will never regret.

It is very true that it is no easy task to learn the material presented in this book. There is no short cut to mastering the forms and syntax of the Latin language. Do not have any qualms, however, about what you are about to do. The rewards that you will reap from this undertaking will benefit you the rest of your life and it will be well worth the effort you put into it now.

At this time you are taking the preparatory steps for your adult life. If you have plans to go on to college or are dreaming of a career that requires training beyond high school, the best service you can perform for yourself is to learn how to study and how to absorb the greatest amount of learning in the shortest possible time. The study of Latin can help you to do this. It trains the memory, it gives you increased word power, it provides the opportunity to develop your reasoning powers, and strengthens your reading skills.

Due to modern technology in the fields of transportation and communication, the world is becoming smaller and smaller. Therefore, it is becoming increasingly more important to know the languages of other lands. The study of Latin is invaluable if you wish to learn other languages, for it makes it possible for you to acquire an understanding of the very nature of language. Latin is the perfect specimen language. It is predictable in its syntax and within two years one can learn all there is to know about Latin grammar. Then from Latin, you can branch out into the Romance languages—French, Italian, Spanish, Portuguese and Rumanian. The study of these languages is greatly enhanced and facilitated by knowledge of "the mother tongue."

More than half of the words of the English language come directly or indirectly from Latin, and it has been estimated that you can add from 500–1,000 English words to your vocabulary every year you study Latin. One of the greatest assets you can have when you enter the marketplace is the gift of speech. Being well-spoken can be a great advantage to you in job interviews and on the job itself. The study of Latin can improve your speaking skills by making you well versed in proper grammar and providing you with a colorful vocabulary. In the same way the study of Latin can help your writing skills. Completing questionnaires and writing reports and summaries are important aspects of many jobs. Learning how to do this can be one of the bonuses derived from language study.

The study of Latin will initiate you into a great heritage—not only the study of the language itself, but the knowledge of the culture and civilization of Rome will enrich your life and touch upon many other fields of endeavor—art, music, mythology, literature, architecture and law.

Educated people of all nations have studied Latin for two thousand years. Don't you want to be in this number?

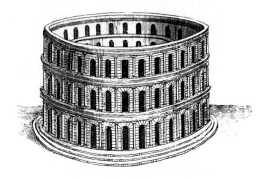

CONTENTS

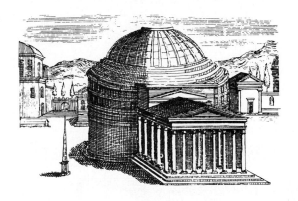

Wall with garden from House of Livia, Terme Museum, Rome

INTRODUCTION

Both Latin and English, as well as most modern European languages, the Slavic languages, and some Near Eastern languages, are descendants of the same parent-language; this parent-language is usually called *Indo-European*. But although the two languages are basically similar in structure, the differences between them far outweigh the similarities. There are two reasons for this: one is that Latin represents a much earlier stage of development; the other is that the Latin which we read is a highly artificial creation developed by the Romans for literary and political purposes and is consequently somewhat different in construction from any language used for everyday purposes.

INFLECTION

It is characteristic of the older languages of the Indo-European group that they express the relation of words to each other (syntax) by changes in the endings of the words rather than, as in English and other younger languages, by word order and the use of prepositions and auxiliary verbs. These changes of endings are called *inflection*. The inflection of nouns, adjectives, and pronouns is called *declension*, that of verbs *conjugation*.

English words are inflected very little: a normal English verb has only three forms, e.g. *make, makes, made* (all other uses are dealt with by the use of such auxiliaries as *is, was, will, has, should* and *might*). An English noun has four forms, e.g. *boy, boy's, boys, boys'*. A regular transitive verb in Latin has more than a hundred forms; a regular noun has twelve.

CASES OF NOUNS

A Latin noun has six cases; their basic uses are as follows:

1. **The Nominative** names the subject of the sentence, i.e. whatever the statement or question is about: The *boy* runs.

2. The **Vocative** is the case of direct address: Look, *Marcus!*

3. The **Genitive** is used to enable a noun to qualify another noun in some way; most of its uses are represented in English by prepositional phrases with *of*; the gardens *of Caesar*; part *of the army*; love *of life*; a man *of distinction*.

4. The **Dative** expresses the object indirectly affected by the action of a verb or by the quality of an adjective (*to* or *for* in English): I gave a book *to him*. He did it *for you*. She is unfriendly *to me*. This is suitable *for warfare*.

5. **The Accusative** limits the action of the verb in various ways, i.e. it tells how far the action of the verb extends: She went *home*. I ran a *mile*. He saw a *bird*. I stayed three *days*.

6. The **Ablative,** having taken over the functions of three separate cases of the parent Indo-European language, has three basic uses: It expresses separation (*from*): He comes *from New York*. She fainted *from hunger*. This book was written *by* (i.e. comes *from*) *Dickens*. It expresses location, either in space or in time (*in, on, at*): *at seven o'clock; on Tuesday; in Italy*. It expresses the instrument by which, or the circumstances under which, an action takes place (*with*): She jumped *with joy*. We dig *with shovels*. He came *with his father*.

GENDER OF NOUNS

In English, gender is determined by sex: words naming males are nouns of the masculine gender, words naming females are nouns of the feminine gender, and words naming things are nouns of the neuter gender. In Latin, too, nouns naming males and females are masculine and feminine respectively, and many names of things are neuter. There are also, however, a great many names of things, inanimate objects, abstract qualities, names of actions, etc., which are not neuter, but masculine or feminine.

TENSES OF VERBS

A Latin verb has six tenses, one of which, the perfect, is used in two different ways. Here are the uses of the tenses:

Present tenses: The *present* describes an action as going on in the present, or as generally true: *He is sleeping. A rolling stone gathers no moss.* The *perfect* describes an action as completed by the present time: *We have come to see the city.*

Past tenses: The *perfect* is also used, like the English past tense, merely to state that an action took place in the past, without further qualifying it: *I arrived yesterday.* The *imperfect* describes an action as going on (not completed) at some time in the past: *When I arrived, he was leaving.* The *pluperfect* describes an action as already completed by some time in the past: *When I arrived, he had left.*

Future tenses: The *future* describes an action as taking place in the future: *He will refuse to go.* The *future perfect* describes an action as completed by some time in the future: *By this time tomorrow I shall have met my friend.* The future and future perfect tenses are much more common in Latin than in English. "I'm going when the sun sets" must be changed to "I shall go when the sun will have set" in order to be translated into Latin.

PRONUNCIATION OF LATIN

The Alphabet. The Latin alphabet is like the English, except that it has no *j* or *w*. The division of the letters into vowels and consonants is the same as in English, except that *i*, when it occurs between vowels or before a vowel at the beginning of a word, is a consonant. The letter *y* is always a vowel, and occurs only in words of Greek origin.

Vowels. Each vowel in Latin has two sounds, long and short. The quantity of a vowel is indicated by a line (called a *macron*) above it if it is long; short vowels are unmarked. The vowels are pronounced as follows:

LONG	SHORT
ā as in *father*	a as in *idea*
ē as in *obey*	e as in *bet*
ī as in *machine*	i as in *sit*
ō as in *note*	o as in *omit*
ū as in *rule* (never as in pupil)	u as in *put*

The letter *y* is pronounced like the French *u* or the German *ü* (form the lips as if to say *oo*, but say *ee* instead).

Diphthongs. Latin has six diphthongs (combinations of two vowels to make a single sound), pronounced as follows:

ae like *aye*	*eu* like *ay-oo*, said as one syllable
au like *ow* in *now*	*oe* like *oy* in *joy*
ei as in *neighbor*	*ui* like *uee* in *queen*

Consonants. The consonants are pronounced as in English, with the following exceptions:

bs is pronounced like *ps*
bt is pronounced like *pt*
c is always hard, as in *came* (never soft, as in city)
ch is pronounced as in *character*
g is always hard, as in *go* (never soft, as in gem)

gu before a vowel is pronounced as in *anguish*

i (when a consonant) is like *y* in *youth*

ph is pronounced as in *philosophy*

s is pronounced as in *sit* (it never has the z sound, as in busy)

su before a vowel is sometimes pronounced like *sw*, as in *suave*

th is pronounced as in *thick* (not as in this)

v is pronounced like *w*

z is like *dz* in *adze*

The letters *x* and *z* are called *double consonants* (as representing *ks* and *dz*). Every consonant must be sounded in pronouncing a Latin word; doubled consonants should not be run together but pronounced separately.

Syllabification. Each Latin word has as many syllables as it has vowels or diphthongs. Consonantal *i* is not counted as a vowel, nor is *u* when it has the sound of English *w* after *g*, *q*, and sometimes *s*.

> **ae di fi′ ci um   du o dē vī gin′tī   gau′di um   iu′be ō**
> **lin′gua   per suā′de ō   su′us**

The rules for the division of Latin words into syllables are:

1. A consonant between two vowels or diphthongs is pronounced with the following syllable: **dē′li gō   nu′me rus   o′cu lus   Trō iā′nus**

2. In a group of two or more consonants, only the last consonant is pronounced with the following syllable; but if the last consonant in the group is *h*, *l*, or *r*, preceded by *c*, *g*, *p*, *b*, *d*, or *t*, both these consonants are usually pronounced with the following syllable:

> **a gri′co la   am′plus   ap pro pin′quō   Co rin′thus**
> **dif fi cul′tās   quat tu or′de cim   tem pes′tās**

3. Of the double consonants, *x* goes with the preceding syllable, *z* with the following: **aux i′li um   gā′za**

4. In a compound word the prefix is separated from the rest of the word: **cōn scrī′bō   in ter′e ō**

The last syllable of a Latin word is called the *ultima*, the next to last the *penult*, and the one before that the *antepenult*.

Length of Syllables. Syllables are classified as long or short, depending on the length of time it takes to pronounce them. The Romans thought that it took twice as long to pronounce a long syllable as it did a short one. Since we are used to making such distinctions in length of syllables only in singing, it is difficult for us to reproduce this pronunciation; but we must learn to identify long syllables in order to accent words correctly. A syllable which contains a long vowel or a diphthong is said to be *long by nature*. A syllable whose vowel is followed by two or more consonants or by a double consonant (*x* or *z*) is said to be *long by position*. Other syllables are *short*. If a short vowel is followed by two consonants, the first of which is *c*, *g*, *p*, *b*, *d*, or *t*, and the second of which is *l* or *r*, the syllable is *common*: i.e., it may be treated as either long by position or short.

Accents. A word of two syllables is accented on the first. In words of three or more syllables the accent is on the penult if it is long (either by nature or by position); if the penult is short the accent falls on the antepenult. Except in monosyllables the ultima is never accented.

ca la′mi tās   fa cul′tās   ge′nus   oc′ci dō   oc cī′dō

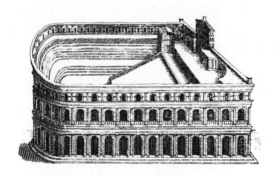

ITALIA

Roman Roads

0   50   100   150
Scale of Miles

Danuvius Fl.

Lacus Venetus

Helvetii

RHAETIA

NORICUM

GALLIA TRANSALPINA

Lepontii

Venonetes

Salassi

Euganei

Carni

PANNONIA

Mediolanum

GALLIA

VENETIA

ISTRIA

Ligures

Placentia

CISALPINA

Duria Fl.

ILLYRICUM

Rubicon Fl.

Florentia

Metaurus

UMBRI

Picentes

Mare Adriaticum

CYRNOS (CORSICA)

Etrusci

Lacus Trasumenus

Tarquinii

Veii

Cures

Sabini

Alba

Roma

Praeneste

Marsi

Ostia

M. Albanus

Alba Longa

TIUM

Samnites

APULIA

Ardea

VOLSCI

Cannae

SARDOS (SARDINIA)

CAMPANIA

Caudium

VIA APPIA

Herculaneum

Pompeii

M. Vesuvius

Brundisium

Mare Tyrrhenum

Lucani

Bruttii

M A R E

Sicani

SICILIA

M. Aetna

NUMIDIA

Carthago

Sicali

Syracusae

COSSURA

N O S T R U M

AFRICA

Zama

MELITA

1

First Declension
Nominative Case

Villa of the Mysteries, Pompeii

> Ipsa scientia potestas est.
> *Knowledge itself is power.*—BACON

——Forms ——

THE FIRST DECLENSION

Nouns whose stem ends in **-ā** belong to the first declension; they may be recognized by the **-ae** ending of the genitive singular. First declension nouns are declined like **puella,** *girl.*

CASES		SINGULAR	ENDINGS
NOMINATIVE:	puel'la	*a girl (the girl)*	**-a**
GENITIVE:	puel'lae	*of a girl (the girl)*	**-ae**
DATIVE:	puel'lae	*to (for) a girl (the girl)*	**-ae**
ACCUSATIVE:	puel'lam	*a girl (the girl)*	**-am**
ABLATIVE:	puel'lā	*	**-ā**

		PLURAL	
NOMINATIVE:	puel'lae	*girls (the girls)*	**-ae**
GENITIVE:	puellā'rum	*of girls (the girls)*	**-ārum**
DATIVE:	puel'līs	*to (for) girls (the girls)*	**-īs**
ACCUSATIVE:	puel'lās	*girls (the girls)*	**-ās**
ABLATIVE:	puel'līs	*	**-īs**

* Because of its many uses no standard translation can be given for the ablative case.

The base of a first declension noun is found by dropping the **-ae** ending of the genitive singular; the endings are then added to this base.

——Syntax ——

THE NOMINATIVE CASE

Subject. The subject of a verb is in the nominative case.
Predicate Nominative. A noun used with a linking verb to define or make a statement about the subject is in the nominative; such a noun is called *a predicate nominative.*

> Gallia est prōvincia. *Gaul is a province.*

— Vocabulary —

agri'cola, -ae, m., *farmer*
a'qua, -ae, f., *water*
fē'mina, -ae, f., *woman*
fortū'na, -ae, f., *fortune, chance*
Gal'lia, Gal'liae, f., *Gaul*
īn'sula, -ae, f., *island*
Īta'lia, Īta'liae, f., *Italy*
lin'gua, lin'guae, f., *tongue, language*
lit'tera, -ae, f., *letter* (of alphabet)
  in plural, *letter* (epistle), *letters*

memo'ria, -ae, f., *memory*
nātū'ra, -ae, f., *nature*
poē'ta, -ae, m., *poet*
prōvin'cia, -ae, f., *province*
puel'la, -ae, f., *girl*
sil'va, -ae, f., *forest*
vī'ta, -ae, f., *life*

est, *is, there is*
sunt, *are, there are*

House of Poseidon and Amphitrite, Herculaneum

〰〰〰〰〰〰〰〰〰〰〰〰〰〰〰〰〰〰〰〰〰〰〰〰

Helps and Hints. In the vocabularies the genitive singular ending is given after the nominative to show the declension: "m." stands for masculine gender, "f." for feminine.

〰〰〰〰〰〰〰〰〰〰〰〰〰〰〰〰〰〰〰〰〰〰〰〰

—*Word Study*—

Latin has no articles (i.e., no words for *a, an,* or *the*); consequently **puella** may be translated by *girl, a girl,* or *the girl,* depending on the context.

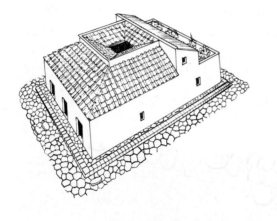

Design of an atrium house. On either side of the entrance there were often shops. The rooms went off the atrium or main court, in the center of which was an impluvium, a square basin into which rainwater was received through an overhead skylight. The Tablinum, the repository of family images and records, might serve as an office for the head of the family.

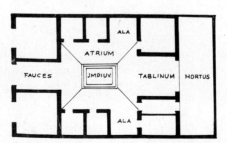

Nouns of the first declension are feminine unless, like **agricola** and **poēta,** they are the terms for male beings.

—Exercises—

A. Decline each of the nouns in the vocabulary like **puella.**

B. Pronounce, give case and number, and translate.

1. fēminīs (*dative*)   2. Ītalia   3. puellae (*three ways*)   4. memoriam   5. silvās   6. linguārum   7. īnsulam   8. Poētae sunt agricolae.   9. Sunt litterae.   10. Gallia est prōvincia.

C. Translate, giving case and number.

1. nature (*accusative*)   2. of the women   3. for the girl   4. of fortune   5. of life   6. letter (*four ways*)   7. for the poets   8. There is water.   9. The province is Gaul.   10. The farmers are poets.

Fountain in the garden of a Pompeian house. Note the artificial cascade and the stone masks into which lanterns could be put at night.

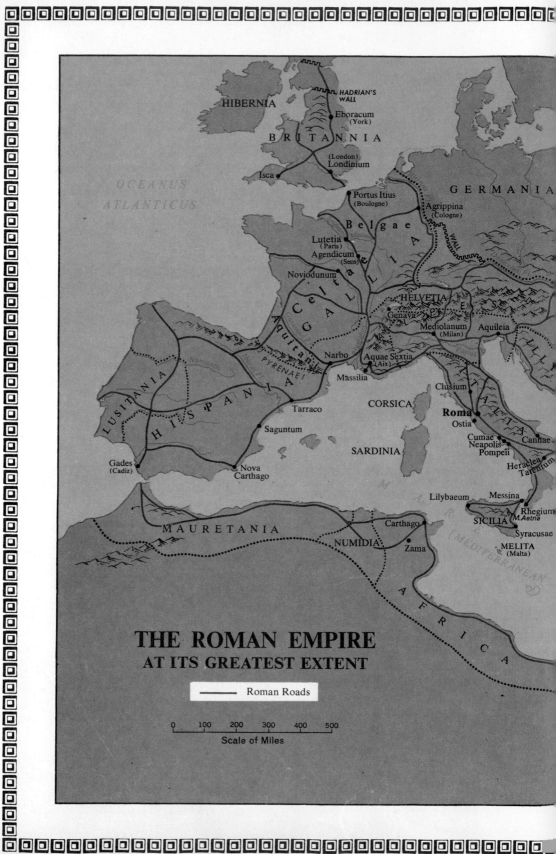

THE ROMAN EMPIRE
AT ITS GREATEST EXTENT

——— Roman Roads

0   100   200   300   400   500
Scale of Miles

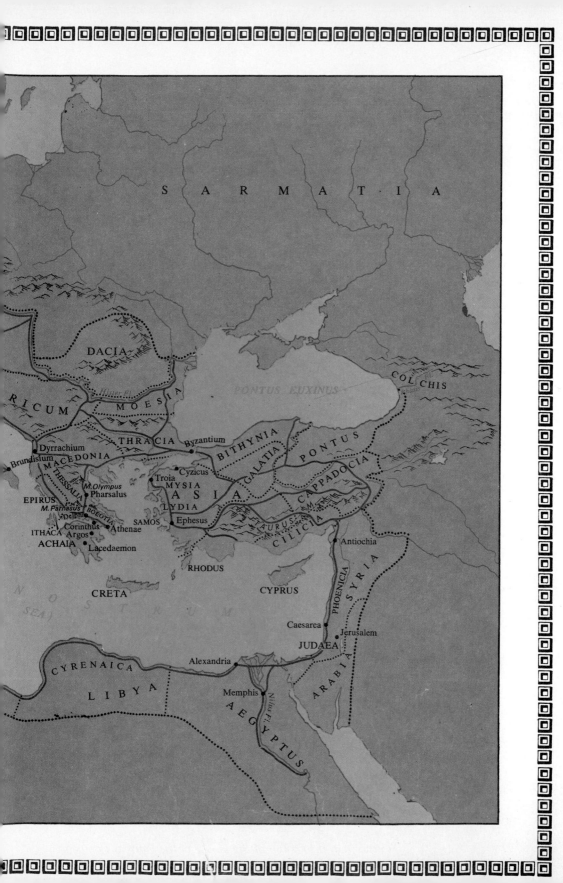

SARMATIA

DACIA

COLCHIS

PONTUS EUXINUS

Phasis

RICUM

MOESIA

Hister Fl.

THRACIA

Byzantium

BITHYNIA

Dyrrachium

PONTUS

GALATIA

Brundisium

MACEDONIA

THESSALIA

Cyzicus

Troia

M.Olympus

MYSIA

CAPPADOCIA

Pharsalus

ASIA

EPIRUS

M.Parnasus

LYDIA

Delphi

BOEOTIA

SAMOS

TAURUS

CILICIA

Corinthus

Athenae

Ephesus

ITHACA

Argos

ACHAIA

Lacedaemon

Antiochia

RHODUS

PHOENICIA

SYRIA

CRETA

CYPRUS

NOSTRUM

SEA)

Caesarea

Jerusalem

JUDAEA

CYRENAICA

Alexandria

ARABIA

LIBYA

Memphis

Nilus Fl.

AEGYPTUS

2

Present Tense
Agreement of Verbs
Direct Object

A view from the atrium of the House of the Faun at Pompeii

Gutta cavat lapidem.
Dripping hollows out rock. —OVID

—Forms—

VERBS

English shows the person and number of a verb by a pronoun subject. In Latin these are shown by the personal endings of the verb, the pronoun subject being expressed only when it shows emphasis or contrast. The personal endings of the active voice are as follows:

	SINGULAR		PLURAL	
1ST PERSON	-ō *or* -m,	*I*	-mus,	*we*
2D PERSON	-s,	*you*	-tis,	*you*
3D PERSON	-t,	*he, she, it*	-nt,	*they*

THE FIRST CONJUGATION

Verbs whose present stem ends in **-ā** belong to the first conjugation. First conjugation verbs are conjugated in the present tense as follows:

	SINGULAR		PLURAL	
1ST PERSON	vo'cō,	*I call*	vocā'mus,	*we call*
2D PERSON	vo'cās,	*you call*	vocā'tis,	*you call*
3D PERSON	vo'cat,	*he, she, it calls*	vo'cant,	*they call*

Helps and Hints. In translating a Latin verb whose subject is not expressed, a glance at the personal ending will show you which English pronoun to choose as subject.

vocās = -s, *you* + vocā-, *call*
vocāmus = -mus, *we* + vocā-, *call*

—Syntax—

VERBS

Latin has no special progressive or emphatic forms. **Vocō** means *I call, I am calling,* or *I do call,* whichever sounds best in the sentence.

AGREEMENT

A verb agrees with its subject in person and number.

> Agricol**a** puellam am**at**.　*The farmer loves the girl*
> Agricol**ae** pugn**ant**.　*The farmers are fighting.*

DIRECT OBJECT

The direct object of a verb (that which receives the action of a verb) is in the accusative case.

> Poētās laudāmus.　*We praise poets.*
> Fēminam spectō.　*I look at the woman.*

Longitudinal section of the House of the Tragic Poet in Pompeii. The east side. (l. to r.) The fauces, atrium, tablinum, and peristyle.

—Vocabulary—

amīci'tia, -ae, f., *friendship*

pa'tria, -ae, f., *country, native land*

a'mō, *I love, I like*
dō, *I give*
lau'dō, *I praise*
nā'vigō, *I sail*
oc'cupō, *I seize, I capture*
pa'rō, *I prepare, I prepare for*
por'tō, *I carry*
pug'nō, *I fight*
spec'tō, *I look at*
vo'cō, *I call*

nōn, (adverb) *not*

et, (conjunction) *and*
sed, (conj.) *but*

ad, *towards, to*
cum, *with*

The west side. Note the funnel-like roofing which collected water for the cistern whose wellhead is seen near the impluvium in the atrium.

—Exercises—

A. Pronounce and translate.

1. vocāmus   2. spectātis   3. parās   4. occupō   5. amant
6. pugnat   7. portant   8. laudāmus   9. parant   10. vocātis
11. spectant   12. occupāmus   13. occupātis   14. dō   15. laudant

B. Translate.

1. you (*pl.*) love   2. we carry   3. I am calling   4. they are seizing   5. you (*sing.*) prepare   6. we are praising   7. they are looking at   8. you (*pl.*) are calling   9. he is fighting   10. we prepare
11. she loves   12. he is seizing   13. they call   14. we carry   15. he
fights

C. Give the construction (i.e., the case and the use in the sentence)
of each noun, and translate.

1. Poēta patriam amat.   2. Litterās nōn portāmus.   3. Amīcitiam
puellae laudant.   4. Fēminae amant silvam.   5. Galliam laudant.

Artificial Island Pavilion, Hadrian's Villa, Tivoli

*Bedroom of a villa excavated
at Boscoreale (near Pompeii).*

6. Ītaliam amāmus. 7. Prōvinciam occupātis. 8. Litterās parātis. 9. Portat puella aquam. 10. Silvam spectās.

~~~~~~

In general, changing the order of the words in a Latin sentence
does not alter its meaning. In English we identify the subject and
the direct object of a verb by their location in the sentence: "The
girl looks at the farmer" is not the same as "The farmer looks at
the girl." In Latin the syntax of a noun is shown by its case endings. The following sentences all mean exactly the same thing,
but with a different emphasis in each sentence.

Puella agricolam spectat. Puella spectat agricolam. Agricolam
puella spectat. Agricolam spectat puella. Spectat puella agricolam. Spectat agricolam puella.

~~~~~~

D. Translate (words in parentheses are to be omitted from the Latin).

1. We praise the poets. 2. The woman and the farmer are looking at the forest. 3. The girls do not carry water. 4. You (*sing.*)
seize the province. 5. The poet praises (his) country. 6. Girls
do not fight. 7. The woman is looking at the island. 8. The
farmer and the poet love (their) native land. 9. Poets praise
friendship. 10. The farmer is calling the girls.

3

Conjugation of Sum
Uses of Sum
Ablative of Place Where
Questions

Fresco with seaside villas, National Museum, Naples

In virtute sunt multi ascensus.

In excellence there are many degrees.—CICERO

——Forms——

THE VERB SUM

The present stem of **sum** is irregular, but it takes the regular personal endings.

PRESENT TENSE

SINGULAR		PLURAL	
sum,	*I am*	**sumus,**	*we are*
es,	*you are*	**estis,**	*you are*
est,	*he, she, it is, there is*	**sunt,**	*they are, there are*

——Syntax——

THE USES OF SUM

Sum is ordinarily used as a linking verb, connecting its subject with a predicate nominative, or with some other kind of predicate.

Gallia est prōvincia. *Gaul is a province.*
Gallia est in Eurōpā. *Gaul is in Europe.*

In the third person it may also be translated by *there is* or *there are.*

Est aqua. *There is water.*
Sunt litterae. *There is a letter.*

THE ABLATIVE OF PLACE WHERE

Location *on* or *in* is shown by the ablative case with the preposition **in.**

In silvā est. *He is in the forest.*
In īnsulā pugnāmus. *We are fighting on the island.*

QUESTIONS

To turn a statement into a question which has a *yes* or *no* answer, add the enclitic **-ne** to the first word.

> Galliane est prōvincia?   *Is Gaul a province?*
> Suntne litterae?   *Are there letters?*

If the question is introduced by an interrogative pronoun, adjective, or adverb, **-ne** is not used.

> Quid puellae spectant?   *What are the girls looking at?*
> Ubi sunt fēminae?   *Where are the women?*

An enclitic (the word is derived from the Greek for "leaning on") must be attached to the end of another word: **suntne, vīllaque.** When an enclitic has been attached to a word, the accent falls on the syllable before the enclitic, whether long or short.

Helps and Hints. Since Latin has no words for *yes* and *no*, questions with the enclitic **-ne** must be answered by a statement or part of a statement:

> Spectantne agricolae silvam?   *Are the farmers looking at the forest?*
> Spectant.   *Yes.*
> Nōn spectant.   *No.*
> Nautae, nōn agricolae, silvam spectant.
>   *No, the sailors are looking at the forest.*
> Vīllam, nōn silvam, spectant.   *No, they are looking at the farmhouse.*

—— Vocabulary ——

Eurō'pa, -ae, f., *Europe*
Germā'nia, -ae, f., *Germany*
Hispā'nia, -ae, f., *Spain*
nau'ta, -ae, m., *sailor*
por'ta, -ae, f., *gate*
Rō'ma, -ae, f., *Rome*
ter'ra, -ae, f., *earth, land*
tu'ba, -ae, f., *trumpet*
vi'a, -ae, f., *road, way*
vīl'la, -ae, f., *farmhouse*

quid?, (interrogative pronoun) *what?*

ubi?, (interrogative adverb) *where?*

-ne, (enclitic interrogative particle)

-que, (enclitic conjunction) *and* (connects words of like syntax; must be translated before the word to which it is attached)

(above) Ostian apartment house. These complexes had about four or five stories usually with shops on the ground floor facing the street. Staircases led from the street to the upper floors and many had inner courtyards.
(below) Street in Trajan's market erected in c. 110 A.D. to replace the shops with living lofts which were destroyed to make room for Trajan's Forum and Basilica.

—— Exercises ——

A. Read the Latin and translate.

1. Agricolae sumus.   2. Fēmina in silvā est.   3. Estisne puellae?
4. Nauta in īnsulā est.   5. Sumus in Germāniā.   6. Nōn sum
puella.   7. Suntne fēminae in silvā?   8. Spectantne nautae fēminās?   9. Nōn sunt portae in vīllā.   10. Agricolae fēminaeque
īnsulam spectant.

B. Translate.

1. The women are in Spain.   2. Are you a farmer?   3. We are in
the farmhouse.   4. Is the girl in the province?   5. The sailor is
looking at the trumpet.   6. Are the farmers carrying water?   7. The
sailors are on the island.   8. Are you (*pl.*) in the forest?   9. They
are not on the road.   10. The girls are not in the farmhouse.

—— Reading ——

Read aloud and translate.

A SAILOR IN ITALY

In viā sunt nautae. Agricolae nautās spectant. Agricola nautam vocat:
AGRICOLA: O nauta, ubi est tua patria?
NAUTA: Mea patria est Germānia; sumus nautae.
AGRICOLA: Ubi est Germānia?
NAUTA: Germānia est in Eurōpā.
AGRICOLA: Estne Hispānia in Eurōpā?
NAUTA: Hispānia etiam est in Eurōpā, sed nōn est prope Germāniam.
    Hodiē ad Hispāniam nāvigāmus, et posteā ad Germāniam. Pa-
    triam nostram amāmus. Valē.

4

Second Declension
Genitive of Possession

Bronze lampstand and lamp from Pompeii

Salus populi suprema lex.

The safety of the people is the highest law.—CICERO

—— *Forms* ——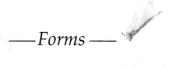

THE SECOND DECLENSION

There are five declensions of Latin nouns. They are distinguished by the ending of the genitive singular. Nouns whose genitive singular ends in **-ae** belong to the first declension **(puella, -ae).** Second declension nouns end in **-ī** in the genitive singular. They are usually masculine if they end in **-us** or **-er** in the nominative singular.

	SINGULAR				ENDINGS
NOM.	amī′cus	fi′lius	pu′er	a′ger	**-us, —**
GEN.	amī′cī	fi′lī	pu′erī	a′grī	**-ī**
DAT.	amī′cō	fi′liō	pu′erō	a′grō	**-ō**
ACC.	amī′cum	fi′lium	pu′erum	a′grum	**-um**
ABL.	amī′cō	fi′liō	pu′erō	a′grō	**-ō**

	PLURAL				
NOM.	amī′cī	fi′liī	pu′erī	a′grī	**-ī**
GEN.	amīcō′rum	filiō′rum	puerō′rum	agrō′rum	**-ōrum**
DAT.	amī′cīs	fi′liīs	pu′erīs	a′grīs	**-īs**
ACC.	amī′cōs	fi′liōs	pu′erōs	a′grōs	**-ōs**
ABL.	amī′cīs	fi′liīs	pu′erīs	a′grīs	**-īs**

—— *Syntax* ——

GENITIVE OF POSSESSION

The genitive case is used to show possession (*of*, *-'s*, or *-s'* in English).

agricolae ager   *the farmer's field, the field of the farmer*
agricolārum ager   *the farmers' field, the field of the farmers*

Roman silver dishes and cups. Tableware from Mindenhall Trove in the British Museum. Cantharus and skyphos from the House of the Menander at Pompeii.

—— Vocabulary ——

a'ger, a'grī, m., *field, territory*

amī'cus, -ī, m., *friend*

an'nus, -ī, m., *year*

cam'pus, -ī, m., *field, plain*

de'a, -ae, f., *goddess**

de'us, -ī, m., *god*

e'quus, e'quī, m., *horse*

fī'lia, -ae, f., *daughter**

fī'lius, fī'lī, m., *son*

gla'dius, gla'dī, m., *sword*

lēgā'tus, -ī, m., *envoy; lieutenant*

lū'dus, -ī, m., *game; school*

nūn'tius, nūn'tī, m., *messenger, message*

pu'er, pu'erī, m., *boy*

ser'vus, -ī, m., *slave*

vir, vi'rī, m., *man; husband*

* In the dative and ablative plural **dea** and **fīlia** have the irregular forms **deābus** and **fīliābus,** to distinguish them from the corresponding forms of **deus** and **fīlius.**

~~~~~~

Helps and Hints. Nearly all nouns of the second declension in
-us and **-er** are masculine. Exceptions are names of cities and
towns in **-us,** names of plants and gems, and a few other words;
all of these are feminine.

~~~~~~

—— Exercises ——

A. Translate and give the construction of each noun.

1. Virī agrōs agricolārum occupant.   2. Fīliās nūntī amat.
3. Equum fīlī vocāmus.   4. Servus tubam lēgātī portat.
5. Nūntius fēminās vocat.   6. Agricolārum amīcī occupant terram.   7. Agrōs in prōvinciā nōn parant.   8. Puerī amīcus gladium
spectat.   9. Fēminae deās laudant.   10. Equī nūntiōs portant.

B. Translate. Watch your noun and verb endings!

1. The boy praises the slave's memory.   2. The women are calling
the lieutenant's friend.   3. The lieutenant is looking at the boys'
horses.   4. The lieutenants seize the farmer's fields.   5. You
(*sing.*) love the messenger's daughter.   6. The boys do not carry
the messenger's trumpets.   7. We love the gods and goddesses.
8. The messengers carry the letter.   9. The slave of the lieutenant
is calling the boy.   10. Are the men fighting in the plains?

~~~~~~

Helps and Hints. To avoid ambiguity, do not place a genitive of
possession between two nouns.
Servus agricolae equum laudat = *The slave praises the farmer's
horse* or *The farmer's slave praises the horse.* To avoid this confusion,
the sentence meaning *The slave praises the farmer's horse* should be
written: Servus equum agricolae laudat, *The farmer's slave praises
the horse* should be: Agricolae servus equum laudat.

~~~~~~

—Reading—

Read aloud and translate.

THE TROJAN WAR

In Asiā est vir clārus. Vir est Anchīsēs. Dea Anchīsēn (*accusative*) amat. Aenēās est fīlius deae et Anchīsae. Aenēae fēmina est Creūsa. Creūsa Aenēāsque fīlium vocant Ascānium.

   Aenēae patria est Trōia. Trōia nōn est in Eurōpā, sed in Asiā. Graecī et virī Trōiae pugnant. Graecī Trōiam occupant. Aenēās Anchīsēn portat. Creūsam fīliumque vocat.

AENĒĀS: "Nōn iam est Trōia. Sed deī deaeque virōs Trōiae amant. Etiam fēminās et puerōs puellāsque amant. Hodiē ad Eurōpam nāvigāmus."

Lamp holder from Herculaneum

Standing lamp

> Aspirat primo Fortuna labori.
> *Fortune smiles upon our first effort.*—VERGIL

REVIEW 1 (LESSONS 1–4)

—Vocabulary Drill—

A. Give the genitive, gender, and meaning of the following nouns.

ager	fēmina	lūdus	puella
agricola	filia	memoria	puer
amīcitia	filius	nātūra	servus
amīcus	fortūna	nauta	silva
annus	gladius	nūntius	terra
aqua	īnsula	patria	tuba
campus	lēgātus	poēta	via
dea	lingua	porta	vīlla
deus	littera	prōvincia	vir
equus			vīta

B. Give the meanings of the following verbs.

amō	nāvigō	portō	sum
dō	occupō	pugnō	vocō
laudō	parō	spectō	

C. Give the meaning of the following words.

et	nōn	quid	sed	ubi
ad	cum			

—Drill on Forms—

A. Decline the following nouns in the singular and plural. Name cases.

nauta	lēgātus	filius

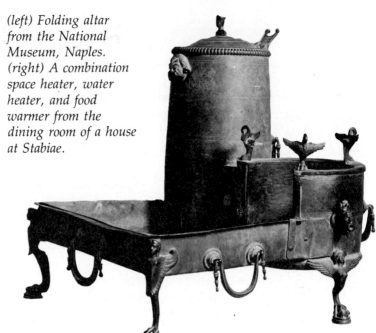

(left) Folding altar from the National Museum, Naples.
(right) A combination space heater, water heater, and food warmer from the dining room of a house at Stabiae.

B. Conjugate the following verbs in the present tense. Give meanings.

pugnō   sum

C. Translate the following verb forms.

1. laudant
2. nāvigās
3. portat
4. damus
5. spectant

6. parās
7. pugnātis
8. amō
9. occupāsne?
10. vocātis

D. Give the Latin for the following.

1. we are carrying
2. they sail
3. he is fighting
4. you (*pl.*) love
5. she gives

6. we look at
7. I am seizing
8. you (*sing.*) praise
9. do you (*pl.*) call?
10. they prepare

E. Give the following forms.

    1. *genitive singular:* via, amīcus, gladius.
    2. *dative singular:* amīcitia, puer, fīlius.
    3. *accusative singular:* patria, equus, ager.
    4. *nominative plural:* porta, nūntius, puer.
    5. *accusative plural:* littera, vir, annus.
    6. *ablative plural:* fortūna, deus, fīlia.

—— Exercises ——

A. Translate.

    1. Fēminae puellaeque nōn nāvigant.
    2. Nūntī amīcus est in silvā.
    3. Poētae deam amant laudantque.
    4. Nautae fīliī in īnsulā sunt.
    5. Gladium fīlī portat.
    6. Fīlia deōs amat.
    7. In campō pugnāmus.
    8. Vir in vīllā est, sed puer est in agrō.
    9. In agrīs estis.
  10. Puerī in lēgātī prōvinciā sunt.

B. Translate.

    1. We look at the lieutenant's sword.
    2. The messengers are in Germany.
    3. You (*pl.*) praise the nature of women.
    4. He is preparing a letter.
    5. The horses carry the boys.
    6. We love the gods.
    7. They are seizing the man's field and farmhouse.
    8. They look at the horses.
    9. We are calling the friends.
  10. The sailors praise the goddess.

5

Second Declension, Neuter; Accusative of Place to Which Ablative of Place from Which

Children carrying implements used in elaborate Roman wedding ceremonies

> Ab ovo usque ad mala.
> *From the egg right to the fruits.* —HORACE
> *(From soup to nuts.)*

—Forms—

THE SECOND DECLENSION, NEUTER

Neuter nouns of the second declension end in **-um** in the nominative singular. They are declined like **verbum,** *word.*

	SINGULAR	ENDINGS	PLURAL	ENDINGS
NOMINATIVE:	ver'bum	-um	ver'ba	-a
GENITIVE:	ver'bī	-ī	verbō'rum	-ōrum
DATIVE:	ver'bō	-ō	ver'bīs	-īs
ACCUSATIVE:	ver'bum	-um	ver'ba	-a
ABLATIVE:	ver'bō	-ō	ver'bīs	-īs

Helps and Hints. In all neuter nouns and adjectives of all declensions, the nominative is always the same as the accusative; and in the plural the ending of these two cases is always **-a.**

—Syntax—

THE ACCUSATIVE OF PLACE TO WHICH

The accusative is used with the prepositions **ad** *to,* **in** *into,* and **sub** *up to,* to indicate *place to which,* i.e., the goal toward which the action of the verb is directed.

> Agricola fīlium in vīllam vocat.
> *The farmer calls his son into the farmhouse.*
> Aquam sub oppidum portāmus.
> *We are carrying water up to the town.*

THE ABLATIVE OF PLACE FROM WHICH

The ablative is used with the prepositions **ā, ab** *away from*, **dē** *down from*, and **ē, ex** *out of*, to indicate *place from which*, i.e., the point from which motion takes place.

Frūmentum ex agrīs portant.   *They carry grain from the fields.*
Nāvigātis ab īnsulā.   *You are sailing from the island.*

—— Vocabulary ——

bel'lum, -ī, neuter, *war*
cae'lum, -ī, n., *sky*
dō'num, -ī, n., *gift*
frūmen'tum, -ī, n., *grain*

op'pidum, -ī, n., *town*
perī'culum, -ī, n., *danger, risk*
rēg'num, -ī, n., *kingdom; kingship*
ver'bum, -ī, n., *word*

ā, ab, (preposition with the ablative) *from, away from*
ad, (preposition with the accusative) *to, toward, near*
dē, (prep. with abl.) *from, down from, about, concerning*
ē, ex, (prep. with abl.) *from, out of*
in, (prep. with acc. of place to which) *into, against*; (with abl. of place where) *in, on*
sub, (prep. with acc. of place to which) *under, up to, to the foot of*; (with abl. of place where) *under, at the foot of*

Sarcophagus relief showing child from infancy to first schooling

M·CORNELIO·M·F·PAL·STATIO·   ·FECER·

— Word Study —

The prepositions listed in the vocabulary may also be used as prefixes on verbs. Certain combinations of letters are hard to pronounce. Many of these occur when a preposition is prefixed to a verb, and often they are changed slightly for the sake of easier pronunciation. It is easier to say "import" than "inport," "support" than "subport," *"appello"* than *"adpello."* This is true in both English and Latin. This change for the sake of easier pronunciation is called *assimilation.*

— Exercises —

A. Translate.

1. ē perīculō 2. in oppidō 3. ad Ītaliam 4. dē caelō 5. sub silvam 6. ā patriā 7. sub rēgnō 8. ad servum 9. in īnsulam 10. ā campō

B. Translate.

1. away from the gate 2. into the water 3. to Europe 4. under the sky 5. from the kingdom 6. up to the town 7. down from the road 8. to school 9. in the field 10. out of the farmhouse

C. Pronounce and translate.

1. Fēminae bellum nōn amant. 2. Frūmentum ex agrīs ad vīllam portāmus. 3. Occupant īnsulam et oppida. 4. Virine puellās in viā spectant? 5. Puerum ad caelum portat deus. 6. Nūntī fīlius in silvam amīcum vocat. 7. Lēgātī gladiōs in rēgnum portant. 8. Est bellum in Eurōpā. 9. Agricolae servī laudant frūmentum. 10. Ab Ītaliā ad īnsulam nāvigātis.

D. Translate.

1. The lieutenants seize the kingdom and (its) towns. 2. The farmer's slaves carry water into the farmhouse. 3. The gods love the gifts of men and women. 4. There is danger of war in Italy. 5. The sailors are sailing from Spain to the islands. 6. The men are calling the boys out of the forest. 7. The girls do not like the words of the messenger. 8. Are the sons of the lieutenant in danger? 9. The farmer's daughters are carrying grain from the field to the road. 10. The men from the province are fighting.

Altar showing wedding scenes: Note the joining of hands at the conclusion of the marriage service, the children taking part in the procession to the bridegroom's house carrying an umbrella and an offering for the sacrifice.

—Reading—

Read aloud and translate.

AENEAS SAILS TO CARTHAGE

Post longum bellum in Asiā, Aenēās cum amīcīs ab Asiā ad Eurōpam nāvigat. Sed perīculum est in Eurōpā. Ab Eurōpā ad Āfricam nāvigat. Est magnum oppidum in Āfricā. Elissa* est rēgīna oppidī. Elissa frūmentum et dona Aenēae amīcīs (*dative*) dat. Elissa Aenēan (*accusative*) amat. Deī Aenēan rēgīnamque dē caelō spectant.

Nautae Aenēae et virī fēminaeque in oppidō sunt amīcī. Sed perīculum est in Āfricā.

* Elissa of Tyre, usually known by her nickname Dido, was the foundress of Carthage in North Africa.

6

Adjectives
Agreement of Adjectives
Adjectives
as Substantives

Portrait in fresco of a husband and wife from a bakery in Pompeii

Nullum magnum ingenium sine mixtura dementiae fuit.
There has not been any great talent without an element of madness.

—SENECA

—Forms—

ADJECTIVES

Adjectives in **-us, -a, -um** belong to the first and second declensions.

	MASCULINE	SINGULAR FEMININE	NEUTER
NOMINATIVE:	ma'lus	ma'la	ma'lum
GENITIVE:	ma'lī	ma'lae	ma'lī
DATIVE:	ma'lō	ma'lae	ma'lō
ACCUSATIVE:	ma'lum	ma'lam	ma'lum
ABLATIVE:	ma'lō	ma'lā	ma'lō

		PLURAL	
NOMINATIVE:	ma'lī	ma'lae	ma'la
GENITIVE:	malō'rum	malā'rum	malō'rum
DATIVE:	ma'līs	ma'līs	ma'līs
ACCUSATIVE:	ma'lōs	ma'lās	ma'la
ABLATIVE:	ma'līs	ma'līs	ma'līs

—Syntax—

AGREEMENT OF ADJECTIVES

An adjective agrees with the noun it modifies in gender, number, and case. This is why a Latin adjective must have forms for all genders, as well as for the cases and numbers. However, an adjective will not necessarily have the same ending as the noun it modifies.

Agricolae sunt malī. *The farmers are bad.*
Fēminae sunt bonae. *The women are good.*

~~~~~~

Helps and Hints. Adjectives may either precede or follow the noun modified. In any phrase, the determining and most significant word comes first. In general, numeral adjectives, adjectives of quantity, and interrogative pronouns tend to precede the words to which they belong. When **sum** is used as the substantive verb, it regularly stands first, or at any rate before its subject.

~~~~~~

ADJECTIVES USED AS NOUNS

In Latin any adjective may be used as a noun; its translation will depend on its gender.

malus,	*a bad man*	malī,	*bad men, the wicked*
mala,	*a bad woman*	malae,	*bad women*
malum,	*a bad thing*	mala,	*bad things, evils*

In English this use of the adjective is mostly restricted to certain plurals: "The good die young." "The poor you have always with you."

—— Vocabulary ——

al'tus, al'ta, al'tum, *high; deep*
bo'nus, bo'na, bo'num, *good*
fe'rus, fe'ra, fe'rum, *wild, fierce, savage*
lā'tus, lā'ta, lā'tum, *wide, broad*
lon'gus, lon'ga, lon'gum, *long*
mag'nus, mag'na, mag'num, *large, great*
ma'lus, ma'la, ma'lum, *bad*
me'us, me'a, me'um, *my, mine*

mul'tus, mul'ta, mul'tum, *much* (pl., *many*)
par'vus, par'va, par'vum, *small, little*
tu'us, tu'a, tu'um, *your, yours* (when speaking to one person)

cum, (prep. with abl.) *with*
sine, (prep. with abl.) *without*

—Word Study—

Cum (in the forms **co-, com-, con-**) is, like the prepositions in Lesson 5, also used as a verb prefix. **Co- (com-, con-)** means *together, completely,* or *forcibly*. Note the meanings of the following compounds:

collaudō   *I praise highly*
comparō   *I put together, I arrange; I prepare eagerly*
comportō   *I carry together, I bring together*
convocō   *I call together, I summon*

A grave monument in the Vatican Museum showing a family portrait

—— *Exercises* ——

A. Decline the following.

ager lātus   bellum magnum   fīlia parva   nauta bonus

B. Translate, giving reasons for the ending of each adjective.

1. Agrī lātī in magnā īnsulā sunt. 2. Bonīne sunt puerī parvī?
3. Deī malōs nōn amant. 4. Puer parvus equōs ferōs vocat ex
agrō. 5. Multī nāvigant ad Ītaliam. 6. Mea fīlia est parva, nōn
magna. 7. Multum frūmentum bonī servī portant. 8. Tua patria
nōn est magna. 9. Viae longae nōn sunt. 10. Multa bella mala
sunt.

C. Translate.

1. Is the good farmer in the small field? 2. Many people like large
gifts. 3. The bad messenger calls the men into the wide plain.
4. A good poet praises great men. 5. Are you sailing to your
large island? 6. Your daughters are looking at the wild horse.
7. There is a large gate in the small town. 8. Are you fighting
with your friends in my farmhouse? 9. The good boys are carrying much water into the big forest. 10. Where are they preparing the long roads?

—— *Reading* ——

Read aloud and translate.

THE GODS CALL AENEAS TO ITALY

Rēgnum Elissae in Āfricā est. Rēgnum est lātum et oppidum est
magnum altumque. Ferī Āfricānī rēgīnam nōn amant. Bellum parant,
sed rēgīnae oppidum nōn occupant.

    Aenēās cum amīcīs ā Siciliā ad Āfricam nāvigat. Elissa Aenēan amat
et vocat: "Meum rēgnum est tuum. Africānī meum rēgnum nōn
amant; in magnō perīculō sumus. Troiānīs meam patriam dō."

    Sed deī Trōiānōs in Ītaliam vocant. Aenēās: "Tuum rēgnum est
magnum et bonum et pulchrum, et Āfricānī sunt malī. Tē et tuum
rēgnum laudō, et tē amō. Sed deī Trōiānōs ad Ītaliam vocant."

7

Imperfect Tense
Future Tense

Sarcophagus showing a woman's funeral

Excitabat fluctus in simpulo.
He was stirring up billows in a ladle.—CICERO
(He was raising a tempest in a teapot.)

—Forms—

Two other tenses besides the present are formed on the present stem of a verb, the *imperfect* tense and the *future* tense.

THE PRESENT TENSE

The present tense is formed by adding the personal endings **-ō, -s, -t, -mus, -tis,** and **-nt** to the present stem of the verb, omitting the **-ā-** of the stem before **-ō,** and shortening it before **-t** and **-nt.**

SINGULAR		PLURAL	
vo'cō,	*I call*	vocā'**mus,**	*we call*
vo'cās,	*you call*	vocā'**tis,**	*you call*
vo'cat,	*he, she, it calls*	vo'cant,	*they call*

THE IMPERFECT TENSE

To form the imperfect tense we add the tense-sign **-bā-** to the present stem, and then add the personal endings **-m, -s, -t, -mus, -tis,** and **-nt,** shortening the **-ā-** of **-bā-** before **-m, -t,** and **-nt.**

SINGULAR		PLURAL	
vocā'**bam,**	*I was calling*	vocābā'**mus,**	*we were calling*
vocā'**bās,**	*you were calling*	vocābā'**tis,**	*you were calling*
vocā'**bat,**	*he, she, it was calling*	vocā'**bant,**	*they were calling*

THE FUTURE TENSE

The future tense is formed by adding the tense-sign **-bi-** to the present stem of the verb, then the personal endings **-ō, -s, -t, -mus, -tis,** and **-nt,** omitting the **-i-** of **-bi-** before **-ō** and changing it to **-u-** before **-nt.**

SINGULAR		PLURAL	
vocā'**bō**,	*I shall call*	vocā'**bimus**,	*we shall call*
vocā'**bis**,	*you will call*	vocā'**bitis**,	*you will call*
vocā'**bit**,	*he, she, it will call*	vocā'**bunt**,	*they will call*

—Syntax—

USE OF TENSES

The Latin imperfect does not have the same meaning as the English past tense; in fact, English has no tense which is the equivalent of the imperfect tense in Latin. The imperfect tense describes an action as incomplete (**imperfectum**, *uncompleted*), i.e., as going on, at some time in the past. There are several ways of translating the imperfect into English: the standard translation of **vocābat** is *he was calling*; but it could also mean *he used to call*, or, very rarely, *he called*. The translation you choose will depend on the context.

The Latin future tense, like the future tense in English, merely states that an action will take place in the future: **vocābō**, *I shall call*, **vocābis**, *you will call*, etc.

Funerary relief showing a butcher shop. Hanging are various cuts including a calf's head. To the left are scales.

— Vocabulary —

appel'lō, *I call, I name*
con'vocō, *I call together, I assemble, I summon*
exspec'tō, *I await, I wait for*
ha'bitō, *I live, I dwell*
labō'rō, *I labor, I suffer, I am hard pressed*

nār'rō, *I tell, I relate*
nūn'tiō, *I announce, I report*
su'perō, *I surpass, I defeat*
vo'lō, *I fly*
vul'nerō, *I wound*

— Exercises —

A. Analyze each form and translate.

1. appellābam, nūntiābis, convocātis   2. occupat, labōrāmus, exspectābunt   3. nāvigāmus, vocābat, volābunt   4. vulnerābis, superābant, nārrāmus   5. spectābit, portābimus, habitābunt   6. laudābās, pugnābātis, parābimus   7. dant, amābit, superābunt   8. vulnerō, appellābit, vocābunt   9. exspectābit, habitābant, volāmus   10. amābō, portābitis, nūntiābās

B. Translate.

1. they will tell, I was laboring, we shall look at   2. we are sailing, he will seize, I am calling together   3. they prepare, they are praising, they were fighting   4. you (*sing.*) were giving, we shall sail, they wound   5. I shall surpass, you (*pl.*) are flying, they will praise   6. he was summoning, we shall call, they carry   7. you (*pl.*) relate, we were fighting, I shall live   8. they will seize, he names, you (*sing.*) were preparing   9. we shall suffer, they were looking at, she was loving   10. I shall wait for, he announces, you (*pl.*) will give

C. Read the Latin and translate.

1. Bonam fortūnam tuam nūntiābō.   2. Agricolae labōrābant in agrīs.   3. Fēminae puerōs puellāsque convocābunt.   4. Meōs fīliōs nōn superābitis.   5. Nauta servum in viā vulnerābit.   6. Deī deaeque in caelō habitābant.   7. Multī lēgātōrum amīcī exspectābant nūntiōs.   8. In vīllā parvā habitābāmus.   9. Spectābam equum meum in campō lātō.   10. Virī in magnā silvā labōrābunt.

D. Translate.

1. We shall sail to the small island. 2. The good sailor will not wound the friend of the girl. 3. They were assembling the men and women. 4. The horses will carry water into the town. 5. The good farmer used to live in a large farmhouse. 6. The boys were preparing the letter. 7. Will you (*pl.*) carry much grain into the road? 8. The messenger's son was looking at my gifts. 9. I was laboring in your fields. 10. The lieutenants used to carry many swords.

——*Reading*——

Read aloud and translate.

THE FALL OF TROY

DĪDŌ: "Meōs tuōsque amīcōs convocābō. Nārrābisne malam fortūnam Trōiae?"

AENĒĀS: "Nārrābō. Cum meō parvō fīliō et fēminā, Creūsā, in oppidō meō habitābam. Vītam bonam Trōiānōrum laudābāmus. Nūntiī bellum nūntiābant: 'Graecī ad Asiam nāvigābunt.' Trōiānī bellum parābant et Graecōs exspectābant. Bellum in patriam meam portābant Graecī. Graecōrum gladiī multōs Trōiānōs vulnerābant. Trōiānī labōrābāmus: Graecī Trōiānōs superābant. Cum Graecīs ferīs pugnābam et multōs vulnerābam. Ō, mala nārrō! Graecī meum oppidum altum occupābant!"

Funerary relief showing a dealer in poultry and vegetables. The monkeys are probably pets brought by sailors.

8

Adjectives in -er
Dative of
Indirect Object

Relief from a sarcophagus showing a greengrocer's shop in Ostia

Nullum saeculum magnis ingeniis clausum est.
To great talents no era is closed.—SENECA

—Forms—

ADJECTIVES IN -ER

Some adjectives of the first and second declension end in **-er** in the masculine nominative singular. These are declined like **miser** *wretched* or **sacer** *sacred*.

		SINGULAR	
	MASCULINE	FEMININE	NEUTER
NOMINATIVE:	mi′ser	mi′sera	mi′serum
GENITIVE:	mi′serī	mi′serae	mi′serī
DATIVE:	mi′serō	mi′serae	mi′serō
ACCUSATIVE:	mi′serum	mi′seram	mi′serum
ABLATIVE:	mi′serō	mi′serā	mi′serō

		PLURAL	
NOMINATIVE:	mi′serī	mi′serae	mi′sera
GENITIVE:	miserō′rum	miserā′rum	miserō′rum
DATIVE:	mi′serīs	mi′serīs	mi′serīs
ACCUSATIVE:	mi′serōs	mi′serās	mi′sera
ABLATIVE:	mi′serīs	mi′serīs	mi′serīs

		SINGULAR	
NOMINATIVE:	sa′cer	sa′cra	sa′crum
GENITIVE:	sa′crī	sa′crae	sa′crī
DATIVE:	sa′crō	sa′crae	sa′crō
ACCUSATIVE:	sa′crum	sa′cram	sa′crum
ABLATIVE:	sa′crō	sa′crā	sa′crō

		PLURAL	
NOMINATIVE:	sa′crī	sa′crae	sa′cra
GENITIVE:	sacrō′rum	sacrā′rum	sacrō′rum
DATIVE:	sa′crīs	sa′crīs	sa′crīs
ACCUSATIVE:	sa′crōs	sa′crās	sa′cra
ABLATIVE:	sa′crīs	sa′crīs	sa′crīs

~~~~~~

Helps and Hints. There is no new difficulty in the declension of these adjectives. The masculine is like **puer** and **ager,** the rest like **magnus.**

Note that **līber** and **miser** retain the **e,** like **puer; pulcher** and **vester** drop it, like **ager.** To remember which words drop the **e** and which keep it, think of English derivatives: *liberate, miserable, puerile, agrarian,* and *pulchritude.* Most second declension adjectives in **-er** drop the **e. Līber** and **miser** are the commonest ones that do not.

~~~~~~

—— *Syntax* ——

INDIRECT OBJECT

The indirect object is put in the dative. It shows *to* or *for* whom or which something is said, given, shown, or done. Notice that in English we often omit the preposition *to* or *for.* The indirect object usually comes before the direct in Latin.

Agricola puerō aquam dat.   *The farmer gives the boy water. (water to the boy.)*
Equō frūmentum parat.   *He is preparing grain for the horse.*

Relief showing a banquet scene with the guests around the banquet table. On the left notice the servants pouring beverages and serving food. On the right are pictured the kitchen and bakery of a Roman house.

Helps and Hints. Do not confuse the dative of the indirect object with the accusative of place to which, which must be used with verbs of motion.

Dōnum puellae dabō.   *I shall give a gift to the girl.*
Aquam ad puellam portābō.   *I shall carry water to the girl.*

——Vocabulary——

lī'ber, lī'bera, lī'berum, *free*
mi'ser, mi'sera, mi'serum, *wretched, unfortunate, poor*
nos'ter, nos'tra, nos'trum, *our, ours*
pul'cher, -chra, -chrum, *beautiful; noble, fine*
sa'cer, -cra, -crum, *sacred, holy*
ves'ter, -tra, -trum, *your, yours* (when speaking to more than one person)

an'te, (prep. with acc.) *before, in front of*
con'trā, (prep. with acc.) *against*
in'ter, (prep. with acc.) *between, among*
ob, (prep. with acc.) *because of, on account of*
per, (prep. with acc.) *through*
post, (prep. with acc.) *after, behind*
prop'ter, (prep. with acc.) *because of, on account of*
trāns, (prep. with acc.) *across, over*

—— Word Study ——

The prepositions **ante, inter, ob, per,** and **trāns** are also used as prefixes on verbs, with the following meanings:

> ante-, *before, forwards*
> inter-, *between, at intervals, to pieces*
> ob-, *towards, to meet, in opposition to*
> per-, *through, completely*
> trāns-, trā-, *across, over, through and through*

—— Exercises ——

A. Decline the following.

agricola miser   puella pulchra   verbum sacrum

B. Read the Latin and translate.

1. Verba deōrum sacra sunt.   2. Equī nostrī sunt parvī pulchrīque.   3. Vestrumne frūmentum servīs dabitis?   4. Propter perīcula ad Germāniam nōn nāvigābimus.   5. Pugnābuntne nostrī in Germāniae campīs?   6. Sunt inter fēminās memoriae amīcitiae magnae.   7. Tua fīlia pulchra caelum spectat.   8. Deīs dōna multa et pulchra dabimus.   9. Amīcī nostrī sunt miserī.   10. Nautae tuum fīlium parvum vulnerant.

〜〜〜〜〜〜〜〜〜〜〜〜〜〜〜〜〜〜〜〜〜〜〜〜〜〜〜〜〜〜〜〜〜〜

Since adjectives are freely used as nouns in Latin, we often find **nostrī,** *our men,* especially in military historians like Caesar. So also **tuī,** *your friends, your family,* etc.

In Latin, as in English, two adjectives modifying the same noun may or may not be connected by a conjunction, depending on the meaning.

> Magnum equum pulchrum spectō.
> *I am looking at a big beautiful horse.*
> Equum magnum et pulchrum spectō.
> *I am looking at a large and beautiful horse.*

But Latin usage differs from English in one respect: we seldom connect *many* with another adjective by a conjunction; Latin nearly always says **multī et . . .**

> Equōs multōs et pulchrōs spectō.
> *I am looking at many beautiful horses.*

~~~~~~

C. Translate.

1. On account of the war, we are without grain.   2. Is our native land free?   3. Our men were fighting in Europe.   4. We shall look at the games with our friends.   5. You (*pl.*) were carrying grain across the fields.   6. We are without water, and we shall suffer. 7. I used to give many beautiful gifts to the goddess.   8. Your poor slaves were laboring in the broad plains.   9. You used to dwell among good friends.   10. Our friends were looking at the beautiful girls.

——Reading——

Read aloud and translate.

AENEAS AT THE CAPTURE OF TROY

Aenēās miseram fortūnam Trōiānōrum pulchrae rēgīnae narrābat.

AENĒĀS: "Graecī Trōiam occupābant. Nostrōs virōs fēmināsque cum amīcīs ad oppidī portam convocābam. Propter perīculum sacra deōrum ad portam portābāmus, et Anchīsae dabāmus. Meī servī frūmentum et aquam parābant. Meīs amīcīs servīsque gladiōs dābam.

"Anchīsēs deōs invocābat: 'Amābātis Trōiam Trōiānōsque. Ubi estis? Spectātisne nostra perīcula? Inter multa perīcula labōrāmus. Nōnne amant deī nostram patriam?'"

> Saepe creat molles aspera spina rosas.
> *Often the prickly thorn produces tender roses.* —OVID

REVIEW 2 (LESSONS 5–8)

—Vocabulary Drill—

A. Give the genitive, gender, and meaning of the following nouns.

bellum	dōnum	oppidum	rēgnum
caelum	frūmentum	perīculum	verbum

B. Give the other nominative singular forms, and the meaning, of the following adjectives.

altus	longus	miser	pulcher
bonus	magnus	multus	sacer
ferus	malus	noster	tuus
lātus	meus	parvus	vester
līber			

Thermopolium at Ostia, a tavern where food and drinks were served. It is located in what was a populous section of the city.

C. Give the meanings of the following verbs.

appellō	habitō	nārrō	superō
convocō	labōrō	nūntiō	volō
exspectō			vulnerō

D. Give the meaning of the following prepositions, and the case or cases with which each is used.

ā, ab	cum	inter	propter
ad	dē	ob	sine
ante	ē, ex	per	sub
contrā	in	post	trāns

——Drill on Forms——

A. Decline the following.

oppidum līberum, perīculum magnum, dōnum pulchrum

B. Decline the following adjectives in all genders, singular and plural.

altus   miser   sacer

C. Conjugate the verb **narrō** in the present, imperfect, and future, giving meanings.

D. Translate the following verb forms.

1. exspectābis
2. vulnerābunt
3. superābant
4. volābam
5. nūntiābitis

6. appellābātis
7. labōrābāmus
8. convocābat
9. nārrābimus
10. habitābō

E. Give the Latin for the following.

1. I shall name
2. we shall assemble
3. he used to live
4. we were telling
5. you (*pl.*) will labor

6. they were waiting for
7. I was reporting
8. you (*pl.*) used to surpass
9. they will fly
10. you (*sing.*) will wound

—Drill on Syntax—

Translate.

1. in your (*one person*) farmhouse
2. on the large island
3. at the foot of the beautiful forest
4. toward my kingdom
5. into the broad field
6. out of your (*more than one person*) province
7. up to the small town
8. down from the long road
9. away from our fatherland
10. to the free land

—Exercises—

A. Translate.

1. Mea fīlia linguam poētārum bonōrum amat.
2. Nostrī tuam patriam superābunt.
3. Fēminae bonae deōs deāsque laudābant.
4. Pulchrae puellae bonōs puerōs exspectābunt.
5. Lēgātī nūntiōs ad parvum oppidum convocābant.
6. Lūdōsne puerōrum in campō lātō spectābimus?
7. Dabisne virō multa et pulchra dōna?
8. Est vīlla magna in oppidō.
9. Nautae labōrant; sunt sine aquā.
10. Aqua est alta et perīculum magnum.

B. Translate.

1. Our field is broad and your forest is large.
2. The messengers will report our good fortune to the lieutenant.
3. Many boys used to sail to the long island.
4. We were carrying many letters through the great forest.
5. The sons and daughters of the good sailor live in the province.
6. The kingdom of God is large and wide.
7. On account of the danger, your small son will carry a sword.
8. The bad men and my friends were fighting.
9. Our men were wounding your friends on the road.
10. We are carrying many beautiful gifts toward the kingdom.

9

Imperfect of Sum
Future of Sum
Ablative of Means or
Instrument

Roman mosaic of a man milking a goat, Imperial Palace, Istanbul

Medici graviores morbos asperis remediis curant.
Doctors cure the more serious diseases with harsh remedies.

—CURTIUS RUFUS

—Forms—

THE IMPERFECT AND FUTURE OF SUM

IMPERFECT TENSE

e'ram,	*I was*	erā'mus,	*we were*
e'rās,	*you were*	erā'tis,	*you were*
e'rat,	*he, she, it was*	e'rant,	*they were*

FUTURE TENSE

e'rō,	*I shall be*	e'rimus,	*we shall be*
e'ris,	*you will be*	e'ritis,	*you will be*
e'rit,	*he, she, it will be*	e'runt,	*they will be*

Relief from France showing a wine shop. Notice the large and small measures hanging over the counter on a rack.

— Syntax —

ABLATIVE OF MEANS OR INSTRUMENT

Means or instrument is expressed by the ablative without a preposition. Notice that it is regularly used of *things*, not persons, and is usually translated by *with* or some other preposition meaning *by means of.*

Servus tubā signum dat.   *A slave gives the signal on a trumpet.*
Deōs multīs linguīs laudābunt.   *They will praise the gods in many languages.*

— Vocabulary —

The following words are all adverbs.

be'ne, *well*
crās, *tomorrow*
cūr (interrogative), *why?*
di'ū, *for a long time, long*
he'rī, *yesterday*
ho'diē, *today*
iam, *now, already*
i'bi, *there, in that place*
in'terim, *meanwhile*

ma'le, *badly*
nunc, *now*
post'eā, *afterwards*
sae'pe, *often*
sem'per, *always*
tum, *then, at that time*
u'bi (relative), *where, when;*
  (interrogative), *where?*

— Exercises —

A. Name the tense, person, and number, and translate.

1. convocābō, sunt, laudābam   2. erātis, dabimus, erat   3. nārrat, eris, nāvigābitis   4. erit, amābāmus, estis   5. nūntiābunt, es, appellāmus

B. Name the tense, person, and number, and translate.

1. you (*sing.*) were, they were flying, I am   2. you (*pl.*) used to seize, we shall be, she was wounding   3. I shall be, they are carrying, I was   4. it is, you (*sing.*) will fight, you (*pl.*) will be   5. he will defeat, we were, you (*pl.*) are waiting for

C. Read the Latin and translate.

1. Puerī semper erunt bonī amīcī. 2. Lēgātī gladiīs diū pugnābant. 3. Ubi erātis herī? Crās ubi eritis? 4. Bonī nautae bene
nāvigābunt. 5. Dōna magna saepe dabant fēminīs. 6. Ītalia lī-
bera semper erit. 7. Equī ferī erant in campō lātō. 8. Erit frūmentum in agrō ubi agricolae labōrant. 9. Cūr vocābās servōs in
oppidum? 10. Virī aquam ad vīllam equīs portābunt.

D. Translate.

1. Meanwhile the boys were awaiting the messenger for a long
time. 2. Will your son always fight with a sword? 3. I was in
Gaul yesterday; will you (*sing.*) be there tomorrow? 4. We often
used to call our friends together with a trumpet. 5. The words
of the gods and goddesses will always be sacred. 6. The unfortunate lieutenant was laboring for a long time. 7. Afterwards we
shall sail to Italy. 8. I was small then; now I am big. 9. Today
we shall seize the town with swords. 10. There were always
many dangers in the great forest.

—— Reading ——

Read aloud and translate.

AENEAS AFTER THE FALL OF TROY

AENĒĀS: "Bellum erat longum; diū labōrābāmus. Nunc nāvigābam ab
  Asiā cum Anchīsā Ascaniōque et sacrīs deōrum Trōiānōrum."
DĪDŌ: "Sed Creūsa ubi erat?"
AENĒĀS: "Ō, nōn aderat! Miser eram sine fēminā meā. Sed interim ab
  Asiā nāvigābāmus ad Thrāciam."
DĪDŌ: "Ubi est Thrācia?"
AENĒĀS: "In Eurōpā est. Sed ibi erat perīculum magnum, et deī Trōiā-
  nōs in altum (*the deep*) vocābant."
DĪDŌ: "Posteā ubi erātis?"
AENĒĀS: "Est in altō īnsula sacra, īnsula deī. Ad īnsulam nāvigābāmus,
  et ibi deus Anchīsae bona verba dabat dē nostrā fortūnā."

10

Principal Parts
of Verbs
Interrogative Particles

Mosaic of edible sea life, National Museum, Naples

Num barbarorum Romulus rex fuit?
Romulus was not a king of barbarians, was he?—CICERO

—Forms—

THE PRINCIPAL PARTS OF A LATIN VERB

1. *the present indicative,* as **vocō**   3. *the perfect indicative,* as **vocāvī**
2. *the present infinitive,* as **vocāre**   4. *the supine,* as **vocātum**

The fixed parts of a verb, to which the different endings are added, are called *stems*. Every regular verb has three stems: *present, perfect,* and *participial, (supine)* to be found in the last three principal parts.

     present **vocā-**   *perfect* **vocāv-**   *supine* **vocāt-**

The first conjugation includes all verbs whose present stem ends in **-ā**. This is obtained by dropping the infinitive ending **-re**.

Dō and **sum** are irregular verbs. The principal parts of **dō** are **dō, dare, dedī, datum;** those of **sum** are **sum, esse, fuī, futūrus.**

—Syntax—

INTERROGATIVE PARTICLES

We have seen that to make the kind of question which may be answered by *yes* or *no* we add the enclitic **-ne** to the first word of the sentence. When a question expects the answer *yes,* some negative word, usually **nōn,** is placed first in the sentence and has the **-ne** attached to it.

     Nōnne puella est pulchra?
      Isn't the girl beautiful? or *The girl is beautiful, isn't she?*

When the answer *no* is expected the question is introduced by **num.**

     Num puella est pulchra? *The girl isn't beautiful, is she?*

— Vocabulary —

am'bulō, ambulā're, ambulā'vī, ambulā'tum, *walk*

clā'mō, clāmā're, clāmā'vī, clāmā'tum, *shout*

cōnfīr'mō, cōnfīrmā're, cōnfīrmā'vī, cōnfīrmā'tum, *strengthen; encourage; declare*

dēmōn'strō, dēmōnstrā're, dēmōnstrā'vī, dēmōnstrā'tum, *show, point out*

lī'berō, līberā're, līberā'vī, līberā'tum, *free, set free*

oppug'nō, oppugnā're, oppugnā'vī, oppugnā'tum, *attack*

ser'vō, servā're, servā'vī, servā'tum, *guard, keep; save*

stō, stā're, ste'tī, stā'tum, *stand*

temp'tō, temptā're, temptā'vī, temptā'tum, *try, attempt*

Ā'frica, -ae, f., *Africa*

A'sia, -ae, f., *Asia Minor*

num, (interrogative particle used in questions expecting a *no* answer)

Center section of Basilica mosaic showing marine life, Aquileia Museum

—— Exercises ——

A. Answer these questions in complete Latin sentences.

1. Nōnne lēgātī oppidum oppugnābunt gladiīs?   2. Num viae ad Germāniam longae erant?   3. Nostrīne in Āfricā erant multī? 4. Nōnne deī erunt amīcī bonōrum?   5. Num ambulābātis herī in silvā?

B. Read the Latin and translate.

1. Fēminae per campōs cum puellīs ambulābant.   2. Puerī puellīs tubam nūntī dēmōnstrant.   3. Dabisne deīs dōna multa et pulchra?   4. Nautaene nostrōs in īnsulā exspectant?   5. Galliae virōs nōn saepe superābāmus.   6. Fēminaene servōs līberābunt? 7. Num vir amīcum puerī vulnerat?   8. Gladius nostrī lēgātī longus est.   9. Laudābam agricolae equōs in agrō.   10. Post bellum clāmābant puerī.

C. Translate.

1. You (*pl.*) are not carrying water to the farmhouse, are you? 2. Are you giving a gift to the sailors today?   3. They are defeating our men now.   4. Gaul, Africa, and Asia were not always provinces.   5. Does the farmer give much grain to (his) horse?   6. The good girl is calling the sailors together.   7. The lieutenants are waiting for a message today.   8. The boy will give many large gifts to (his) friend.   9. Will you (*sing.*) not free the slaves in your country?   10. The lieutenants were fighting with swords.

—— Reading ——

AENEAS CONTINUES HIS TALE

AENĒĀS: "Tum ab īnsulā sacrā ad terram Crētam fortūna Trōiānōs vocābat. Ibi oppidum parābāmus; et nunc Anchīsēs cōnfīrmābat meōs, et clāmābat: 'In Crētā habitābimus. In Crētā stābunt sacra deōrum Trōiānōrum!'"

DĪDŌ: "Cūr hodiē in Crētā nōn estis?"

AENĒĀS: "Dēerat* frūmentum, et misera erat vīta. Et nunc deī Anchīsae viam dēmōnstrābant in Ītaliam, ubi parābant rēgnum Trōiānīs."

* *from* **dēsum, dēesse,** *to be lacking*

11

Formation of Adverbs
Perfect Tense

Distribution of bread, fresco, Pompeii, National Museum, Naples

Divina natura dedit agros, ars humana aedificavit urbes.
The divine nature produced the fields, human skill has built cities.

—TIBULLUS

—Forms—

THE FORMATION OF ADVERBS

Adverbs are normally made from adjectives of the first and second declensions by adding **-ē** to the base:

altē,	*on high, deeply*	longē,	*far off, by far*
lātē,	*widely*	miserē,	*wretchedly, desperately*
līberē,	*freely, frankly*	pulchrē,	*beautifully, nobly*

Not all first and second declension adjectives have regularly formed adverbs. You have already learned that the adverbs of **bonus** and **malus** are **bene** and **male,** and you will see other irregular adverbs later.

Helps and Hints. Do not be disturbed about adverbs formed from first and second declension adjectives ending in **-er.** They follow the rule given; for example, **līber,** *free;* **līberē,** *freely.* (base **līber + ē**).

THE PERFECT TENSE

The perfect tense is the only tense which does not use the regular personal endings **-ō,** or **-m, -s, -t, -mus, -tis,** and **-nt.** Its endings are:

	SINGULAR	PLURAL
1ST PERSON:	**-ī**	**-imus**
2D PERSON:	**-istī**	**-istis**
3D PERSON:	**-it**	**-ērunt** or **-ēre**

These endings are added to the *perfect stem*, which is found by dropping the -ī from the third principal part of the verb: **vocāvī, vocāv-.**

vocā'**vī,**   *I have called, I called*
vocā**vis'tī,**   *you have called, you called*
vocā'**vit,**   *he has called, he called*

vocā'**vimus,**   *we have called, we called*
vocā**vis'tis,**   *you have called, you called*
vocāvē'**runt,**   *they have called, they called*

All regular verbs of the first conjugation are conjugated this way in the perfect tense.

The perfect tense of **sum** is: fuī   fuimus
                                     fuistī   fuistis
                                     fuit   fuērunt

The perfect tense of **dō** is: dedī   dedimus
                                    dedistī   dedistis
                                    dedit   dedērunt

Roman relief, grape treading, Archeological Museum, Venice

—— *Syntax* ——

USE OF THE PERFECT TENSE

The perfect tense represents an act as completed at the time of speaking (*I have prepared*) or merely as having occurred in the past time (*I prepared*). Contrast this with the imperfect, which expresses an action as continued in past time (*I was preparing*).

Frūmentum nunc parāvī.   *I have now prepared the grain.*
Dōnum puellae iam dedit.
  He has already given the gift to the girl.
Tum frūmentum parāvī.   *I prepared the grain then.*
Dōnum puellae dedit herī.   *He gave the gift to the girl yesterday.*

—— *Vocabulary* ——

a'nimus, -ī, m., *mind; spirit*
ar'ma, -ō'rum, n., (pl.) *arms*
auxi'lium, auxi'lī, n., *help, aid*
  auxi'lia, -ō'rum, n., (pl.)
  auxiliary troops, reinforcements
captī'vus, -ī, m., *captive*
cas'tra, -ō'rum, n., (pl.) *camp*
cōnsi'lium, cōnsi'lī, n., *plan, advice*
cō'pia, -ae, f., *plenty, supply*
  cō'piae, -ā'rum, f., (pl.) *forces, troops*

fāma, -ae, f., *rumor, report, reputation*
fu'ga, -ae, f., *flight*
impedīmen'tum, -ī, n., *hindrance*
  impedīmen'ta, -ō'rum, n., (pl.) *baggage*
nu'merus, -ī, m., *number; group*
proe'lium, proe'lī, n., *battle*
sig'num, -ī, n., *sign, signal; military standard*
tē'lum, -ī, n., *weapon*

—— *Word Study* ——

In this lesson you are introduced to a number of words which occur frequently in military histories, particularly those of Caesar. Some of these deserve further explanation:
Auxilia: the plural of **auxilium** means *helps, aids,* or *sources of aid* in ordinary Latin; but as a technical military term it refers to all the non-legionary soldiery in an army, light-armed infantry, cavalry, archers, slingers, etc.

Cōpiae: this word, too, keeps its normal meanings in the plural, *supplies, riches, resources;* but in military terminology a general's resources are the forces at his disposal.

Impedīmenta: from a tactical point of view the pieces of baggage which accompany an army are primarily *hindrances* to rapid maneuvering.

Arma and **castra** (like *trousers* and *scissors* in English) occur only in the plural. Remember to use a plural verb when **castra** is the subject:

> Castra sunt magna.   *The camp is large.*

Arma can be used of *arms* and *weapons* in general; but when contrasted with **tēla** it has more specific meanings:

arma, "defensive arms" as opposed to **tēla,** "offensive weapons," or **arma,** "weapons for close fighting," as opposed to **tēla,** "missiles."

—— Exercises ——

A. Translate, giving both meanings for all perfects.

1. servāvistī, pugnābās, clāmābis   2. fuit, appellāvistis, stetērunt   3. ambulāvī, habitābō, portātis   4. cōnfirmāvī, superābāmus, vocābis   5. nūntiat, nāvigāvērunt, līberāvistī

Relief showing a silversmith's workshop. Notice the finished products, molds, crucible for melting silver, and scales.

B. Translate into Latin.

1. we have tried, they will look at, he awaited 2. I have liked, they have prepared, you (*pl.*) called together 3. he has praised, she was giving, they were pointing out 4. we shall seize, you (*sing.*) will suffer, they attacked 5. he is relating, they will fly, we have wounded

C. Read the Latin and translate.

1. Equī sine aquā herī erant. 2. Dabisne litterās fēminae crās? 3. Arma multa et bona nostrīs dedit. 4. Posteā ad lēgātum portābit nūntium dē perīculīs. 5. Tēlīs pugnāvimus cum Galliae cōpiīs. 6. Cūr puerum tēlō vulnerāvistī? 7. Diū cum meīs amīcīs ambulāvī. 8. Herī in castrīs nostrīs lēgātōs diū exspectābāmus. 9. Multās litterās pulchrē parāvistis. 10. Multī in Eurōpā iam līberī sunt.

D. Translate into Latin.

1. Why were the boys and the slaves fighting in that place? 2. We have freed the small town with our swords. 3. The messengers called the big boys together with (their) trumpets. 4. We shall give gifts to the goddess tomorrow. 5. We were living in the farmhouse for a long time. 6. We carried grain to our friends yesterday. 7. The bad boys were without friends. 8. Many fine horses were standing on the road today. 9. Did you (*sing.*) wound the man with a weapon? 10. The poets were not unhappy.

—— *Reading* ——

Read aloud and translate.

AENEAS COMPLETES HIS TALE

AENĒĀS: "Anchīsēs animōs nostrōs bonīs verbīs cōnfirmāvit: 'Deī signum dedērunt; nostrum rēgnum est in Ītaliā. Est longē ab Āfricā, sed post longam fugam et multōs annōs in Ītaliam nāvigābimus.'

Tum nāvigāvimus in terram ubi habitābant vir fēminaque, captīvī Trōiānī, nostrī amīcī. Iam līberī erant. Fēmina multa et pulchra dōna dedit, et vir bonum cōnsilium dē nostrō rēgnō in Ītaliā. Nautae nostrī arma et cōpiam aquae frūmentīque ab oppidō nostrōrum amīcōrum portāvērunt. Tum ad rēgnum tuum nāvigāvimus."

12

Pluperfect Tense
Future Perfect Tense

A relief showing a cloth merchant's shop

Colossus magnitudinem suam servabit etiam si steterit in puteo.
A giant will keep his size even though he will have stood in a well.

—SENECA

—— Forms ——

PLUPERFECT AND FUTURE PERFECT

Two other tenses besides the perfect are formed on the perfect stem: the pluperfect and the future perfect; these three tenses are called tenses of the *perfect system*.

THE PLUPERFECT TENSE

To form the pluperfect we add the tense-sign **-erā-** to the perfect stem, and then add the personal endings **-m, -s, -t, -mus, -tis,** and **-nt,** shortening the **-ā-** of **-erā-** before **-m, -t,** and **-nt.**

vocā'v**eram,**	*I had called*	vocāverā'**mus,**	*we had called*
vocā'v**erās,**	*you had called*	vocāverā'**tis,**	*you had called*
vocā'v**erat,**	*he had called*	vocā'v**erant,**	*they had called*

THE FUTURE PERFECT TENSE

The future perfect tense is formed by adding the tense-sign **-eri-** to the perfect stem of the verb, then the personal endings **-ō, -s, -t, -mus, -tis,** and **-nt,** omitting the **-i-** of **-eri-** before **-ō.**

vocā'v**erō,**	*I shall have called*	vocāve'**rimus,**	*we shall have called*
vocā'v**eris,**	*you will have called*	vocāve'**ritis,**	*you will have called*
vocā'v**erit,**	*he will have called*	vocāve'**rint,**	*they will have called*

—— Vocabulary ——

audā'cia, -ae, f., *daring, boldness*
car'rus, -ī, m., *wagon, cart*
cū'ra, -ae, f., *care, anxiety*
do'minus, -ī, m., *lord, master*
ino'pia, -ae, f., *lack, want*
ī'ra, -ae, f., *anger*
li'ber, li'brī, m., *book*
lo'cus, -ī, m. (lo'ca, locō'rum, , pl.), *place*

magis'ter, magis'trī, m., *master, teacher*
poe'na, -ae, f., *punishment, penalty*
po'pulus, -ī, m., *people, nation*
so'cius, so'cī, m., *ally, comrade*

—— *Word Study* ——

Dominus and **magister** both mean *master*, but the two words are not interchangeable. **Dominus** is "master" in the sense of "owner," **magister** in the sense of "director."

Populus. The word **populus** in Latin is generally used in the singular, as in the phrase **populus Rōmānus.** It is used in the plural to mean *nations* or *tribes*. Note that *many people* is generally expressed by **multī.**

—— *Exercises* ——

A. Analyze each form and translate.

1. pugnāverat, labōrābunt, ambulāvistī   2. oppugnābat, spectāvērunt, parat   3. portāvī, eram, vocāverit   4. volāvimus, nārrant, dēmōnstrāverās   5. servābit, laudāvistī, stetērunt   6. occupābāmus, exspectāveritis, temptāvistis   7. clāmāverat, superāmus, cōnfirmāverō   8. nāvigābāmus, habitāverint, appellāvērunt   9. līberāvistī, nuntiāverās, dederit   10. convocābant, amāvērunt, vulnerābō

B. Translate.

1. I have wounded, you (*sing.*) were capturing, you (*pl.*) will look at   2. we shall have carried, he shouted, they had set free   3. you (*sing.*) had stood, they will have attacked, we are flying   4. they have praised, we shall name, he guards   5. they will have tried, I shall be, we walk   6. you (*pl.*) have declared, I had given, they told   7. they have fought, he waited for, you (*sing.*) will have called   8. they had surpassed, we shall labor, I have shown   9. you (*pl.*) have prepared, he had liked, we shall have sailed   10. I shall announce, they assembled, he had lived

C. Read the Latin and translate.

1. Meae fīliae auxilium miserō servō dabant.   2. Ob bellī perīculum multa tēla parāverant.   3. Lūdōsne in oppidō hodiē spectābātis?   4. Agricolae magnam frūmentī cōpiam ex agrō portābant.   5. Num nautae miserī ab īnsulā nāvigāverint?   6. Fēminae puellās in campum saepe convocāverant.   7. Virīs signum proelī tubā iam dederō.   8. Crās puerī gladiīs servum malum vulnerābunt.

9. Tum lēgātus bonam fortūnam nostrōrum nūntiāverat.
10. Nūntiī virōs in parvā vīllā herī exspectāvērunt.

D. Translate.

1. The peoples of Europe had not always been free.   2. Haven't the good boys given the poet's books to the teacher?   3. Tomorrow our camp will be in the great forest in Germany.   4. The little girl's books were not large, were they?   5. Won't the masters set (their) slaves free now?   6. Without weapons I shall have fought badly.   7. The farmer's son had already given grain and water to the horses.   8. The lieutenants encouraged our forces when they were being hard pressed for a long time.   9. A large number of our men had carried the baggage into the camp.   10. Do free people often walk with slaves?

—Reading—

Read aloud and translate.

AENEAS INCURS DIDO'S ANGER

Ubi Aenēās Elissae perīcula Trōiānōrum narrāverat, rēgīna clāmāvit: "Magna est audācia tua! Ad multa loca et per perīcula magna nāvigāvistī! Multa dōna tuīs dedī, et nunc fugam ē meō rēgnō parātis."

Magna erat cūra Aenēae: rēginam amābat, sed deī Trōiānōs vocābant in Ītaliam.

Ubi fugam parāverat Aenēās magna erat īra rēgīnae. Misera clāmāvit: "Aenēan virum meum appellāvī, sed Trōiānus malus nōn amāvit miseram Elissam! Iam fugam parāvit; crās ab Āfricā nāvigābit. Semper stābit īra mea inter Trōiānōs et populum meum! Sociī nōn erunt: semper meī in armīs stābunt contrā Trōiānōs, et diū labōrābunt Trōiānī bellīs et proeliīs multīs!"

Sed interim Aenēās erat in altō; ad Ītaliam iam nāvigābat.

Qui non est hodie cras minus aptus erit.

He who is not prepared today will be less so tomorrow. —OVID

REVIEW 3 (LESSONS 9–12)

— *Vocabulary Drill* —

A. Give the genitive, gender, and meaning of the following nouns.

animus	cōnsilium	inopia	poena
arma	cōpia	īra	populus
audācia	cūra	liber	proelium
auxilium	dominus	locus	signum
captīvus	fāma	magister	socius
carrus	fuga	numerus	tēlum
castra	impedīmentum		

B. Give the principal parts and meanings of the following verbs.

ambulō	dēmōnstrō	oppugnō	sum
clāmō	dō	servō	temptō
cōnfīrmō	līberō	stō	

C. Give the meanings of the following adverbs.

bene	hodiē	male	saepe
crās	iam	num	semper
cūr	ibi	nunc	tum
diū	interim	posteā	ubi
herī			

~~~~~~

A *synopsis* of a verb consists of all the forms of a given person and number. The synopsis of **vocō** in the first person singular is:

PRESENT   vocō,   *I call, I am calling, I do call*

IMPERFECT   vocābam,   *I was calling, I called*

FUTURE   vocābō,   *I shall call*

PERFECT   vocāvī,   *I have called, I did call, I called*

PLUPERFECT   vocāveram,   *I had called*

FUTURE PERFECT   vocāverō,   *I shall have called*

~~~~~~

—Drill on Forms—

A. Give a synopsis, with meanings, of the following verbs. (See p. 69.)

1. dō *in the 2d person singular*
2. līberō *in the 3d person singular*
3. stō *in the 1st person plural*
4. vulnerō *in the 2d person plural*
5. sum *in the 3d person plural*

B. Translate.

1. temptābitis
2. dēmōnstrās
3. fueram
4. oppugnāvimus
5. cōnfirmābant

6. dederis
7. ambulāvimus
8. stetērunt
9. servāveritis
10. clāmāverat

C. Translate.

1. she will stand
2. you (*sing.*) had been
3. we were saving
4. they have shouted
5. they will have given
6. you (*pl.*) attack

7. I walked
8. you (*sing.*) will have strengthened
9. we tried
10. you (*pl.*) had shown

—Drill on Syntax—

Translate the words in italics, giving the reason for each case.

1. Where are *the captives?*
2. These men are *captives.*
3. I like *the plan.*
4. What is the plan *of the auxiliary troops?*
5. He gave a sword *to (his) comrade.*
6. He carried a sword *to the place.*
7. They carried their baggage *in carts.*

8. They guarded their baggage *in the camp.*
9. They carried their baggage *into the camp.*
10. They carried their baggage *from the camp.*

—— *Exercises* ——

A. Translate.

1. Nōnne nostrōs superāvistis audāciā cōpiārum vestrārum?
2. Est in oppidō nostrō cōpia frūmentī sed aquae inopia.
3. Lēgātī arma servāverant longē ab castrīs.
4. Lēgātus populō cōnsilia sociōrum līberē nūntiāvit.
5. Captīvōrum cūra magna erat, sed animōs cōnfirmāvimus.
6. Cūr nūntius signum proelī tubā dederit?
7. Fāma dē sociōrum fugā lātē longēque volāverat.
8. Ibi erant castra magna nostrārum cōpiārum.
9. Magnae erunt īrae deōrum in malōs.
10. Puer gladiō miserum servum altē vulnerāverat.

B. Translate.

1. After the battle signal our men shouted.
2. We shall carry a report far and wide concerning the great battle.
3. Not many people have walked through the forest, have they?
4. Where is the camp of our allies?
5. Did you (*pl.*) wound the unfortunate sailor deeply with your weapons?
6. Afterwards we shall have strengthened the spirits of our men with good words.
7. There was not a lack of water in our camp, but we were without grain.
8. The wretched captives freely pointed out the way to our camp.
9. The lieutenant had already attacked the small town without the help of the allies.
10. The baggage will be in the town, but we shall carry our arms into camp.

13

Imperative Mood
Vocative Case

Relief of a knife-seller's shop

Ora et labora.
Pray and labor.—ST. BENEDICT

—Forms—

MOODS

Every Latin verb has five attributes: tense, voice, mood, person, and number. In the forms which you have learned you have seen examples of all six tenses (present, imperfect, future, perfect, pluperfect, and future perfect), all three persons (first, second, and third), and both numbers (singular and plural); but so far you have learned only one voice, the active, and one mood, the indicative.

Latin verbs have three moods, the indicative, the subjunctive, and the imperative. The indicative, as you have seen, is used to make statements and to ask questions. The subjunctive (which you will learn later) is used to describe unreal actions. The imperative is used for commands.

THE IMPERATIVE MOOD

The present imperative singular in Latin is regularly the same as the present stem, **vocā,** *call.* The plural adds **-te** to the singular, **vocāte,** *call.* The singular form is used when one person is addressed; the plural is used when more than one person is addressed. The imperatives of **sum** are **es** and **este.**

THE VOCATIVE CASE

The vocative case is used for direct address. It is rarely the first word in a sentence and is usually set off by commas. The vocative case in Latin is the same as the nominative in all declensions, except for second declension singular nouns ending in **-us** or **-ius.** Nouns of the second declension singular ending in **-us** have **-e** as the vocative ending, as **amīce,** *O friend!* But **filius,** and proper nouns ending in **-ius,** have the vocative ending in **-ī: fīlī** *son:* **Iūlī,** *Julius.**

*The masculine vocative singular of **meus** is **mī.**

~~~~~~

Helps and Hints. The imperative and vocative frequently occur in the same sentence. *Come here, boys. Fight hard, soldiers.* Usually the imperative comes first in the sentence and the vocative second. Remember that the plural of *all* Latin nouns has the vocative the same as the nominative.

~~~~~~

—— Vocabulary ——

cau'sa, -ae, f., *reason, cause*
epis'tula, -ae, f., *letter, epistle*
fā'bula, -ae, f., *story*
hō'ra, -ae, f., *hour*
Iū'lia, -ae, f., *Julia*

Iū'lius, -ī, m., *Julius*
Lū'cius, Lū'cī, m., *Lucius*
Mār'cus, -ī, m., *Marcus*
pecū'nia, -ae, f., *money*
rēgī'na, -ae, f., *queen*

al'bus, -a, -um, *white*
amī'cus, -a, -um, *friendly*
grā'tus, -a, -um, *pleasing, welcome; grateful*
inimī'cus, -a, -um, *unfriendly, hostile* (inimī'cus, -ī, m., *enemy*)
ni'ger, ni'gra, ni'grum, *black*
no'vus, -a, -um, *new*
parā'tus, -a, -um, *ready, prepared*
vē'rus, -a, -um, *true*

—— Word Study ——

Iūlia, Iūlius. Iūlius is a Roman family name. A Roman girl was not given a name of her own, but was known simply by the family name in the feminine form. All the daughters of the Julius family would be called Julia. To distinguish between them they might be given nicknames or, if there were many of them, they were given numbers.

Lūcius and **Mārcus** are Roman first names. Because of the practice of naming boys after their fathers, grandfathers or paternal uncles, there were only 18 given names in use in the classical period, and only about half of these were common.

—— *Exercises* ——

A. Give the present active imperative second person singular of:

dō   nāvigō   pugnō   spectō   dēmōnstrō

B. Give the present active imperative second person plural of:

portō   labōrō   clāmō   stō   pugnō

(top) Pavement mosaic indicating an office of Carthage shipowners. (bottom) The Square of the Corporations at Ostia.

C. Give the vocative singular of:

vir	Iūlia	puer	Lūcius	agricola
puella	Mārcus	nauta	fīlius	captīvus

D. Give the vocative plural of:

rēgīna	dea	socius	amīcus	dominus
nūntius	fēmina	servus	poēta	fīlia

E. Read the Latin and translate.

1. Līberā, domine, servōs; bonī virī sunt. 2. Crās castra occupā-verimus. 3. Dā, Iūlia, pecūniam servō amīcō. 4. Per silvam diū ambulāvimus. 5. Spectāte rēgīnam; pulchra est. 6. Multī nūntiō epistulās dederant. 7. Parāvistīne, mī fīlī, epistulam? 8. Crās, virī, nāvigābimus; parāte vestra arma. 9. Rēgīna puellīs parvīs pulchra dōna dabat. 10. Lēgātus tubā signum dedit.

F. Translate.

1. Why are the letters not welcome, my queen? 2. Tell the story of your dangers, Marcus. 3. We are ready; sail to the island, sailors. 4. Lucius had walked with his friends through the forest for a long time. 5. My sons, give money to your friends. 6. They carried the money into the town yesterday. 7. Boys, carry water to the black horses. 8. Tomorrow we shall seize the camp and the town. 9. Julia was beautiful but unfriendly. 10. Julia, are you the daughter of Lucius Julius?

—— Reading ——

Read aloud and translate.

LAVINIA

Ubi Trōiānī in Ītaliam nāvigāverant, Amāta erat rēgīna Latīnōrum. Lāvīnia erat fīlia Amātae et Latīnī. Lāvīniam Aenēas amāvit, sed Turnus, dominus Rutulōrum et socius Latīnōrum, Lāvīniam diū amābat. Amātae Turnus grātus erat, Aenēas nōn grātus. Inter Troiānōs et Latīnōs erat longum bellum. Causa bellī erat Lāvīnia.

Latīnī castra Aeneadārum oppugnābant. Turnus clāmāvit: "Tua fāma, Aenēa (*vocative*), mī inimīce, est magna. Nunc convocā tuōs sociōs et dēmōnstrā audāciam Troiānōrum."

14

Third Declension

Relief from France showing a fullery (cloth finishing and laundering establishment)

Otium sine litteris mors est et hominis vivi sepultura.
Leisure without literature is death, or rather
the burial of a living man.—SENECA

— Forms —

THE THIRD DECLENSION

All nouns and adjectives whose genitive singular ends in **-is** belong
to the third declension.

	SINGULAR		ENDINGS
NOMINATIVE:	frā'ter	so'ror	—
GENITIVE:	frā'tris	sorō'ris	**-is**
DATIVE:	frā'trī	sorō'rī	**-ī**
ACCUSATIVE:	frā'trem	sorō'rem	**-em**
ABLATIVE:	frā'tre	sorō're	**-e**
	PLURAL		
NOMINATIVE:	frā'trēs	sorō'rēs	**-ēs**
GENITIVE:	frā'trum	sorō'rum	**-um**
DATIVE:	frā'tribus	sorō'ribus	**-ibus**
ACCUSATIVE:	frā'trēs	sorō'rēs	**-ēs**
ABLATIVE:	frā'tribus	sorō'ribus	**-ibus**

The vocative of the third declension is like the nominative.

— Vocabulary —

cele'ritās, celeritā'tis, f.,
  swiftness, speed
cōn'sul, cōn'sulis, m., *consul*
dux, du'cis, m., *leader*
frā'ter, frā'tris, m., *brother*
imperā'tor, imperātō'ris, m.,
  commander, general
impe'rium, impe'rī, n., *command,*
  military power, government

mā'ter, mā'tris, f., *mother*
mī'les, mī'litis, m., *soldier*
pa'ter, pa'tris, m., *father*
rēx, rē'gis, m., *king*
so'ror, sorō'ris, f., *sister*

dēlec'tō, -ā're, -ā'vī, -ā'tum,
  please

mox, adverb, *soon*

—Word Study—

Imperium. Originally Rome was ruled by a king, who alone held the power to rule. This power was called the **imperium,** and was symbolized by the **fascēs,** a bundle of rods tied around an axe, representing the king's right to inflict corporal or capital punishment.

Cōnsul. After the overthrow of the monarchy (509 B.C.) the **imperium** was given to elected officials, the consuls. Two consuls were elected annually. The word **imperium** came more and more to mean "the power to command armies," since the officials who held it also served as generals in war time.

Imperātor. Since Roman armies were led by consuls or praetors, Latin has no separate word for *general.* However, when a consul or a praetor by his successes showed clearly that he held the imperium (which was thought of almost as a magical power), he might be acclaimed **imperātor,** *wielder of the imperium,* by his troops. He was allowed to use **imperātor** as a title with his name. This title was later taken as a name by the Roman emperors. For convenience, **imperātor** may be translated merely as *general* or *commander.*

Relief showing a smith and his assistant

—— Exercises ——

A. Decline.

cōnsul bonus   māter mea   dux novus

B. Translate.

1. Ducēs novōs mīlitēs in castra mox vocābunt.   2. Lēgātus laudāvit cōnsulis fīliōs.   3. Pater meus amīcus erat cōnsulum in
Ītaliā.   4. Mīlitēs in agrō post castra diū pugnābant.   5. Nārrā,
Iūlia, fābulam tuō frātrī parvō.   6. Ubi imperātor cōpiās Galliae
superāvit?   7. Multa et pulchra dōna dederāmus nostrae sorōrī.
8. Post proelium erit novus imperator.   9. Fāma dē nostrī imperātōris bonā fortūnā latē longēque volāverat.   10. In vīllā, māter,
Iūliam exspectā; ad oppidum ambulābō.

C. Translate.

1. The books of the great poet pleased my brother well.   2. Marcus
is the leader of many soldiers.   3. The consul's sisters were looking at many broad fields.   4. Lucius called (his) brothers and
sisters from the wide forest into the town.   5. The general used
to fight in battle with (his) soldiers.   6. The people used to give
the military power to the consuls.   7. Where was the consul's
father?   8. The teacher gave (his) little sister beautiful gifts.   9. We
shall soon sail to the kingdom of the great king.   10. The boys
were praising (their) fathers and mothers.

—— Reading ——

Read aloud and translate.

TURNUS ASSEMBLES THE RUTULIANS

Turnus, dux Rutulōrum, in magnō oppidō Ardeā cum patre Daunō
et sorōre Iūturnā habitābat. Tum alta et magna in agrō Latīnō Ardea
stābat. Posteā oppidum parvum erat, sed Rōmānīs sacrum. Saepe
cōnsulēs Rōmānī dona pulchra deīs Ardeae dabant.

   Ubi Aeneadae in Ītaliam navigāverant, fāma dē Trōianōrum fugā
longē lātēque per Ītaliam volāverat, sed Turnum nōn dēlectāvit. Dux
Rutulōrum populum convocāvit, animōs mīlitum cōnfīrmāvit et bellum parāvit.

15

Third Declension, Neuter
Ablative of Manner

Chart of measures on one of the buildings in the market place, Leptis Magna

> Materiam superabat opus.
> *The workmanship was better than the subject matter.*—OVID

—— *Forms* ——

THIRD DECLENSION NEUTER

Neuter nouns of the third declension, like all neuters in Latin, have the same form in the nominative and the accusative, the nominative and accusative plural ending in **-a**.

		SINGULAR		ENDINGS
NOMINATIVE:	nō'men	i'ter	tem'pus	—
GENITIVE:	nō'min**is**	iti'ner**is**	tem'por**is**	**-is**
DATIVE:	nō'min**ī**	iti'ner**ī**	tem'por**ī**	**-ī**
ACCUSATIVE:	nō'men	i'ter	tem'pus	—
ABLATIVE:	nō'min**e**	iti'ner**e**	tem'por**e**	**-e**

		PLURAL		
NOMINATIVE:	nō'min**a**	iti'ner**a**	tem'por**a**	**-a**
GENITIVE:	nō'min**um**	iti'ner**um**	tem'por**um**	**-um**
DATIVE:	nōmi'**nibus**	itine'**ribus**	tempo'**ribus**	**-ibus**
ACCUSATIVE:	nō'min**a**	iti'ner**a**	tem'por**a**	**-a**
ABLATIVE:	nōmi'**nibus**	itine'**ribus**	tempo'**ribus**	**-ibus**

—— *Syntax* ——

ABLATIVE OF MANNER

The manner in which an action is performed is expressed by the ablative with **cum**. If the noun is modified by an adjective, **cum** may be omitted; if it is used, the word order must be: adjective, **cum,** noun:

Litterās cum dīligentiā parāvit.   *He prepared the letter with care.*
Litterās magnā dīligentiā parāvit.   ⎱ *He prepared the letter*
Litterās magnā cum dīligentiā parāvit. ⎰ *with great care.*

Do not confuse the Ablative of Manner with the Ablative of Means.

Cum audāciā pugnāvīstī.   *You fought with boldness.*
(ABLATIVE OF MANNER)
Tēlīs pugnāvīstī.   *You fought with weapons.*
(ABLATIVE OF MEANS)

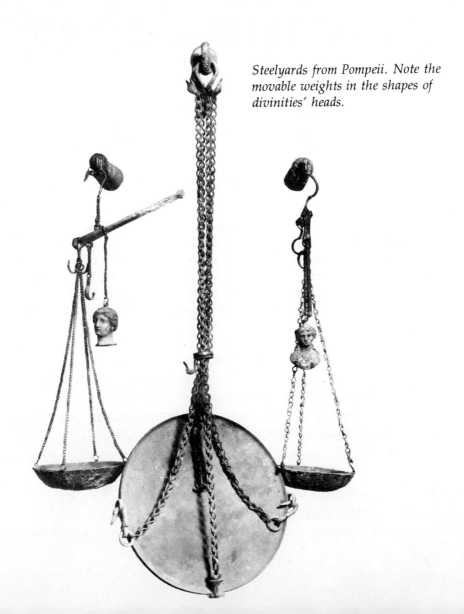

Steelyards from Pompeii. Note the movable weights in the shapes of divinities' heads.

—— Vocabulary ——

Cae'sar, Cae'saris, m., *Caesar*
ca'put, ca'pitis, n., *head*
car'men, car'minis, n., *song, poem*
cor'pus, cor'poris, n., *body*
dīligen'tia, -ae, f., *diligence, care*
flū'men, flū'minis, n., *river, stream*
i'ter, iti'neris, n., *march, journey; route*
nō'men, nō'minis, n., *name*
tem'pus, tem'poris, n., *time*
vul'nus, vul'neris, n., *wound*

Germā'nus, -a, -um, *German*
Grae'cus, -a, -um, *Greek*
Hispā'nus, -a, -um, *Spanish*
Rōmā'nus, -a, -um, *Roman, of Rome*

—— Word Study ——

Caesar. Most Roman men had three names, the **praenōmen,** the **nōmen** and the **cognōmen.** The **praenōmen** is the *first name* or *given name,* e.g., **Lūcius, Mārcus.** The **nōmen** is the *family name,* e.g., **Iūlius.** The **cognōmen** is a kind of *nickname,* designating the branch of the family to which the man belonged. It often described some physical characteristic or commemorated some famous deed. Caesar is a cognomen of the Julius family; the full name of the famous Caesar was Gaius Julius Caesar.

Rōmānus. The genitive of **Rōma** is not used to indicate possession; *Rome's* or *of Rome* is expressed by the adjective **Rōmānus:**

mīles Rōmānus	*a soldier of Rome*
cōpiae Rōmānae	*the forces of Rome*

Populus Rōmānus means either the Roman nation as a whole, or the common people as distinguished from the senatorial nobility. Decrees, etc., were issued in the name of the Senate and the Roman People (**Senātus Populusque Rōmānus,** abbreviated **S.P.Q.R.**).

—— Exercises ——

A. Decline the following.

corpus magnum	carmen vērum	caput meum

B. Read the Latin and translate.

1. Caesar erat imperātor magnus in Galliā. 2. Germānī magnā cum audāciā nostra castra oppugnābunt. 3. Mīlitēs cum dīligentiā in oppidō arma parābant. 4. Mātrum carmina fīliās dēlectāverint. 5. Nautae Graecī nōn nāvigābant magnā celeritāte. 6. Nōnne flūmen erat lātum et longum et pulchrum? 7. Lūcī Iūlī Caesaris fīliae nōmen erit Iūlia. 8. Populus Rōmānus imperium cōnsulibus grātē dedit. 9. Corpora Rōmānōrum magna nōn erant. 10. Post bellum nōmen novum cōnsulī dabimus.

C. Translate.

1. The teachers did not often look at the boys with great friendliness. 2. Men of Rome, fight with great diligence! 3. Did the messenger give the battle signal on a trumpet? 4. There was a horse's body on the road. 5. The Spanish always used to fight with great boldness. 6. A great king in Germany was a friend and ally of the Roman People. 7. The German forces had fought in the camp of the Romans. 8. The journey to the Spanish town is long, but we shall walk with great speed. 9. The troops of Rome attacked the German camp with long weapons. 10. Why did you carry the grain to town in a wagon, Marcus?

— Reading —

Read aloud and translate.

ROMAN SCHOOLS

In lūdō Rōmānō erant puerī sed nōn multae puellae. Sī lūdus bonus erat, puerī magistrō pecūniam dabant. Magister saepe erat servus fīdus. Docēbat puerōs grammaticam, rhētoricam, arithmēticam. Laudābat puerōs sī discipulī bonī erant. Puerōs malōs et nōn studiōsōs castigābat. Paedagōgus puerōs exspectābat et librōs portābat. Fortūna puerōrum nōn mala erat sī puerī bonī erant.

Puellae domī erant. Mātrēs puellās artēs domesticās docēbant. Nōnne vīta puellārum bona erat?

Hodiē in patriā nostrā puerī et puellae in lūdō sunt. In multīs lūdīs cīvēs librōs comparant. Fortūna vestra bona est. Nunc magna cōpia librōrum bonōrum est sed tum librī paucī erant.

16

Third Declension,
I-Stems

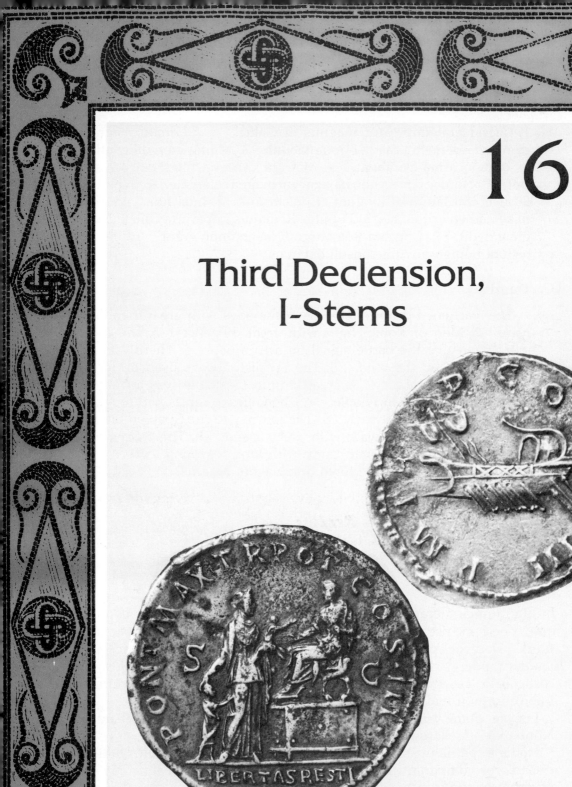

(l.) Silver Denarius of Hadrian (r.) Bronze Sestertius of Hadrian

O praeclarum custodem ovium lupum!
An excellent protector of sheep, the wolf!— CICERO

Wax tablet from Pompeii

—Forms—

THIRD DECLENSION I-STEMS

A group of nouns which have **-ium** instead of **-um** in the genitive plural are called i-stem nouns of the third declension. Also some neuter nouns of the third declension have **-ī** in the ablative singular instead of **-e,** and **-ia** in the nominative and accusative plural. I-stems include the following:

Masculine or feminine nouns
1. ending in **-ēs** or **-is** in the nominative singular and having the same number of syllables in the genitive singular

> hostis, hostis, m.,   *enemy*
> caedēs, caedis, f.,   *murder*

2. ending in **-ns** or **-rs** in the nominative singular

> īnfāns, īnfantis, m.,   *baby*
> mors, mortis, f.,   *death*

3. of one syllable in the nominative singular whose base ends in two consonants

> nox, noctis, f.,   *night*

Neuter nouns
Neuter nouns ending in **-al** or **-e** in the nominative singular (like **animal** and **mare**): these show the **-i-** of the stem in the ablative singular **-ī,** the nominative and accusative plural **-ia,** and the genitive plural **-ium.**

DECLENSION OF I-STEMS

	SINGULAR			ENDINGS M. & F.	NEUT.
NOMINATIVE:	ig'nis	urbs	ma're	—	—
GENITIVE:	ig'nis	ur'bis	ma'ris	-is	-is
DATIVE:	ig'nī	ur'bī	ma'rī	-ī	-ī
ACCUSATIVE:	ig'nem	ur'bem	ma're	-em	—
ABLATIVE:	ig'ne	ur'be	ma'rī	-e	-ī
	PLURAL				
NOMINATIVE:	ig'nēs	ur'bēs	ma'ria	-ēs	-ia
GENITIVE:	ig'nium	ur'bium	ma'rium	-ium	-ium
DATIVE:	ig'nibus	ur'bibus	ma'ribus	-ibus	-ibus
ACCUSATIVE:	ig'nēs	ur'bēs	ma'ria	-ēs	-ia
ABLATIVE:	ig'nibus	ur'bibus	ma'ribus	-ibus	-ibus

—— Vocabulary ——

a'nimal, animā'lis, n., *animal*
cī'vis, cī'vis, m. or f., *citizen,*
  fellow citizen
fī'nis, fī'nis, m., *end, boundary*
  fī'nēs, fī'nium, m., *territory*
gēns, gen'tis, f., *family, clan,*
  nation
hos'tis, hos'tis, m., *enemy*

ig'nis, ig'nis, m., *fire*
ma're, ma'ris, n., *sea*
mōns, mon'tis, m., *mountain, hill*
mors, mor'tis, f., *death*
nā'vis, nā'vis, f., *ship*
pā'nis, pā'nis, m., *bread*
pōns, pon'tis, m., *bridge*
urbs, ur'bis, f., *city*

—— Word Study ——

Hostis. Both **hostis** and **inimīcus** (the adjective used as a noun) mean
enemy. **Hostis** is an enemy of the state or a public enemy, and **inimīcus**
is a personal enemy. In English we often use "enemy" in the singular
as a collective noun, to designate a hostile army or nation. Such a
collective use should be translated by the Latin plural.

Hostēs oppidum oppugnant. { *The enemy is attacking the town.*
{ *The enemy are attacking the town.*

—Exercises—

A. Decline.

mare nostrum   mōns altus   nāvis longa

B. Read the Latin and translate.

1. Per multās terrās mariaque portāvimus nostrōs deōs ad Ītāli-am. 2. Nōnne dederās pānem multīs cīvibus Rōmānīs? 3. In marī multae nāvēs frūmentum ad īnsulam portābant. 4. In flūmine erat pōns ab īnsulā ad urbem. 5. Erunt semper Caesaris proeliōrum memoriae in Galliā. 6. In agrō Rōmānō erant viae ā montibus ad mare. 7. In hostium castrīs erant multī cīvēs vestrī. 8. Est semper in proeliō perīculum mortis. 9. In Galliae fīnibus erant multī populī. 10. Suntne multa animālia in marī?

C. Translate.

1. There is a long bridge on a beautiful river in Germany. 2. Horses are good and friendly animals. 3. The ships were sailing through the sea toward the land. 4. There was a beautiful city in the territory of the Greeks. 5. On the bridge was a soldier on a white horse. 6. The mountains in Gaul are high and beautiful. 7. Marcus often used to call our fellow citizens into the city. 8. The soldiers will carry (their) weapons from the gates of the city. 9. They attacked the enemy's city with fire. 10. Were you (*pl.*) looking at the fires on the mountain?

—Reading—

Read aloud and translate.

APPIUS CLAUDIUS

Ōlim erat vir Rōmānus, Appius Claudius nōmine. Magnum et longum aquaeductum aedificāvit. Rōmānī aquaeductum ab nōmine Appī ap-pellāvērunt. Aquaeductus bonam aquam in urbem Rōmam portāvit.

Appius Claudius etiam longam et bonam viam ad oppidum Ītaliae Capuam aedificāvit. Rōmānī viam "Appiam" appellāverunt. Erant multae aliae viae in Ītaliā sed Via Appia praecipuē clāra erat.

In Viā Appiā multī Rōmānī ambulābant. Agricolae frūmentum portābant et amīcōs salūtābant. Inter fēminās et virōs erant puerī et puellae; cum amīcīs in viā clāmābant. Magnus numerus agricolārum in vīllīs prope Viam Appiam habitābat. Diū labōrābant, et multum frūmentum carrīs ad vīllās portābant. Vīta agricolārum erat bona.

Appius Claudius patriam amābat et cum hostibus Rōmānōrum semper pugnābat. Via et aquaeductus in Ītaliā hodiē manent.

An olive press from Pompeii. The olives were bruised in a mill. The oil from the first pressing was used for perfumes and cosmetics; from the second, cooking; and from the third, illumination.

Tarditas et procrastinatio odiosa est.
Delay—putting things off until tomorrow—is hateful.—CICERO

REVIEW 4 (LESSONS 13–16)

—Vocabulary Drill—

A. Give the genitive, gender, and meaning of the following nouns.

animal	dīligentia	hōra	mīles	pōns
caput	dux	hostis	mōns	rēgina
carmen	epistula	ignis	mors	rēx
causa	fābula	imperātor	nāvis	soror
celeritās	finis	imperium	nōmen	tempus
cīvis	flūmen	iter	pānis	urbs
cōnsul	frāter	mare	pater	vulnus
corpus	gēns	māter	pecūnia	

B. Give the nominative singular forms, and the meaning, of the following adjectives.

albus	grātus	niger	parātus
amīcus	inimīcus	novus	vērus

C. Give the meanings of the following words.

amīcē	grātē	mox	vērē
dēlectō	inimīcē	parātē	

—Drill on Forms—

A. Give the following forms.

1. *vocative singular:* Mārcus, tempus, Iūlius
2. *genitive singular:* imperium, vulnus, nāvis
3. *dative singular:* deus, dīligentia, celeritās
4. *accusative singular:* iter, vir, dux
5. *ablative singular:* mare, gēns, pecūnia

6. *vocative plural:* nūntius, animal, flūmen
7. *genitive plural:* cīvis, māter, fābula
8. *dative plural:* epistula, gladius, rēx
9. *accusative plural:* caput, imperator, causa

B. Give a synopsis in the active indicative and imperative (where applicable), with meanings of:

1. dēlectō *in the third person singular*
2. dō *in the third person plural*
3. sum *in the second person singular*
4. vulnerō *in the second person plural*
5. stō *in the first person plural*

C. Decline throughout.

animal nigrum   rēx amīcus   celeritās nova

——Drill on Syntax ——

Translate the words in italics, giving the reason for each case.

1. The sailors are *in a ship.*
2. We carried our grain to Africa *in a ship.*
3. The messenger gave the signal *on a trumpet.*
4. The messenger gave the signal *on the mountain.*
5. The Germans fought *with boldness.*
6. The Germans fought *with weapons.*
7. They gave gifts *to the cities.*
8. They carried water *to the cities.*
9. The road *to Germany* is long.
10. Where are you, *son?*

—— Exercises ——

A. Translate.

1. Cīvēs gladiīs in proeliō contrā mīlitēs pugnāvērunt.
2. Puerī Rōmānī magnā cum dīligentiā hodiē epistulās parant.
3. Pulchrae erant fīliae nostrī imperātōris.
4. Rēx bonus servīs pecūniam dōnaque dabat.

5. Captīvōs Rōmānōs in castrīs servābāmus.
6. Crās, frāter, nāvigābis trāns mare ad patriam nostram.
7. Occupāvistīne equum meum in itinere?
8. Post proelium mīlitēs cum celeritāte ad castra arma portāvērunt.
9. Sorōrēs ducis in viā diū ambulābant.
10. Imperātor spectābat hostium castra in monte.

B. Translate.

1. The songs of the soldiers in the Roman camp pleased the leaders.
2. Will the Roman people soon give a new name to our king?
3. Where did you seize my friend's new horses?
4. The envoy will carry to the German king the message about the danger of war.
5. The journey from Germany to Italy is long.
6. Carry your swords to the camp now, Marcus and Lucius.
7. Caesar often used to fight against the enemy in Gaul.
8. We walked toward the wide river for a long time.
9. Have you not looked at the many weapons of the lieutenant?
10. Our camp is always in a large field.

Sarcophagus of P. Nonius Zethus, a miller, showing a grain mill worked by a donkey, and various measures, sieve, and scoop.
Aug. (Augustalis) indicates member of a priesthood for an imperial cult of freedmen.

Second Conjugation

A funeral urn showing an oculist examining one of his patients

Quos amor verus tenuit, tenebit.
Those whom true love has held, it will go on holding
——SENECA.

——*Forms*——

THE SECOND CONJUGATION

Verbs whose present stem (found by dropping **-re** from the second principal part) ends in **ē** belong to the second conjugation. They are conjugated like **moneō, monēre, monuī, monitum,** *advise, warn:*

INDICATIVE MOOD
PRESENT TENSE

SINGULAR	PLURAL
mo'neō	monē'**mus**
mo'nēs	monē'**tis**
mo'net	mo'nent

IMPERFECT TENSE

monē'**bam,** etc.	monēbā'**mus,** etc.

FUTURE TENSE

monē'**bō,** etc.	monē'**bimus,** etc.

PERFECT TENSE

mo'nuī, etc.	monu'**imus,** etc.

PLUPERFECT TENSE

monu'**eram,** etc.	monuerā'**mus,** etc.

FUTURE PERFECT TENSE

monu'**erō,** etc.	monue'**rimus,** etc.

PRESENT IMPERATIVE

mo'nē	monē'**te**

Notice that **moneō** is conjugated in exactly the same way as **vocō**, except that the stem vowel is not dropped, but only shortened, before **-ō** in the present active indicative first person singular **moneō**.

—— Vocabulary ——

Helvē'tius, -a, -um, *Helvetian, of the Helvetians*

ha'beō, habē're, ha'buī, ha'bitum, *have; hold*
ma'neō, manē're, mān'sī, mān'sum, *stay, remain*
mo'neō, monē're, mo'nuī, mo'nitum, *warn; advise, inform*
mo'veō, movē're, mō'vī, mō'tum, *move;* castra movēre, *to break camp*
se'deō, sedē're, sē'dī, ses'sum, *sit*
te'neō, tenē're, te'nuī, ten'tum, *hold*
ti'meō, timē're, ti'muī, ——, *fear, be afraid*
vi'deō, vidē're, vī'dī, vī'sum, *see*

—— Exercises ——

A. Analyze each form and translate.

1. vidēbam, vīdit, vīdēbunt, vīderātis   2. timēmus, timuimus, timet, timuit   3. sedēbō, sēderant, mānserat, manēbunt   4. tenēbat, tenuerit, mōvit, movet   5. portābitis, laudāvistis, timēbātis, nūntiāverās   6. parat, vīdī, dedī, appellāvit   7. timuistī, tenuistis, habuī, vidēbāmus   8. es, cōnfirmāverō, monēbat, mānsērunt   9. oppugnābāmus, convocāvit, dat, sēdimus   10. habuit, fuit, habuerat, tenuerimus

B. Translate.

1. we were warning, they had warned, he will see   2. I shall fear, you had seen, they will have   3. we have sat, they have sat, I sit   4. we were holding, they remain, I shall have sat   5. you had, you will have, they will have   6. he was, you will remain, they had warned   7. she has seen, they had feared, we are moving   8. will you give? will they not stand? they were not calling, were they?   9. he announced, we shall have stood, you have saved   10. he had moved, we shall have moved, they will remain

C. Give synopses in the indicative, with meanings, of the following:

1. maneō *in the first person singular*   2. videō *in the third person singular*   3. habeō *in the third person plural*

D. Read the Latin and translate.

1. Mīlitēs ducem tenēbunt in oppidō.   2. Imperātor Rōmānus castra crās movēbit.   3. Populus Rōmānus imperium semper tenēbat. 4. Cōnsulēs monēbō dē bellī perīculō.   5. Stāte, virī, in viā et ducem exspectāte.   6. Post proelium miserī captīvī mortem timuērunt.   7. Saepe nāvem pulchram vīdimus.   8. Diū sedēbant in villā frātrēs agricolae.   9. Māterne tua in urbe manēbit? 10. Nōnne parātis, puellae, nunc librōs novōs?

E.   Translate.

1. We stayed on the mountain for a long time.   2. The soldiers will soon break camp.   3. Lucius, are you holding the small animal?   4. Girls, warn the farmer; there is a fire in the farmhouse. 5. Our father saw a long river in Spain.   6. My brother is sitting on the small bridge.   7. The enemy do not fear our men.   8. The captives do not have much money, do they?   9. The consuls will have warned the citizens of the danger.   10. Tell the boys a story about Julius Caesar.

—— *Reading* ——

Read aloud and translate.

A BRAVE WATER BOY

Lūcius, lēgātus Caesaris, in vīllā agricolae amīcī sedēbat et agricolae fīliīs fābulam dē bellō Gallicō nārrābat.

"Erat cum nostrīs cōpiīs puer Gallus. In proeliō ad mīlitēs aquam cibumque parvō carrō portābat. Mortem nōn timēbat. In castrīs cum mīlitibus labōrābat.

"Diū in fīnibus Aeduōrum mānsimus. Nostrās cōpiās Caesar in castrīs ad flūmen Ararim tenēbat. Cum Helvētiīs pugnābat et hostēs exspectābat.

"Hostēs cōpiās flūmen navibus trānsportābant. In flūmine nōn erat pōns. Ubi de flūmine puer aquam portābat, signa Helvētiōrum vīdit et nostrōs dē perīculō magnā cum celeritāte monuit. Helvētiī castra nostra oppugnāvērunt, sed parātī erāmus. Puerum Caesar laudāvit. Est hodiē cīvis Rōmānus."

18

Third Declension, Adjectives Ablative of Accompaniment

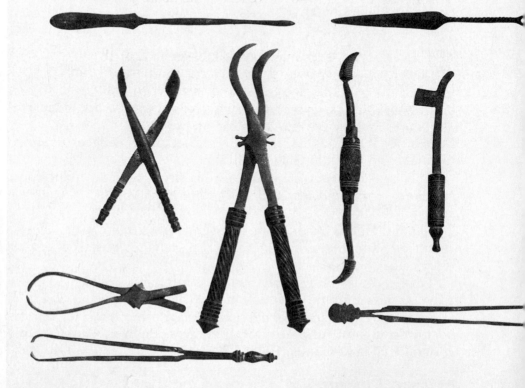

Surgeon's tools found at Pompeii

Patria est communis omnium parens.

Our native land is the common parent of us all.—CICERO

—— Forms ——

ADJECTIVES OF THE THIRD DECLENSION

These adjectives are declined like third declension **i**-stem nouns. Like the neuter **i**- stems, they always have **-ī** in the ablative singular.

Third declension adjectives of three terminations end in **-er** in the masculine nominative singular, **-is** in the feminine, and **-e** in the neuter. They are declined like **celer,** *swift.*

| | SINGULAR | | | PLURAL | | |
	M.	F.	N.	M.	F.	N.
NOM.	ce′ler	ce′leris	ce′lere	ce′lerēs	ce′lerēs	cele′ria
GEN.	ce′leris	ce′leris	ce′leris	cele′rium	cele′rium	cele′rium
DAT.	ce′lerī	ce′lerī	ce′lerī	cele′ribus	cele′ribus	cele′ribus
ACC.	ce′lerem	ce′lerem	ce′lere	ce′lerēs	ce′lerēs	cele′ria
ABL.	ce′lerī	ce′lerī	ce′lerī	cele′ribus	cele′ribus	cele′ribus

Adjectives of two terminations end in **-is** in both the masculine and the feminine nominative singular, and in **-e** in the neuter (**brevis, breve**). Adjectives of two terminations are declined like adjectives of three terminations, except that they have no separate form for the masculine nominative and vocative singular.

| | SINGULAR | | PLURAL | |
	M. & F.	N.	M. & F.	N.
NOMINATIVE:	bre′vis	bre′ve	bre′vēs	bre′via
GENITIVE:	bre′vis	bre′vis	bre′vium	bre′vium
DATIVE:	bre′vī	bre′vī	bre′vibus	bre′vibus
ACCUSATIVE:	bre′vem	bre′ve	bre′vēs	bre′via
ABLATIVE:	bre′vī	bre′vī	bre′vibus	bre′vibus

Adjectives of one termination have the same form for the nominative and vocative singular of all three genders. All third declension adjectives which do not end in **-er** or **-is** in the masculine nominative singular are adjectives of one termination.

	SINGULAR		PLURAL	
	M. & F.	N.	M. & F.	N.
NOMINATIVE:	au'dāx	au'dāx	audā'cēs	audā'cia
GENITIVE:	audā'cis	audā'cis	audā'cium	audā'cium
DATIVE:	audā'cī	audā'cī	audā'cibus	audā'cibus
ACCUSATIVE:	audā'cem	au'dāx	audā'cēs	audā'cia
ABLATIVE:	audā'cī	audā'cī	audā'cibus	audā'cibus

—Syntax—

THE ABLATIVE OF ACCOMPANIMENT

Accompaniment is expressed by the ablative with **cum,** *with, along with, in company with.* **Puella cum mātre est.** *The girl is with her mother.*

∽∽∽∽∽∽∽∽∽∽∽∽∽∽∽∽∽∽∽∽∽∽∽∽∽∽∽∽∽∽∽∽∽∽∽∽∽

Do not confuse the ablative of accompaniment with the ablative of means or the ablative of manner.

Oppidum cum sociīs oppugnāvērunt.   *They attacked the town with their allies.*
(ABLATIVE OF ACCOMPANIMENT)
Oppidum tēlīs oppugnāvērunt.   *They attacked the town with weapons.*
(ABLATIVE OF MEANS)
Oppidum cum audāciā oppugnāvērunt.   *They attacked the town with boldness.*
(ABLATIVE OF MANNER)

∽∽∽∽∽∽∽∽∽∽∽∽∽∽∽∽∽∽∽∽∽∽∽∽∽∽∽∽∽∽∽∽∽∽∽∽∽

—Vocabulary—

ā'cer, ā'cris, ā'cre, *sharp, fierce*
au'dāx, audā'cis,* *bold, daring*
bre'vis, bre've, *short*
Britan'nus, -a, -um, *British*
ce'ler, ce'leris, ce'lere, *swift*
fa'cilis, fa'cile, *easy*
for'tis, for'te, *brave*

Gal'lus, -a, -um, *Gallic*
gra'vis, gra've, *heavy; severe, serious*
om'nis, om'ne, *all, every*
po'tēns, poten'tis,* *powerful*
si'milis, si'mile, *like, similar*
Trōiā'nus, -a, -um, *Trojan*

*The genitive singular of adjectives of one termination must be learned, since the base cannot be found from the nominative singular.

—— Word Study ——

Adjective Prefixes. Used with an adjective the prefix **in** means *not;* **inimīcus = in + amīcus,** *not friendly;* therefore, *unfriendly.* The prefix **per** means *very.* What are the meanings of the following adjectives?

imparātus, -a, -um	perlongus, -a, -um
ingrātus, -a, -um	permagnus, -a, -um
pergrātus, -a, -um	permultus, -a, -um

The Suffixes -ia and -tia. An abstract noun is often made from an adjective by the addition of **-ia** or **-tia** (*-ness, -ship*) to the base or stem of the adjective. **Amīcitia** (*friendship, friendliness*) is formed from the adjective **amīcus** in this way.

The Suffix -tās. The noun **celeritās** is derived from **celer.** The suffix **-tās, -tātis,** feminine, performs the same function of making an abstract noun from an adjective. Like **-ia** and **-tia,** it may be translated *-ness.* What would be the meanings of the following nouns?

brevitās, brevitātis, f.	lībertās, lībertātis, f.
grātia, grātiae, f.	miseria, miseriae, f.
gravitās, gravitātis, f.	potentia, potentiae, f.
inimīcitiā, inimīcitiae, f.	vēritās, vēritātis, f.

—— Exercises ——

A. Decline the following.

animus ācer   rēgīna fortis   rēgnum potēns

B. Read the Latin and translate.

1. Māter cum fīliō fortī manēbit.   2. Rēx potēns et rēgīna cum fīliābus sedent.   3. Frāter cōnsulis tuō patrī tēla dabit.   4. Breve est iter ad oppidum, et magnā cum celeritāte ambulāmus. 5. Omnēs īnsulam in flūmine Britannō spectābant.   6. Dux audāx tenēbat in castrīs cōnsulem cum frātribus sorōribusque.   7. Omnēs sociī cum Caesare pugnābant.   8. Nostrī tēlīs gravibus hostēs vulnerāverint.   9. Ducēs fortēs cum omnibus cōpiīs oppida magna oppugnāverant.   10. Vīdī omnia in castrīs.

〰〰〰〰〰〰〰〰〰〰〰〰〰〰〰〰〰〰〰〰〰〰〰〰〰

Omnēs and **omnia,** when used as nouns, are usually translated *everyone* and *everything*. Remember that these words are plural in Latin.

Suntne omnēs in nave? *Is everyone on the ship?*

〰〰〰〰〰〰〰〰〰〰〰〰〰〰〰〰〰〰〰〰〰〰〰〰〰

C. Translate.

1. The sons of the consul remained in the fields with the men.
2. The women are sitting on the bridge across the river.   3. The brave messenger warned the citizens about the dangers.   4. The small girls were afraid of everything.   5. The beautiful songs of the British girls pleased the Roman soldiers.   6. The weapons of the bold lieutenant are heavy.   7. Everyone was looking at the powerful soldier.   8. The road from our farmhouse to your city is not short.   9. Look at the wounds on the body of the horse, father.   10. The Trojan soldiers fought with heavy swords.

—— Reading ——

CORIOLĀNUS

Coriolānus malus cīvis erat sed bonus mīles. Rōmānī nūllum frūmentum habēbant et timēbant magnam famem. Iam rēx in Siciliā Rōmānīs multum frūmentum dederat sed Coriolānus frūmentum pauperibus nōn dabat. Itaque pauperēs Coriolānum ex urbe exturbāvērunt.

Posteā Coriolānus dux Volscōrum erat et cum mīlitibus Rōmānīs pugnābat. Rōmānōs multīs pugnīs superāvit. Rōmānī clāmāvērunt: "Mox Coriolānus Rōmam occupābit."

Tum māter Coriolānī et uxor et fīliī fīliaeque ex urbe properāvērunt. Māter Coriolānum ōrāvit et obsecrāvit: "Dā, fīlī, salūtem Romae." Respōnsum Coriolānī erat: "Salūtem, māter, dabō urbī meae. Servāvistī Rōmam sed tuum fīlium posthāc numquam vidēbis." Tum Coriolānus cum mīlitibus ab urbe properāvit.

19

Passive Voice, First Conjugation

Pont du Gard, France, Roman Aqueduct and Bridge, 19 B.C.

Amor tussisque non celantur.
Love, and a cough, are not concealed. —OVID

—*Forms*—

THE PASSIVE VOICE

When the subject of the verb is not performing the action, but is being acted upon, the verb is in the passive voice.

In the present system the passive is conjugated like the active, but with a different set of personal endings.

	SINGULAR	PLURAL
1ST PERSON	-or, -r	-mur
2D PERSON	-ris, -re	-minī
3D PERSON	-tur	-ntur

PRESENT PASSIVE INDICATIVE

vo'**cor**,	*I am called*	vocā'**mur**,	*we are called*
vocā'**ris**,	*you are called*	vocā'**minī**,	*you are called*
vocā'**tur**,	*he is called*	vocan'**tur**,	*they are called*

IMPERFECT PASSIVE INDICATIVE

vocā'**bar**,	*I was being called*
vocābā'**ris**,	*you were being called*
vocābā'**tur**,	*he was being called*
vocābā'**mur**,	*we were being called*
vocābā'**minī**,	*you were being called*
vocāban'**tur**,	*they were being called*

FUTURE PASSIVE INDICATIVE

vocā'**bor**,	*I shall be called*	vocā'**bimur**,	*we shall be called*
vocā'**beris**,	*you will be called*	vocabi'**minī**,	*you will be called*
vocā'**bitur**,	*he will be called*	vocābun'**tur**,	*they will be called*

PRESENT PASSIVE IMPERATIVE

vocā'**re**,	*be called!*	vocā'**minī**,	*be called!*

THE PERFECT TENSES IN THE PASSIVE

Perfect tenses in the passive are formed by combining the perfect passive participle (made from the last one of the principal parts) with forms of **sum** for the perfect, **eram** for the pluperfect, and **erō** for the future perfect.

PERFECT   *I have been (was) called, etc.*

vocātus (-a, -um)	{ sum es est	vocātī (-ae, -a)	{ su'mus es'tis sunt

PLUPERFECT   *I had been called, etc.*

vocātus (-a, -um)	{ e'ram e'rās e'rat	vocātī (-ae, -a)	{ erā'mus erā'tis e'rant

FUTURE PERFECT   *I shall (will) have been called, etc.*

vocātus (-a, -um)	{ e'rō e'ris e'rit	vocātī (-ae, -a)	{ e'rimus e'ritis e'runt

—— *Syntax* ——

AGREEMENT OF PERFECT PASSIVE

In the perfect system the perfect passive participle must agree with the subject in gender, number, and case (the case will, of course, be nominative).

Puer vocātus est.   *The boy has been called. The boy was called.*
Puellae vocātae erant.   *The girls had been called.*

—— *Exercises* ——

A. Analyze each Latin form and translate.

1. parāvit, nūntiābitur, līberāta est 2. convocābāmur, cōnfīrmāvistis, vocātum erat 3. data erunt, appellāberis, amābuntur 4. dantur, dabuntur, dedimus 5. vulnerātus es,

vulnerābāminī, exspectāberis   6. amābiminī, superātī erimus,
amātae   erant   7. occupāta   sunt,   occupāta   est,   servātur
8. pugnāvimus, vulnerābunt, pugnāverāmus   9. portāberis, por-
tātum erat, portor   10. spectantur, laudātī sumus, parāvī

B. Translate.

1. you are being wounded, it will be announced   2. they were
being called, I had been praised   3. she will be carried, they have
been saved   4. he has been defeated, we are being freed   5. they
were being carried, you will be praised   6. The fields had been
seized.   7. The women have been praised.   8. The boys have
been called.   9. The money had been given.   10. The mothers
will be loved.

(left) From the Stabian Baths, Pompeii. (right) Hot Room.

C. Read the Latin and translate.

1. Mīlitum animī signō proelī cōnfirmātī erant. 2. Multa et pulchra dōna rēgīnae potentī dantur. 3. Caesaris mors cīvibus miserīs nūntiātur. 4. Cūr fortēs amīcī nōn laudātī sunt? 5. Bonae fēminae semper amātae sunt. 6. Cīvēs Rōmānī saepe ad campum convocābantur. 7. Pōns longus in urbe Britannīs et Gallīs dēmōnstrābitur. 8. Servī Helvētiī crās līberābuntur. 9. Fābulae dē lēgātō audācī semper nārrābuntur. 10. Castra magnā cum audāciā oppugnāta sunt.

D. Translate.

1. Why are the letters not being prepared with care? 2. The wretched captives were being kept in the town. 3. Everyone has been called to the mountain. 4. Tomorrow the city will have been captured; soon we shall break camp. 5. The camp was being attacked with many weapons. 6. The death of the general will be reported far and wide. 7. The brave soldier had been wounded with a heavy weapon. 8. Haven't the enemy been defeated in Germany? 9. Everything was carried into camp. 10. The fields of the good farmer have been seized.

—— *Reading* ——

ALEXANDER'S HORSE

Alexander Magnus, rēx Macedoniae, equum fortem et celerem habēbat. Būcephalus appellātus est. Rēgem in proelium semper portābat. Armīs signōque proelī delectābātur. Ubi mīlitēs rēgis Būcephalum audācem inter hostēs vidēbant, animī cōnfirmābantur et virī clamābant, "Būcephalus nōn est animal, sed similis deō."

Fābula dē equō memoriā diū tenēbātur. Alexander cum potentī duce Indōrum pugnābat. Rēx miserē labōrābat. Būcephalus multīs tēlīs hostium vulnerātus erat. In corpore equī erant gravia vulnera. Mors aderat, sed animal forte nōn timēbat. Alexandrum sine iniūriā ad castra portāvit. Tum animam exspīrāvit.

Posteā in fīnibus Indōrum stābat oppidum Macedonicum. Nōmen oppidī erat Būcephala.

20

Second Conjugation, Passive
Ablative of Personal
Agent

Mosaic, Terme Museum, Rome

A cane non magno saepe tenetur aper.
A boar is often held by a not-so-large dog.—OVID

—Forms—

THE PASSIVE OF THE SECOND CONJUGATION

In the second conjugation the passive is formed in the same way as in the first conjugation.

PRESENT PASSIVE INDICATIVE

mo'ne**or**	monē'**mur**
monē'**ris**	monē'**minī**
monē'**tur**	monen'**tur**

IMPERFECT PASSIVE INDICATIVE

monē'**bar,** etc.	monēbā'**mur,** etc.

FUTURE PASSIVE INDICATIVE

monē'**bor,** etc.	monē'**bimur,** etc.

PERFECT PASSIVE INDICATIVE

mo'nit**us, -a, -um sum,** etc.	mo'nit**ī, -ae, -a su'mus,** etc.

PLUPERFECT PASSIVE INDICATIVE

mo'nit**us, -a -um e'ram,** etc.	mo'nit**ī, -ae, -a erā'mus,** etc.

FUTURE PERFECT PASSIVE INDICATIVE

mo'nit**us, -a, -um e'rō,** etc.	mo'nit**ī, -ae, -a e'rimus,** etc.

PRESENT PASSIVE IMPERATIVE

monē'**re**	monē'**minī**

—Syntax—

THE ABLATIVE OF PERSONAL AGENT

With a passive verb the person by whom the action is performed is expressed by the ablative with the preposition **ā** or **ab**. **Ā** or **ab** in this case is always translated *by*.

> Puer bonus ā patre laudātus est.
> *The good boy was praised by his father.*

~~~~~~

Do not confuse the ablative of agent with the ablative of means. The ablative of agent is usually a person and is preceded by **ā** or **ab**. The ablative of means is usually an object, and is used without a preposition.

> Ā mīlite vulnerātus est.   *He was wounded by a soldier.*
>   (ABLATIVE OF AGENT)
> Tēlō vulnerātus est.   *He was wounded by a weapon.*
>   (ABLATIVE OF MEANS)

~~~~~~

Pons Aemilius, Rome

THE PREDICATE ACCUSATIVE

A verb of making or naming may take a predicate accusative in addition to its direct object.

Vocāvit fīlium Mārcum.　*He called his son Marcus.*

In the passive such verbs may take a predicate nominative.

Puer vocātur Mārcus.　*The boy is called Marcus.*

—— *Vocabulary* ——

aes'tās, aestā'tis, f., *summer*
hi'ems, hi'emis, f., *winter*
lūx, lū'cis, f., *light*

pāx, pā'cis, f., *peace*
sa'lūs, salū'tis, f., *safety, welfare*
vōx, vō'cis, f., *voice*

dē'beō, dēbē're, dē'buī, dē'bitum, *owe; ought*
do'ceō, docē're, do'cuī, doc'tum, *teach; show*
prohi'beō, prohibē're, prohi'buī, prohi'bitum, *prevent, keep . . . from . . .*
respon'deō, respondē're, respon'dī, respōn'sum, *reply, answer*
reti'neō, retinē're, reti'nuī, reten'tum, *hold back*
ter'reō, terrē're, ter'ruī, ter'ritum, *frighten*

—— *Word Study* ——

The Prefixes prō- (por-) and re- (red-). The prefix **prō-** or **por-** means *in front, forward, forth,* or *for.*

> **prohibeō = pro + habeō,**　*I hold out in front = I hold off = I prevent*

The prefix **re-** or **red-** means *back, again, against.*

retineō = re + teneō,　*I hold back*

Notice that in compounds the **-a** and **-e** of **habeō** and **teneō** are changed to **-i.**

Here are some verbs compounded with these two prefixes:

proclāmō,	*I shout forth*	removeō,	*I move back*
prōmoveō,	*I move forward*	renūntiō,	*I bring back a message*
prōvideō,	*I foresee, I provide for*		
prōvocō,	*I call forth*	repugnō,	*I fight against*
remaneō,	*I stay behind*	revocō,	*I call back*

—— Exercises ——

A. Analyze each form and translate.

1. habēmur, monētur, datae sunt   2. vīdērunt, videntur, retinē-tur   3. tenēbātur, tenuerant, retinuī   4. mōvī, mōtus est, movē-bitur   5. habēbās, timueris, servābit   6. mōvit, vīdit, dedit   7. mōverint, mōtī erāmus, timuerāmus   8. mōtum est, dabuntur, monitī sumus   9. vulnerābitur, līberāta eris, vocātī erātis   10. fuimus, erātis, fuerant

B. Translate.

1. he had been moved, I am held   2. you were held, they will be seen   3. they will have been frightened, she was warned   4. it is shown, they were being held   5. he has been held back, it has been prevented   6. they are warned, she has been moved   7. he had been held back, he will be seen   8. he is frightened, you have been defeated   9. he will be called, I shall be saved   10. they were moved, we were freed

C. Read the Latin and translate.

1. Hiemēs in Āfricā brevēs sunt.   2. Tuam fīliam ā flūmine retinu-imus.   3. Puellae ā puerīs in equīs territae sunt.   4. Hostēs ā ducibus vidēbantur.   5. Nostrī magnā cum celeritāte ā nūntiō vo-cābantur ex castrōrum portīs.   6. Dē perīculō hiemis in Germāniā ab amīcō bonō monēberis.   7. Cōpiae Rōmānae bellum parāverant et multa oppida in Gallōrum fīnibus occupābant.   8. Rōma ā Gallīs gentibus diū oppugnāta erat.   9. Multam pecūniam vestrīs amīcīs dēbēmus.   10. Multae et pulchrae urbēs in Hispāniā ā nostrīs amīcīs vīsae sunt.

D. Translate.

1. The farmer's daughter was waiting for her mother on the bridge.   2. Many large cities had been seized by the forces of the Roman consul.   3. The king's sisters were carried by a wagon to the ship.   4. The German camp was seen by the brave lieuten-ant.   5. The horses in the field were frightened by the boys' voices.   6. The wretched slaves owed money to their master.   7. Now I shall give the battle signal on my trumpet.   8. They wounded many soldiers of the enemy with weapons and saved

Rome.   9. The dangers of a winter on the sea were reported to the Roman sailors.   10. The general had been warned about the fire on the mountain.

—Reading—

ALEXANDER AND PORUS

Alexandrī et cōpiārum Graecārum magnum iter erat per fīnēs Persārum Indōrumque. Graecī ad flūmen Hydaspem ab imperātōre prōmōtī erant. Ibi flūmen lātum hostēs Graecīs prohibuit. Trāns flūmen stābant mīlitēs Indī, virī ingentēs. Multae erant cōpiae. Pōrus, rēx Indōrum, in proelium elephantō portābātur et magna pulchraque arma tenēbat.

Tum Alexander mīlitēs trāns flūmen mōvit. Omnēs Graecī, ubi rēgem Indōrum vīdērunt, ferō animō et corpore magnō territī sunt. Acriter pugnātum est. Et Pōrus et Alexander fortiter pugnāvit. Sed Pōrus superātus est et posteā erat socius Alexandrī.

Plan of the Baths of Caracalla, dedicated in 216 A.D.

N. Main Entrance
a. Shops
Q. Nymphaea
P. Rooms opening on colonnade
R. Heated Rooms
T. Libraries (Greek and Latin)
S. Stadium
V. Water Tanks
z. Aqueduct
b. Entrances to the baths
L. Dressing Rooms
A. Frigidarium
B. Central Hall
C. Tepidarium
D. Caldarium
G. Palaestra
F. Exedrae
c and E. Lecture Halls

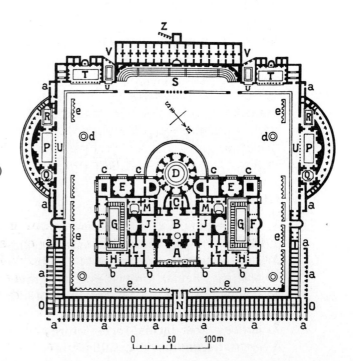

Non est ad astra mollis e terris via.
There is no easy way from the earth to the stars.—SENECA

REVIEW 5 (LESSONS 17–20)

—Vocabulary Drill—

A. Give the genitive, gender, and meaning of the following nouns.

aestās   lūx   salūs   hiems   pāx   vōx

B. Give the other nominative singular forms (or the genitive singular, for adjectives of one termination) and the meaning of the following adjectives.

ācer	brevis	facilis	gravis	potēns
audāx	celer	fortis	omnis	similis

C. Give the principal parts and meanings of the following verbs.

dēbeō	moneō	respondeō	teneō
doceō	moveō	retineō	terreō
habeō	prohibeō	sedeō	timeō
maneō			videō

—Drill on Forms—

A. Give the following forms.

1. *genitive singular:* pāx, hiems, salūs
2. *dative singular:* salūs, Helvētius, aestās
3. *accusative singular:* lūx, vōx, Gallus
4. *ablative singular:* brevis, potēns, grave
5. *nominative plural:* pāx, Trōiānus, audāx
6. *genitive plural:* celer, similis, ācer
7. *dative plural:* facilis, fortis, omnis
8. *accusative plural:* vox, salūs, breve

B. Give a synopsis in the active and passive, indicative and imperative, of:

   1. portō *in the 2d person plural*   2. doceō *in the 2d person singular*

C. Decline.

   1. Gallus audāx   2. aestās brevis

A model of the Baths of Caracalla (plan on p. 113). Note the size of the complex, particularly the large areas of park and garden for strolling, and the roofing arrangements.

—Drill on Syntax—

Translate the words in italics, giving the reason for each case.

1. They gave money *to the citizens.*
2. They carried water *to the citizens.*
3. He was wounded *by an enemy.*
4. He was wounded *by a sword.*
5. We attacked the town *with great speed.*
6. We attacked the town *with our allies.*
7. We attacked the town *with many weapons.*
8. I called my son *Lucius.*
9. My son is called *Lucius.*

—Exercises—

A. Translate.

1. Bona fortūna nostrōrum nautārum cīvibus nūntiābitur.
2. Signum datum est; tum mīlitēs castra hostium oppugnāvērunt. 3. Ignem vestrum, mīlitēs, portāte ad hostium urbēs.
4. Poena inimīcārum gentium erit gravis. 5. Misera animālia in
viīs oppidī sedēbant. 6. Multae nāvēs in flūmine vīsae sunt sub
ponte lātō. 7. Num multī puerī vīsī erant in magnā nāve?
8. Urbēs ā multīs cīvibus cum ducibus oppugnābantur. 9. Cum
lēgātō fortī erant cōnsulēs audācēs. 10. Est longa via ā meō oppidō ad vestram urbem.

B. Translate.

1. Because of the lack of bread the sailors were not staying in the
town. 2. Everything on the ships was seen by everyone. 3. The
brave citizens stayed in camp with the soldiers for a long time.
4. Many ships used to sail to the enemy's territory. 5. The mountains in Italy are not high, but they are beautiful. 6. The death
of the general was announced to the wretched soldiers by the
lieutenant. 7. Lucius, see the fires on the mountain and in the
forests! 8. Caesar had warned the citizens about the dangers of
winter. 9. The long bridge was seen by the brave boys. 10. They
had called the boy Marcus Julius; the girl was called Julia.

21

Numerals

Arch of Constantine, Rome

Etiam capillus unus habet umbram.
Even one hair has a shadow.—PUBLILIUS SYRUS

—Forms—

Ūnus, Duo, and Trēs

Ūnus, *one*, is declined like **malus** except in the genitive and dative singular.

	MASCULINE	FEMININE	NEUTER
NOMINATIVE:	ū'nus	ū'na	ū'num
GENITIVE:	ūnī'us	ūnī'us	ūnī'us
DATIVE:	ū'nī	ū'nī	ū'nī
ACCUSATIVE:	ū'num	ū'nam	ū'num
ABLATIVE:	ū'nō	ū'nā	ū'nō

Duo, *two*, is declined as follows:

	MASCULINE	FEMININE	NEUTER
NOMINATIVE:	du'o	du'ae	du'o
GENITIVE:	duō'rum	duā'rum	duō'rum
DATIVE:	duō'bus	duā'bus	duō'bus
ACCUSATIVE:	du'ōs,	du'ās	du'o
ABLATIVE:	duō'bus	duā'bus	duō'bus

Trēs, *three*, is a regular third declension adjective except that it has, of course, no singular. The endings are added to the base **tr-.**

	M. & F.	N.
NOMINATIVE:	trēs	tria
GENITIVE:	trium	trium
DATIVE:	tribus	tribus
ACCUSATIVE:	trēs	tria
ABLATIVE:	tribus	tribus

CARDINAL NUMERALS

ū'nus, -a, -um, *one*, (I)
du'o, du'ae, du'o, *two*, (II)
trēs, tri'a, *three*, (III)
quat'tuor, *four*, (IV or IIII)
quin'que, *five*, (V)
sex, *six*, (VI)
sep'tem, *seven*, (VII)
oc'tō, *eight*, (VIII)

no'vem, *nine*, (IX or VIIII)
de'cem, *ten*, (X)
ūn'decim, *eleven*, (XI)
duo'decim, *twelve*, (XII)
vīgin'tī, *twenty*, (XX)
cen'tum, *one hundred, a hundred*, (C)
mil'le, *one thousand, a thousand*, (M)

Except for **ūnus, duo,** and **trēs,** the cardinal numerals up through **centum** are indeclinable; **mille** is indeclinable also. This means these adjectives do not change their forms to indicate gender, number, and case.

quinque puerī   *five boys*
quinque puellārum   *of five girls*
ā quinque oppidīs   *from five towns*

ORDINAL NUMERALS

prī'mus, -a, -um,   *first*
secun'dus, -a, -um,   *second*
ter'tius, -a, -um,   *third*
quār'tus, -a, -um,   *fourth*
quīn'tus, -a, -um,   *fifth*

sex'tus, -a, -um,   *sixth*
sep'timus, -a, -um,   *seventh*
octā'vus, -a, um,   *eighth*
nō'nus, -a, -um,   *ninth*
de'cimus, -a, -um,   *tenth*

Ordinal numerals agree in gender, number, and case with the noun they modify.

—— *Vocabulary* ——

Britan'nia, -ae, f., *Britain*
cē'na, -ae, f., *dinner*
fenes'tra, -ae, f., *window*
Grae'cia, -ae, f., *Greece*
Helvē'tia, -ae, f., *Helvetia*
    (modern Switzerland)
iniū'ria, -ae, f., *wrong, injustice*
mēn'sa, -ae, f., *table*
pug'na, -ae, f., *fight*
sel'la, -ae, f., *chair, seat*
Sici'lia, -ae, f., *Sicily*

Trō'ia, -ae, f., *Troy*
victō'ria, -ae, f., *victory*

at'que, ac. (conj.) *and*
aut, (conj.) *or* aut . . . aut . . .,
    either . . . or . . .
quod, (conj.) *because*
sī, (conj.) *if*

Just as **aut . . . aut . . .** means
    either . . . or . . ., so **et . . . et**
    . . . means *both . . . and . . .*

—— Word Study ——

Mēnsa. Since the top of a Roman table could be removed and used as a tray to serve a new course, **mēnsa** can also mean *course*. The *dessert course*, consisting usually of fruits and nuts, was called **secunda mēnsa.**

Atque. Of the three words which you have learned for *and:*

et expresses simple connection,

-que a close connection (which we often express by an unemphatic *and*, sometimes barely pronounced, as in salt 'n' pepper),

atque an emphasized close connection (e.g. She is beautiful *and* intelligent). Hence **atque** may sometimes be translated *and also, and even,* or *and besides*.

—— Exercises ——

A. Read the Latin and translate.

1. Octō parvōs puerōs Germānōs in magnō oppidō vīdimus. 2. Decem virī post victōriam tenēbantur captīvī. 3. Sī pugna fuerit ācris, cōpiae Germānae superābuntur. 4. Quīnque puerī et quattuor puellae in agrīs manēbant. 5. Vīgintī equī in agricolae agrīs vīsī sunt. 6. Propter rēgis iniūriās cum populīs Siciliae pugnābant. 7. Sī deī nostrīs victōriam dederint, duo oppida magna ā duce occupābuntur. 8. Agricolae vīta misera nōn est quod et lātōs agrōs et multam pecūniam habet. 9. Britannī in silvīs agrīsque habitābant; nunc habent magnās urbēs. 10. Grātī sumus quod est magna cēna in nostrā mēnsā.

B. Translate.

1. The camp of the German troops was seized by the Roman soldiers. 2. We used to like the queen of Sicily, but we do not like the king. 3. If they defeat the enemy in Europe, our soldiers will then remain in our country. 4. We shall be unhappy if there is not a large dinner tomorrow. 5. The camp was guarded by the consul's forces. 6. If we fight in Helvetia, we shall defeat the Helvetian forces. 7. Nine slaves were walking toward the farmer's house. 8. A thousand soldiers broke camp and moved the heavy baggage across the river. 9. We praise the king and queen because they love the people. 10. There is a table with six chairs near the window in our farmhouse.

In clauses beginning with *if* in English we usually use the present tense when the future or future perfect would be more accurate. In a sentence like "If I'm in town tomorrow I'll meet you," "if I'm in town" really means "if I shall be in town."

Latin is much more accurate in its use of tenses than English, and always uses the future or future perfect if future time is meant.

Sī hostēs superāverimus, castra occupābimus.
If we defeat the enemy, we shall seize their camp.

—— *Reading* ——

THE KINGS OF ROME

In vīllā sub montibus Faliscīs post secundam mēnsam pater Rōmānus quattuor filiīs fābulās dē patriā in lūcem (*until dawn*) nārrābat. Hiems erat et in sellīs ad ignem sedēbant. Per fenestrās mōns Sōracte albus vidēbātur.

"Pater," clāmāvit ūnus ex puerīs, "nārrā fābulam aut dē Aeneā aut 5 dē rēgibus Rōmānīs."

"Fābulā," respondit pater, "mī cāre filī, dē rēgibus dēlector. Septem erant rēgēs Rōmānī. Rōmulus prīmus erat. Tum urbs nova in monte Palātiō asȳlum erat servōrum atque malōrum, et cīvibus nōn erant fēminae. Sed fābula dē fēminīs Sabīnīs longa est et posteā nārrābitur. 10

"Post mortem Rōmulī populus Numae imperium dedit. Numa sacra cūrāvit.

"Sed prīma lūx adest. Crās, sī bonī fueritis, fābulam dē quīnque rēgibus reliquīs nārrābō."

22

Third Conjugation
Apposition

Relief showing the Praetorian Cohort, the emperor's personal bodyguard

Culpam poena premit comes.
Punishment closely follows crime as its companion.—HORACE

— *Forms* —

THE THIRD CONJUGATION

Verbs whose second principal part ends in **-ere** belong to the third conjugation. The present stem is found by dropping the **-ō** of the first principal part; the perfect stem is found in the same way as in the first two conjugations, by dropping the **-ī** of the third principal part.

The present system of third conjugation verbs differs from that of the first two conjugations in the following ways:

1. In the present tense, since adding the personal endings directly to a stem ending in a consonant would make pronunciation awkward, an **i** or a **u** is inserted between the stem and most of the endings: **regō, regere,** present stem **reg-.**

re'gō	re'g*i***mus**
re'g*i*s	re'g*i***tis**
re'g*i*t	re'g*u***nt**

2. In the imperfect tense the tense sign is **-ēbā-** instead of just **-bā-.**

regē'bam	regēbā'mus
regē'bās	regēbā'tis
regē'bat	regē'bant

3. In the future tense the tense sign is **-ē-,** shortened before **-t** and **-nt,** and becoming **-a-** in the first person singular.

re'gam	regē'mus
re'gēs	regē'tis
re'get	re'gent

The perfect system is formed exactly as in the other conjugations.

PERFECT:	rēx'ī, etc.	rēx'imus, etc.
PLUPERFECT:	rēx'eram, etc.	rēxerā'mus, etc.
FUTURE PERFECT:	rēx'erō, etc.	rēxe'rimus, etc.

The present active imperative regularly adds an **-e** to the stem for the singular, and an **-ite** for the plural.

re'ge	re'gite

—Syntax—

APPOSITION

A noun used to describe another noun or a pronoun is said to be its appositive, or to be in apposition with it. An appositive must refer to the same person or thing as the noun or pronoun to which it applies; it agrees with its noun or pronoun in case. The appositive usually follows its noun or pronoun.

Puella fratrem Mārcum amat.　*The girl loves her brother Marcus.*

A noun may be in apposition with an understood subject.

Cōnsul mīlitēs dūcō.　*I, the consul, am leading the soldiers.*
I, as consul, am leading the soldiers.

An appositive can be used to indicate time.

Caesar puer magnam audāciam habuit.
Caesar, when a boy, had great boldness.
Caesar, while still a boy, had great boldness.

—Vocabulary—

a'gō, a'gere, ē'gī, āc'tum, *do, drive*
cō'gō, cō'gere, coē'gī, coāc'tum, *collect; compel*
dēfen'dō, dēfen'dere, dēfen'dī, dēfēn'sum, *defend*
dū'cō, dū'cere, dūx'ī, duc'tum, *lead*
ge'rō, ge'rere, ges'sī, ges'tum, *bear, carry on, wear*
mit'tō, mit'tere, mī'sī, mis'sum, *send, let go*
pō'nō, pō'nere, po'suī, po'situm, *put, place*
re'gō, re'gere, rēx'ī, rēc'tum, *rule*
relin'quō, relin'quere, relī'quī, relic'tum, *leave, leave behind*
sur'gō, sur'gere, surrēx'ī, surrēc'tum, *rise, stand up*
trā'dō, trā'dere, trā'didī, trā'ditum, *hand over (down), surrender*
vin'cō, vin'cere, vī'cī, vic'tum, *conquer, defeat*

— Word Study —

Cōgō. The two distinct meanings of **cōgō (co- + agō)** come from the two meanings of the prefix **co-,** *together* and *forcibly*: to drive together is to collect; to drive forcibly is to compel.

Dūcō. The present active imperative second person singular of **dūcō** is **dūc** (not **dūce**).

Trādō. In compounds **dō, dare, dedī, datum** becomes **-dō, -dere, -didī, -ditum.**

Two of the verbs in this lesson are commonly used in military idioms.

bellum gerere,   *to wage war*   castra pōnere,   *to pitch camp*

— Exercises —

A. Analyze the form, and translate.

1. dūxī, ēgerat, gessit   2. mīsī, dēfenderit, coēgimus   3. vīcistī, surrēxerint, rēxerat   4. pōnet, relinquēmus, trādit   5. regite, dēfendit, posuerat   6. coēgistī, relīquī, dūxerit   7. trādidit, mīsērunt, vīcerant   8. agēbat, gere, surgent   9. mittimus, mīsimus, ēgerās   10. relinquit, vincent, gerēbant

B. Translate.

1. we shall send, he had risen   2. you have ruled, I did   3. he has put, we have compelled   4. he handed over, we led   5. stand up! he was bearing   6. you are leaving behind, he defended   7. he had conquered, you will let go   8. I shall drive, they place   9. you will have collected, we had surrendered   10. did he carry on? are they not handing down?

C. Read the Latin and translate.

1. Bonī agricolae cēna erat in mēnsā ad fenestram.   2. Dux noster, Lūcius, auxilium ad cōpiās magnā cum celeritāte mīsit.   3. Surgite, virī fēminaeque; equōs videō rēgis atque rēgīnae.   4. Nostrī oppidum nōn relinquent sed patriam defendent.   5. Cīvēs pecūniam coēgērunt, et Marcus dōna multa captīvīs trādet.   6. Cūr auxilia trāns flūmen cum novīs cōpiīs relīquērunt?   7. Rōmānī multa bella cum Germānīs gessērunt.   8. Hodiē castra in campō posuimus;

crās post proelium castra movēbimus.   9. Decem virī pugnam relīquērunt et ā lēgātō vīsī sunt.   10. Cūr post castra mīlitēs relīquit imperātor?

D. Translate.

1. Why had they moved the troops, with the auxiliary forces, out of the town across the river?   2. The boys were sending letters to their friends across the sea.   3. A powerful king used to rule the fierce tribes in the territory of the Britons.   4. The general with his soldiers had defended Lucius, the consul's brother.   5. The soldiers had pitched camp on a high mountain.   6. Marcus, our leader, will defend the wretched soldier.   7. Why didn't the Roman people send aid to its allies across the sea?   8. Caesar, while commander, waged war with the Gauls.   9. Caesar's soldiers conquered the enemy in Gaul and even in Germany.   10. The enemy have surrendered their arms to our leader, Caesar's lieutenant.

—— *Reading* ——

THE KINGS OF ROME (continued)

Pater fīliīs fābulam dē rēgibus Rōmānīs nārrābat: "Tertius rēx erat Tullus Hostīlius. Bellum cum Albānīs gessit. In bellō Albānō trēs frātrēs Rōmānī, Horātiī, patriam defendērunt. Cum tribus frātribus Albānīs, Curiātiīs, pugnāvērunt. Cīvēs Rōmānī Albānīque pugnam spectāvērunt. Diū pugnātum est. Trēs Curiātiī vulnerātī erant. Ūnus 5 ex Horātiīs vīvus relictus est, sed Curiātiōs vīcit et necāvit. Cīvēs surrēxērunt et Horātium in urbem magnō cum gaudiō duxērunt. Albānī urbem Albam Longam Tullō trādidērunt. Rēx Rōmānus Albam vāstāvit.

"Quārtus rēx erat Ancus Marcius. Post mortem Ancī Lūcius Tar- 10 quinius Priscus rēgnum occupāvit. Multa bella gessit et Serviō Tulliō, sextō rēgī, magnum agrum trādidit. Servius populum bene rēxit et urbī Rōmae multa dedit. Post mortem Servī fīlius Tarquinī Priscī, Tarquinius Superbus, rēgnum obtinuit. Bene appellātus est. Superbus malusque erat rēx. Brūtus, pater patriae, Tarquinium Superbum ab 15 urbe rēgnōque ēgit."

23

Third Conjugation, Passive Objective Genitive

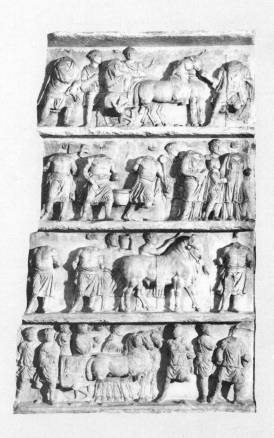

Frieze from Arch of Trajan at Beneventum: A triumphal procession

Trahimur omnes laudis studio.
*We are all led on by our eagerness for praise—*CICERO

—— Forms ——

THIRD CONJUGATION PASSIVE

The present system of the third conjugation forms its passive by adding the passive personal endings to the same bases as in the active except that in the second person singular the inserted vowel is **-e-** instead of **-i-**.

PRESENT

re'**gor**	re'g**imur**
re'g**eris**	regi'**minī**
re'g**itur**	regu**n'tur**

IMPERFECT

regē'**bar**, etc.	regēba'**mur**, etc.

FUTURE

re'**gar**	regē'**mur**
regē'**ris**	regē'**minī**
regē'**tur**	rege**n'tur**

PRESENT IMPERATIVE

re'g**ere**	regi'**minī**

The perfect system in the passive is like that of the other conjugations.

PERFECT

rēc'**tus, -a, -um sum**, etc.	rēc'**tī, -ae, -a su'mus**, etc.

PLUPERFECT

rēc'**tus, -a, -um e'ram**, etc.	rēc'**tī, -ae, -a erā'mus**, etc.

FUTURE PERFECT

rēc'**tus, -a, -um e'rō**, etc.	rēc'**tī, -ae, -a e'rimus**, etc.

—Syntax—

THE OBJECTIVE GENITIVE

The objective genitive is used as if it were the object of a noun or adjective containing some idea of action.

> dux cōpiārum, *the leader of the forces* (dūcit cōpiās)
> cūra agrōrum, *care for the fields*
> fuga malōrum, *flight from evils*

—Vocabulary—

antī'quus, -a, -um, *former, ancient, old-fashioned, old*
clā'rus, -a, -um, *clear, bright; famous*
fīni'timus, -a, -um, *neighboring*
pau'cī, -ae, -a, *few, a few*
re'liquus, -a, -um, *remaining, the rest of*

cē'dō, cē'dere, ces'sī, ces'sum, *move; yield, give way*
cōnsti'tuō, cōnstitu'ere, cōnsti'tuī, cōnstitū'tum, *set up; decide, determine*
conten'dō, conten'dere, conten'dī, conten'tum, *strive, struggle; hasten*
dē'ligō, dēli'gere, dēlē'gī, dēlēc'tum, *choose*
discē'dō, discē'dere, disces'sī, disces'sum, *go away, depart, leave*
excē'dō, excē'dere, exces'sī, exces'sum, *go out, leave*
redū'cō, redū'cere, redūx'ī, reduc'tum, *lead back*

—Word Study—

Antīquus is rarely used to mean "old." **Virī antīquī** means not "old men" but *men of old* or *old-fashioned men*.

Reliquus. The genitive is not used with this adjective. The *of* of *rest of* is part of the meaning of the adjective.

> reliquae cōpiae, *the rest of the troops*

Discēdō. The prefix **dis-** or **dī-** means *apart, in different directions*. In compounds, **cēdō** generally means *go*, hence it is intransitive.

— Exercises —

A. Analyze each form and translate.

1. positus est, reductī sunt   2. cōgēbantur, trādita sunt
3. dēfendar, vincētur   4. ducta est, dēligitur   5. missī erunt, re-
gar   6. relinquēris, gestum erat   7. ācta erat, dūcar
8. cōnstituētur, cesserant   9. vincimur, cōgentur   10. excessērunt,
agēbāris

B. Translate.

1. they have been set up, we shall be chosen   2. it is being sent,
you will be handed over   3. she has been defended, he will be
ruled   4. I am left behind, you will be led back   5. it will have
been carried on, they have been collected   6. they will be placed,
I shall be conquered   7. you have departed, she has stood up
8. he is being driven, we shall not go out   9. they were being led,
we have been let go   10. they had yielded, it has been decided

C. Read the Latin and translate.

1. Ā paucīs mīlitibus ducēs tēlīs victī sunt.   2. Et nautae et mīlitēs
cum celeritāte Gallōs gladiīs vīcērunt.   3. Paucī in auxiliōrum Gallōrum castrīs relictī erant.   4. Nōmina virōrum antiquōrum memoriā tenēmus.*   5. Caesar ā populō cōnsul dēlēctus est.
6. Reliquōs mīlitēs et magna auxilia Caesar ex oppidō ad castra
redūxit.   7. Oppida fīnitima ā nostrīs oppugnāta sunt.   8. Castra
nostra ad pontem in īnsulā parvā posita erant.   9. Mīsī clārī poētae
librum ad meum amīcum.   10. Sī magnā cum audāciā pugnābimus, hostēs vincentur.

D. Translate.

1. The large wagon was driven to the city by the rest of the
boys.   2. After the war the people chose Lucius as king.   3. Stand
up, men; the general and his friends are walking toward our
camp.   4. The German auxiliaries were being led back through
the forest by the brave leader.   5. If we leave the town, we shall
hasten to the small farmhouse across the river.   6. The men of
old had great care for their fields.   7. Our men have not been

* **Memoriā teneō** (*I hold by means of memory*), *I remember.*

conquered in battle by the enemy.   8. Our messengers were sent into the town by the lieutenant.   9. The citizens will always remember the ancient battles.   10. In the towns and in the plains we shall fight with great daring against our enemies.

——Reading——

CINCINNATUS

In numerō virōrum Rōmānōrum antīquōrum est Cincinnātus. Ab Rōmānīs nōmen Cincinnātī memoriā semper tenēbātur. Acer dux mīlitum in bellō erat; in pāce agricola bonus. In parvā villā habitābat, et cūrā agrōrum dēlectābātur. Ubi in castrīs nōn erat, vītam in agrīs agēbat.   5

Rōmānī cum fīnitimīs bellum gerēbant. Cōnsul cum cōpiīs Rōmānīs in montibus miserē labōrābat. Quīnque ex mīlitibus nūntiī ad urbem contendērunt et cīvibus perīculum nūntiāvērunt:

"Sī auxilium ad cōnsulem nōn mīseritis, cōnsul cum reliquīs cōpiīs vincētur."   10

Tum ab cīvibus Cincinnātus dux dēlēctus est et cum novīs cōpiīs ex urbe contrā hostēs excessit. Mīlitēs cōnsulis servātī sunt; arma ab hostibus sunt trādita. Posteā Cincinnātus ad villam in triumphō reductus est.

Model of a covered battering ram used against fortifications

24

Third Conjugation, I-Stem
Ablative of Separation

Model of a catapult, a siege machine worked by torsion for shooting arrows

Gladiator in arena consilium capit.
*The gladiator is making his plan in the arena
(i.e., too late).*—SENECA

—Forms—

I-Stem Verbs of the Third Conjugation

A few important verbs of the third conjugation have present stems ending in **i**; the **i** does not appear in the other two stems. If you will remember that in the third conjugation the present stem is found by dropping the **-ō** from the first principal part you will have no trouble distinguishing **i**-stem verbs from the others. With both **regō, regere** and **capiō, capere** the **-ere** tells you that the verbs belong to the third conjugation; the first principal parts tell you that **capiō** is an **i**-stem and that **regō** is not. In the conjugation of an **i**-stem verb, the **i** of the stem is changed to **e** in the second principal part, the present passive indicative second person singular, and in the present active and passive imperative second person singular.

ACTIVE		PASSIVE	
	PRESENT INDICATIVE		
ca′pio	ca′pimus	ca′pior	ca′pimur
ca′pis	ca′pitis	ca′peris	capi′minī
ca′pit	ca′pi*u*nt	ca′pitur	capi*u*n′tur
	IMPERFECT INDICATIVE		
capiē′bam, etc.	capiēbā′mus, etc.	capiē′bar, etc.	capiēbā′mur, etc.
	FUTURE INDICATIVE		
ca′piam	capiē′mus	ca′piar	capiē′mur
ca′piēs	capiē′tis	capiē′ris	capiē′minī
ca′piet	ca′pient	capiē′tur	capien′tur
	PERFECT INDICATIVE		
cē′pī, etc.	cē′pimus, etc.	cap′tus **sum**, etc.	cap′tī su′mus, etc.

PLUPERFECT INDICATIVE

cē'peram,	cēperā'mus,	cap'tus e'ram,	cap'tī erā'mus,
etc.	etc.	etc.	etc.

FUTURE PERFECT INDICATIVE

cē'perō,	cēpe'rimus,	cap'tus e'rō,	cap'tī e'rimus,
etc.	etc.	etc.	etc.

PRESENT IMPERATIVE

| ca'pe | ca'pite *capture!* | ca'pere | capi'minī *be captured!* |

——Syntax——

ABLATIVE OF SEPARATION

Separation, when no motion is implied, is expressed by the ablative with **a, ab,** or without a preposition. The preposition is generally used with persons and concrete nouns, and omitted before abstract nouns.

Dēfendimur ā finitimīs Gallīs.   *We are defended from the neighboring Gauls.*
Cōnsulem omnī cūrā līberābitis.   *You will free the consul from all care.*

——Vocabulary——

acci'piō, acci'pere, accē'pī, accep'tum, *receive, accept*
ca'piō, ca'pere, cē'pī, cap'tum, *take, capture*
cōnfi'ciō, cōnfi'cere, cōnfē'cī, cōnfe'ctum, *accomplish, finish*
coni'ciō, coni'cere, coniē'cī, coniec'tum, *hurl; throw together*
cu'piō, cu'pere, cupī'vī, cupī'tum, *wish, want, desire*
fa'ciō, fa'cere, fē'cī, fac'tum, *make, do*
fu'giō, fu'gere, fū'gī, fu'gitum, *flee, flee from*
ia'ciō, ia'cere, iē'cī, iac'tum, *throw*
inci'piō, inci'pere, incē'pī, incep'tum, *begin*
interfi'ciō, interfi'cere, interfē'ci, interfec'tum, *kill*

—— Word Study ——

Compounds. Remembering prefixes, you should have no trouble with the meanings of the compound verbs in this lesson.

> accipiō = ad- + capiō,   *take to oneself = receive, accept*
> incipiō = in- + capiō,   *take on = begin*
> cōnficiō = cōn- + faciō,   *do completely = accomplish, finish*
> interficiō = inter- + faciō,   *make into pieces, destroy = kill*
> coniciō = con- + iaciō,   *throw together, throw forcibly = hurl*

Fac. The present active imperative singular of **faciō** is **fac** (as that of **dūcō** is **dūc**).

Fugiō may be used either transitively or intransitively.

> Hostēs fugiunt.   *The enemy are fleeing.*
> Hostēs fugiunt nostrōs.   *The enemy are fleeing from our men.*

—— Exercises ——

A. Translate.

1. capientur, accipiet 2. cōnfēcimus, incipiam 3. cupīvistis, coniciēbātis 4. interfēcerat, fēcimus 5. fugient, iacta sunt 6. interficiēbam, acceptī erant 7. facta erunt, cōnficiunt 8. incipitur, fugimus 9. cupīverās, coniciēbās 10. cēpit, iactum erat

B. Translate.

1. we shall accomplish, he was beginning 2. they have fled, they desire 3. it has been hurled, they will take 4. we have received, I shall make 5. they were throwing, you are killing 6. it will be thrown, it has been finished 7. they will have thrown together, I shall have begun 8. we were capturing, you will be killed 9. we want, he has accepted 10. we do, he killed

C. Read the Latin and translate.

1. Sī cōnsilium cēperimus,* bellum diū nōn gerētur. 2. Quod Germānī nostrōs semper fugiēbant, iter in Germāniam

*__consilium capere,__ *to form* (or *make*) *a plan*

fēcimus.*   3. Hodiē, mīlitēs, prohibēte Gallōs castrīs nostrīs.
4. Populus Rōmānus ducēs cōnsulēs appellābat.   5. Magnā cūrā
līberābimur sī mīlitēs nostram urbem ab hostibus dēfenderint.
6. Cīvēs Rōmānī clārae victōriae memoriam servāvērunt.   7. Gallī
tēla coniciēbant et nostrī multa vulnera accēpērunt.   8. Iūlius Caesar, nostrārum cōpiārum dux, imperātor factus est.   9. Aut hostium oppidum capiēmus aut ab hostibus interficiēmur.   10. Sī
labōrābimus magnā cum dīligentiā multum cōnficiēmus.

D. Translate.

1. If we make a good plan, our sailors will capture many ships.
2. The leaders of the Roman people were called consuls.   3. Men
of Rome, shall we make Lucius our king?   4. The queen, because
she was good, received many beautiful gifts from the grateful
people.   5. Leave the forest, boys, and you will free me from
great care.   6. We hurled many weapons and kept the enemy
from our town.   7. Two boys and five girls were sitting on chairs
near the large table.   8. A thousand soldiers and a hundred auxiliary troops were marching from Italy to Gaul.   9. The neighboring tribes are both savage and hostile, but we shall defend our city
from the dangers of war.   10. A few bad boys were throwing
books through the teacher's window.

——Reading——

PYRRHUS AND FABRICIUS

Rōmānī cum Pyrrho, rēge Epīrī, bellum gerēbant. Ab rēge multīs
proeliīs victī sunt. Multī mīlitēs Rōmānī captī sunt. Rōmānī captīvōs
ā Pyrrhō līberāre cupiēbant et ad rēgem lēgātōs mīsērunt. Ūnus ex
lēgātīs fuit Fabricius, vir bonus et in bellō fortis; clārum erat Fabricī
nōmen, sed vir nōn magnam pecūniam habuit. Pyrrhus Fabricium
benignē accēpit; fāma ducis Rōmānī rēgem dēlectāvit.

"Fabricī," inquit (*says*) Pyrrhus, "sī pacem cum meā patriā faciēs,
pecūniam accipiēs; captīvōs līberābō et meōs mīlitēs ab iniūriā prohi-
bēbō. Eris socius meus."

Sed Fabricius patriam, nōn pecūniam, amābat. Respondit, "Sī,
Pyrrhe, tua dona accēperō, meam amīcitiam nōn cupiēs. Et Rōmānī
et tuī magnō cum honōre bellum cōnficient. Tum amīcī erimus."

*iter facere, *to make a march, to march*

Rident stolidi verba Latina.
Fools laugh at the Latin language.—OVID

REVIEW **6** (LESSONS 21–24)

——*Vocabulary Drill*——

A. Give the genitive, gender, and meaning of the following nouns.

cēna   fenestra   iniūria   mēnsa   pugna   sella   victōria

B. Give the other nominative forms, and the meanings, of the following adjectives.

antīquus   clārus   fīnitimus   paucī   reliquus

C. Give the principal parts and meanings of the following verbs.

accipiō	contendō	faciō	pōnō
agō	cupiō	fugiō	redūcō
capiō	dēfendō	gerō	regō
cēdō	dēligō	iaciō	relinquō
cōgō	discēdō	incipiō	surgō
cōnficiō	dūcō	interficiō	trādō
coniciō	excēdō	mittō	vincō
cōnstituō			

D. Give the meanings of the following conjunctions.

atque   aut   quod   sī

——*Drill on Forms*——

A. Give the following forms.

1. *vocative singular:* Graecia, clārus, victōria
2. *genitive singular:* reliqua, sella, antīquum
3. *dative singular:* Trōia, Sicilia, iniūria
4. *genitive plural:* fenestra, trēs, septem
5. *accusative plural:* pugna, fīnitimum, pauca

B. Give a synopsis in all tenses, indicative and (where applicable) imperative, of:

1. interficiō *in the first person singular, active voice*
2. mittō *in the second person singular, passive voice*
3. faciō *in the third person singular, active voice*
4. accipiō *in the first person plural, passive voice*
5. pōnō *in the second person plural, active voice*
6. agō *in the third person plural, passive voice*

—— Drill on Syntax ——

Translate the words in italics, giving the reason for each case.
1. He was freed *from all care.*
2. He defended his daughter *from the danger.*
3. I gave the book to my son *Marcus.*
4. We freed the captives *from the soldiers.*
5. We have preserved the memory *of the great battle.*
6. They kept the enemy *from the town.*
7. Julius, *our consul,* was in the city.
8. Caesar was the leader *of the forces.*

—— Exercises ——

A. Translate.

1. Omnēs Germānī ē nostrā urbe Rōmā excēdent.   2. Rēx ā bonīs servīs dēfendēbātur.   3. Sī tēla hostium nostrīs ducibus trādita erunt, pācem diū habēbimus.   4. Cōpiae hostium tēlīs nostrōrum mīlitum vulnerātae sunt. 5. Quod rēgīna per portam ambulā- verat, cīvēs surrēxērunt. 6. Ad ignem sedēbāmus, et pater fābulam dē bellō nārrābat.   7. Ubi nūntium dē perīculō bellī accēpimus, iter per magnam silvam in Germāniam fēcimus. 8. Trēs puerōs, Mārce, cum tuō amīcō et quinque puellās vīdī. 9. Magnā cum dīligentiā Gallōs inimīcōs ab nostrīs castrīs prohibēbāmus. 10. Caesaris clārās victōriās memoriā semper tenēbimus.

B. Translate.

1. Our men pitched camp yesterday; today they will break camp and march with great speed to Gaul.   2. If Marcus leaves the city

tomorrow he will not receive the king's gift. 3. Weapons were being hurled toward our town by a thousand soldiers of the enemy. 4. We shall pitch camp tomorrow; then we shall defend our city from the enemy with arms. 5. The king had ruled the people for a long time, and he was loved by everyone in the kingdom. 6. Caesar, our leader, has been made consul by the Roman people. 7. Before the battle the soldiers were preparing the weapons. 8. He has sent many letters to the commander in Gaul, but the commander has not replied. 9. Julia, my sister, wants aid from the queen of the city. 10. The boys and girls wanted either a large dinner or many gifts.

The emperor Hadrian built an elaborate series of fortifications across the north of England to protect the fertile midlands from raiding Picts of Scotland.

25

Demonstratives Is, Hic, Ille
Ablatives of Time

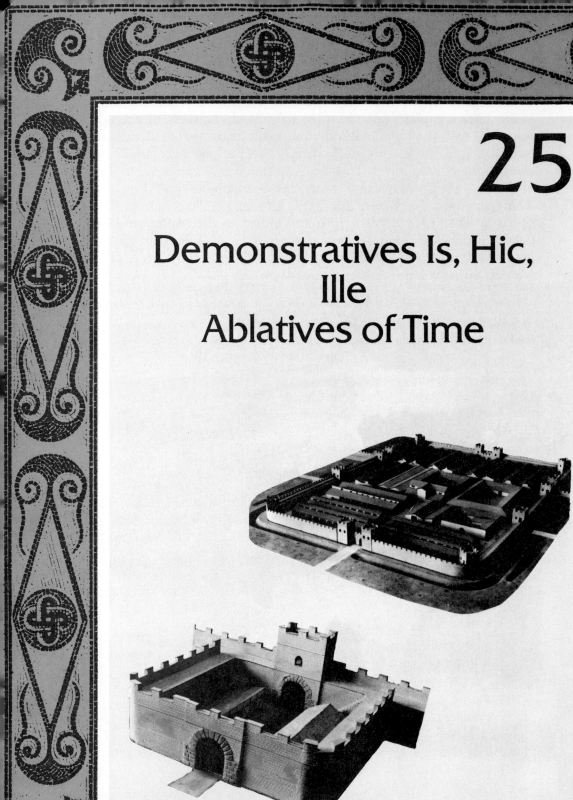

Models of milecastle and cavalry fort on Hadrian's Wall

Inhumanitas omni aetate molesta est.
Inhumanity is harmful in every age.—CICERO

—— Forms ——

DEMONSTRATIVES

The demonstratives point out a person or an object. They are used either as adjectives or pronouns. As adjectives they agree with and modify nouns: **is puer,** *that boy.* As pronouns they are used alone: **videō eum,** *I see him.* The most common demonstrative adjectives are **is,** *this, that,* **hic,** *this,* and **ille,** *that.*

| | SINGULAR | | | PLURAL | | |
	M.	F.	N.	M.	F.	N.
NOM.	is	e'a	id	e'ī	e'ae	e'a
GEN.	e'ius	e'ius	e'ius	eō'rum	eā'rum	eō'rum
DAT.	e'ī	e'ī	e'ī	e'īs	e'īs	e'īs
ACC.	e'um	e'am	id	e'ōs	e'ās	e'a
ABL.	e'ō	e'ā	e'ō	e'īs	e'īs	e'īs
NOM.	hic	haec	hoc	hī	hae	haec
GEN.	hu'ius	hu'ius	hu'ius	hō'rum	hā'rum	hō'rum
DAT.	huic	huic	huic	hīs	hīs	hīs
ACC.	hunc	hanc	hoc	hōs	hās	haec
ABL.	hōc	hāc	hōc	hīs	hīs	hīs
NOM.	il'le	il'la	il'lud	il'lī	il'lae	il'la
GEN.	illī'us	illī'us	illī'us	illō'rum	illā'rum	illō'rum
DAT.	il'lī	il'lī	il'lī	il'līs	il'līs	il'līs
ACC.	il'lum	il'lam	il'lud	il'lōs	il'lās	il'la
ABL.	il'lō	il'lā	il'lō	il'līs	il'līs	il'līs

—— Syntax ——

ABLATIVE OF TIME WHEN

The time when an action occurs is expressed by the ablative without a preposition.

Tertiā hōrā ē castrīs excessērunt.   *They left camp at the third hour.*

ABLATIVE OF TIME WITHIN WHICH

The time within which an action occurs is also expressed by the ablative without a preposition.

> Tribus annīs ad Āfricam nāvigābimus.
> *We shall sail to Africa within three years.*
> Multa oppida ūnō annō capta sunt.
> *Many towns were taken in one year.*

—— Vocabulary ——

e'ques, e'quitis, m., *horseman, knight;* pl., *cavalry*

pe'des, pe'ditis, m., *foot soldier;* pl., *infantry*

is, e'a, id, *this, that; he, she, it*
hic, haec, hoc, *this; the latter*
il'le, il'la, il'lud, *that; the former*

bi'bō, bi'bere, bi'bī, ——, *drink*
cur'rō, -ere, cucur'rī, cur'sum, *run*

dī'cō, -ere, dīx'ī, dic'tum, *say, tell*

e'dō, -ere, ē'dī, ē'sum, *eat*

pe'tō, -ere, petī'vī, petī'tum, *seek; beg; ask; attack; aim at*

scrī'bō, -ere, scrīp'sī, scrīp'tum, *write*

ō'lim, (adv.) *formerly, once upon a time; some day*

—— Word Study ——

Eques, *knight.* The word for horseman or cavalryman may also designate a knight, a member of the wealthy business class among the Romans. In primitive times the title had been given to a man wealthy enough to provide himself with a horse for battle but by the classical period the knights had little connection with horses.

Is, hic, ille. The demonstrative adjectives **hic** and **ille** point out the position of the words they modify as present or near the speaker (**hic**), or absent or more remote from the speaker (**ille**).

Hic and **ille** may also be used to mean *the latter* and *the former* respectively.

Is does not suggest any specific location, but merely indicates that the noun it modifies has already been mentioned or is to be defined.

> Hoc oppidum magnum, illud parvum est.
> *This town (here) is large; that one (there) is small.*

Oppidum Gallōrum vīdī; id oppidum parvum erat.
I saw a town of the Gauls; this (or that) town was small.

Dīcō. The present active imperative singular of **dīcō** is **dīc** (like **dūc** and **fac** it lacks the final **e**).

——Exercises——

A. Give the case and translate.

1. huius peditis   2. illīus cēnae   3. hārum iniūriārum   4. eae pugnae   5. cum eō equite   6. ab eīs cōnsulibus   7. ad illās fenestrās   8. sub illō ponte   9. ad haec flūmina   10. quintō annō

B. Translate.

1. this table   2. of that victory   3. with these tribes   4. to that mountain   5. on this bridge   6. by means of these names   7. this light   8. by this horseman   9. of these voices   10. within three years

Mosaic of a Nile scene, Palestrina

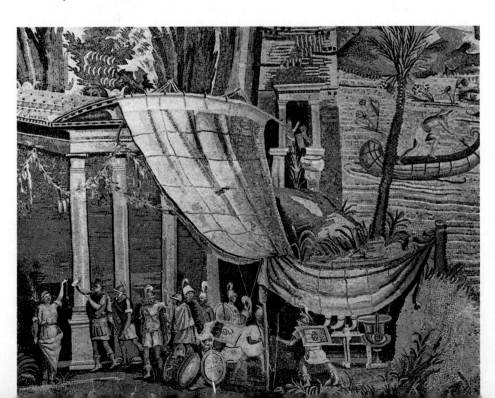

C. Read the Latin and translate.

1. Agricolae fīlia cēnam in mēnsā ad fenestram posuit.   2. Parvum animal in silvā equitēs fugiēbat.   3. Patriam nostram magnā cum audāciā dēfendēmus.   4. Eī equī magnā cum celeritāte ex agrō in viam currēbant.   5. Quīnque annīs ille rēx bonus servōs miserōs līberāverit.   6. Ōlim nostrī multīs proeliīs equitēs hostium vincēbant.   7. Mittite hās epistulās ad vestrōs amīcōs; mox respondēbunt.   8. Illā aestāte peditēs Rōmānī cum illīs hostibus diū pugnāverant.   9. Hae sellae sunt magnae, illae parvae.   10. Cīvēs huius oppidī Germānōs peditēs cēperant et ad castra dūcēbant.

D. Translate.

1. The commander left the infantry in the camp and led the cavalry into battle.   2. In summer we shall send our sons to Italy.   3. The enemy surrendered (its) arms to our infantry at the seventh hour.   4. Much bread was eaten by the wretched captives in the Roman camp.   5. These boys were running down from the mountain at the tenth hour.   6. Our infantry and cavalry waged war with a powerful enemy in Spain.   7. This little girl is writing a letter to (her) brother.   8. The enemy's cavalry attacked our infantry with (their) weapons.   9. These wretched boys are seeking bread, but those girls have given them water.   10. Did that horseman say many things to the lieutenant?

—— *Reading* ——

BAUCIS AND PHILEMON

Ōlim Iuppiter et Mercurius in Phrygiā iter faciēbant. Nōn deī vidēbantur (*seemed*), sed hominēs. Nox aderat. Hī deī longō itinere dēfessī erant. Cibum vīnumque ab multīs petēbant, sed omnēs inimīcī erant. Tum parvam vīllam in colle vīdērunt. Hōc tempore in hāc vīllā habitābant bonus vir Philēmon et bona fēmina Baucis. Erant veterēs et līberōs nōn habēbant. Inopiā magnā labōrābant, sed deōs amābant. Magnā cum amīcitiā deōs recēpērunt, sellās posuērunt, et cēnam parāvērunt. Deī līberē grātēque ēdērunt et bibērunt.

   Post cēnam Iuppiter virō fēminaeque, "Sum," inquit, "Iuppiter. Multa dōna dabō. Omnēs bonōs fēlīcēs faciam."

   Fīnem potentia deōrum nōn habet.

26

Personal Pronouns

Dancers—Tomb of Triclinium, Tarquinia

Vos vestros servate, meos mihi linquite mores.

You cling to your own ways and leave mine to me. —PETRARCH

—— Forms ——

PERSONAL PRONOUNS

The First Person Pronouns are **ego,** *I,* and **nōs,** *we.*

	SINGULAR	PLURAL
NOMINATIVE:	e'go	nōs
GENITIVE:	me'ī	nos'trī, nos'trum
DATIVE:	mi'hi	nō'bīs
ACCUSATIVE:	mē	nōs
ABLATIVE:	mē	nō'bīs

The Second Person Pronouns are **tū,** *you (s.),* and **vōs,** *you (pl.).*

	SINGULAR	PLURAL
NOMINATIVE:	tu	vōs
GENITIVE:	tu'ī	ves'trī, ves'trum
DATIVE:	ti'bi	vō'bīs
ACCUSATIVE:	tē	vōs
ABLATIVE:	tē	vō'bīs

The Third Person. Latin has no personal pronoun for the third person, *he, she, it, they.* It is usually provided for by the demonstrative pronoun **is, ea, id.**

Hic or **ille** may be used as a personal pronoun when specific location is indicated.

Id factum est ab hōc, non ab illā.

This was done by him (this man here), not by her (that woman there).

—— Syntax ——

AGREEMENT OF PRONOUNS

We call the noun for which a pronoun stands its antecedent. A pronoun agrees with its antecedent in gender and number.

Sī erit pānis in mēnsā, eum edēmus; sī aqua, eam bibēmus.
If there is bread on the table, we shall eat it; if there is water, we shall drink it.

The genitive of the personal pronouns is not used to indicate posses-sion; instead we use the possessive adjectives **meus, noster, tuus, vester.** The genitives **meī, nostrī, tuī,** and **vestrī** are used as objective genitives (see Lesson 23): **timor vester,** *your fear,* **timor vestrī,** *the fear of you.*

You will learn the use of the forms **nostrum** and **vestrum** in Lesson 29.

When first and second person pronouns are used in the ablative of accompaniment, the **cum** is placed after the pronoun and the two are written as one word: **mēcum, nōbīscum, tēcum, vōbīscum.**

Vōbīscum ambulābimus.   *We shall walk with you.*

—— Vocabulary ——

auctō'ritās, -tā'tis, f., *authority, influence, prestige*
a'vis, a'vis, f., *bird*
ca'nis, ca'nis, m. or f., *dog*
clā'mor, clāmō'ris, m., *shout, noise*
iū'dex, iū'dicis, m., *juror, judge*

la'pis, la'pidis, m., *stone*
le'giō, legiō'nis, f., *legion*
līber'tās, -tā'tis, f., *freedom, liberty*
nox, noc'tis, f., *night*
prīn'ceps, prīn'cipis, m., *chief*
ti'mor, timō'ris, m., *fear*

—— Word Study ——

Canis is not an **i**-stem. It is an exception to the rule that masculine and feminine third declension nouns which have the same form in the nominative and genitive singular are **i**-stems.

Clāmor, timor. The suffix **-or, -ōris, m.** on a word-root gives us the name of an action or quality. Thus the noun **clāmor** is the name of the action of the verb **clāmō, timor** the name of the action of the verb **timeō.** Other such nouns derived from roots you have learned are:

amor, amōris, m.,   *love*
terror, terrōris, m.,   *fright, terror*

Legiō. The legion was a Roman military unit. Its enrollment varied from 4,200 to 6,000 men during the classical period.

——Exercises——

A. Translate the italicized words.

1. Ad urbem *mēcum* ambulābant.   2. Librum *eīs* dedit.   3. *Cum eīs* ambulābō.   4. *Mē et tē* vīdit.   5. *Ego tibi* dōnum dabō.   6. *Vōbīscum* currēbat.   7. *Id vōbīs* dedērunt.   8. *Tē et illum* ad oppidum dūcam.   9. *Eōrum* prīnceps *vōs* dūcēbat.   10. *Huius amīcī* nāvigābant.

In English, politeness requires that we put the first person after the second and third. In Latin the first person precedes the second and the second precedes the third.

> Ego et tū ambulābāmus.   *You and I were walking.*
> Ego et hic ad īnsulam nāvigāmus.
>   *He and I are sailing to the island.*
> Tū et ille cucurrerātis.   *You and he had run.*
> Haec mihi et tibi et eī dant.
>   *They give these things to you, him, and me.*

Notice also the agreement of the verbs in person and number.

B. Translate the italicized words.

1. He was walking *with her*.   2. Give the book *to me*.   3. I gave the money *to him*.   4. He saw *you and us*.   5. *He and I* can go *with you* (*sing.*).   6. *Their* friends came *with us*.   7. *His* horse ran toward *me*.   8. *You and I* looked at *him*.   9. We were seen *by them*.   10. I gave *it to you* (*pl.*).

C. Read the Latin and translate.

1. Eius frāter mihi pecūniam dabit.   2. Clāmor equitum mē et meam sorōrem terrēbat.   3. Prīnceps legiōnem octāvam cum multīs equitibus ad haec castra dūxit.   4. Illae puellae ad flūmen nōbīscum ambulābunt.   5. Eōrum equī in nostrōs agrōs cucurrerant.   6. Mihi, domine, lībertātem dā; servus miser sum.   7. Iūdicis amīcī tē et tuōs frātrēs vocābant.   8. Caesaris auctōritās

cīvēs nostrōs cōnfirmāvit. 9. Illā nocte noster prīnceps legiōnem ad hunc montem dūxit. 10. Prīnceps mē vīdit et mihi hunc gladium dedit.

D. Translate.

1. At night many fires were seen on that high mountain. 2. He had written a letter to her but he did not send it. 3. Within five years you and I will see many Spanish chiefs in our country. 4. Many white birds were flying towards that small island. 5. His sister gave me bread, but I gave her a stone. 6. The enemy will surrender to us (their) arms and horses. 7. The judge was walking with my father and my mother. 8. A dog was given to Marcus's sister, and she gave it to me. 9. Lucius, run with me to the camp of the Tenth Legion. 10. That black dog was drinking water under the boy's chair.

—Reading—

THE BOY AND THE APPLES

Erat in agrō arbor; in eā pōma multa erant. Puer pōma vīdit. Prīmā lūce in arborem ascendit et duo pōma ab arbore edēbat. Sed agricola, quī puerum vīderat, magnum canem in agrum dūxit.

Tum puer perterritus est et magnō clāmōre locum complēvit; sed nōn erat auxilium. Agricola appropinquāvit et puerum ita monuit: "Pōma nōn tua sunt. Cūr pōma aliēna ab arbore removēbās? Nōn aequum erat. Fūr es, et canis fūrēs mordēbit. Cūr nōn es bonus puer?" Tum puer exclāmat: "Numquam iterum fūr erō. Nunc canem ex agrō ēdūc."

Agricola rīsit et canem abdūxit. Puer incolumis relictus est, et pōma nōn iam* ēdit. Bonum cōnsilium agricolae memoriā tenuit neque posteā ab arbore eius pōma āmōvit.

* **Iam** with a negative means *longer*: **nōn iam,** *no longer*

27

Relative Pronoun

Mosaic of actors dressing, Pompeii

Non omnes qui habent citharam sunt citharoedi.
Not all those who own a musical instrument are musicians. —VARRO

—Forms—

THE RELATIVE PRONOUN—qui, quae, quod, *who, which*

	SINGULAR			PLURAL		
	MASC.	FEM.	NEUT.	MASC.	FEM.	NEUT.
NOM.	quī	quae	quod	quī	quae	quae
GEN.	cu′ius	cu′ius	cu′ius	quō′rum	quā′rum	quō′rum
DAT.	cui	cui	cui	qui′bus	qui′bus	qui′bus
ACC.	quem	quam	quod	quōs	quās	quae
ABL.	quō	quā	quō	qui′bus	qui′bus	qui′bus

—Syntax—

AGREEMENT OF THE RELATIVE PRONOUN

A relative pronoun agrees with its antecedent in gender, number, and person, but its case is determined by its use in its own clause.

Virum quī aderat vīdī. *I saw the man who was present.*
Porta quam vidēs lāta est. *The gate which you see is wide.*
Fēminae sunt quās dēlēgit. *They are the women whom he chose.*
Ego quī haec vōbīs dīcō sum vester rēx.
   I who say these things to you am your king.

Notice that **quī** in the first example is masculine gender, singular number, third person, like its antecedent **virum,** but it is *nominative* as subject of the verb **aderat.** In the second example **quam** is feminine gender, singular number, third person, to agree with **porta,** but *accusative* because it is the object of the verb **vidēs.**

In the ablative of accompaniment the **cum** is usually attached to the relative, **quōcum, quācum, quibuscum.**

The translation of the relative pronoun

NOMINATIVE:	MASCULINE AND FEMININE	*who*
	NEUTER	*which*
GENITIVE:	MASCULINE AND FEMININE	*whose, of whom*
	NEUTER	*of which*
DATIVE:	MASCULINE AND FEMININE	*to whom*
	NEUTER	*to which*
ACCUSATIVE:	MASCULINE AND FEMININE	*whom*
	NEUTER	*which*
ABLATIVE:	MASCULINE AND FEMININE	*from, by,* or *with, whom*
	NEUTER	*in, on, at, from, by,* or *with, which*

A clause introduced by a relative pronoun is called a relative clause. A third person pronoun antecedent of a relative pronoun is often omitted in Latin.

Quī auxilium dat vērus est amīcus.   *He who gives help is a true friend.*

—— Vocabulary ——

cī′vitās, -tā′tis, f., *citizenship, citizenry, state*

ho′mō, ho′minis, m., *man, human being*

hor′tus, -ī, m., *garden*

la′bor, labō′ris, m., *difficulty, hardship; work*

lēx, lē′gis, f., *law*

multitū′dō, multitū′dinis, f., *great number, crowd*

pars, par′tis, f., *part, direction*

pēs, pe′dis, m., *foot*

vir′tūs, virtū′tis, f., *manliness, bravery, courage*

Musicians, Tomb of the Leopards, Tarquinia

—— Word Study ——

Homō, vir. Homō means *man* as opposed to animals or inanimate objects; **vir** means *man* as opposed to woman.

> Animālia fera sunt sed hominēs sunt fortēs.
> *Animals are fierce, but men are brave.*
> Virī proelia amāvērunt, fēminae timuērunt.
> *The men loved battles; the women feared them.*

Vir may also mean *hero*.

> Virī antīquī vēram virtūtem habēbant.
> *The heroes of old used to have real courage.*

—— Exercises ——

A. Translate the italicized words.

1. Tū, *quī amās* . . .   2. Frāter imperātōris *quem vīdī* . . .
3. Flūmen, *quod est lātum* . . .   4. Mīlitēs *quibus victōriam nūntiāvī* . . .   5. Nautae, *quōrum nāvēs erant* . . .   6. Animālia, *quae sedēbant* . . .   7. Eques *ā quō pedes vulnerātus est* . . .   8. Fēminae *quās spectāvī* . . .   9. Peditēs *quibuscum discēdēbāmus* . . .   10. Mea fīlia, *cui dedī* . . .

B. Translate the italicized words.

1. This is a town *in which* many people . . .   2. I, *who am your sister* . . .   3. I see some girls *who are* . . .   4. Give back the money *which* you took.   5. He was killed by a man *whose friends* were . . .
6. He spoke to the messengers *with whom you were leaving.*   7. We captured a city *which is* in . . .   8. The farmers *whom we saw* . . .
9. The women *to whom I gave* . . .   10. I know a boy *whose name is* . . .

C. Read the Latin and translate.

1. Eōs mīlitēs vīdī quī in magnō bellō pugnāverant.   2. Gravia erant ea tēla quae portābāmus.   3. Quī magnam virtūtem habet vir est vērē.   4. Ea legiō quae ā Mārcō ducta est bene pugnāvit.
5. Ubi sunt puellae fēminaeque quibuscum ambulābās?   6. Vōbīs

154

qui cīvēs Rōmānī estis multa dē cīvitātis lēgibus cōnsul dīcet.
7. Caesar, cuius cōpiae ab Ītaliā discessērunt, nunc est in Galliā.
8. Mīlitēs ā quibus castra dēfēnsa sunt cum virtūte pugnāvērunt.
9. Dux cui perīculum nūntiātum est ad castra currit.   10. Legiōnem
ad flūmen quod in prōvinciā est dūxit.

D. Translate.

1. The man whom you sent to the general has reported the victory.   2. I saw those slaves who had been led to the city.   3. The people whose courage you praised are now citizens.   4. You who live in farmhouses do not like the life of the city.   5. Those rivers which you were looking at in Gaul are wide and deep.   6. In Helvetia I have seen a large city in which many people live.   7. He who is not my friend is my enemy.   8. I sent my friend the books which I had written.   9. Behind the farmhouse there was a large garden, in which the farmer and (his) sons were working.   10. Did you see the men to whom I gave the money?

— *Reading* —

THE KING'S STORYTELLER

Servus rēgis antīquī omnī nocte quīnque fābulās dominō narrābat. Ūnā nocte rēx magnā cūrā mōtus est; etiam post octō fābulās nōn requiēvit. Itaque rūrsus petīvit octō fābulās, id quod servum nōn dēlectāvit. "Quod cupīvistī, domine, iam factum est."

Respondit rēx, "Fābulae quās mihi narrāvistī erant multae sed 5 brēvēs. Longam cupiō fābulam quae multa verba habet."

Servus tum incēpit: "Ōlim erat agricola quī magnam pecūniam habēbat. In oppidō pecūniam virō dedit et accēpit centum ovēs. Dum ea animālia redūcit, appropinquat ad flūmen sine pontibus in quō est eō diē magna aquae cōpia; itaque modum nōn videt quō ovēs per 10 aquam aget. Tandem vīdit scapham, in quā ab agricolā duo animālia posita et portāta sunt."

Ubi haec verba dīxit, tacuit servus. Eum rēx hōc modō obsecrāvit: "Dīc mihi reliquam fābulam tuam."

Respondit ille, "Flūmen et altum et lātum, scapha parva est, atque 15 sunt multa animālia. Sī dūxerit hic agricola omnia animālia trāns flūmen, fābulam quam incēpī ad fīnem dūcam."

28

Interrogative Pronoun
Interrogative Adjective

Mosaic—Roman tragic masks, Gregorian Museum, Vatican, Rome

Quid rides? . . . De te fabula narratur.

What are you laughing at? The joke's on you. —HORACE

—Forms—

THE INTERROGATIVE PRONOUN

	SINGULAR	
	MASCULINE AND FEMININE	NEUTER
NOMINATIVE:	quis	quid
GENITIVE:	cu'ius	cu'ius
DATIVE:	cui	cui
ACCUSATIVE:	quem	quid
ABLATIVE:	quō	quō

		PLURAL	
	MASCULINE	FEMININE	NEUTER
NOMINATIVE:	quī	quae	quae
GENITIVE:	quō'rum	quā'rum	quō'rum
DATIVE:	qui'bus	qui'bus	qui'bus
ACCUSATIVE:	quōs	quās	quae
ABLATIVE:	qui'bus	qui'bus	qui'bus

THE INTERROGATIVE ADJECTIVE

Quī, quae, quod meaning *which?, what?* followed by a noun, is declined exactly like the relative pronoun.

—Syntax—

USE OF THE INTERROGATIVE

The interrogative pronoun is used to ask questions, either direct or indirect. The English equivalents are as follows: NOM., *who? what?* GEN., *whose? of whom?* DAT., *to* or *for whom?* ACC., *whom? what?* ABL., *by* or *with whom?* or *in, on, at, by,* or *with what?* The singular and plural are the same in English. *Who saw . . . ?* in Latin can be **Quis vīdit?** or **Quī vīdērunt?**

—— Vocabulary ——

ci'bus, -ī, m., *food*

mo'dus, -ī, m., *measure, degree; manner, way*

mū'rus, -ī, m., *wall*

ni'hil, n., (defective noun) *nothing**

vī'num, -ī, n., *wine*

āmit'tō, -ere, āmī'sī, āmis'sum, *lose*

commit'tō, -ere, -mī'sī, -mis'sum, *entrust;* (with proelium) *begin a battle, join battle*

expel'lō, -ere, ex'pulī, expul'sum, *drive out, drive away*

red'dō, -ere, red'didī, red'ditum, *give back, restore*

—— Word Study ——

Modus. The phrases **quō modō (quōmodo),** *by what way?, in what manner?, how?,* and **quem ad modum,** *to what degree?, how?,* are used frequently in Latin.

> Quō modō id fēcit?   *How did he do it?*
>
> Quem ad modum territus es?   *How were you frightened?*

Committō. The two distinct meanings of this word come from the two meanings of the prefix **com-,** *together* and *completely. To let go completely* is *to entrust; to let a battle go together* is *to join battle.*

—— Exercises ——

A. Translate the italicized words.

1. *Quid* vīdistī? 2. *Quī* ambulant? 3. *Quae* fēcistis? 4. *Quis* pugnat? 5. *Quōrum equī* erant in agrō? 6. *Cum cuius amīcō* ambulās? 7. *Cum quō amīcō* nāvigāvit? 8. *A quibus* ductī sunt? 9. *Cui* pecūniam dedit? 10. *Quibus mīlitibus* haec dīxit?

---

* A defective word is one whose inflection is incomplete. **Nihil** has no plural and no genitive, dative, or ablative singular.

B. Translate the italicized words.

1. *Whom* were they defending?   2. *To which farmer* did you give the money?   3. *What* is in the road?   4. *In what land* is Rome? 5. *With whom* is he fighting?   6. *In(to) which direction* were you sailing?   7. *Whose* friend is he?   8. *With which weapon* was he wounded?   9. *To whom* are you saying this?   10. *To whose brother* did you entrust the money?

Mosaic showing children's games

Combat of the Gladiators—relief, National Museum, Rome

C. Read the Latin and translate.

1. Quis vīdit prīncipem cuius amīcus ex oppidō expulsus est?
2. Quibus pecūniam et dōna commīsistis?   3. Quam legiōnem dūcēbat ex castrīs ad flūmen?   4. Cum quibus proelium crās com-
mittēmus?   5. Cīvis malus cīvitātem āmīsit, sed posteā eī reddita
est.   6. Quid in hortō post vīllam vīdistī? Nihil vīdī.   7. In quam
partem fēminae ambulābant?   8. Cuius equī in nostrō agrō currunt?   9. Quō modō ex urbe expulistis hostēs quī eam oppugnābant?   10. Quī agricolae bibunt vīnum et aquam in vīllā?

D. Translate.

1. Who gave back freedom and citizenship to the unhappy captives?   2. To whose father did you owe that money?   3. By whom
was the little girl frightened?   4. What gift did the farmer's daughter give to the consuls?   5. To whom were you giving those books
I wrote?   6. In which direction were those boys whom you saw
running?   7. What was the judge saying to the citizens?   8. How
did you lose the wine you were carrying?   9. What did she write
in the letter which you have?   10. Which general will lead the
infantry into battle?

——— Reading ———

SCIPIO AFRICANUS MINOR

Ōlim in hortō Cicerō et Q. Mūcius, iūdex Rōmānus, sedēbant. Hic illī
multa dē C. Laeliō, clārō virō Rōmānō, et dē verbīs nārrābat, quae
verba Laelius dē Scipiōnis virtūte cum amīcīs fēcerat.

AMĪCUS: Quō modō, Laelī, mortem tuī cārī amīcī Scipiōnis accēpistī?

LAELIUS: Sine, amīce, dolōre. Quid is quī vītam bonam ēgit dē morte
timet? In caelō Scipiō malum nōn habēbit. Sed quid dē eius vītā
dīcam: dē pietāte in mātrem, līberālitāte in sorōrēs, bonitāte in
servōs? Scipiō erat vir bonus et fortis quī patriam amābat. Quī
imperātor antīquus omnēs hās virtūtēs habēbat?

AMĪCUS: Vēra dīcis, Laelī. Sed hunc bonum quis malus interfēcit?

LAELIUS: Is quem lēx et pāx nōn dēlectant, vir inimīcus patriae, Carbō.

AMĪCUS: Quam bonus vir interfectus est!

Ut sementem feceris ita metes.

As you sow so will you reap.—CICERO

REVIEW 7 (LESSONS 25–28)

—Vocabulary Drill—

A. Give the genitive, gender, and meaning of the following nouns.

auctōritās	homō	lībertās	pedes
avis	hortus	modus	pēs
canis	iūdex	multitūdō	prīnceps
cibus	labor	mūrus	timor
cīvitās	lapis	nihil	vīnum
clāmor	legiō	nox	virtūs
eques	lēx	pars	

B. Give the principal parts and meanings of the following verbs.

āmittō	committō	dīcō	expellō	reddō
bibō	currō	edō	petō	scrībō

—Drill on Forms—

A. Give the following forms.

1. *genitive singular:* eques, hōmo, quis
2. *dative singular:* multitūdō, pēs, ego
3. *accusative singular:* virtūs, nihil, quis
4. *ablative singular:* iūdex, cīvitās, hic
5. *nominative plural:* labor, pedes, ille
6. *genitive plural:* canis, pars, avis
7. *dative plural:* lapis, prīnceps, quis
8. *accusative plural:* virtūs, modus, similis

B. Give a synopsis of the following verbs in the indicative and (where applicable) the imperative, active and passive, with meanings.

1. **reddō** *in the third person singular.* 2. **moveō** *in the second person singular.* 3. **iaciō** *in the second person plural.*

C. Translate:

1. biberant
2. expulsa est
3. redditum erit
4. scrībet

5. edēbāmus
6. petītus sum
7. dicta erant
8. currēs

D. Translate.

1. he has eaten
2. we were writing
3. it was lost
4. they will drink

5. he is being driven out
6. we were running
7. it had been said
8. you had been sought

—— Exercises ——

A. Translate.

1. Eōs nautās quī ad terram nāvigābant spectāvit.   2. Quī sunt illī virī quibuscum pugnābātis?   3. Cuius frūmentum agricola carrō ab agrō portat?   4. Dē quō imperātōre hominēs haec dīcunt? 5. Virōs antīquōs, quōrum virtūtēs magnae erant, amābant deī omnēs.   6. Ad quem amīcum illās litterās scrīpsistī?   7. Captīvīs reddidit bonus cōnsul omnēs agrōs quōs āmīserant.   8. In quam partem currēbat is agricola cuius equus āmissus erat?   9. Servum cui prīnceps lībertātem cīvitātemque dederat spectāvimus. 10. Unum pedem in proeliō āmīserat mīles miser.

B. Translate.

1. What did they put on the head of the general who defeated the German forces?   2. Formerly he used to work in summer and in winter in that farmer's fields.   3. Are these the boys with whom you were defending your camp?   4. The women in the garden are eating bread; they will not drink the wine.   5. Man is the animal which dwells in cities.   6. The Gauls and the Romans are fighting, but within seven years the former will have been defeated and the latter will march to the city.   7. Soldiers, defend this town in which we all live.   8. The women were frightened by wild animals, but the men killed them.   9. To whom was the victory of our legions reported, to the general, or to his lieutenant?   10. The animals who were fleeing from the fierce dogs ran into the forest.

29

Fourth Declension
Partitives

Statuettes of clown slaves

Dente lupus, cornu taurus petit.
The wolf attacks with his fang, the bull with his horn.—HORACE

—*Forms*—

THE FOURTH DECLENSION

This declension consists of those nouns whose genitive singular ends in **-ūs.** Those ending in **-us** in the nominative singular are masculine, with a few exceptions. Those whose nominative ends in **-ū** are neuter. Masculine and feminine nouns of the fourth declension are declined like **passus,** *pace.*

	SINGULAR	PLURAL	ENDINGS
NOMINATIVE:	pas'sus	pas'sūs	-us, -ūs
GENITIVE:	pas'sūs	pas'suum	-ūs, -uum
DATIVE:	pas'suī	pas'sibus	-uī, -ibus
ACCUSATIVE:	pas'sum	pas'sūs	-um, -ūs
ABLATIVE:	pas'sū	pas'sibus	-ū, -ibus

Neuter nouns of the fourth declension are declined like **cornū,** *horn.*

NOMINATIVE:	cor'nū	cor'nua	-ū, -ua
GENITIVE:	cor'nūs	cor'nuum	-ūs, -uum
DATIVE:	cor'nū	cor'nibus	-ū, -ibus
ACCUSATIVE:	cor'nū	cor'nua	-ū, -ua
ABLATIVE:	cor'nū	cor'nibus	-ū, -ibus

The vocative endings of the fourth declension are like the nominative.

The Declension of Domus. Besides its normal fourth declension forms, **domus** has some endings of the second declension.

	SINGULAR	PLURAL
NOMINATIVE:	do'mus	do'mūs
GENITIVE:	do'mūs	do'muum
DATIVE:	do'muī	do'mibus
ACCUSATIVE:	do'mum	do'mōs
ABLATIVE:	do'mō	do'mibus

Rarely used, but seen occasionally, are second declension forms for the genitive and dative singular and genitive plural (**domī, domō, domōrum**) and fourth declension forms for the ablative singular and accusative plural (**domū, domūs**).

——Syntax——

PARTITIVES

The Genitive of the Whole (Partitive Genitive). The genitive is used to denote the whole of which a part is mentioned.

> Pars exercitūs in Galliam iter fēcit.
> *Part of the army marched into Gaul.*
> Erant duo frātrēs, quōrum Mārcus mīles, Lūcius nauta erat.
> *There were two brothers, of whom Marcus was a soldier,*
> *Lucius a sailor.*

The **-um** forms of the genitive plural of the personal pronouns (**nostrum, vestrum**) are used as partitive genitives.

> Pars nostrum in castrīs mānsit.   *Part of us stayed in the camp.*
> Quis vestrum haec fēcit?   *Which of you has done these things?*

The partitive genitive is frequently used with **nihil.**

> Nōs nihil cibī, vōs nihil vīnī habētis.
> *We have no food (nothing of food), and you have no wine (nothing of wine).*
> Est nihil reliquī.   *There is nothing left (nothing of remaining).*

The partitive idea is sometimes expressed by the ablative of place from which with **dē** or **ex,** especially with cardinal numerals and **paucī.**

> Ūnus ex puerīs in vīllā erat.
> *One of the boys was in the farmhouse.*
> Paucōs dē equīs agricolae dedimus.
> *We gave a few of the horses to the farmer.*

Either construction can be used with **multī.**
Remember, the English expressions *rest of* and *all of* are not partitive in Latin.

> Reliquī nautae in nāve mānsērunt.
> *The rest of the (The remaining) sailors stayed in the ship.*
> Omnēs fēminae territae sunt.
> *All of (All) the women were frightened.*

—— Vocabulary ——

adven'tus, -ūs, m., *arrival, approach*
cor'nū, -ūs, n., *horn, wing (of an army)*
cur'sus, -ūs, m., *running; course, quick motion*
do'mus, -ūs, f., *house, home*
exer'citus, -ūs, m., *army*
ex'itus, -ūs, m., *departure, way out; end, outcome*
fluc'tus, -ūs, m., *wave*
im'petus, -ūs, m., *attack*
ma'nus, -ūs, f., *hand; band (of men)*
occā'sus, -ūs, m., *setting, downfall, a going down*
pas'sus, -ūs, m., *pace*
por'tus, -ūs, m., *harbor, port*
senā'tus, -ūs, m., *senate*
ū'sus, -ūs, m., *use; advantage; practice, experience*

—— Word Study ——

Gender of Fourth Declension Nouns. Except for **domus, manus,** and names of trees, all of which are feminine, nearly all fourth declension nouns in **-us** are masculine.
Impetum facere in with accusative means *to attack.*
Passus. The pace (two steps) was a Roman unit of measurement, about five feet long; a mile was a thousand paces (**mille passūs**).

—— Exercises ——

A. Translate.

1. quis cīvium   2. in magnīs fluctibus   3. nihil vīnī   4. magna pars urbis   5. paucae de fēminīs   6. septem ex puellīs   7. multī mīlitum   8. adventū nostrī exercitūs   9. ā parte vestrum   10. impetum fēcit in equitēs

B. Translate.

1. the rest of the army   2. all of the men   3. part of our band   4. which of us   5. by means of a fierce attack   6. many of the

women   7. the leader of their army   8. nothing left   9. ten of the men   10. no water

C. Read the Latin and translate.

1. Fluctūs magnī erant sed dē marī in portum sine perīculō nāvigāvimus.   2. Decem ex mīlitibus erant et magnī et fortēs. 3. Suntne multī passūs inter portum et domōs oppidī? 4. Multitūdō cīvium diū exspectāvit adventum cōnsulum ā quibus lēgēs bonae factae erant.   5. Quis nostrum gladiō rēgem malum petet?   6. Quod animal illa cornua magna gerēbat quae in vīllā tuā vīdī?   7. Paucī ex nostrīs equitibus nihil cibī equīs dabant. 8. Manus peditum labōrābat in ponte cuius pars cōnfecta non erat.   9. Parvum animal quod in silvā vīdimus magnō timōre nostrī occupātum est.   10. Caesaris exercitus impetum fēcit in cōpiās Germānās.

D. Translate.

1. Have you fled because of your fear of us?   2. Which of you led the army out of the camp into the plains?   3. The tenth legion was attacked by bands of Spanish foot soldiers.   4. Whose garden did you see in that city yesterday?   5. The wretched captives, who had no food, were waiting for the arrival of our general. 6. What did the leader of the army say to those soldiers who had attacked the town?   7. Eight of the boys were led back to (their) fathers' houses by the teacher.   8. Many of the girls gave back the rest of the money which the men had given to them.   9. The foot soldiers made an attack, and all of the enemy ran down from the mountain toward the river.   10. The consul reported to the senate the arrival of the enemy's army.

—— *Reading* ——

A TRIP TO THE CITY

Marcus, cuius pater agricola erat, in agrīs ā prīmā lūce ad sōlis occāsum labōrābat. Frūmentum cōgēbat quod ad urbem Rōmam carrīs portābātur. Hoc iter facere saepe cupiēbat quod Rōmam nōn vīderat.

Ōlim pater, "Quod, mī fīlī," inquit, "mihi auxilium multōs diēs dedistī, tē mēcum ad urbem dūcam." Ubi frūmentum coāctum est, ā

Relief showing a scene from Roman comedy. An angry father is restrained from
chastising drunken son returning from a banquet supported by his personal slave.
Son will be saved by this slave's tricks. (Flute player is accompanist for play.)

vīllā discessērunt. Post quīnque hōrās pater fīliusque eius in viīs urbis
ambulābant. Ibi hominēs quī ab omnibus prōvinciīs convēnerant
vīdērunt.

Eō diē per Viam Sacram cum mīlitibus veniēbat in triumphō imperātor clārus. Propter eius adventum magnī clāmōrēs cīvium audiēbantur.
Marcus servum vīdit quī gladium post tergum tenēbat et ad imperātōrem
currēbat. Magnā vōce Marcus clāmāvit, "Spectāte, Rōmānī! Illum
servum malum capite! Ducem nostrum interficiet. Vīdī . . . !" Sed
servus nōn iam aderat.* Fūgerat!

Marcus, quod vītam ducis servāverat, ab omnibus laudātus est et
ob virtūtem magnum praemium accēpit.

* from **adsum**

30

Fourth Conjugation
Accusative of Extent
of Space
Accusative of Duration
of Time

Model of the Theatre of Marcellus

Non est ars quae ad effectum casu venit.

That which achieves its effect by accident is not art.—SENECA

—Forms—

THE FOURTH CONJUGATION

Verbs whose present stem ends in ī belong to the fourth conjugation, and may be recognized by the **-īre** of the second principal part. They are conjugated like **audiō, audīre, audīvī, audītum,** *hear.*

The present system of the fourth conjugation is formed like that of third conjugation **i-**stems. The **-ī-** of the stem is shortened before a vowel or a final **-t.**

1. **Present.** The personal endings are added directly to the present stem, except that a **-u-** is inserted in the third person plural.

	ACTIVE		PASSIVE	
	SINGULAR	PLURAL	SINGULAR	PLURAL
	au'diō	audī'mus	au'dior	audī'mur
	au'dīs	audī'tis	audī'ris	audī'minī
	au'dit	au'diunt	audī'tur	audiun'tur

2. **Imperfect.** As in the third conjugation, the tense sign is **-ēbā-.**

audiē'bam, etc.   audiē'bar, etc.

3. **Future.** The tense sign, as in the third conjugation, is **-ē-,** shortened before **-t** and **-nt,** and becoming **-a-** in the first person singular.

au'diam   au'diar
au'diēs, etc.   audiē'ris, etc.

The perfect system of the fourth conjugation is formed in the same way as that of the other conjugations.

PERFECT	audī'vī, etc.	audī'tus **sum,** etc.
PLUPERFECT	audī'veram, etc.	audī'tus e'ram, etc.
FUT. PERFECT	audī'verō, etc.	audī'tus e'rō, etc.

The imperative is formed in the same way as in the first and second conjugations.

ACTIVE		PASSIVE	
au'dī	audī'**te** (*hear!*)	audī'**re**	audī'**minī** (*be heard!*)

—— *Syntax* ——

ACCUSATIVE OF EXTENT OF SPACE AND ACCUSATIVE OF DURATION OF TIME

Extent of space (how far?) and duration of time (how long?) are expressed by the accusative without a preposition.

> Mīlle passūs cucurrit. *He ran a mile.*
> Domus mea est vīgintī pedēs ā vīllā tuā.
> *My house is twenty feet from your villa.*
> In urbe quīnque annōs mānsimus.
> *We stayed in the city for five years.*

—— *Vocabulary* ——

mī'lia, mī'lium, n. pl., *thousands*

au'diō, -ī're, -ī'vī, -ī'tum, *hear, listen to*

conve'niō, -ī're, convē'nī, conven'tum, *come together, assemble*

dor'miō, -ī're, -ī'vī, -ī'tum, *sleep*

impe'diō, -ī're, -ī'vī, -ī'tum, *hinder*

inve'niō, -ī're, invē'nī, inven'tum, *come upon, find*

mū'niō, -ī're, -ī'vī, -ī'tum, *fortify, build*

perve'niō, -ī're, pervē'nī, perventum, *reach, arrive*

ve'niō, -ī're, vē'nī, ven'tum, *come*

et'iam, (adv.) *also, even*

ta'men, (adv. postpositive)* *nevertheless, yet, still*

nam, (conj.) *for*

---

* A postpositive adverb or conjunction may not come first in its own clause; usually it comes second.

> Clāmōrēs audīvimus, puerōs tamen nōn invēnimus.
> *We heard the shouts, yet we did not find the boys.*

—Word Study—

Mīlia, *thousands,* which is declined regularly as a third declension neuter **i**-stem (like the plural of **mare**), differs from all other Latin numerals in that it is a noun rather than an adjective. Consequently it cannot modify a noun, but must be used with a partitive genitive. It has no singular; you remember that **mīlle,** *a thousand,* is, like most cardinal numerals, an indeclinable adjective.

> Mīlle mīlitēs vulnerātī sunt. *A thousand soldiers were wounded.*
> Quattuor mīlia mīlitum vulnerāta sunt.
> *Four thousand soldiers were wounded.*
> Quattuor mīlia ex mīlitibus *four thousand of the soldiers*
> Mīlle passūs ambulāvistī. *You walked a mile.*
> Quīnque mīlia passuum ambulāvistī. *You walked five miles.*

Perveniō. Although we say *arrive at* or *arrive in* in English, **perveniō,** being a verb of motion, takes an accusative of place to which, not ablative of place where.

> Brevī tempore ad portum pervēnimus.
> *Within a short time we arrived at the harbor (we reached the harbor).*

> Tertiā hōrā in castra pervēnērunt.
> *They arrived in camp (reached camp) at the third hour.*

—Exercises—

A. Analyze each form and translate.

1. audīs, audiētur, audītur, audiēmus 2. veniēbat, convēnērunt, perveniunt, vēnerant 3. mūniēbāmus, mūnīvērunt, mūnītum erat, mūniam 4. impedient, impedītus sum, invēneram, pervenient 5. conveniēbant, audītus erit, mūnīvimus, veniētis

B. Translate.

1. we shall hear, they are building 2. he has been hindered, they were coming together 3. she had arrived, I shall have come 4. it has been fortified, you were finding 5. they are listening to, we shall come together

C. Translate the italicized words.

1. I saw *a thousand girls.* 2. I saw *five thousand boys.* 3. I saw *three thousand of the soldiers.* 4. They came *one mile.* 5. They came

ten miles. 6. He spoke *to four thousand citizens.* 7. They fought *with eight thousand foot soldiers.* 8. *Two thousand captives were found* in the camp. 9. We carried the weapons *of one thousand soldiers.* 10. He lived in Europe *for twenty years.*

D. Read the Latin and translate.

1. Decem hōrās urbem oppugnāverant et Graecōs, quī gravibus armīs impedītī sunt, vīcerant. 2. Lēgātus quī dē pāce missus erat quīnque mīlia passuum ad oppidum fīnitimum vēnit. 3. Propter fluctūs in marī dux octō hōrās in portū mānserat. 4. Brevī tempore multī Rōmānōrum in urbem nostram convenient. 5. Quis vestrum audiēbat imperātōrem ubi vōs dē victōriā docēbat? 6. Decem ex agricolīs frūmentum mīlle passūs ad flūmen portāvērunt. 7. Nautae quī ad urbem vēnērunt nāvēs in portū relīquerant. 8. Māter mea ad agricolae vīllam septimā hōrā pervēnit et trēs hōrās manēbat. 9. Iter faciēmus multa mīlia passuum

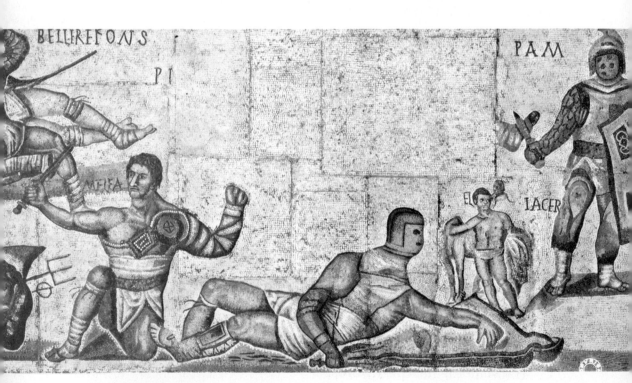

Fighting gladiators

ad fīnēs nostrōrum sociōrum in Eurōpā.   10. Quōs invēnistī ubi in castra pervēnistī?

E.   Translate.

1. We remained in camp for four hours, for we had not heard the signal.   2. We have come a mile and yet we have not found a river.   3. For many years she waited; yet the letters from him did not come.   4. We carried the grain and water to the horses many miles across the plains.   5. Ten thousand of the enemy were captured, for they fought badly because there was no food in their camp.   6. They are building a large camp in the territory of the friendly Gauls.   7. The attacks of our infantry were hindered by the enemy's boldness.   8. I saw three thousand men who had come from a neighboring city.   9. In my farmhouse there are the horns of many animals which I found in the woods.   10. What did you hear when you arrived at the villa of the consul?

——Reading——

A CITY IS TAKEN BY A HORSE

Ōlim fīlius rēgis Trōiānī per Graeciam iter faciēbat. Ibi rēgīnam pulchram Graecōrum vīdit et statim amāvit. Posteā eam trāns mare ad urbem Trōiam dūxit.

Īrātī ob rēgīnae discessum prīncipēs Graeciae multās nāvēs parāvērunt. Atque ad illam urbem cum multīs et fortibus cōpiīs nāvigāvērunt.

Post novem annōs tamen ab hostibus nōn superāta erat Trōia propter virtūtem Trōiānōrum. Itaque decimō annō clārus imperātor Graecus cōnsilium novum et audāx cēpit. Mīlitēs eius iussū magnum equum ligneum fēcērunt, cuius corpus erat cavum. Ille exercituī, "In hōc equō cavō," inquit, "partem peditum nostrōrum pōnēmus. Hoc animal, sī in urbem ductum erit, nōbīs victōriam dabit."

Ubi Trōiānī dē mūrīs magnitūdinem animālis spectāvērunt, terrēbantur paucī. Multī tamen clāmābant, "Nōnne sacer est hic equus? Movēte eum per portās urbis ad templa deōrum, nam sine hōrum auxiliō urbem nostram nōn bene dēfendere poterimus."

Sed equus, quem in urbem accēpērunt Trōiānī, non pācem sed arma hostium portābat. Hōc modō id quod hominēs nōn decem annīs fēcerant, ūnā nocte cōnfēcit equus.

31

Fifth Declension
Formation of Adverbs

A bronze of a retiarius

Fallaces sunt rerum species.
The appearances of things are deceptive. — SENECA

—— *Forms* ——

THE FIFTH DECLENSION

Nouns whose stem ends in ē (shortened after a consonant and before a vowel) belong to the fifth declension; they may be recognized from the **-ēī** or (after a consonant) **-eī** ending of the genitive singular. They are declined like **diēs,** *day,* and **rēs,** *thing.*

	SINGULAR	PLURAL	SINGULAR	PLURAL	ENDINGS	
NOM.	di'ēs	di'ēs	rēs	rēs	-ēs	-ēs
GEN.	diē'ī	diē'rum	re'ī	rē'rum	-ēī, -eī	-ērum
DAT.	diē'ī	diē'bus	re'ī	rē'bus	-ēī, -eī	-ēbus
ACC.	di'em	di'ēs	rem	rēs	-em	-ēs
ABL.	di'ē	diē'bus	rē	rē'bus	-ē	-ēbus

The vocative endings of the fifth declension are like the nominative.

FORMATION OF ADVERBS

You have learned that adverbs are formed from adjectives of the first and second declensions by adding **-ē** to the base. Adjectives of the third declension form their adverbs by adding **-ter** or **-iter** to the base (if the base ends in **t,** only **-er** is added). Study the formation of the following adverbs.

ācriter,	*sharply, fiercely*	fortiter,	*bravely*
audacter,	*boldly, rashly*	graviter,	*deeply, severely*
breviter,	*briefly*	potenter,	*powerfully*
celeriter,	*swiftly*	similiter,	*in like manner, similarly*

—— *Vocabulary* ——

a'ciēs, aciē'ī, f., *straight line; line of battle*
di'ēs, diē'ī, m., *day*
iā'nua, -ae, f., *door*
lec'tus, -ī, m., *bed, dining couch*

merī'diēs, -ē'ī, m., *midday, noon; south*
rēs, re'ī, f., *thing, affair, matter*
spēs, spe'ī, f., *hope*

frūmentārius, -a, -um, *having to
do with grain*
pūb'licus, -a, -um, *belonging to
the people, public*

i'taque, (conj.), *and so, therefore*
ne'que, nec, (conj.), *and . . . not,
nor*

— Word Study —

Gender. Fifth declension nouns are all feminine, with the exception of **diēs** and **merīdiēs.** In certain idiomatic expressions, however, **diēs** may be feminine: **diē cōnstitūtā,** *on the appointed day.*
Rēs. *Thing* is really never a good translation for **rēs,** and vice versa (e.g. *many things* is **multa,** not **multae rēs**). The meaning *thing* is given because **rēs** has so many possible translations in English that no other English word will cover them. (Depending on the context, **rēs** in the singular may mean *fact, business, function, science, property, profit,* etc.; in the plural it may mean *the physical universe, conditions, circumstances, deeds,* etc.)

Four idiomatic uses of **rēs:**

> rēs frūmentāria, reī frūmentāriae, f.,   *grain supply, forage*
> rēs pūblica, reī pūblicae, f.,   *commonwealth, state, republic*
> rēs gestae, rērum gestārum, f., pl.,   *deeds, accomplishments*
> rēs novae, rērum novārum, f. pl.,   *revolution*

Multō diē (*at much day*) is an idiom for *late in the day;* similarly **multā nocte** means *late at night.*

— Exercises —

A. Decline.

1. haec aciēs   2. bonus diēs   3. exercitus fortis   4. rēs gestae
5. ūna spēs   6. quae manus?   7. rēs pūblica   8. duo cornua
9. mīlle passūs   10. mīlia passuum

B. Read the Latin and translate.

1. Lēgēs reī pūblicae nostrae sunt bonae.   2. Imperātor mīlitēs in agrōs ob rem frūmentāriam mīsit.   3. Hostēs fortēs sunt; magnā tamen cum audāciā pugnābimus.   4. Ante merīdiem peditēs tertiae aciēī bene pugnābant.   5. Cōnsul cīvibus multa dē rē pūblicā

dīxerat.　6. Merīdiē cibus datus est duōbus mīlibus cīvium. 7. Hostēs cum nostrā prīmā aciē sine spē pugnābant.　8. Rēs gestae huius populī sunt multae et magnae.　9. Domum ūnīus ē cōnsulibus vīderimus.　10. Multō diē ad iānuam domūs meae pervēnērunt.

C. Translate.

1. He was sleeping in the bed which was between the two windows.　2. He also informed the ambassador about the great hope of the citizens for peace.　3. At the arrival of the queen, all of the men who were sitting down stood up.　4. The rest of our first line of battle was driven away by the fierce attack of the Germans.　5. The boys were throwing stones down from one of the high houses into the street.　6. The army of one of the two generals remained in the plain for many hours.　7. In my country the days are short in winter and long in summer.　8. The soldiers broke camp late at night on account of the lack of food.

——— *Reading* ———

A GRATEFUL GHOST

Puella Graeca cum patre mātreque iter per montēs Āsiae faciēbat, quod ex patriā fugere propter bellum coāctī erant. Multōs post diēs ad villam antīquam et pulchram vēnērunt, in quā hominēs iam dūdum nōn habitābant. Itaque ibi semper manēre constituērunt.

Multā nocte magna vōx nōmen patris ex silvā clāmāvit. Pater, "Absum," respondit atque ob timōrem reliquam noctem sub lectō iacēbat. Secundā nocte in silvam vocāta est mater. Eī vocī ex fenestrā, "Crās veniam," respondit, et dormīre temptābat. Tertiā nocte appellāta est puella, quae nihil dīxit, sed in silvam contendit.

Ibi brevī tempore alba ossa hūmāna vīdit. Mox ossa surrēxērunt atque ad eam ambulāre incipiēbant. "Quis es?" inquit puella territa.

"Ōlim huius vīllae dominus eram," respondit. "Hōc in locō ab animālī interfectus sum, nec posteā corpus meum invenīrī potuit. Itaque centum annōs nocte per hanc silvam ambulō. Sī ossa mea sub terrā posueris, discēdam."

"Miser homo," inquit puella, "id quod petis faciam." Adventū diēī patrem vocāvit et eius auxiliō ossa sub terrā posuit. Posteā vōx in silvā nōn iam audīta est.

32

Inquam; Possum Infinitives

Gilt bronze helmet and greaves from the gladiators' barracks in Pompeii

Stultum est timere quod vitare non potes.
It is foolish to fear that which you cannot avoid.—PUBLILIUS SYRUS

—Forms—

INQUAM

The defective verb **inquam,** *I say,* has only five commonly used forms.

PRESENT	PERFECT
in'quam, *I say*	
in'quis, *you say*	
in'quit, *he says*	in'quit, *he said*
in'quiunt, *they say*	

Inquam, inquis, etc. are used only to introduce direct quotations; they played the part of quotation marks for the Romans, who used little punctuation. They never come before the quotation, but are usually placed after its first word or phrase.

POSSUM

The verb **possum, posse, potuī, ——,** *I am able, I can,* is a compound of **potis,** *able,* and **sum,** *I am.* In the present system, **potis** becomes **pot-** before an **e,** and **pos-** before an **s.**

PRESENT		IMPERFECT		FUTURE	
pos'sum	pos'sumus	po'teram	poterā'mus	po'terō	pote'rimus
po'tes	potes'tis	po'terās	poterā'tis	po'teris	pote'ritis
po'test	pos'sunt	po'terat	po'terant	po'terit	po'terunt

The perfect system is regular.

  po'tuī, etc.   potu'eram, etc.   potu'erō, etc.

There are no imperatives.

PRESENT PASSIVE INFINITIVE

The present passive infinitive is formed in the first, second, and fourth conjugations by changing the final **-e** of the present active infinitive to **-ī**. In the third conjugation the **-ere** of the present active infinitive is replaced by **-ī**.

ACTIVE		PASSIVE	
vocāre,	*to call*	vocārī,	*to be called*
monēre,	*to warn*	monērī,	*to be warned*
regere,	*to rule*	regī,	*to be ruled*
capere,	*to take*	capī,	*to be taken*
audīre,	*to hear*	audīrī,	*to be heard*

—— Syntax ——

INFINITIVE WITH SUBJECT ACCUSATIVE

Iubeō must, and **cogō** and **prohibeō** may be followed by an infinitive phrase (infinitive with an accusative subject).

> Mīlitēs coēgērunt agricolam vīllam relinquere.
> *The soldiers forced the farmer to leave his farmhouse.*
> Cōnsul cīvēs convenīre iussit.
> *The consul ordered the citizens to assemble.*
> Nōs ad Āfricam nāvigāre prohibēbunt.
> *They will prevent us from sailing to Africa.*

THE COMPLEMENTARY INFINITIVE

Some verbs need an infinitive to complete their meaning, e.g. **possum, cōnstituō** (when it means *decide*), and **dēbeō** (when it means *ought*).

> Castra movēre cōnstituērunt.   *They decided to break camp.*
> Dēbēmus audīre cōnsulem.   *We ought to listen to the consul.*
> Hoc dīcī potest.   *This can (is able to) be said.*

—— Vocabulary ——

gau'dium, gau'dī, n., *joy, gladness*
offi'cium, offi'cī, n., *duty*
prae'mium, prae'mī, n., *reward*
praesi'dium, praesi'dī, n., *guard, garrison*
ter'gum, -ī, n., *back*

ab'sum, abes'se, ā'fuī, āfūtū'rus, *be absent, be distant, be away*

ad'sum, ades'se, ad'fuī, adfūtū'rus, *be present, be near*
conti'neō, -ē're, -ti'nuī, -ten'tum, *hold together, restrain, bound*
in'quam, in'quis, in'quit, in'quiunt, *say*
iu'beō, -ēre, ius'sī, ius'sum, *order, bid*
pos'sum, pos'se, po'tuī, ——, *be able, can*
susti'neō, -ē're, -ti'nuī, -ten'tum, *hold up, hold in check, withstand*

—— *Exercises* ——

A. Translate.

1. poterit, potuerit, possumus 2. potuistis, potes, poterant
3. aberit, aderat, āfuerāmus 4. adfuerimus, possunt, aberunt
5. adest, potestis, āfuērunt 6. potest continēre 7. Iussimus
puerōs venīre. 8. poterāmus audīre 9. Coēgit hominem labōrāre. 10. poterunt invenīre

B. Translate.

1. we are able, he can, you will be able 2. they were able, she
could, I had been able 3. he was absent, they are present, they
are away 4. he will be able, they can, I shall have been able
5. we shall be away, he was near, they have been away 6. You
were able to flee. 7. they could withstand 8. He forced the men
to fight. 9. I ordered the messenger to run. 10. They will be able
to sleep.

C. Read the Latin and translate.

1. Mea vīlla abest duo mīlia passuum ab urbe. 2. Prīnceps praemia magnō cum gaudiō accēpit. 3. Hostēs in nōs impetum fēcērunt quī ā nostrīs equitibus sustentus est. 4. Caesar praesidium
mīlitum in ponte relīquit. 5. "Quis vestrum," inquit lēgātus, "hās
litterās ad imperātōrem portāre poterit?" 6. Paucī aderant, et
multī aberant. 7. Cōnsul cīvibus, "Nōn dēbēmus, "inquit, "discēdere ā nostrō officiō." 8. Poterō ad tuam urbem venīre crās, sī
pecūniam invēnerō. 9. Equitēs iussī sunt continēre equōs ferōs;
paucī dē hīs tamen celeriter ad campōs fūgērunt. 10. Prīncipēs
quī novās rēs cupiēbant cīvitātem relinquere coāctī sunt.

D. Translate.

1. We decided to fortify that large camp which we had captured from the enemy.   2. The slaves were forced to give back to the master part of the reward which he had given them.   3. Who will flee with me from this wretched place?   4. The messenger said to the general, "The garrison will remain on the bridge for two days."   5. We shall not be able to be present, but we shall send our sons and daughters.   6. "An evil man cannot be truly great," said the judge to the citizens.   7. The attack of the German cavalry was held in check by our men, who were fighting fiercely.   8. The republic ought not to be overcome by the attack of one man who desires a revolution.   9. "The duties of the Roman consuls," said the teacher, "were many and not easy."   10. The father ordered (his) sons to send all of the money to the farmers.

—— Reading ——

A SISTER SAVES HER BROTHERS

Iūlia parva puella Rōmāna erat, quae duōs frātrēs habēbat. Cum eīs semper esse cupiēbat; illī tamen eam discēdere iubēbant. "Puellās," inquiunt, "in lūdōs nostrōs nōn accipimus, nam nōs paene virī sumus."

Prīmō aestātis diē, frātrēs ad mare ambulāre cōnstituērunt, nam propter magnum aestum nāre cupiēbant. Iūlia etiam cum eīs ambulāre incipiēbat, sed mox, quod illī currēbant, ab eīs relicta est. In villā patris manēre recūsāvit et cum cane, quī propter aetātem gravis erat et iam currere nōn poterat, post frātrēs discessit. Hī neque eam neque canem vidēbant.

Ubi ad mare vēnit Iūlia, frātrēs magnō cum clāmōre in aquā nābant. Illa post saxum sedēbat et eōs spectābat.

Subitō ūnus dē puerīs clāmāvit: "Polypus meōs pedēs capit!" Ad eum nāvit frāter, quem quoque polypus cēpit. Iūlia magnō timōre ad villam cucurrit; iam currēbat etiam canis. Ad mare vocat patrem, ā quō puerī ē magnō mortis perīculō servātī sunt. Itaque posteā frātrēs sorōrem in lūdōs semper accipiēbant.

Summary of Case Uses

Nominative
1. Subject of a verb (Lesson 1)
   Puerī currunt.   *The boys are running.*
2. Predicate Nominative or Subjective Complement (Lessons 1, 20)
   Caesar erat consul.   *Caesar was consul.*
   Puer appellātur Mārcus.   *The boy is called Marcus.*

Vocative
1. For direct address (Lesson 13)
   Venī, Lūcī, ad vīllam.   *Come to the farmhouse, Lucius.*

Genitive
1. Of possession (Lesson 4)
   Mātrēs puellārum adsunt.   *The girls' mothers are here.*
2. Objective (Lesson 23)
   Noster timor bellī est magnus.   *Our fear of the war is great.*
3. Of the whole (Partitive) (Lesson 29)
   Pars urbis est pulchra.   *Part of the city is beautiful.*

Dative
1. Of the indirect object (Lesson 8)
   Equitibus equōs dat.   *He is giving horses to the horsemen.*

Accusative
1. Of the direct object (Lesson 2)
   Exercitum videō.   *I see an army.*
2. Of place to which (Lesson 5)
   Ad oppidum veniunt.   *They are coming to the town.*
3. Predicate Accusative (Objective Complement) (Lesson 20)
   Fīlium meum vocāvī Lūcium.   *I have called my son Lucius.*
4. Of extent of space (Lesson 30)
   Tria mīlia passuum cucurrī.   *I ran three miles.*
5. Of duration of time (Lesson 30)
   Duās hōrās mānsit.   *He waited two hours.*
6. Subject of an infinitive (Lesson 32)
   Coēgit virōs discēdere.   *He forced the men to leave.*
7. Subjective complement in an infinitive phrase (Lesson 32)
   Prohibet servum esse cīvem.
     He keeps the slave from being a citizen.

Ablative
Showing separation

1. Of place from which (Lesson 5)
   Ab īnsulā nāvigāmus.   *We are sailing from the island.*
2. Partitive place from which (Lesson 29)
   Duo dē puerīs absunt.   *Two of the boys are absent.*
3. Of separation (Lesson 24)
   Cīvēs timōre līberāvit.   *He freed the citizens from fear.*
4. Of personal agent (Lesson 20)
   Hoc factum est ā Caesare.   *This was done by Caesar.*

Showing location
1. Of place where (Lesson 3)
   In urbe manet.   *He is staying in the city.*
2. Of time when (Lesson 25)
   Tertiā hōrā discessērunt.   *They left at the third hour.*
3. Of time within which (Lesson 25)
   Tribus diēbus discēdēmus.   *We shall leave within three days.*

Showing instrument or circumstances
1. Of means or instrument (Lesson 9)
   Tēlō vulnerātus est.   *He was wounded by a weapon.*
2. Of accompaniment (Lesson 18)
   Vēnī cum meīs amīcīs.   *I came with my friends.*
3. Of manner (Lesson 15)
   Dōnum magnō gaudiō accēpit.   *He received the gift with great joy.*

Mosaic of an animal show from late imperial villa at Piazza Armerina

Per varios usus artem experientia fecit.

Through different exercises practice has brought skill.—MANILIUS

REVIEW **8** (LESSONS 29–32)

—*Vocabulary Drill*—

A. Give the genitive, gender, and meaning of the following nouns.

aciēs	exitus	merīdiēs	praesidium
adventus	fluctus	mīlia	rēs
cornū	gaudium	occāsus	senātus
cursus	iānua	officium	spēs
diēs	impetus	passus	tergum
domus	lectus	portus	ūsus
exercitus	manus	praemium	

B. Give the principal parts and meanings of the following verbs.

absum	conveniō	inveniō	possum
adsum	dormiō	iubeō	sustineō
audiō	impediō	mūniō	veniō
contineō	inquam	perveniō	

C. Give the meaning of:

etiam	itaque	neque	tamen
frūmentārius	nam	pūblicus	

—*Drill on Forms*—

A. Give the following forms.

1. *genitive singular:* merīdiēs, praemium, manus
2. *dative singular:* spēs, ūnus, cornū
3. *accusative singular:* aciēs, passus, virtūs
4. *ablative singular:* rēs, tergum, impetus
5. *nominative plural:* rēs, gaudium, domus
6. *genitive plural:* diēs, praemium, mīlia
7. *accusative plural:* officium, fluctus, cornū
8. *ablative plural:* rēs, exercitus, duo

B. Decline throughout: aciēs, exercitus

C. Give a synopsis of:

1. iaciō *in the active indicative first person singular, with meanings*
2. inveniō *in the passive indicative third person singular, with meanings*
3. possum *in the indicative third person plural, with meanings*
4. absum *in the indicative first person plural, with meanings*

D. Translate.

1. impediēbant
2. dormiam
3. mūnīverant
4. audiuntur
5. vēnerint
6. inquit
7. potuistī
8. convēnimus
9. āfuit
10. mūnīta sunt
11. aderimus
12. pervēnērunt
13. inventus erat
14. dormīre
15. veniētisne?

E. Translate.

1. we shall be present
2. he was listening to
3. they will be able
4. they were hindered
5. she was sleeping
6. he said
7. we have arrived
8. he is absent
9. will you build?
10. to come together
11. we shall build
12. they were found
13. you could
14. he will arrive
15. come! (*sing.*)

—Drill on Syntax—

Translate.

1. for five days
2. a thousand boys
3. three thousand men
4. to free from fear
5. quickly and bravely
6. nine of the soldiers
7. within two years
8. at night
9. by our cavalry
10. with much joy

—— *Exercises* ——

A. Translate.

1. Duo mīlia cīvium illīus oppidī verba prīncipis trēs hōrās audī-vērunt; tum illum dēlēgērunt rēgem.   2. Mīlitēs quī in aciē pug-nāre ob telōrum timōrem nōn possunt hostēs prohibēre mūrō cogentur.   3. Septimō diē peditēs tēlīs castra oppugnāvērunt et ducem hostium cēpērunt.   4. Legiōnēs paucīs diēbus aderunt cum auxiliīs sī Germānī victī erunt.   5. Puer quī Mārcus vocātur iter ab hōc oppidō tria mīlia passuum per silvam ad urbem magnam fēcit.   6. "Tēla vestra, virī," inquit, "dē nāve conicite; hostēs ad-sunt et vōs fortēs esse dēbētis."   7. Manus equitum in urbem merīdiē vēnit, sed nihil cibī eīs datum est.   8. Ubi legiōnēs nostrās vīdērunt, eī quī cīvēs servōs esse coēgerant cum celeritāte fūgē-runt.   9. Canis albus sub mēnsā in hortō diū dormiēbat.   10. Tertia aciēs in monte post castra ā lēgātō sōlis occāsū continēbātur.

B. Translate.

1. Many beautiful gifts were given to the queen by the citizens of the kingdom.   2. Caesar ordered the cavalry to make an attack on the wing of the enemy.   3. We decided to remain with our friends in Spain for a few days.   4. Where are the men who were ordered to work with me in the fields?   5. After the arrival of the messen-ger from the general, our forces waited in camp for the legions. 6. The first line of battle ran towards the enemy and attacked them fiercely.   7. The messenger who had carried my letter for two miles was killed by a weapon.   8. Within six days we shall march through the enemy's territory with great speed.   9. When he left Gaul, the leader said, "Men, we have conquered the enemy and freed our allies from fear of attacks."   10. Many of our horses desire grain and water, which we are not able to find tonight.

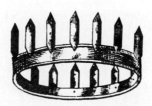

33

Comparison of Adjectives Quam Ablative of Comparison

Colosseum, Rome

Risu inepto res ineptior nulla est.
There is nothing more foolish than a foolish laugh.—CATULLUS

—Forms—

REGULAR COMPARISON OF ADJECTIVES

An adjective has three degrees, positive (e.g. *strong, certain*), comparative (e.g. *stronger, more certain*), and superlative (e.g. *strongest, most certain*).

The Comparative Degree. Latin adjectives regularly form the comparative by adding **-ior** (masculine and feminine) and **-ius** (neuter) to the base of the positive.

POSITIVE		COMPARATIVE	
potens	*strong*	potentior, potentius	*stronger*
certus	*certain*	certior, certius	*more certain*

The Superlative Degree. The superlative is regularly formed by adding **-issimus, -issima, -issimum** to the base of the positive.

potentissimus, -a, -um	*strongest*
certissimus, -a, -um	*most certain*

The Declension of the Comparative and Superlative. An adjective in the comparative degree is declined as a third declension consonant-stem.

	SINGULAR		PLURAL	
	MASC. & FEM.	NEUTER	MASC. & FEM.	NEUTER
NOMINATIVE:	cer'tior	cer'tius	certiō'rēs	certiō'ra
GENITIVE:	certiō'ris	certiō'ris	certiō'rum	certiō'rum
DATIVE:	certiō'rī	certiō'rī	certiō'ribus	certiō'ribus
ACCUSATIVE:	certiō'rem	cer'tius	certiō'rēs	certiō'ra
ABLATIVE:	certiō're	certiō're	certiō'ribus	certiō'ribus

The superlative is declined like **malus, -a, -um.**

—Syntax—

COMPARISON

Quam is used like *than* in English to join the two words which are being compared. The Latin usage differs from the English in that the word following **quam** must be in the same case as the word with which it is being compared.

Rōmānī dīligentiōrēs quam Germānī erant.
The Romans were more diligent than the Germans.
Haec via est longior quam illa.
This road is longer than that.
Nōn vīdī puerum potentiōrem quam eum.
I have not seen a boy more powerful than he.
Caesaris castra ampliōra erant quam Britannōrum.
Caesar's camp was larger than the Britons'.

ABLATIVE OF COMPARISON

When the noun or pronoun with which another is compared is in the nominative or accusative, **quam** may be omitted and the second noun or pronoun put into the ablative.

Rōmānī dīligentiōrēs Germānīs erant.
The Romans were more diligent than the Germans.
Haec via longior illā est.
This road is longer than that.
Nōn vīdī puerum potentiōrem eō.
I have not seen a boy more powerful than he.

Translation of the Comparative and Superlative

The comparative may be translated with *too* or *rather*.

Hic mōns est altior.
$\begin{cases} \text{\textit{This mountain is higher.}} \\ \text{\textit{This mountain is too high.}} \\ \text{\textit{This mountain is rather high.}} \end{cases}$

The superlative may be translated with *very*.

Hic mōns est altissimus.
$\begin{cases} \text{\textit{This mountain is the highest.}} \\ \text{\textit{This mountain is most high.}} \\ \text{\textit{This mountain is very high.}} \end{cases}$

—— Vocabulary ——

ae'quus, -a, -um, *level; fair, just;
   like, equal*
am'plus, -a, -um, *large, ample*
bar'barus, -a, -um, *foreign,
   strange, barbarous*
cer'tus, -a, -um, *sure, certain*
dī'ligēns, dīligen'tis, *careful,
   diligent*
fē'lix, fēlī'cis, *happy, lucky*
inī'quus, -a, -um, *uneven; unfair;
   unfavorable*

iūs'tus, -a, -um, *right, just*
lae'tus, -a, -um, *happy, joyful,
   glad*
nō'tus, -a, -um, *famous, well-
   known*
trīs'tis, -e, *sad, grim*
ū'tilis, -e, *useful, profitable*

quam, (conj. and adv.) *as, than,
   how?*

——Exercises ——

A. Translate.

1. Via longior est.   2. Iter longius est.   3. Puerī sunt
dīligentissimī.   4. Poeta est tristissimus.   5. Ō fēlīcissime di-
ērum!   6. Lēgēs sunt iūstissimae.   7. Erat fortior quam Mārcus.
8. Nōn erat fortior Lūciō.   9. Mōns est altissimus.   10. Potentior
est prīncipibus.

B. Translate.

1. The girl is very brave.   2. This is the shortest of all rivers.
3. He was stronger than the soldier.   4. I saw the very powerful
consul.   5. He gave it to the bolder general.   6. They were with
the very famous poet.   7. It is on the highest hill.   8. His house
is rather ample.   9. I see a very happy woman.   10. The laws are
too unfair.

C. Read the Latin and translate.

1. Haec via brevior est quod montēs paucī sunt.   2. Iter ā meā
vīllā ad urbem rēgīnae est longissimum.   3. Gladiī ūtiliōrēs quam
librī in proeliō sunt.   4. Dē monte altiōre nostrī amīcī castra hostium dīligenter spectābant.   5. Lēgēs nostrae aequiōrēs lēgibus
Germānōrum sunt.   6. Iūdicēs nōtissimī cum fīliīs et fīliābus ad
nostram urbem venient.   7. Hic lapis ā fortiōre quam tē iactus

est.   8. Paucīs diēbus cōpiae amplissimae ad finēs barbarōrum iter longissimum fēcērunt.   9. Fīliī meī certē dīligentiōrēs quam tuī sunt.   10. Fortissimī Germānōrum ad rēgem potentem missī sunt.

D. Translate.

1. They were throwing very heavy stones down from the windows.   2. These girls are more careful than those boys, but the boys are faster.   3. We were not able to find the place, because the journey was very long.   4. This large fierce animal ought to be killed by a sword heavier than mine.   5. This river is very wide, but it is not very deep.   6. I have seen swords heavier than those of the Roman soldiers.   7. On that day we decided to walk to this very well-known place.   8. The camp was pitched at the foot of a mountain which was very high.   9. Caesar was the most diligent of all the generals in the Roman army.   10. The foreign boys were stronger than those in this city.

—— Reading ——

ARION AND THE DOLPHIN

Arīon erat amplissimus poēta Graecus, cuius fāma erat nōtissima in omnibus terrīs. Ab patriā ad Ītaliam Siciliamque pervēnerat et carminibus multās urbēs laetās fēcit. Populī barbarī eī dōna dedērunt. Multīs rēgibus fēlīcior erat. Animālia fera eius carmine dēlectābantur; ad multam noctem stābant et id magnō cum gaudiō audiēbant. Hiems discesserat et Arīon patriam nāve petēbat. Sed mare erat tūtius quam nāvis, nam nautae gladiīs in poētam impetum fēcērunt. Hic ab illīs fugit et in aquam saluit. Arīon tamen, ubi saliēbat, carmen tristissimum et pulcherrimum canēbat. Delphīnus quī hoc carmen audīvit poētam servāvit et in tergō ad patriam portāvit.

34

Comparison of Adjectives in -er, -eus, -ius, -ilis
Dative with Adjectives

Inner view of Colosseum, Rome

Simia quam similis, turpissima bestia, nobis!
How like us is that very ugly beast the monkey!—CICERO

——*Forms*——

COMPARISON OF ADJECTIVES IN -ER

All adjectives which end in **-er** in the masculine nominative singular, regardless of their declension, form the superlative by adding **-rimus, -rima, -rimum** to the masculine nominative singular of the positive (not to the base). The comparative is regular.

POSITIVE	COMPARATIVE	SUPERLATIVE
pulcher, pulchra, pulchrum	pulchrior, -ius	pulcherrimus, -a, -um
celer, celeris, celere	celerior, -ius	celerrimus, -a, -um

COMPARISON OF ADJECTIVES IN -EUS OR -IUS

Adjectives of the first and second declensions which have **i** or **e** before the **-us** ending form the comparative and superlative by using the adverbs **magis,** *more,* and **maximē,** *most.*

POSITIVE	COMPARATIVE	SUPERLATIVE
idōneus, -a, -um	magis idōneus, -a, -um	maximē idōneus, -a, -um
suitable	*more suitable*	*most suitable*

Such adjectives are compared thus to avoid forms which would be awkward to pronounce (just as we say "more beautiful" instead of "beautifuler").

COMPARISON OF SOME ADJECTIVES IN -ILIS

Facilis, *easy,* **difficilis,** *difficult,* **similis,** *like,* and **dissimilis,** *unlike,* form the superlative by adding **-limus, -lima, -limum** to the base of the positive. The comparative is regular.

POSITIVE	COMPARATIVE	SUPERLATIVE
facilis, -e	facilior, -ius	facillimus, -a, -um
difficilis, -e	difficilior, -ius	difficillimus, -a, -um
similis, -e	similior, -ius	simillimus, -a, -um
dissimilis, -e	dissimilior, -ius	dissimillimus, -a, -um

These are the only common adjectives in **-ilis** to have this form of the superlatives. The others are regular.

ūtilis, -e   ūtilior, -ius   ūtilissimus, -a, -um

——Syntax——

DATIVE WITH ADJECTIVES

The dative is used to complete the meaning of some adjectives, e.g.

amīcus	difficilis	fīnitimus	nōtus	propinquus	similis
inimīcus	fidēlis	grātus	pār	proximus	dissimilis
facilis		idōneus	propior		ūtilis

Caesar amīcus Mārcō, inimīcus Lūciō est.
   Caesar is friendly to Marcus, but unfriendly to Lucius.
Fīnitimī Gallīs sunt Germānī.
   Neighboring to the Gauls are the Germans.
Prīnceps barbarōrum pār Caesarī nōn est.
   The chief of the barbarians is not equal to Caesar.

But, if the adjective is used as a noun, it requires the genitive:

Caesar amīcus Mārcī, inimīcus Lūcī est.
   Caesar is Marcus' friend but Lucius' enemy.

——Vocabulary——

au'reus, -a, -um, *golden*
cu'pidus, -a, -um, *eager, desirous*
dex'ter, dex'tra, dex'trum, *right*
diffi'cilis, -e, *difficult*
dissi'milis, -e, *unlike*
dū'rus, -a, -um, *hard, harsh*
fidē'lis, -e, *faithful, loyal*
idō'neus, -a, -um, *suitable*
nō'bilis, -e, *of high birth, noble,
   well-known*
pār, pa'ris, *equal*
pos'terus, -a, -um, *following, next*

propin'quus, -a, -um, *near,
   nearby*
propior, -ius, *nearer*
proximus, -a, -um, *nearest, next*
sinis'ter, sinis'tra, sinis'trum, *left*
va'lidus, -a, -um, *strong*
ma'gis (adv.), *more, more greatly*
magno'pere (adv.), *greatly*
max'imē (adv.), *most, most
   greatly, especially*
ni'si (conj.), *unless, if . . . not,
   except*

——Word Study——

Cupidus. The objective genitive, not the dative, is used with **cupidus.**

Cupidus pecūniae est. $\begin{cases} \textit{He is desirous of money.} \\ \textit{He is eager for money.} \end{cases}$

Posterus. As an adjective this word is seldom seen except in expressions of time: **posterō diē,** *the next day,* **posterō annō,** *in the following year.* As a noun in the masculine plural, **posterī, posterōrum, m.,** it means *posterity, descendants.*

Propinquus. Used as a noun **propinquus, -ī, m.,** means *relation* or *kinsman.*

——Exercises——

A. Compare the following, giving all nominative singular forms of all three degrees.

acer, celer, difficilis, dissimilis, facilis, idōneus, līber, miser, niger, nōbilis, pulcher, similis, ūtilis

B. Read the Latin and translate.

1. Cūr Mārcī amīcus mihi inimīcissimus est?   2. Nautae patriae nostrae hodiē dissimillimī sunt eīs quī in marī inter Britanniam et Galliam nāvigābant.   3. Noster exercitus cupidissimus pācis erat; posterō annō tamen fortiter pugnāvit.   4. Rōma est pulcherrima urbium mihi nōtārum.   5. Mīlitēs quī in proeliō superātī erant fidēlissimī imperātōrī erant.   6. Lēx tua est magis idōnea bellō quam pācī; mea aequē grāta cīvibus et mīlitibus est.   7. Num potes invenīre equum nōbiliōrem quam meum?   8. Ubi oppidum propinquum vīderam, posterō diē litterās ad meōs propinquōs scrīpsī.   9. Nōn pugnābit nisi eī gladium longiōrem dederis. 10. Hortus in quō ambulāmus est propinquus hortīs Caesaris.

C. Translate.

1. A small white dog is sleeping in a chair in the garden which is near our villa.   2. The next day, those bad sailors were throwing stones at (towards) the consul's house.   3. Oughtn't you to be more friendly to Julia's kinsmen?   4. When we attacked the en-

emy's left wing the battle was very fierce and many very brave men were killed. 5. This sword is harder than that; it is also longer and wider. 6. If your friends will not be faithful to the commonwealth, they will be the most wretched of all men. 7. Which of these girls is most like the queen? 8. The noble chief was very similar to the king of that country. 9. This work is not very difficult for me, but it is more difficult than yours. 10. Marcus was stronger than Lucius, but Lucius was braver.

—— Reading ——

A SOLDIER TELLS ABOUT HIS DEEDS

Marcus in exercitū Caesaris mīles validus fuerat. In proeliīs acerrimīs pugnaverat, et vulnus gravissimum accēperat; itaque posterō annō ab imperātore in Ītaliam missus erat. Nunc in parvō oppidō cum fīliō, Lūciō, fīliāque pulcherrimā habitābat. Marcus Lūciō sorōrīque eius fabulās dē bellō saepe nārrābat.

Lūcius, quī fābulās patris audīre cupīvit, "Fortissimusne," inquit, "mīles erās?"

Eī respondit Marcus, "Audī, Lūcī, haec. Caesar, ubi Helvētiōs ē Galliā expulit, in fīnēs Germānōrum iter longissimum faciēbat. Lēgātum idoneum mittere cōnstituit cum epistulā ad legiōnem nōnam, quae in castrīs relicta erat. Mē epistulam portāre iussit. Posterā nocte per silvās contendēbam. Tum in mē vigintī hominēs impetum acerrimum gladiīs fēcerunt . . ."

"Quid fēcistī, pater?" clāmāvit Lūcius.

"Contrā eōs diū magnā cum virtūte pugnāvī. Septem hostēs interfēcī; quīnque vulnerāvī; reliquī ab eō locō fūgērunt. Post multās horās ad castra vēnī et ducī legiōnis epistulam dedī. Hanc ob rem ā Caesare laudātus sum. Nōnne fortissimus eram?"

Lūcius patrem spectāvit sed nihil dīxit.

35

Irregular Comparison of Adjectives

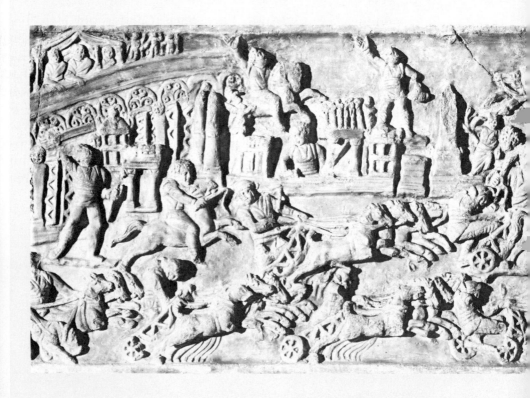

Relief showing a chariot race

Bonitas non est pessimis esse meliorem.

It is not goodness to be better than the worst. — SENECA

——*Forms*——

IRREGULAR COMPARISON OF ADJECTIVES

A few very common adjectives have irregular comparatives and superlatives (like *good, better, best; bad, worse, worst* in English). These must be learned carefully.

bo'nus, -a, -um, *good*	me'lior, me'lius, *better*	op'timus, -a, -um, *best*
ma'lus, -a, -um, *bad*	pe'ior, pe'ius, *worse*	pes'simus, -a, -um, *worst*
mag'nus, -a, -um, *great*	ma'ior, ma'ius, *greater*	max'imus, -a, -um, *greatest*
par'vus, -a, -um, *small*	mi'nor, mi'nus, *smaller*	mi'nimus, -a, -um, *smallest*
mul'tī, -ae, -a, *many*	plū'rēs, plū'ra, *more*	plū'rimī, -ae, -a, *most*

Some other adjectives are defective in their comparison, lacking either a positive, a comparative, or a superlative.

Lacking a positive

——	exte'rior, exte'rius, *outer*	extrē'mus, -a, -um, *outermost, farthest, last, end of*
——	īnfe'rior, īnfe'rius, *lower*	īn'fimus, -a, -um *or* ī'mus, -a, -um, *lowest, bottom of*
——	inte'rior, inte'rius, *inner*	in'timus, -a, -um, *inmost*
——	pri'or, pri'us, *former, earlier*	prī'mus, -a, -um, *first, foremost*
——	pro'pior, pro'pius, *nearer*	prox'imus, -a, -um, *nearest, next*
——	supe'rior, supe'rius, *higher*	sum'mus, -a, -um, *highest, top of*
——	ulte'rior, ulte'rius, *farther*	ul'timus, -a, -um, *farthest*

Lacking a comparative
mul'tus, -a, -um, *much*   ——   plu'rimus, -a, -um, *most*

Lacking a superlative
se'nex, se'nis, *old*   senior, *older*   ——

—— Vocabulary ——

plūs, plū'ris, n., *more, a larger*
   amount
me'dius, -a, -um, *middle of*
se'nex, se'nis, *old (masculine only)*

nā'tū, *by birth*
pro'pe, (adv.) *nearly, almost;*
   (prep. w. acc.) *near*

——Word Study ——

Defective comparisons

Multus. To replace the missing comparative of **multus** we use the noun **plūs, plūris, n.,** with a genitive of the whole (partitive genitive).

> Da mihi plūs cibī.   *Give me more food (more of food).*

Senex. To provide a superlative for **senex,** use **maximus nātū,** *oldest (greatest by birth).* **Maior nātū** is sometimes used for the comparative instead of **senior. Senex** has no neuter or feminine. It is not an **i**-stem. **Medius,** like **reliquus,** contains within itself the partitive idea **of;** it is not used with the genitive.

> in mediō campō   *in the middle of the plain*

The same is usually true of **summus,** and frequently of **extrēmus, īmus,** and **īnfimus.**

> in summō monte   *on top of the mountain*
> in extrēmā viā   *at the end of the road*

—— Exercises ——

A. Translate.

   1. more girls 2. more wine 3. the oldest soldier 4. to the top of the house 5. in the middle of the camp 6. from the bottom of the river 7. near the town 8. nearer to the town 9. next to the town 10. at the end of the island

B. Read the Latin and translate.

   1. Mīlitēs ā dextrō cornū fortiōrēs in proeliō quam hostēs erant.
   2. Erat fidēlis amīcīs quī in ponte nocte captī sunt. 3. Hī librī

meliōrēs sunt illīs; ab optimō poētā scrīptī sunt. 4. Posterō diē equitēs flūminī propiōrēs erant quam peditēs, quī sub monte erant. 5. Num Lūcius maior nātū tuōrum fīliōrum est? 6. Castra maxima ab eōrum exercitū trāns illud flūmén posita sunt. 7. Nāvēs Rōmānōrum dissimillimae nāvibus hostium erant. 8. Senex quī in hōc oppidō habitat quīnque mīlia passuum ad mediam silvam hodiē ambulāvit. 9. Fēlix nōn est is quī fēlīcior miserrimīs est. 10. Suntne plūrēs cīvēs in hāc urbe quam in illā?

C. Translate.

1. The right wing of our army was coming towards the large plain. 2. At midnight shouts were heard in the middle of the town. 3. The cavalry on our left wing are nearer to the camp than to the river. 4. This man is better than the worst people; but shall we call him good? 5. The teacher is very eager for more books. 6. Very many citizens were not able to flee when the town was taken. 7. From the top of the mountain we can look at the sea across the plains. 8. In that town we shall find more horses and more grain. 9. Which is the oldest of your three sons? 10. Near the bridge which is next to the town the river is very deep.

—— Reading ——

ANDROCLES AND THE LION

Androclus erat servus quī cum dominō inīquō ad urbem in Āfricā pervēnit. Ob plūrimās iniūriās dominī ad fugam in ultimōs montēs coāctus est. In summō monte in maximā spēluncā habitābat.

Ōlim Androclus ubi cibum petēbat leōnem vidit. Maximus erat eius timor et in interiōrem partem spēluncae fūgit. Sed leō nōn ferus erat, et vēnit in spēluncam maximā cum difficultāte, nam in pede erat spīna, quae eī magnum dolōrem faciēbat. Tum Androclī misericordia erat maior timōre; leō signīs auxilium petēbat. Androclus spīnam vulnere expressit. Leō grātissimus erat atque hī duo, vir animalque, in spēluncā trēs annōs habitāvērunt et erant optimī amīcī.

36

Comparison of Adverbs
Ablative of Degree of Difference
Temporal and Causal Clauses

A Renaissance drawing of a Roman Circus showing five different circus games

Canis timidus vehementius latrat quam mordet.

A timid dog barks more violently than it bites.—CURTIUS RUFUS

—— *Forms* ——

COMPARISON OF ADVERBS

The Comparative. For the comparative of an adverb we use the neuter accusative singular of the comparative of the adjective from which it is derived.

bene,	*well*	melius,	*better*
celeriter,	*swiftly*	celerius,	*more swiftly*
līberē,	*freely*	līberius,	*more freely*
male,	*badly*	peius,	*worse*
similiter,	*similarly*	similius,	*more similarly*
validē,	*strongly*	validius,	*more strongly*

The Superlative. The superlative of an adverb is formed by changing the **us** of the superlative adjective to **ē**.

optimus	optimē	*best*
celerrimus	celerrimē	*most swiftly*
līberrimus	līberrimē	*most freely*
pessimus	pessimē	*worst*
simillimus	simillimē	*most similarly*
validissimus	validissimē	*most strongly*

Adverbs which have no corresponding adjectives

diū,	*for a long time*	saepe,	*often*
diūtius,	*for a longer time, any longer*	saepius,	*more often*
diūtissimē,	*for the longest time*	saepissimē,	*most often*

—— *Syntax* ——

Accusative as Adverb. Since all accusatives are used in one way or another to limit the action of a verb, all accusatives might be called adverbial. This is why the accusative singular of the comparative adjective is used as a comparative adverb. Similarly, to form the adverbs of some adjectives in the positive degree we merely put them into the neuter accusative singular (instead of giving them an adverbial ending, **-ē** or **-ter**).

facile, *easily;* multum, *much;* prīmum, *for the first time*

ABLATIVE OF DEGREE OF DIFFERENCE

The ablative is often used adverbially with comparatives, also with **ante** and **post,** to express the degree of difference.

Multō fortius pugnat.
  He fights much more bravely. (literally, *more bravely by much.*)
Paulō ante vēnit.   *He came a little while ago.* (literally, *before by a little*).
Multīs post annīs Germānī Rōmam oppugnāvērunt.
  Many years later the Germans attacked Rome. (Literally, *afterward by many years*).

QUAM WITH THE SUPERLATIVE

Quam is used with the superlative to express *as . . . as possible.*

Venīte quam prīmum.   *Come as soon as possible.*

Some form of **possum** is to be understood, and is sometimes expressed, with this construction.

Venīte quam prīmum potestis.   *Come as soon as you can.*

TEMPORAL AND CAUSAL CLAUSES

You have already been using subordinate clauses introduced by **ubi,** *when,* and **quod,** *because.* Clauses introduced by **ubi,** *when,* are called temporal clauses. Temporal clauses may also be introduced by **ut,** *as, when,* **postquam,** *after* (**post,** *later,* **quam,** *than*), and **simul atque,** *as soon as, at the same time as.* Clauses introduced by **quod,** *because,* are called causal clauses; they may also be introduced by **ut,** *as, since.*

—— *Vocabulary* ——

pau'lum, -ī, n., *a little*

coti'diē, (adv.) *daily, every day*
de'inde, (adv.) *then, next*

e'ō, (adv.) *there, to that place*
hūc, (adv.) *here, to this place*
il'lūc, (adv.) *there, to that place there*

nōn'dum, (adv.) *not yet*
num'quam, (adv.) *never*
pae'ne, (adv.) *almost*
quō, (interr. adv.) *where to?, to what place?*
si'mul, (adv.) *at the same time*
sta'tim, (adv.) *at once, immediately*
tan'dem, (adv.) *at length, at last, finally*

at'que, (conj.) *as (after* aequē, pariter, *and* simul)
post'quam, (conj.) *after*
ut, (conj.) *how, as, when, since*

—— Exercises ——

A. Translate.

1. much more fiercely   2. as fiercely as possible   3. a little more often   4. as soon as possible   5. Where is he?   6. Where is he walking (to)?   7. after many years   8. many years later   9. on the right wing   10. two paces longer

〰〰〰〰〰〰〰〰〰〰〰〰〰〰〰〰〰〰〰〰〰〰〰〰〰

Prīmō is used as an ablative of time when, *at first*. It is also used to modify other words in the ablative of time when in the following idioms:

> prīmā aestāte,   *at the beginning of summer*
> prīmā lūce,   *at daybreak*   prīmā nocte,   *early in the night*

〰〰〰〰〰〰〰〰〰〰〰〰〰〰〰〰〰〰〰〰〰〰〰〰〰

B. Read the Latin and translate.

1. Ut in hortō ambulābam vīdī avēs quibus pulchriōrēs numquam vīderam.   2. Paucīs diēbus ante, reī pūblicae pecūniam dare tandem coāctus erat.   3. Prīmō ad urbem quam celerrimē cucurrī; deinde victōriam prīncipī nūntiāvī.   4. Prīmā nocte cīvēs in oppidum omnia animālia dūcere cōnstituērunt.   5. Simul atque in silvam vēnit, magnopere territa est clāmōribus.   6. Postquam ad summum montem pervēnērunt, facillimē poterant vidēre ignēs.
7. Mīlitēs Caesaris multō fortius quam Germānī in Galliā conten-

dēbant.　8. Lēgātī officia quam dīligentissimē facere dēbent.
9. Prīmā aestāte nostrī cum hostibus in Galliā diū atque acriter
pugnābant.　10. Fēmina aquam minus facile quam servus portāre
poterat.

C. Translate.

1. You will never be able to see my friends if you do not run as
quickly as possible.　2. She had not yet seen a more friendly
woman than Julia's mother.　3. After you finished your work,
what did you do next?　4. The animals on the top of the mountain
immediately ran toward the river as soon as they saw the fires.
5. As there was danger of war, Caesar led the troops very quickly
from Italy into Gaul.　6. They broke camp at daybreak and
marched many miles through the territory of the Romans.　7. On
the next night we remained in the city and watched the games.
8. The　Germans were much larger than the Gauls, but the latter
fought more bravely.　9. A few days later, the right wing of our
army easily forced the enemy to leave the camp.　10. Our commander ought to wage war as fiercely as possible.

—— *Reading* ——

HANNIBAL CROSSES THE RHONE

Hannibal, nōtissimus Carthāginiēnsium imperātor, postquam urbem
in Hispāniā, Saguntum, cuius populus erat socius Rōmānōrum, cēpit,
bellum cum Rōmānīs in Ītaliā gerere cōnstituit.

　Multīs cum equitibus et peditibus et elephantīs itineribus maximīs
per Pȳrēnaeōs montēs ad flūmen Rhodanum tandem pervēnit. Ibi
cōnsul Rōmānus ad ostium flūminis castra posuerat et hostēs cotīdiē
exspectābat.

　Hannibal nāvēs quam celerrimē coēgit et exercitum trāns flūmen
dūcere parābat. Sed prīmō Hannōnem cōpiārum partem quam prīmum flūmen trādūcere et ā tergō impetum in Rōmānōs facere iussit.

　Simul Hannibal nāvibus reliquās cōpiās trādūxit et partem equitum
ad castra Rōmāna mīsit. Simul atque Rōmānī hostēs vīdērunt, proelium equestre statim commīsērunt. Illī hostēs nōn facile vīcērunt, sed
tandem Carthāginiēnsēs in fugam dedērunt.

Diligentia maximum etiam mediocris ingeni subsidium.
Diligence is a very great help even to a mediocre intelligence.

— SENECA

REVIEW 9 (LESSONS 33–36)

— Vocabulary Drill —

A. Give the other nominative forms, and the meanings, of the following adjectives.

aequus	dīligēns	inīquus	posterus
amplus	difficilis	iūstus	propinquus
aureus	dissimilis	laetus	senex
barbarus	dūrus	medius	sinister
certus	fēlix	nōbilis	summus
cupidus	fidēlis	nōtus	tristis
dexter	idōneus	par	ūtilis
			validus

B. Give the meaning of:

atque	magnopere	numquam	quam
cotīdiē	multum	paene	quō
deinde	nātū	postquam	simul
eō	nisi	prīmum	statim
hūc	nōndum	prope	tandem
illūc			ut

— Drill on Forms —

A. Compare the following adjectives, giving all nominative singular forms of all three degrees.

dīligēns	ūtilis	parvus	miser
malus	nōbilis	magnus	bonus
pulcher	celer	facilis	similis
ācer	iūstus	longus	dūrus

B. Compare the following adverbs.

bene	lātē	celeriter	facile
ācriter	magnopere	male	fidēliter
saepe	miserē	longē	diū

C. Give the following forms.

1. *the genitive masculine singular of the comparatives of* dūrus, bonus, *and* idōneus
2. *the dative feminine singular of* aureus, dexter, *and of the superlative of* nōbilis
3. *the accusative masculine singular of* pār, fēlix, *and of the comparative of* malus
4. *the ablative feminine singular of* fidēlis, ūtilis, *and of the comparative of* dīligēns
5. *the nominaive neuter plural of* dīligēns, pār, *and of the comparative of* parvus
6. *the genitive neuter plural of* iūstus *and of the comparatives of* facilis *and* multī
7. *the dative feminine plural of* barbarus, difficilis, *and of the superlative of* ācer
8. *the accusative masculine plural of* senex, sinister, *and of the comparative of* dissimilis

—Drill on Syntax—

A. Translate.

1. prīmā nocte
2. post paucōs diēs
3. fēlicissimus hominum
4. multīs post annīs
5. amīcior mihi
6. pariter atque
7. in īmō marī
8. quam facillimum
9. finitimī Rōmānōrum
10. tribus pedibus altior

B. Translate.

1. as soon as
2. more money
3. on the right wing
4. too unfairly
5. more horses
6. at daybreak
7. rather badly
8. most like the king
9. eager for food
10. every day

—Exercises—

A. Translate.

1. Simul atque ad summum montem pervēnī, "Quam pulchra," inquam, "est haec terra in quā habitāmus!" 2. Ut perīculum bellī multō maius est, dēbēmus in oppidum et plūs frūmentī et plūra arma portāre. 3. Prīmā lūce ad extrēmam silvam quam celerrimē cucurrērunt, atque postquam eō pervēnērunt pulcherrimam urbem vīdērunt. 4. Quod Mārcus in lūdīs cotīdiē gladiō pugnat dextra manus paulō maior est sinistrā. 5. Ille rēx, quī imperī cupidissimus est, pār est ducibus cīvitātum Graecārum; sed Caesaris pār nōndum est. 6. Prīmō mīlitēs ab hostium dextrō cornū cum nostrīs diū atque ācriter pugnāvērunt; deinde paulum cessērunt; tandem fūgērunt. 7. Mārcus prope duōbus pedibus altior quam soror est; sed illa multō pulchrior est. 8. Ut ambulābat in hortō quī proximus est flūminī tum prīmum vīdit eam puellam quam amat. 9. Tū quī maximus deōrum es, mē audī et fac mē fēlīciōrem. 10. Iubē, Lūcī, puerōs quam prīmum venīre, nam magister in lūdō diūtius manēre nōn potest.

B. Translate.

1. That book is too big; don't you have a book more suitable for this boy, who is rather small? 2. As soon as the cavalry on the right wing saw the enemy they attacked their left wing as fiercely as possible. 3. My sister is very like your daughter, who is not unlike Julia; which is the most beautiful of these girls? 4. As the consul will not stay much longer, you ought to arrive in the city as soon as possible. 5. In early summer they came to the middle of a very large forest, and there they saw animals whose horns were much bigger than those which are known to us. 6. Caesar's friend is much more friendly to me than to you; nevertheless he likes you a little. 7. After they fought long and fiercely in the plain next to the forest, they could not fight any longer. 8. Marcus is the tallest of my father's brothers. 9. With his left hand he was holding a heavy stone; with his right he aimed at the chief of the barbarians with a much heavier stone. 10. I first saw that very large bird as I was walking to the top of the mountain near our city.

37

Demonstratives Ipse, Idem
Irregular Adjectives
Ablative of
Specification

Model of the Forum of Septimius Severus at Leptis Magna

Aliena nobis, nostra plus aliis placent.
*Other people's things are more pleasing to us, and
ours to other people.*—PUBLILIUS SYRUS

—Forms—

IPSE AND ĪDEM

The intensive demonstrative adjective **ipse, ipsa, ipsum,** *myself, your-self, himself, herself, itself (ourselves, yourselves, themselves),* is declined like **ille** except in the neuter nominative and accusative singular.

	SINGULAR			PLURAL		
NOM.	ip'se	ip'sa	ip'sum	ip'sī	ip'sae	ip'sa
GEN.	ipsī'us	ipsī'us	ipsī'us	ipsō'rum	ipsā'rum	ipsō'rum
DAT.	ip'sī	ip'sī	ip'sī	ip'sīs	ip'sīs	ip'sīs
ACC.	ip'sum	ip'sam	ip'sum	ip'sōs	ip'sās	ip'sa
ABL.	ip'sō	ip'sā	ip'sō	ip'sīs	ip'sīs	ip'sīs

The demonstrative adjective **īdem,** *the same,* is a compound of **is** with the suffix **-dem,** with some changes in spelling to make pronunciation easier.

SINGULAR

NOMINATIVE:	ī'dem	ea'dem	i'dem
GENITIVE:	eius'dem	eius'dem	eius'dem
DATIVE:	eī'dem	eī'dem	eī'dem
ACCUSATIVE:	eun'dem	ean'dem	i'dem
ABLATIVE:	eō'dem	eā'dem	eō'dem

PLURAL

NOMINATIVE:	eī'dem	eae'dem	ea'dem
GENITIVE:	eōrun'dem	eārun'dem	eōrun'dem
DATIVE:	eīs'dem	eīs'dem	eīs'dem
ACCUSATIVE:	eōs'dem	eās'dem	ea'dem
ABLATIVE:	eīs'dem	eīs'dem	eīs'dem

IRREGULAR ADJECTIVES

The following first and second declension adjectives are declined like
ūnus, with **-īus** in the genitive and **-ī** in the dative singular. The
plurals are regular, like that of **malus.**

> al'ter, al'tera, al'terum, *the other (of two), second*
> neu'ter, neu'tra, neu'trum, *neither*
> nūl'lus, -a, -um, *no, not any*
> sō'lus, -a, -um, *only, alone*
> tō'tus, -a, -um, *whole, entire*
> ūl'lus, -a, -um, *any*
> u'ter, u'tra, u'trum, *which (of two)?*

A'lius, a'lia, a'liud, *other, another,* is also declined like the above
adjectives, except that (like **ille**) it has **-ud** in the neuter nominative
and accusative singular.

Uter'que, utra'que, utrum'que, *each (of two),* is declined throughout
like **uter** with the suffix **-que** added.

—— Syntax ——

THE ABLATIVE OF SPECIFICATION

The ablative without a preposition is used to show in what respect
the quality of a noun, adjective, or verb applies.

> Rēx nōmine erat. *He was king in name (with respect to name).*
> Mārcus tibi pār virtūte est. *Marcus is equal to you in courage.*

—— Vocabulary ——

her'ba, -ae, f., *grass*
subsi'dium, subsi'dī, n., *aid,
   support*
to'ga, -ae, f., *toga*
vic'tor, victō'ris, m., *victor*

aliēnus, -a, -um, *belonging to
   another, another's*
quis'que, quid'que, *each one*
un'de, (rel. adv.) *whence, from
   where, from which,* (interr.
   adv.) *whence?, where from?*
un'dique, *from everywhere, from
   all sides, on all sides*

—Word Study—

Alius, alter. Alius and **alter,** when repeated, have special meanings.

> alius . . . alius . . . *one . . . another*
> alter . . . alter . . . *the one . . . the other*

Imperātor aliam partem agit, aliam lēgātus.
A commander plays one part, a lieutenant another.
Duōs frātrēs habeō; alter Mārcus, alter Lūcius vocātur.
I have two brothers; the one is called Marcus, the other Lucius.

If it appears in two different cases, **alius** may also be translated *some . . . one; some . . . another.*

> Aliī in aliam partem ambulābunt.
> *Some will walk in one direction, some in another.*

Alter is used similarly.

> Alter in alteram partem ambulabit.
> *The one will walk in one direction, the other in the other.*

Alter, *second,* may be used as an ordinal numeral, instead of **secundus.**
Toga. The toga was the white wool trapezoidal outer garment of a Roman citizen, and had to be worn at all political or religious functions. It was forbidden to respectable women and to foreigners.

—Exercises—

A. Translate.

1. utrīus puellae?　2. alterī mīlitī　3. cīvium ipsōrum　4. utrīque puerō　5. in ipsā villā　6. ab eādem urbe　7. aliud oppidum　8. alterum oppidum　9. equus alterīus　10. equus aliēnus

B. Translate.

1. of the farmer himself　2. on the same day　3. which wing (of the army)?　4. another's authority　5. each hand　6. the other house　7. another house　8. towards the city itself　9. other citizens　10. of the entire town

C. Read the Latin and translate.

1. Uterque puer equōs in agrō spectābat, sed neuter eōs capere poterat.   2. Sōlī mīlitī quī in hāc pugnā nōn interfectus est rēx praemium dedit vīllam agrōsque lātissimōs.   3. Agricola duōs fīliōs habēbat, quōrum alter Mārcus appellātus est, alter Lūcius. 4. Uterque exercitus castra eōdem tempore relīquit; alter in Helvētiam, alter ad Ītaliam contendit.   5. Caesar ipse cōpiās in proelium contrā hostēs semper dūcēbat.   6. Utrum animal corpore maius est?   7. Sōlī cīvēs Rōmānī togās gerere poterant.   8. Eādem nocte quisque clāmōrēs per tōtīus urbis viās audīvit.   9. Unde vēnērunt eae nāvēs quās ipse in mediō flūmine vīdī?   10. Sī alter cōnsul exercitum redūxerit victōrem, quid praemī cuique mīlitī dare dēbēmus?

D. Translate.

1. After the shouts of the soldiers were heard from all sides, some citizens ran to the gates of the town, and others remained in the middle of the streets.   2. We shall surrender our arms to Caesar alone; we shall yield to no other commander.   3. The one dog was in the garden; we found the other in the grass behind the farmhouse.   4. The same poet has written a book about the nature of things; which one of you (two) has seen it?   5. Caesar himself saw the enemy, and at the same time the auxiliary troops ran from the camp.   6. He finally was able to find each one of the boys who had thrown the stones.   7. The king ruled the people of the whole nation fairly for many years.   8. Tell me this: which boy is stronger in courage?   9. The commander of the garrison was sitting on a horse in the middle of the field.   10. Neither daughter wanted to walk with the mother to the town.

—— Reading ——

HANNIBAL ENCAMPS AT THE TICINUS

Post proelium equestre cum Rōmānīs ad Rhodanum Hannibal cōpiās Carthāginiēnsēs trāns Alpēs maximā cum difficultāte dūxit. In hīs montibus altissimīs aliae gentēs Gallōrum Hannibalī amīcae, aliae inimīcae erant. Ubi ad summās Alpēs exercitus pervēnit, in castrīs biduum remānsit et imperātor ipse mīlitibus campōs Ītaliae quī sub montibus vidērī poterant dēmōnstrāvit. Posteā omnēs ad flūmen Ticīnum brevī tempore pervēnērunt.

Hōc locō Hannibal cōpiās convocāvit. "Mīlitēs," inquit, "sī eundem animum habueritis quem quisque vestrum habēbat in priōribus rēbus, vincētis. Ab ultimīs fīnibus terrārum vīgintī annīs hūc pervēnistis. Hōc annō per montēs flūminaque tōtīus Hispāniae magna itinera fēcistis. Mox fortūna vōbīs labōrum fīnem dabit. Atque vestra erunt praemia quibus ampliōra dī hominibus numquam dedērunt."

Panorama of Ancient Rome showing Colosseum and Circus Maximus

38

Subjective and Objective Infinitives

Basilica in the Forum of Septimius Severus at Leptis Magnis

Aliquando et insanire iucundum est.
It is sometimes pleasant even to act like a madman.—SENECA

—Forms—

INFINITIVES

The infinitive has three tenses; present, perfect and future, and it has both voices, active and passive. There is no future passive infinitive.

Present Infinitive. The forms of the present infinitive, active and passive, have been given in Lesson 32.

Perfect Active Infinitive. The perfect active infinitive is formed by adding **-isse** to the perfect stem.

vocāvis'se,	*to have called*
monuis'se,	*to have warned*
rēxis'se,	*to have ruled*
cēpis'se,	*to have taken*
audīvis'se,	*to have heard*

Perfect Passive Infinitive. The perfect passive infinitive is like the perfect passive indicative, but with **esse** replacing **sum, es, est,** etc.

vocātus, -a, -um esse,	*to have been called*
monitus, -a, -um esse,	*to have been warned*
rēctus, -a, -um esse,	*to have been ruled*
captus, -a, -um esse,	*to have been taken*
audītus, -a, -um esse,	*to have been heard*

Future Active Infinitive. The future active infinitive is formed by adding **-ūrus, -ūra, -ūrum** to the stem of the fourth principal part. **Esse** is sometimes added.

vocātū'rus, -a, -um esse,	*to be about to call*
monitū'rus, -a, -um esse,	*to be about to warn*
rēctū'rus, -a, -um esse,	*to be about to rule*
captū'rus, -a, -um esse,	*to be about to take*
audītū'rus, -a, -um esse,	*to be about to hear*

SUMMARY OF INFINITIVES

	ACTIVE	PASSIVE
PRESENT	vocāre monēre regere capere audīre	vocārī monērī regī capī audīrī
PERFECT	vocāvisse monuisse rēxisse cēpisse audīvisse	vocātus esse monitus esse rēctus esse captus esse audītus esse
FUTURE	vocātūrus esse monitūrus esse rēctūrus esse captūrus esse audītūrus esse	

— Syntax —

SUBJECTIVE AND OBJECTIVE INFINITIVES

The infinitive may be used as a noun, and so can be the subject or direct object of a verb. As a noun the infinitive is neuter singular nominative or accusative.

Laudārī est grātum.   *It is pleasant to be praised.*
                        Being praised is pleasant.
Tē nāvigāre docēbō.   *I shall teach you to sail.*
                        I shall teach you sailing.
Timuit manēre in silvā.   *He feared to remain in the forest.*
                            He was afraid to remain in the forest.
Lūdōs spectāre puerōs dēlectāvit.   *It pleased the boys to watch*
                                      the games.
                                      Watching the games pleased
                                      the boys.
Amō ambulāre.   *I like to walk. I like walking.*
Cupīvit discēdere.   *He desired to depart.*
Labōrāre incēpit.   *He began to work. He began working.*

Parant venīre. *They are preparing to come.*
Temptābam vidēre urbem. *I was trying to see the city.*

For the other two uses of the infinitive see Lesson 32.

——Vocabulary——

clau'dō, clau'dere, clau'sī, clau'sum, *shut, close*
crēs'cō, crēs'cere, crē'vī, crē'tum, *grow, increase*
dēsis'tō, dēsis'tere, dēs'titī, dēs'titum, *leave off, stop*
du'bitō, -ā're, -ā'vī, -ā'tum, *doubt; hesitate*
fran'gō, fran'gere, frē'gī, frāc'tum, *break*
īn'struō, īnstru'ere, īnstrūx'ī, īnstrūc'tum, *pile up, draw up; equip*
iun'gō, iun'gere, iūnx'ī, iūnc'tum, *join*
la'vō, lavā're, lā'vī, lau'tum, *wash*
lū'dō, lū'dere, lū'sī, lū'sum, *play; mock*
pre'mō, pre'mere, pres'sī, pres'sum, *press; crush, overpower*
pro'bō, -ā're, -ā'vī, -ā'tum, *prove; approve of*
reci'piō, reci'pere, recē'pī, recep'tum, *accept, receive; take back*
remit'tō, remit'tere, remī'sī, remis'sum, *send back, let go back*
remo'veō, removē're, remō'vī, remō'tum, *move back*
tra'hō, tra'here, trāx'ī, trāc'tum, *draw, drag*
va'leō, valē're, va'luī, va'litum, *be well, be strong*

——Word Study——

Claudō. In compounds **claudō** becomes, **-clūdō, -clūdere, -clūsī, -clūsum: inclūdō,** *shut in,* etc.

Dubitō, when it means *hesitate,* takes a complementary infinitive.

Dubitavērunt ex urbe excēdere. *They hesitated to leave the city.*

Premō. In compounds **premō** becomes **-primo, -primere, -pressī, -pressum: exprimō,** *press out,* etc.

Valeō. The present active imperatives of **valeō** are used as parting salutations: **valē, valēte,** *goodbye, farewell.*

"Valē," inquit, "amīce." *He said, "Farewell, friend."*

Valēre iubeō is *I bid farewell.*

Socium valēre iussit. *He bade his companion farewell.*

—— Exercises ——

A. Translate, naming the use of each infinitive.

1. Nōn poterant trahere carrum.   2. Dēbēs claudere iānuam.
3. Cupisne   lūdere?   4. Cōnstituērunt   dōnum   recipere.
5. Poterant removērī.   6. Puerōs currere iubēbit.   7. Mīlitēs ambulāre coāctī sunt.   8. Poterāsne epistulam remittere?   9. Lavārī parāverant.   10. Mīlitēs iter facere iubentur.

B. Translate, naming the use of each infinitive.

1. You ought to listen to me.   2. They will start to flee.   3. He has decided not to finish the wall.   4. Caesar ordered the men to be led into camp.   5. Are you afraid to see him?   6. They forced the line of battle to depart.   7. Do you hesitate to come?   8. It ought to be placed here.   9. We shall begin to build a camp. 10. He was preparing to sail.

C. Read the Latin and translate.

1. Lēgātus postquam aciem instrūxit legiōnem impetum facere in hostēs iussit.   2. Bonum nōn est omnia timēre.   3. Uter lēgātus mīlitēs ā sinistrō cornū ē pugnā excēdere coēgit? 4. Omnēs fēminae et puellae puerīque longē ā proeliō remōtī erant.   5. "Valē," inquit, "ad aliam īnsulam crās sōlus discēdam."   6. Nōs numerō mīlitum superant; dēbēmus tamen pugnāre quam fortissimē.
7. Pater statim utrumque fīlium gladium frangere coēgit.   8. Eīdem equī frūmentum multa mīlia passuum per tōtam silvam trahere potuērunt.   9. Imperātor ipse equitēs ad castra remittī iussit.
10. Fēminae optimae dīligentiam fīliārum laudāre dēbent.

D. Translate.

1. "I have come myself as quickly as possible," he said, "because I want to see my friends."   2. The poet, who was writing another book, could not be found.   3. "It is bad to be sent from the city," said the consul.   4. The barbarian king compelled the people to give money to the state alone.   5. When he left the farmhouse he bade (his) brothers and sisters farewell.   6. If you cannot come to me, I shall come to you.   7. The bravest of our soldiers cannot be defeated by any enemy.   8. Each one ought to defend (his) country from all enemies with great courage.   9. We were not able to

drag the body of the horse from the road.　10. Which consul (of the two) ordered that those books be thrown into the fire?

—— Reading ——

THE BATTLE OF TRASIMENE

Flamīnius cōnsul mīlitēs per agrum quī est inter urbem Cortōnam et lacum Trasumēnum dūcēbat. Hōc locō Hannibal exercitum Rōmānum exspectābat et in collibus capere temptābat. Hoc cōnficere potuit atque exercitus Rōmānus maximō proeliō oppressus est, et cōnsul interfectus est.

Post proelium decem mīlia mīlitum fugā Rōmam petīvērunt, sed itinera ab hostibus clausa erant. Aliī novam aciem īnstruere cupiēbant, aliī bellō quam prīmum dēsistere. Tandem nūntiōs remittere cōnstituērunt. Hī pervenīre ad urbem nōn facile potuērunt.

Interim ibi ad prīmum hostium victōriae nūntium timor cīvium magnopere crēscēbat. Undique clāmōrēs mātrum eōrum quī in proeliō interfectī sunt audīrī poterant. Tum patrēs M. Pompōnium, ūnum ex senātōribus, populō calamitātem nūntiāre iussērunt. "Pugnā," inquit, "magnā victī sumus." Hīs vērō Rōmānī dīcuntur verba tristiōra numquam audīvisse.

Interior of the Basilica Julia in the Roman Forum as it appeared about 300 A.D.

39

Indirect Statement
Tenses of Infinitives
Ablative of Cause

The remains of the Basilica at Pompeii

Credula vitam spes fovet et melius cras fore semper dicit.
Credulous hope supports our life, and always says that
tomorrow will be better.—TIBULLUS

—*Syntax*—

INDIRECT STATEMENTS

Indirect statements in Latin, used as objects of verbs of saying, thinking, knowing, perceiving, or the like (expressed or implied), have an *infinitive* with the subject in the *accusative* case; i.e. they are infinitive phrases, (Lesson 32).

> Dīcit Caesarem esse fortem.   *He says that Caesar is brave.*

Latin has no word for the introductory *that.*

> Putō puellās librōs lēgisse.   *I think that the girls have read the books.*
> Vīdit nāvēs vēnisse.   *He saw that the ships had come.*

The time of the infinitive is relative to the main verb; i.e., the present infinitive is used to show *the same time as* the main verb; the perfect infinitive is used to show *time before* the main verb; the future infinitive is used to show *time after* the main verb.

> Sciō eum hoc vidēre.   *I know that he is seeing this.*
> Sciō eum hoc vīdisse.   *I know that he has seen this.*
> Sciō eum hoc vīsūrum esse.   *I know that he will see this.*
>
> Scīvī eum hoc vidēre.   *I knew that he was seeing this.*
> Scīvī eum hoc vīdisse.   *I knew that he had seen this.*
> Scīvī eum hoc vīsūrum esse.   *I knew that he would see this.*

THE ABLATIVE OF CAUSE

The ablative, usually without a preposition, may be used to express cause.

> Hoc fēcī amōre vestrī.   *I did it from love of you.*
> Timōre animālium silvam relīquērunt.
>   *They left the forest from fear of the animals.*
> Inopiā cibī labōrābant.   *They were suffering from lack of food.*
> Quā rē hoc dīcitis?   *For what reason do you say this?*

The preposition **dē** is used in the expression **quā dē causā,** *for which reason.*

> Nūllam aquam invēnit, quā dē causā īnsulam relinquere coāctus est.
> *He found no water, for which reason he was forced to leave the island.*

—— *Vocabulary* ——

accē'dō, accē'dere, acces'sī, acces'sum, *approach, go to*
cognōs'cō, cognōs'cere, cognō'vī, cog'nitum, *learn, find out*
crē'dō, crē'dere, crē'didī, crē'ditum, *believe, trust*
exīs'timō, -ā're, -ā'vī, -ā'tum, *think, suppose, consider*
intel'legō, intelle'gere, intellēx'ī, intellēc'tum, *understand*
iū'dicō, -ā're, -ā'vī, -ā'tum, *judge, consider*
le'gō, le'gere, lē'gī, lēc'tum, *choose; gather; read*
negō, -āre, -āvī, -ātum, *deny, say . . . not*
nes'ciō, nescī're, nescī'vī, nescī'tum, *not know*
obti'neō, obtinē're, obti'nuī, obten'tum, *hold (against opposition)*
perti'neō, pertinē're, perti'nuī, ——, *pertain; extend*
pu'tō, -ā're, -ā'vī, -ā'tum, *think*
sci'ō, scī're, scī'vī, scī'tum, *know*
sen'tiō, sentī're, sēn'sī, sēn'sum, *feel, realize*
spē'rō, -ā're, -ā'vī, -ā'tum, *hope*

a'pud, (prep. w. acc.) *among, at the house of, in the presence of*
cir'cum, (prep. w. acc.) *around*
prae'ter, (prep. w. acc.) *beyond, besides, except*
prō, (prep. w. abl.) *in front of, on behalf of, in exchange for, instead of*

—— *Word Study* ——

Accēdō is used with the accusative of place to which.
Cognōscō. The basic sense of this word is *begin to know.* Consequently in the perfect system it can mean *know.*

PERFECT	cognōvī,	*I have learned, I know*
PLUPERFECT	cognōveram,	*I had learned, I knew*
FUTURE PERFECT	cognōverō,	*I shall have learned, I shall know*

Crēdō takes an indirect object of the person to whom belief or trust is given.

Tibi crēdō.   *I believe you. I trust you.*

Nesciō is normally used instead of **nōn sciō.**

Spērō. Unlike *hope* in English, this verb is not used with a complementary infinitive, but with an indirect statement, usually with a future active infinitive.

Mē vīsūrum esse tē spērō.   *I hope to see you (I hope that I shall see you).*

——*Exercises*——

A. Translate.

1. Dīcō tē iānuam claudere dēbēre.   2. Crēdisne eum cōpiās īnstrūctūrum?*   3. Intellegunt nōs lūsisse.   4. Exīstimābam exercitum posse superāre hostēs.   5. Nōs pecūniam receptūrōs esse spērat.   6. Hostēs accēdere scīvit.   7. Cognōvit mē ventūrum esse.   8. Dīcit puerōs mittī.   9. Putat mīlitēs pugnāvisse.   10. Sciō vōs hoc probāre.

B. Translate.

1. We know that he was killed.   2. He says that Lucius is being sent.   3. He wants to say to them that we shall yield.   4. Do you think that the men have ceased to fight?   5. Caesar says that the army is approaching.   6. I know that he will send it.   7. I think that he is judging us.   8. They believed that our army would defeat the enemy.   9. I hear that our friends have sailed.   10. He knows that we can play.

C. Read the Latin and translate.

1. Quod mīlitēs esse paucōs cognōverat, monuit ducem difficile futūrum esse hostēs superāre.   2. Ipsīs cīvibus hanc victōriam magnam vōs dēbēre nūntiāre putō.   3. Dīxit omnēs agricolās circum hoc oppidum inopiā cibī et aliārum rērum labōrāre.

* The **esse** is frequently omitted from the future active infinitive. It is sometimes omitted from the perfect passive infinitive.

4. Rōmānōs victūrōs hostēs crēdimus quod scīmus hōs illīs parēs nōn esse virtūte.   5. Apud cōnsulēs tōtī cīvitātī dīximus Lūcium virum bonum esse; alterum illud malum fēcisse.   6. Servōs tuōs in agrōs urbī proximōs dūcī putō.   7. Omnēs Rōmānī Caesarem

Basilica and Column of Trajan

maximum imperātōrum fuisse intellegunt.   8. Cōnsulī ipsī agrōs Helvētiōrum mīlia passuum duo ā flūmine abesse nūntiant. 9. Ītaliam patriam poetārum magnōrum esse sciunt.   10. Mīlitēs in summō monte manēre iussōs esse audīvimus.

D. Translate.

1. I hope to sail to Italy next summer; I hear that the cities there are very beautiful.   2. The leaders know that the enemy is approaching and that many soldiers have left the camp from fear of death.   3. We understand that the best wines by far are always placed on the table at Marcus's house.   4. The people hoped that the consuls would lead the army around the enemy's camp that day.   5. We said to him that we were unable to sail because of the large waves.   6. We all believe that many good books have been written by that poet; but which of us has read them? 7. Everyone knows that Rome has always been and is now a very great city.   8. We bade our comrades farewell and said to them that we hoped to see them within a few years.   9. He himself says that the ambassadors have been sent to the Gauls.   10. Our native land is like our mother, for which reason we think that we ought to fight on her behalf.

— *Reading* —

FABIUS APPOINTED DICTATOR

Ubi in urbe nūntiātum est Rōmānōs graviter superātōs esse, multitūdō fēminārum in Forō stābat circum eōs quī ā proeliō vēnerant et nūntium dē virīs et fīliīs petēbat. Sed nihil certī cognōvērunt.

Illō tempore patrēs Q. Fabium Maximum dictātōrem ob perīculum facere cōnstituērunt. Fabius dīxit cīvēs Rōmānōs multa sacra deīs facere dēbēre. Haec illī fēcērunt.

Fabius nova cōnsilia bellī cēpit. Nam scīvit Hannibalem esse imperātōrem meliōrem quam cōnsulēs Rōmānōs. Itaque exercitum Rōmānum proelium cum hostibus committere prohibēbat; itinera in summīs montibus magnā cum cūrā faciēbat.

Haec autem cōnsilia cīvibus nōn grāta erant. Multī enim Rōmānī exīstimābant Fabium hostēs proeliō superāre posse, et exercitum Rōmānum in collēs fugere vidēre nōn cupiēbant.

40

Reflexives
Dative of Reference
Dative of Purpose
Double Dative

Emperor Marcus Aurelius, 2nd century, A.D., Rome

In alio pediculum, in te ricinum non vides.
You see a louse on someone else, but not a tick on yourself.
— PETRONIUS

— *Forms* —

REFLEXIVE PRONOUNS

The third person reflexive pronoun is declined as follows:

	SINGULAR	PLURAL
GENITIVE:	su'ī	su'ī
DATIVE:	si'bi	si'bi
ACCUSATIVE:	sē (or) sē'sē	sē (or) sē'sē
ABLATIVE:	sē (or) sē'sē	sē (or) sē'sē

The reflexives of the first and second persons are supplied from the declension of **ego** and **tū; meī,** *of myself,* **tuī,** *of yourself,* and so on. When **cum** is used with the ablative of reflexive pronouns it is attached to them, as it is to personal pronouns: **mēcum, tēcum, sēcum,** etc.

— *Syntax* —

The reflexive pronouns refer to the subject of the sentence or of the clause in which they stand.

The reflexive of the third person serves for all genders and numbers.

> Sē vulnerāvit. *He wounded himself.*
> Iūlia dīxit sē id vīdisse. *Julia said that she had seen it.*
> But
> Eum vulnerāvī. *I wounded him.*
> Putō eam vīdisse id. *I think that she has seen it.*

REFLEXIVE ADJECTIVES

The reflexive adjective is **suus, sua, suum.** It is declined like **magnus.** It is used to refer back to the subject of the clause in which it stands, or to the subject of the main verb of the sentence. It is rarely used in the nominative case. When the English *his* (or *her*) is not reflexive, the genitive of the pronoun **is, ea, id** is used.

Suum equum in agrum dūxit.   *He led his horse into the field.*
Suōs fīliōs ad oppidum mīsērunt.   *They sent their sons to the town.*
But
Eius equum in agrum dūxī.   *I led his horse into the field.*
Eōrum fīliōs ad oppidum dūximus.   *We took their sons to the town.*

DATIVE OF REFERENCE

The dative is used to show to whose advantage or disadvantage the action of the verb is performed.

Habē tibi illud praemium.   *Keep that reward for yourself.*

DATIVE OF PURPOSE; DOUBLE DATIVE

A dative expressing purpose is sometimes coupled with a dative of reference in a construction which is called the double dative.

Duās legiōnēs praesidiō oppidō relīquit.
He left two legions as a guard (for a guard) for the town.
Equitēs Caesarī auxiliō erant.
The cavalry served as an aid (were for an aid) to Caesar.

The words most commonly used as datives of purpose are:

auxiliō,   *for an aid*   praesidiō,   *for a guard*
cūrae,   *for a care, worry*   subsidiō,   *for a support*
impedīmentō,   *for a hindrance*   ūsuī,   *for an advantage*

—— Vocabulary ——

ar'bor, ar'boris, f., *tree*
col'lis, col'lis, m., *hill*
cupi'ditās, cupiditā'tis, f., *greed, desire*
glō'ria, -ae, f., *fame, glory*
lī'berī, -ō'rum, m. pl., *children*
lū'na, -ae, f., *moon*
mo'ra, -ae, f., *delay*
negō'tium, negō'tī, n., *trouble; task, business*

senā'tor, senātō'ris, m., *senator*
sōl, sō'lis, m., *sun*
stel'la, -ae, f., *star*
tur'ris, tur'ris, f., *tower**
ven'tus, -ī, m., *wind*

suus, -a, -um, (refl. poss. adj.) *his, her, its, their*

suī, sibi, sē, (refl. pron.) *himself, herself, itself, themselves*

* **Turris** keeps the **-i** of its stem in the accusative singular: **turrim.**

—Word Study—

Cupiditās is frequently used with an objective genitive.

cupiditās potestātis   *a desire for power*

Līberī, *children.* This is merely the adjective **līber** used as a plural noun. It came to mean *children* because a Roman houseold was composed of the father, the mother, free persons, and slaves, and the free persons were of course the children of the family.

Recipiō, used with a reflexive pronoun for its object, means *to take oneself back, return, retreat.*

mē recipiō,   *I return*
tē recipis,   *you return*
sē recipit,   *he returns, etc.*

Sōlis occāsus (*the going down of the sun*) means *sunset,* either as a time (*sundown*) or a direction (*west*).

—Exercises—

A. Translate.

1. Cum suīs sociīs vēnit.   2. Suum amīcum vīdit.   3. Putāmus eum id factūrum.   4. Negāvit sē posse venīre.   5. Eius soror hoc dīxit.   6. Suae matrī vīnum dedit.   7. Eius matrī dedī cibum. 8. Suās cōpiās hūc dūxit.   9. Eōrum librī relīctī sunt.   10. Putat sē dēbēre discēdere.

B. Translate.

1. We know that she is present.   2. He thinks that he can do it. 3. I believe that they have found it.   4. They sent their letters here.   5. They said that he had been sent there.   6. Have you seen his horse?   7. We came with them.   8. The boys praised themselves.   9. Their father was wounded.   10. The senator said that he would come.

C. Read the Latin and translate.

1. Cōnsul dīxit illum senātōrem sēcum ad Āfricam nāvigātūrum. 2. Alter poēta multa dē lūnā et sōle, alter dē ventīs et fluctibus scrīpsit; utrīus librum legēs?   3. Virī optimī sē nōn laudant.

The Roman Forum with the Temple of Saturn

4. Helvētiī nūntium mīsērunt magnam suārum cōpiārum partem ē fīnibus excessisse. 5. Suae mātrī sē pecūniam invenīre nōn potuisse dīxit. 6. Sōlis occāsū prīma aciēs ā lēgātīs in castra reducta erat. 7. Gallī et Germānī quī trāns flūmen habitant inter sē contendunt. 8. Lūcius "Senātōrī," inquit, "auxiliō cupiō esse in urbe." 9. Puella sē litterās ab ipsō poētā accēpisse dīxit. 10. Puerī nihil vidēre poterant, nam nox sine stellīs aut lūnā erat.

D. Translate.

1. As soon as they saw his horse, they began to retreat. 2. The senator was saying that he desired to read that poet's books. 3. We hope that the men from Britain will arrive in our land tomorrow. 4. He hesitated to say to his father that there would be a delay. 5. I have heard that the winds are very strong, and I do not think that we shall reach the island. 6. My business today is very difficult, but I hope to see you after noon. 7. "Fight as bravely and as fiercely as possible," said the general to his troops, "and we shall defeat our enemy today." 8. Eagerness for money has compelled many men to do unfair things. 9. The bravest foot soldier had been sent from the town as an aid to the messengers. 10. As soon as they realized that the enemy was approaching, the soldiers ran to the top of the tower.

—— *Reading* ——

MINUCIUS LEFT IN CHARGE

Hannibal sē trāns collēs recēperat et Fabius sōlus in urbem Rōmam discesserat et exercitum cum magistrō equitum, nōmine Minuciō, relīquerat, quī sē in agrō Lārīnātī tenēbat et praesidiō fīnitimīs oppidīs erat. Sed Minucius, quod nōn crēdēbat cōnsilia Fabī victōriae esse idōnea, ob cupiditātem glōriae suōs mīlitēs contrā hostēs ēdūcere cōnstituit.

Castra Rōmānōrum in colle altō et tūtō locō posita erant. Sōlis occāsū ea Minucius in campōs proximōs hostibus mōvit. Hannibal ipse intellēxit sē proelium commissūrum nōn cum eōdem duce; castra sua propius hostēs mōvit et proelium parābat. Alter exercitus vidēbat alterum aciem īnstruere et magna erat cupiditās pugnae.

Nocte Hannibal equitēs ad castra Rōmāna mīsit. Hās cōpiās autem equestrēs nūllō negōtiō suīs castrīs Rōmānī prohibuērunt.

Nec verbum verbo curabis reddere fidus interpres.
*As a true translator you will take care not to
translate word for word.*—HORACE

REVIEW 10 (LESSONS 37–40)

—Vocabulary Drill—

A. Give the genitive, gender, and meaning of the following nouns.

arbor	līberī	senātor	turris
collis	lūna	sōl	ventus
cupiditās	mora	stella	victor
glōria	negōtium	subsidium	
herba		toga	

B. Give the other nominative singular forms, and the meanings, of the following adjectives and pronouns.

aliēnus	ipse	quisque	tōtus
alius	neuter	sōlus	ūllus
alter	nūllus	suus	uter
īdem			uterque

C. Give the principal parts and meanings of the following verbs.

accēdō	frangō	lūdō	recipiō
claudō	īnstruō	negō	remittō
cognōscō	intellegō	nesciō	removeō
crēdō	iūdicō	obtineō	sciō
crēscō	iungō	pertineō	sentiō
dēsistō	lavō	premō	spērō
dubitō	legō	probō	trahō
exīstimō		putō	valeō

D. Give the meaning of:

apud	prō
circum	unde
praeter	undique

—Drill on Forms—

A. Make a copy of the following box, and fill in the blanks with the proper forms of the infinitives of **lavō, obtineō, trahō, recipiō,** and **sentiō.**

TENSE	ACTIVE	PASSIVE
PRESENT		
PERFECT		
FUTURE		

B. Give the following forms.

1. *genitive singular:* negōtium, cupiditās, alter
2. *dative singular:* suī, collis, sōlus
3. *accusative singular:* sōl, īdem, turris
4. *ablative singular:* arbor, ipse, suī
5. *nominative plural:* negōtium, victor, uterque
6. *genitive plural:* senātor, collis, tōtus
7. *dative plural:* ventus, arbor, suī
8. *accusative plural:* stella, ūsus, toga

—Drill on Syntax—

A. Translate, identifying the use of each infinitive.

1. Did you decide to close the door?   2. He was not able to drag the cart.   3. Do you think that they have learned this?   4. They ordered the soldier not to kill the women.   5. We believed that he had been sent back.   6. He hoped that I would read the book.   7. I think that the children have grown.   8. We know that they are being sent back.   9. They ought to believe you.   10. He hesitated to retreat.

B. Translate the italicized words.

1. *His* children came.   2. I reported *it* to *their* friends.   3. He said that *he* was able to do *it*.   4. Caesar led *his* troops to the town.

5. I saw *their* army. 6. We know that *they* will see *us*. 7. They say that *they* desire *this*. 8. He finished *his* business. 9. *Their* friends were coming. 10. I hope that *you* will do *it*.

—— *Exercises* ——

A. Translate.

1. Exīstimō eōs ad hoc oppidum tribus diēbus ventūrōs esse.
2. Intellegō vōs putāre nōs nōn posse venīre. 3. Omnēs spērāmus nostrum exercitum fortem hostēs barbarōs in Galliā et Germaniā superātūrum. 4. Propter inōpiam frūmentī Caesar ibi tōtam aestātem manēre nōn poterat. 5. Imperātor suīs mīlitibus sē illō diē pugnāre cupere dīxit. 6. Sē multa dē sōle et lūnā et stellīs cognōvisse dīcēbat. 7. Suum frātrem multō fortiōrem meō patre esse putābat. 8. Caesar parvam peditum manum praesidiō pontī relīquisse dīcitur. 9. Sōlis occāsū barbarī sē ad summum collem recipere coāctī sunt. 10. Nescīvēruntne hī cīvēs suam cupiditātem rērum aliēnārum inīquam esse?

B. Translate.

1. We knew that they had put the money in the ships and that the sailors were preparing to sail. 2. The small girl hesitated to play with the larger children. 3. My friend had been sent by his father as an aid to the lieutenant in Gaul. 4. The woman could not believe that her son had left the camp. 5. We saw that the citizens were frightened by the letter from the consul. 6. They do not suppose that they are equal to us in courage, do they? 7. The chief of the town thought that that very high tower would act as a hindrance (would be for a hindrance) to our men. 8. I do not believe that this very good boy has mocked the teachers. 9. The senators learned that the two armies of the Gauls had been joined to each other. 10. Few men thought that a man could walk on the moon.

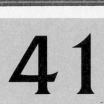

41

Participles

Jordan: Petra, The Treasury, 2nd century, A.D.

> Quam se ipse amans—sine rivali!
> *Himself loving himself so much—without a rival!*—CICERO

—Forms—

PARTICIPLES

There are three participles in Latin, the present and future in the active voice, and the perfect in the passive voice. (There is also a future passive participle, which will be taken up in a later lesson.)

Present Active Participle. The present active participle is formed as follows:

1. First and second conjugations: add **-ns** to the present stem.

> **vocō,** present stem **vocā** + **ns** = **vocāns,**   *calling*
> **moneō,** present stem **monē** + **ns** = **monēns,**   *warning*

2. Third and fourth conjugations: add **-ēns** to the present stem.

> **regō,** present stem **reg** + **ēns** = **regēns,**   *ruling*
> **capiō,** present stem **capi** + **ēns** = **capiēns,**   *taking*
> **audiō,** present stem **audī** + **ēns**   **audiēns,**   *hearing*

Perfect Passive Participle. The perfect passive participle is the fourth principal part declined as a first and second declension adjective (like **malus, -a, -um**).

> vocātus, -a, -um,   *having been called*
> monitus, -a, -um,   *having been warned*
> rēctus, -a, -um,   *having been ruled*
> captus, -a, -um,   *having been taken*
> audītus, -a, -um,   *having been heard*

Future Active Participle. This is formed by adding **-ūrus, -ūra, -ūrum** to the stem of the fourth principal part.

> vocātūrus, -a, -um,   *about to call*
> monitūrus, -a, -um,   *about to warn*
> rēctūrus, -a, -um,   *about to rule*
> captūrus, -a, -um,   *about to take*
> audītūrus, -a, -um,   *about to hear*

Sum has only one participle, the future active, **futūrus, -a, -um.**

SUMMARY OF PARTICIPLES

	ACTIVE		PASSIVE	
PRESENT	vocāns	*calling, while calling*		
	monēns	*warning, while warning*		
	regēns	*ruling, while ruling*		
	capiēns	*taking, while taking*		
	audiēns	*hearing, while hearing*		
PERFECT			vocātus	*called, having been called*
			monitus	*warned, having been warned*
			rēctus	*ruled, having been ruled*
			captus	*taken, having been taken*
			audītus	*heard, having been heard*
FUTURE	vocātūrus	*about to call*		
	monitūrus	*about to warn*		
	rēctūrus	*about to rule*		
	captūrus	*about to take*		
	auditūrus	*about to hear*		

DECLENSION OF PARTICIPLES

The perfect passive and future active participles are declined like first and second declension adjectives. The present active participle is declined like a third declension adjective, except that it has **-e** in the ablative singular.

	SINGULAR		PLURAL	
	MASC. & FEM.	NEUTER	MASC. & FEM.	NEUTER
NOMINATIVE:	vo'cāns	vo'cāns	vocan'tēs	vocan'tia
GENITIVE:	vocan'tis	vocan'tis	vocan'tium	vocan'tium
DATIVE:	vocan'tī	vocan'tī	vocan'tibus	vocan'tibus
ACCUSATIVE:	vocan'tem	vo'cāns	vocan'tēs	vocan'tia
ABLATIVE:	vocan'te	vocan'te	vocan'tibus	vocan'tibus

—Syntax—

PARTICIPLES

Functions. The participle shares the characteristics of two other parts of speech. A participle is like a verb in that it expresses an action and has tense and voice. It also takes a direct object if it is active and transitive. It is like an adjective in that it has gender, number, and case, and modifies a noun.

Tenses. The tenses of the participle, like those of the infinitive, are relative to the time of the main verb. The present participle describes an action contemporaneous with that of the main verb, the perfect an action prior to that of the main verb, and the future an action after that of the main verb. Latin observes these distinctions very carefully.

TRANSLATION OF PARTICIPLES

The basic translations of the participles are as follows:

PRESENT ACTIVE: vocāns, *calling, while calling*
PERFECT PASSIVE: vocātus, *called, having been called*
FUTURE ACTIVE: vocātūrus, *about to call, going to call,*
  intending to call, destined to call

PARTICIPLES REPLACING CLAUSES

Latin makes a much greater use of participles than English, often using a participle where English would use a clause. Consequently we must often translate a Latin participle by a clause.

Equum inventum rēdūxit.
> *When he had found his horse, he led it back.*
> *Since he had found his horse, he led it back.*
> *He led back his horse, which he had found.*

—Vocabulary—

addū'cō, addū'cere, addūx'ī, adduc'tum, *lead to; influence*
circumve'niō, circumvenī're, circumvē'nī, circumven'tum, *surround,*
  come around
commo'veō, commovē're, commō'vī, commō'tum, *move thoroughly,*
  upset, alarm

com'pleō, complē're, complē'vī, complē'tum, *fill up, complete*
cōnspi'ciō, cōnspi'cere, cōnspex'ī, cōnspec'tum, *look at attentively, observe closely*
dēfi'ciō, dēfi'cere, dēfē'cī, dēfec'tum, *fail; revolt, desert*
dīmit'tō, dimit'tere, dīmī'sī, dīmis'sum, *let go away, send away, dismiss*
ēnūn'tiō, ēnūntiā're, ēnūntiā'vī, ēnūntiā'tum, *report, announce*
expō'nō, expō'nere, expo'suī, expo'situm, *set forth; explain*
in'citō, -ā're, -ā'vī, -ā'tum, *stir up, arouse*
intermit'tō, intermit'tere, intermī'sī, intermis'sum, *stop, pause; interrupt; lose (time)*
occī'dō, occī'dere, occī'dī, occī'sum, *kill, cut down*
op'primō, oppri'mere, oppres'sī, oppres'sum, *crush, overpower*
trādū'cō, trādū'cere, trādūx'ī, trāduc'tum, *lead across*

—— Word Study ——

Dēficiō, when it means *revolt* or *desert,* takes the ablative of place from which, usually with **ab.**
Trādūcō may take two objects.

      Exercitum flūmen trādūxit.   *He led the army across the river.*

—— Exercises ——

A. Translate in as many ways as you can.

1. Puerōs lūdentēs vīdī.   2. Equitēs in proeliō victōs ad urbem mīsit.   3. Erat pugnātūrus.   4. Castra oppugnāta capientur. 5. Poētam sub arbore sedentem vīdimus. 6. In silvam trāctī, fugere temptant. 7. Imperātor hostēs superātōs esse putāns discessit. 8. Puella hōs librōs lectūra est.   9. Aciem īnstrūctam dūxit in proelium. 10. Cōnspectūrus sum hanc domum.

B. Translate, using participles wherever possible.

1. He was wounded while he was fighting in Europe.   2. Having collected the infantry, he led them across the river.   3. I heard the soldiers who were shouting.   4. I am about to dismiss him.   5. I am about to desert from the army.   6. He was about to kill the

animal.   7. He carried the money which he had found to the city.   8. I saw him as he was about to depart.   9. He interrupted the work that had been begun.   10. When he had defeated the enemy he let them go away (dismissed them).

C. Read the Latin and translate.

1. Litterās portāns ad Caesarem mediā nocte vēnit.   2. In castra vēnērunt ducem occīsūrī, sed prohibitī sunt.   3. In mediō monte stābam audiēns virōs clāmantēs.   4. Cōnsul mīlitēs timēns urbem relinquere cōnstituit.   5. Germānī fidēlēs suum ducem interfectum portantēs ad oppidum veniunt.   6. Pedes prō castrīs pugnāns gladium āmīsit.   7. Caesar suās cōpiās hostium cornū dextrum opprimentēs vīdit.   8. Territī puerī, hīs verbīs commōtī, sē recipere ad patrēs cōnstituērunt.   9. Hostēs ad urbem accēdentēs oppressūrī sumus.   10. Prīma aciēs castra oppugnābat, sed secunda aciēs, in colle instructa, hostēs exspectābat.

(upper) A late republican denarius (silver coin) of Longinus. Reverse, a man casting his ballot. The tablet bears the letter U for **uti rogas,** *a favorable vote. Obverse, Vesta. (lower) Denarius of Quintus Cassius. Reverse, a voting urn, curule chair (magistrate's bench) and tablet with A,* **absolvo,** *(I acquit) and C,* **condemno.** *Obverse, Liberty.*

D. Translate, using participles wherever possible.

1. He reported that he had seen near the bridge the bodies of four men killed in the battle.   2. Having observed the camp closely, he decided to attack it.   3. We shall easily be able to surround those soldiers who were wounded in the battle.   4. The lieutenant, because he had been dismissed by the general, decided to desert from the army.   5. I hope that the little boys who have been frightened by those noises will come to our farmhouse in a short time.   6. He said that that part of the river was filled up with large stones.   7. The right wing, near the river, was equal to the enemy in courage, but the left wing, fighting in the plain, was being overpowered.   8. Having been influenced by the words of the senator, the Roman people praised its faithful generals who were about to depart.   9. Holding the sword with her wounded hand, the brave girl was waiting for her brothers.   10. At midnight Caesar gave the letter to the messenger who was standing in front of the camp.

—— *Reading* ——

FABIUS RESCUES MINUCIUS

Adductus hāc minōre victōriā Minucius, magister equitum, imperium simile eī dictātōris Fabiī petēbat. Ā populō convocātō hoc imperium Minuciō datum est. Hic cum suīs mīlitibus ē castrīs ēductīs impetum Hannibalis exspectābat. Fabius tamen suōs in castrīs tenēns rem cōnspiciēbat.

   Collis parvus erat inter castra Rōmānōrum et Poenōrum. Hannibal sēnsit sē dēbēre eum occupāre. Itaque cum paucīs ex militibus ad collem accessit et eum occupāvit. Prīmum Minucius ipse equitibus* impetum in hostēs fēcit, sed Hannibal labōrantibus suīs subsidiō plūrēs mīsit et Rōmānōs circumveniēbat. Deinde Minucius commōtus legiōnēs īnstrūctās in proelium ēdūxit. Hannibal mittēns auxilia peditum equitumque mox tōtam aciem complēverat. Aciēs Rōmāna maximē labōrābat. Tum legiōnēs Fabiī velut caelō dēmissae ad auxilium sē ostendērunt et aciem Poenōrum oppressērunt.

* Ablative of means; people are often treated as instruments in military writings.

42

Subjunctive Mood

The interior of the late imperial curia (Senate House) at Rome

Facilius per partes in cognitionem totius adducimur.
We are more easily led part by part to an understanding
of the whole. —SENECA

——Forms——

THE SUBJUNCTIVE

The subjunctive mood has four tenses, present, imperfect, perfect, and pluperfect.

The present subjunctive is formed as follows:

First conjugation: The **-ā-** of the present stem is changed to **-ē-** and the personal endings are added.

ACTIVE		PASSIVE	
SINGULAR	PLURAL	SINGULAR	PLURAL
vo'cem	vocē'mus	vo'cer	vocē'mur
vo'cēs	vocē'tis	vocē'ris	vocē'minī
vo'cet	vo'cent	vocē'tur	vocen'tur

Second, third, and fourth conjugations: -ā- and the personal endings are added to the present stem.

mo'neam	moneā'mus	mo'near	moneā'mur
mo'neās	moneā'tis	moneā'ris	moneā'minī
mo'neat	mo'neant	moneā'tur	monean'tur
re'gam	regā'mus	re'gar	regā'mur
re'gās	regā'tis	regā'ris	regā'minī
re'gat	re'gant	regā'tur	regan'tur
ca'piam	capiā'mus	ca'piar	capiā'mur
ca'piās	capiā'tis	capiā'ris	capiā'minī
ca'piat	ca'piant	capiā'tur	capian'tur
au'diam	audiā'mus	au'diar	audiā'mur
au'diās	audiā'tis	au'diar	audiā'minī
au'diat	au'diant	audiā'tur	audian'tur

Sum and its compounds have an irregularly formed present subjunctive.

sim	sī'mus
sīs	sī'tis
sit	sint

The imperfect subjunctive. All four conjugations, and **sum,** form the imperfect subjunctive by adding the personal endings to the present active infinitive (with the final **-e** lengthened).

	ACTIVE	PASSIVE		ACTIVE	PASSIVE
1ST.	vocā'rem	vocā'rer	2ND.	monē'rem	monē'rer
	vocā'rēs	vocārē'ris		monē'rēs	monērē'ris
	vocā'ret	vocārē'tur		monē'ret	monērē'tur
	etc.	etc.		etc.	etc.
3RD.	re'gerem	re'gerer		ca'perem	ca'perer
	re'gerēs	regerē'ris		ca'perēs	caperē'ris
	re'geret	regerē'tur		ca'peret	caperē'tur
	etc.	etc.		etc.	etc.
4TH.	audī'rem	audī'rer	SUM	essem	
	audī'rēs	audīrē'ris		essēs	
	audī'ret	audīrē'tur		esset	
	etc.	etc.		etc.	

The perfect active subjunctive. All verbs form the perfect active subjunctive in the same way. They add **-erī-** and the personal endings to the perfect stem.

1ST.	2ND.	3RD	
vocā'verim	monu'erim	rex'erim	cē'perim
vocā'verīs	monu'erīs	rex'erīs	cē'perīs
vocā'verit	monu'erit	rex'erit	cē'perit
etc.	etc.	etc.	etc.

4TH.	SUM
audī'verim	fu'erim
audī'verīs	fu'erīs
audī'verit	fu'erit
etc.	etc.

The perfect passive subjunctive. The perfect passive subjunctive is the perfect passive participle used as a subjective complement with the present subjunctive of **sum.**

1ST.	2ND.	3RD.		4TH.
vocā'tus sim	mo'nitus sim	rēc'tus sim	cap'tus sim	audī'tus sim
vocā'tus sīs	mo'nitus sīs	rēc'tus sīs	cap'tus sīs	audī'tus sīs
vocā'tus sit	mo'nitus sit	rēc'tus sit	cap'tus sit	audī'tus sit
etc.	etc.	etc.	etc.	etc.

The pluperfect active subjunctive. Add the personal endings to the perfect active infinitive (lengthening the final -e).

1st.	2nd.	3rd.	
vocāvis′sem	monuis′sem	rēxis′sem	cēpis′sem
vocāvis′sēs	monuis′sēs	rēxis′sēs	cēpis′sēs
vocāvis′set	monuis′set	rēxis′set	cēpis′set
etc.	etc.	etc.	etc.

4th.	SUM
audīvis′sem	fuis′sem
audīvis′sēs	fuis′sēs
audīvis′set	fuis′set
etc.	etc.

The pluperfect passive subjunctive uses the perfect passive participle with the imperfect subjunctive of **sum.**

1st.	2nd.
vocā′tus es′sem	mo′nitus es′sem
vocā′tus es′sēs	mo′nitus es′sēs
vocā′tus es′set	mo′nitus es′set
etc.	etc.

3rd.		4th.
rēc′tus es′sem	cap′tus es′sem	audī′tus es′sem
rēc′tus es′sēs	cap′tus es′sēs	audī′tus es′sēs
rēc′tus es′set	cap′tus es′set	audī′tus es′set
etc.	etc.	etc.

Relief showing jurors and scribes, and speaker pleading a law case

—Syntax—

TRANSLATIONS OF THE SUBJUNCTIVE

In modern English the subjunctive is seldom used. Many Latin subjunctives must therefore be translated by English indicatives or infinitives. For this reason no standard translation of the subjunctive can be given. You will learn how to translate each kind of subjunctive clause when it is presented.

—Vocabulary—

au'rum, -ī, n., *gold*
fer'rum, -ī, n., *iron*
pī'lum, -ī, n., *javelin*

scū'tum, -ī, n., *shield*
tribū'nus, ī, m., *tribune*
val'lēs, val'lis, f., *valley*

ar'mō, -ā're, -ā'vī, -ā'tum, *arm, equip*
cōnsis'tō, cōnsis'tere, cōn'stitī, cōn'stitum, *halt; take a stand*
er'rō, -ā're, -ā'vī, -ā'tum, *wander; make a mistake*

perfi'ciō, perfi'cere, perfē'cī, perfec'tum, *finish, accomplish*
perter'reō, perterrē're, perter'ruī, perter'ritum, *terrify*

nē, (adv.) *not*
vē'rō, *in truth, indeed; but*

au'tem, (postpositive conj.) *but, however; and, moreover*
e'nim, (postpositive conj.) *for*
vel, (conj.) *or*

—Word Study—

Ferrum is often used to mean *sword, swords,* or *weapons,* particularly in the phrase **ferrō et igne,** *by fire and sword.*
Pīlum. This is the heavy *javelin* of the Roman legionary, which he hurled during the charge, before the hand-to-hand sword fighting.
Scūtum: a large rectangular *shield,* curved like part of a cylinder; it would protect completely a man kneeling behind it. It was made of hide stretched over a wooden frame, with a hemispherical iron boss in the center to deflect heavy missiles.
Tribūnus. The **tribūnus mīlitum** was a Roman officer, commissioned

by a vote of the people. Unlike the **lēgātī,** who formed the general's staff, the **tribūnī** were assigned to particular legions. Each legion had six **tribūnī,** who took turns commanding it.

Vel, aut. Aut is used when the two terms being joined are contrasted or opposed (*or else*).

> Vincēs aut vincēris.   *You will conquer, or else be conquered.*

Vel is used when an alternative is offered as a matter of choice.

Hic locus est urbs vel oppidum.
> *This place is a city or, if you like, a town (or at least a town).*

Like **aut . . . aut . . .,** **vel . . . vel . . .** can mean   *either . . . or . . .*

—— Exercises ——

Give synopses, in the subjunctive only, of the following verbs.

1. armō *in the first person singular, active and passive*
2. terreō *in the second person singular, active and passive*
3. dūcō *in the third person singular, active and passive*
4. perficiō *in the first person plural, active and passive*
5. sentiō *in the second person plural, active and passive*
6. iungō *in the third person plural, active and passive*
7. sum *in the third person singular*
8. possum *in the third person plural*

A relief from Germany showing a covered wagon

43

Hortatory Subjunctive

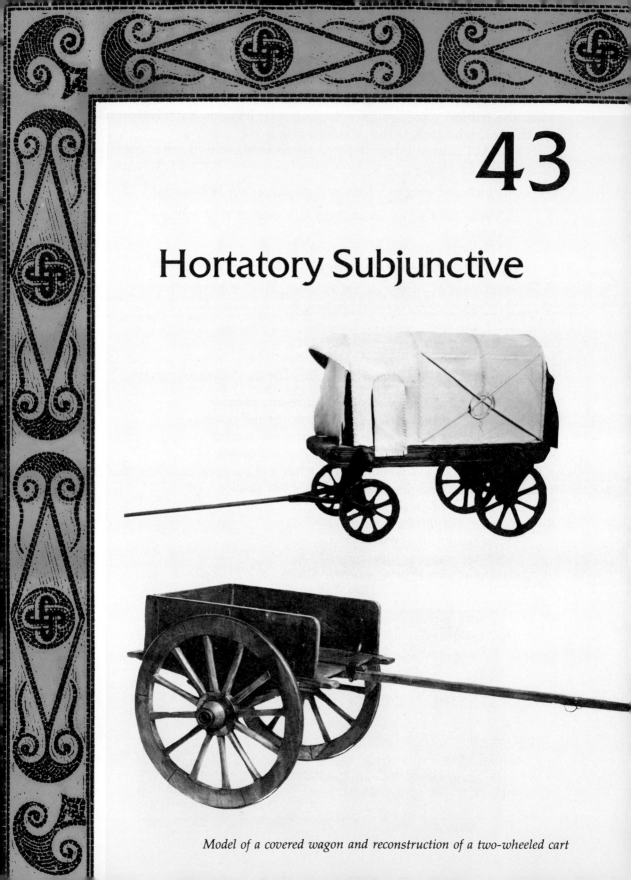

Model of a covered wagon and reconstruction of a two-wheeled cart

Qui dedit beneficium taceat; narret qui accepit.

Let him who has given a favor be silent; let him who has received it tell it.—SENECA

——Syntax——

THE HORTATORY SUBJUNCTIVE

A command or exhortation may be expressed in Latin by the present subjunctive, usually translated in English by *let*. The negative in Latin is expressed by **nē**.

Captīvī hūc addūcantur.   *Let the captives be led to this place.*
Nē coniciant peditēs pīla.   *Let the foot soldiers not throw their javelins.*

——Vocabulary——

cala'mitās, calamitā'tis, f., *disaster, misfortune*

condi'ciō, condiciō'nis, f., *terms, condition*

cōnsuētū'dō, cōnsuētū'dinis, f., *habit, custom*

difficul'tās, difficultā'tis, f., *difficulty*

īnsi'diae, -ārum, f., *trap, ambush, plot*

iū'dicium, iūdi'cī, n., *judgment, trial*

or'bis, or'bis, m., *circle, wheel*

potes'tās, potestā'tis, f., *power*

re'giō, regiō'nis, f., *direction; district, region*

sententia, -ae, f., *opinion*

vadum, -ī, n., *ford, shallows*

ca'lidus, -a, -um, *hot*

frī'gidus, -a, -um, *cold*

subitō, (adv.) *suddenly*

um'quam, (adv.) *ever*

——Word Study——

Orbis terrārum (*the circle of lands*) was the Roman name for the territories lying around the Mediterranean Sea; the phrase then came to mean *world,* in the sense of the inhabited areas of the world. The world as a globe is **tellus, tellūris, f.**

—Exercises—

A. Translate.

1. Conveniant omnēs. 2. Nē pugnēmus. 3. Mihi pecūniam det. 4. Cōnsulem audiāmus. 5. Nē frangātur. 6. Nē venīre dubitent. 7. Discēdāmus. 8. Nē equōs incitēmus. 9. Nē terreātur. 10. Nōs nē videat.

B. Translate.

1. Let him hear us. 2. Let them not find it. 3. Let her not hear this. 4. Let him not see them. 5. Let us go away. 6. Let her give them food. 7. Let them not play. 8. Let us announce this. 9. Let's sit here. 10. Let him not fear to come.

C. Read the Latin and translate.

1. Prō patriā nostrā omnēs maximā cum virtūte pugnēmus. 2. Nē umquam audiat vōs perīculum fūgisse. 3. Ipsī frūmentum ab illīus agricolae agrīs portēmus. 4. Discēdant illī puerī in viā lūdentēs. 5. Verbīs eius senātōris nōtī nē commoveāmur, sed nostrās sententiās dīcāmus sine timōre. 6. Ad hanc vallem nē veniant sine aquā et cibō. 7. Nostrās condiciōnēs pācis accipiant, et maneant semper nōbīs amīcī. 8. Labor hodiē cōnficiātur; crās enim labōrāre nōn cupiēmus. 9. Illā nocte nihil vīdimus; post enim sōlis occāsum erat nūlla lūx lūnae aut stellārum. 10. Captus est mīles hūc veniēns rēgem interfectūrus.

D. Translate.

1. Let them not ever think that they have defeated me. 2. Let her always believe that her sons were killed in the war. 3. Let us all look at the army as it marches to the camp. 4. Let us hope that the enemy will not surpass us in number of cavalry. 5. Let the tribune not hear that you deserted from the legion. 6. Let the judgments of our famous judge be accepted by all the citizens. 7. I hope that your children will learn many things about the world and its regions. 8. "Let him not hesitate to speak his opinion about the plot," said the consul. 9. Let us halt in this little valley, far from the enemy's camp. 10. Let that tribune not lead his forces into the territory of the enemy.

—— Reading ——

ATALANTA

Ōlim in longinquā terrā habitābat potēns rēx, nōmine Schoeneus. Eius fīlia, Atalanta, celerrima omnium mortālium erat. Quod Atalanta tam pulchra erat, multōs procōs habēbat. Fortūna autem procōrum mala erat. Omnī procō Schoeneus "Sī Atalantam," inquit, "certāmine pedum vīceris, tum eam in mātrimōnium dūcere poteris; sī Atalanta tē vīcerit, poena mors erit."

Tandem ad rēgiam Schoeneī vēnit Hippomenēs, quī Atalantam in mātrimōnium dūcere cupiēbat. Schoeneus eī condiciōnēs prōposuit. Inde Hippomenēs auxilium ā Venere ōrāvit, quae eī tria aurea pōma dedit. Tum Hippomenēs dīxit sē ad certāmen esse parātum.

Dum haec geruntur, omnēs amīcī rēgis ad certāmen convēnērunt. Signum tubā datur. Magnō cursū Atalanta et Hippomenēs ēmicant. Atalanta autem celerior est itaque Hippomenēs ūnum ex tribus pōmīs proicit. Atalanta pōmum tollit et tum Hippomenēs prior est. Mox tamen Atalanta propter celeritātem suam eum superātūra est. Hippomenēs igitur secundum pōmum dēmittit, sed iterum Atalanta pōmum tollit et eum cōnsequitur. Nunc ad mētam appropinquant. Ōrāns auxilium ā deā, Hippomenēs tertium pōmum proicit. Atalanta id quoque tollit sed spatium ad mētam brevius est. Hippomenēs est victor. Prō poenā mortis Hippomenēs Atalantam in mātrimōnium dūcit.

Mosaic from Terme Cisiarii at Ostia showing two-wheeled cart drawn by mules, probably the usual mode of transport.

44

Adverbial Clause of Purpose
Relative Clause of Purpose

Model of a Roman freight ship

Legum servi sumus ut liberi esse possimus.
*We are slaves of the laws in order that we may be able
to be free.*—CICERO

—Syntax—

ADVERBIAL CLAUSE OF PURPOSE

The subjunctive is used in Latin to express purpose. The present subjunctive is used if the main verb is present, future, or future perfect. The imperfect subjunctive is used if the main verb is in the imperfect, perfect, or pluperfect. An adverbial clause of purpose is introduced by **ut** if it is affirmative and **nē** if it is negative.

Pugnābāmus ut urbem defenderēmus.
We were fighting to defend the city.
so as to defend the city.
in order to defend the city.
that we might defend the city.
so that we might defend the city.
in order that we might defend the city.

Pugnāmus nē superēmur.
We are fighting so as not to be defeated.
that we may not be defeated.
so that we may not be defeated.
in order that we may not be defeated.

RELATIVE CLAUSES OF PURPOSE

The relative clause of purpose is introduced by the relative pronoun instead of by **ut**. It is used to name the purpose of its antecedent, rather than the purpose of the whole clause.

Mīsit nūntiōs quī regiōnis cōnsuētūdinēs cognōscerent.
He sent messengers to learn the customs of the district.
who were to learn the customs of the district.
Librī scrībuntur quōs legāmus.
Books are written for us to read.
which we may read.

When the purpose contains some comparative idea, the clause is introduced by **quō** (Ablative of Degree of Difference).

Cōnsulī appropinquābō quō melius ōrātiōnem audiam.
 I shall go near to the consul in order to hear his speech better. . . . *the better to hear his speech.* Literally: . . . *by which the better I may hear his speech.*

The infinitive is never used to express purpose.

—— Vocabulary ——

altitū'dō, altitū'dinis, f., *height, depth*

centu'riō, centuriō'nis, m., *centurion*

do'lor, dolō'ris, m., *grief, pain, suffering*

flōs, flō'ris, m., *flower*

fos'sa, -ae, f., *ditch*

ge'nus, ge'neris, n., *kind, sort, class, race*

hīber'na, -ōrum, n., (pl.) *winter quarters*

iūs, iū'ris, n., *right, justice, law*

lātitū'dō, lātitū'dinis, f., *width*

magnitū'dō, magnitū'dinis, f., *size, greatness*

mēns, men'tis, f., *mind*

mercā'tor, mercātō'ris, m., *merchant, trader*

o'nus, o'neris, n., *burden*

o'pus, o'peris, n., *work*

ōrā'tiō, ōrātiō'nis, f., *speech*

val'lum, -ī, n., *rampart*

—— Word Study ——

Centuriō. A centurion was the highest ranking non-commissioned officer in the Roman army. As his title implies, he was originally in charge of a hundred soldiers; but in practice centurions' duties varied widely. A centurion might on occasion even be left in charge of a legion.

Fossa, vāllum. In fortifying a camp Roman soldiers dug a *trench* (**fossa**) around the outside of a large square area, throwing the dirt toward the inner side. A palisade of wooden stakes was then set in the top of this long mound of dirt; the mound and the palisade together made up what was called the **vāllum.**

The adverb **magnopere** is a contraction of the ablative of manner **magnō opere,** *with great effort.*

—— Exercises ——

A. Translate.

1. I shall send a messenger to report this. 2. I sent a messenger to report this. 3. He will have come to hear us. 4. Men were sent to defend the bridge. 5. I shall send men to defend the bridge. 6. He has come to see them. 7. He had fled so as not to be killed. 8. They are fleeing so as not to be killed. 9. They will come to look at you. 10. Will you come with me to warn them?

B. Read the Latin and translate.

1. Pugnēmus fortiter ut ā duce laudēmur. 2. Mercātōrēs ad nostram urbem vēnērunt ut pecūniam facerent. 3. Magnā cum dīligentiā aquam in hortum portāvit ut flōrēs crēscerent. 4. Multās ōrātiōnēs scrīpsit quās aliī dīcerent. 5. Celerrimē cucurrit nē ā suō patre caperētur. 6. Paulō ante nautae missī erant quī ad Britanniam cum illō mercātōre nāvigārent. 7. Nūntius ad urbem missus est quī cīvēs dē perīculīs monēret. 8. Illa fēmina veniet ad urbem nōn ut lūdōs spectet sed ut ipsa spectētur. 9. Prīmā lūce prīnceps barbarus ad mediam silvam accessit nē ab equitibus invenīrētur. 10. Hortus tuus meum magnitūdine superat; labōrābō autem ut meum pulchriōrem tuō faciam.

C. Translate.

1. We sent the boys to the town to watch the games. 2. I had sailed many miles to come to this place because I had hoped to find my brother here. 3. The consuls, departing from the city, left a tribune and two thousand soldiers to be (for) a guard to the citizens. 4. I shall give you food to eat and wine to drink. 5. They fought long and fiercely in order to defeat a very powerful army of the Gauls. 6. I shall send my sister to the city to see the king and queen. 7. I want to fight bravely so that I may be equal to my father in boldness. 8. The messenger ran very quickly to report to the centurion that the enemy were approaching the camp. 9. Let my father come as soon as possible to lead me back to my native land. 10. These boys will read many books in order to learn as much as possible about the moon and stars.

——Reading——

CROESUS AND HIS SON

Inter fābulās quae nōbīs trāditae sunt dē Croesō rēge est haec: Croesus, quī maximum rēgnum et magnam cōpiam aurī habēbat, nōn tamen erat laetus, quod eius fīlius vocem nōn habēbat. Medicōs ad sē undique vocābat, sed nēmō eōrum vōcem puerō miserō dare poterat. Tandem Croesus ad urbem Delphōs īre cōnstituit, ut cōnsilium ab ōrāculō rogāret. Ad illum oppidum itinere longō pervēnit. Postquam sē sacrō in flūmine lāvit et ad ōrāculum accessit, tum haec verba ā rēge audīta sunt: "Ubi puer vocem habēbit, homō interficiētur." Ōrāculum intellegere semper erat difficillimum, sed multī existimāvērunt fīlium rēgis mox ē vītā excessūrum esse. Croesus igitur trīstissimus factus est.

Multīs post annīs Croesī hostēs rēgnum maximīs cum cōpiīs oppugnābant. Ūnus ex hīs hostibus ad rēgem cucurrit ut eum interficeret. Fīlius perterritus hostem armātum vīdit et exclāmāvit, "Num rēgem interficiēs?" Croesus tamen gladiō occīsus est. Hōc modō ōrāculum probātum est vērum.

Painting of a landing scene

Assiduus usus uni rei deditus et ingenium et artem saepe vincit.
*Constant practice devoted to one subject often outdoes both
intelligence and skill.*—CICERO

REVIEW **11** (LESSONS 41–44)

——*Vocabulary Drill*——

A. Give the genitive, gender, and meaning of the following nouns.

altitūdō	flōs	magnitūdō	potestās
aurum	fossa	mēns	regiō
calamitās	genus	mercātor	scūtum
centuriō	hīberna	onus	sententia
condiciō	īnsidiae	opus	tribūnus
cōnsuētūdō	iūdicium	ōrātiō	vadum
difficultās	iūs	orbis	vallēs
dolor	lātitūdō	pīlum	vāllum
ferrum			

B. Give the principal parts and meanings of the following verbs.

addūcō	cōnsistō	errō	opprimō
armō	cōnspiciō	expōnō	perficiō
circumveniō	dēficiō	incitō	perterreō
commoveō	dīmittō	intermittō	trādūcō
compleō	ēnūntiō	occīdō	

C. Give the meanings of the following.

autem	enim	nē	umquam
calidus	frīgidus	subitō	vel
			vērō

——*Drill on Forms*——

A. Give a synopsis in the indicative, subjunctive, and imperative of:

1. laudō *in the first person singular, active.*
2. moveō *in the second person singular, passive.*

3. dūcō *in the third person singular, active.*
4. iaciō *in the first person plural, passive.*
5. inveniō *in the second person plural, active.*
6. sum *in the third person plural.*

B. Make a copy of the following box and fill the blanks with the proper forms of the participles of **incitō, habeō, dīcō, perficiō,** and **mūniō.**

TENSE	ACTIVE	PASSIVE
PRESENT		
PERFECT		
FUTURE		

——Drill on Syntax——

Translate.

1. I want to see you.   2. I came to see you.   3. It is good to see you.   4. He had come to see you.   5. We are afraid to see you. 6. It pleases me to see you.   7. They ordered him to see you. 8. They will come to see you.   9. She was able to see you.   10. He sent men to see you.

——Exercises——

A. Translate.

1. Tribūnus "Prīmā lūce," inquit, "mīlitēs castra muniant fossā vāllōque." 2. Nē putēmus nostrās mentēs meliōrēs quam Gallōrum esse.   3. Nāvem inventūrī sumus quā mercātōrēs aurum nostrum ad patriam portent.   4. Nūntiō in silvam errātūrō viam ad urbem dēmōnstrāvī; ille autem mihi nihil dīxit.   5. Ut deae mēns nōbīs amīca sit, puellae dēligantur quae mēnsam ex aurō factam ad eam portent.   6. Mīlitēs scūta pīlaque portantēs iter ad vadum quam celerrimē faciant, nē circumveniantur.   7. Magnā cum celeritāte currit ut ignem in summō colle videat.   8. In mēnsā

exponāmus cibōs vīnaque optima nē hic prīnceps potentissimus nōbīs inimīcus sit.   9. Nē audiat magister tē id opus optimum intermīsisse quod herī incēpistī.   10. Barbarī fossam lapidibus complēre incēpērunt ut cōpiās trādūcerent et castra occupārent.

B. Translate.

1. Let us all be friendly to these men, who are here to see our city.   2. He was wounded as he was about to hurl his javelin at the chief of the barbarians.   3. Let not your grief be too great, for I know that your brother will come to find you.   4. Let the enemy put their shields and javelins in the ditch across the valley; then let them surrender themselves to us.   5. The goddess equipped her son with a shield made out of gold, for she was anxious about his safety (his safety was for an anxiety to her).   6. We took a cart with which to carry our wounded to the camp.   7. Your grain will be of use (for a use) to us, and we shall make bread for you to eat.   8. He will send a messenger to the enemy's camp to carry the terms of peace.   9. It is very difficult to believe that these flowers, chosen with care, will not please your mother.   10. That centurion came to our camp to report to the tribunes the ambush of the German army.

Model of harbors at Ostia

45

Indirect Commands

Appian Way—remains of the Temple of Hercules and the Villa of the Quintilii

Exigo a me non ut optimis par sim, sed ut malis melior.
I require myself not to be equal to the best, but to
be better than the bad.—SENECA

—— Syntax ——

INDIRECT COMMANDS

Verbs of asking, advising, and commanding are followed by indirect commands. In English these are usually infinitives. Latin uses the subjunctive in the same tenses as adverbial clauses of purpose (see Lesson 44). Indirect Commands are also called Substantive Clauses of Purpose.

Cases with Verbs of Asking, Advising, and Commanding. Three different constructions are used for the person asked, advised, or commanded to do something.

Dative (indirect object): **imperō, mandō, persuadeō.**

Mihi persuāsit ut venīrem. *He persuaded me to come.*

Accusative (direct object): **moneō, ōrō, rogō.**

Mē monuit nē venīrem. *He warned me not to come.*

Ablative with a Preposition (place from which): **petō, postulō, quaerō.**

Ā mē petit ut veniam. *He is asking me to come.*

Reflexives in Indirect Commands. In an indirect command the reflexive pronoun has as its antecedent the subject of the verb of asking, advising, or commanding which governs the indirect command.

Ab eīs petīvit nē sē vulnerārent. *He begged them not to wound him.*

—— Vocabulary ——

im'perō, -ā're, -ā'vī, -ā'tum, *order, command*
man'dō, -ā're, -ā'vī, -ā'tum, *command, instruct; entrust*
ō'rō, -ā're, -ā'vī, -ā'tum, *beg*
persuā'deō, persuādē're, persuā'sī, persuā'sum, *persuade*
pos'tulō, -ā're, -ā'vī, -ā'tum, *demand*
quae'rō, quae'rere, quaesī'vī, quaesī'tum, *seek; inquire, ask*
ro'gō, -ā're, -ā'vī, -ā'tum, *ask*

er'gō, (adv.) *therefore*

praete'reā, (adv.) *besides,
besides that*

pro'cul, (adv.) *at some distance*

an, (conj.) *or*

an'nōn, (conj.) *or not*

—— Word Study ——

Imperō and **rogō** may take a direct object in place of an indirect command.

> Tibi pecūniam imperābō.   *I shall order money from you.*
> Mē cibum rogāvit.   *He asked me for food.*

An, annōn. An is used in double questions when the two halves cannot both be true.

> Ad Ītaliam veniēs, an in Britanniā manēbis?
>   *Will you come to Italy, or remain in Britain?*
> Ad Ītaliam veniēs annōn?   *Will you come to Italy or not?*

—— Exercises ——

A. Translate.

1. He had begged me not to sail (**ōrō** and **petō**).   2. We shall persuade them to remain.   3. I asked him to depart (**petō, quaerō, and rogō**).   4. He influenced me to fight.   5. They were demanding of me that I yield.   6. I advise you not to walk.   7. He commanded them to halt (**imperō** and **mandō**).   8. We warn you to flee.   9. They are instructing her not to run.   10. He ordered that the work be finished (**imperō** and **iubeō**).

B. Read the Latin and translate.

1. Petitisne ā mē ut ad Hispāniam vōbīscum nāvigem?   2. Tribūnīs imperat ut itinere Helvētiōs prohibeant.   3. Ille prīnceps barbarus frātrī persuādēbit ut rēgnum in cīvitāte occupet.   4. Caesar ab eīs postulāvit ut decem ex prīncipibus ad sē addūcerentur. 5. Agricolam senem addūcere temptābant ut sibi pecūniam daret.   6. Tē rogābō ut hās litterās ad cōnsulem portēs. 7. Petīvēruntne ā Germānīs nē sēcum pugnārent, an cōnstituērunt bellum gerere?   8. Cōnsul cōpiās barbarās monuit ut iter per fīnēs Gallōrum maximā cum celeritāte facerent.   9. Dux mandat ut

omnēs Aeduī sibi tēla et arma omnia trādant.   10. Cīvēs mīlitēs rogāvērunt nē castra prope urbem pōnerent.

C. Translate.

1. The senators had instructed the consuls to defend the state from all dangers.   2. She is asking her father to give her the money. 3. The leader with great difficulty persuaded the soldiers to fight in that valley.   4. He begged his mother not to send him to that school.   5. The tribune has ordered grain from the farmers and wine from the merchants.   6. The messenger demanded of the boys that they lead him through the great forest.   7. We command you to complete this work; therefore it ought to be begun at once.   8. Caesar let some farmers go away, but he warned others to carry the grain to the camp in carts.

——*Reading*——

THE STORY OF REGULUS

Rōmānī antīquī bella longa cum Carthāginiēnsibus gerēbant. Haec gēns erat audāx et potēns, quam Rōmānī maximē timēbant. Senātus Rōmānus putābat hostēs ē Siciliā urbem Rōmam ipsam oppugnātūrōs esse. Propter hoc perīculum Rōmānī cōnsilium audācissimum cēpērunt. Cōnsulem Rēgulum cum exercitū in Āfricam mīsērunt ut Carthāginem caperet.

Carthāginiēnsēs paucīs proeliīs victī celeriter pācem rogābant. Sed Rōmānī eōs inīquās condiciōnēs accipere coēgērunt. Mox autem rursus pugnāre cōnstituērunt; nōn sōlum Rōmānōs superāvērunt sed etiam Rēgulum cēpērunt. Ducem captum Rōmam redīre iussērunt ut pax meliōribus condiciōnibus cōnstituerētur. "Lībertātem tibi reddēmus," inquiunt, "sī nostrī captīvī ā Rōmānīs remittentur. Si nōn remittentur, ad nōs quam celerrimē venīre dēbēs."

Itaque quid fēcit Rēgulus? Sē haec factūrum esse cōnfirmāvit, et sine morā ad senātum discessit. Senātōribus, "Captīvōs," inquit, "reddere nōn dēbētis. Sunt enim fortēs, ego autem nōn iam validus sum. Vōs sine mē facile eōs superātūrōs esse existimō. Hostēs autem sine mīlitibus captīs bellum diūtius gerere nōn poterunt."

Brevī tempore Rēgulus Carthāginem rediit, et ab Carthāginiēnsibus crūdēlissimē interfectus est.

46

Clauses after Verbs of Fearing
Sequence of Tenses

Dress of Roman matron and a consul in toga and senatorial boots

Sedit qui timuit ne non succederet.

He who feared he would not succeed sat still.—HORACE
(For fear of failure, he did nothing.)

——*Syntax*——

CLAUSES AFTER VERBS OF FEARING

In English we use an indirect statement after verbs of fearing: "I fear
that he is coming." Latin uses the subjunctive. After verbs of fearing
an affirmative clause is introduced by **nē,** a negative clause by **nē nōn**
or **ut.**

> Timeō nē veniat.   *I fear that he is coming (lest he come).*
> Timeō nē nōn veniat.   *I fear that he is not coming.*
> Timeō ut veniat.   *I fear that he is not coming.*

If you will remember that a clause after a verb of fearing expresses
the wish that the person fearing has in mind, you will have no trouble.

SEQUENCE OF TENSES

You have already learned that in purpose clauses and indirect commands the present subjunctive is used after present and future main
verbs, and the imperfect subjunctive after past verbs. In other kinds
of clauses we may need to express an action prior to that of the main
verb (e.g., "I fear that he has come," "I feared that he had come");
for this we use the perfect or pluperfect subjunctive. *Sequence of tenses*
is the term used for the tense relationship between the main verb and
the subjunctive in a subordinate clause.
Primary Sequence. If the verb of the main clause is in a present or
future tense, the verb in the subjunctive is in:
1. the present tense, if its action takes place at the same time as, or
   after, that of the main verb.
2. the perfect tense, if its action is over with by the time of that of the
   main verb.
Secondary Sequence. If the verb of the main clause is in a past tense,
the verb in the subjunctive is in:
1. the imperfect tense, if its action takes place at the same time as, or
   after, that of the main verb.
2. the pluperfect tense, if its action is over with by the time of that of
   the main verb.

TENSES OF THE MAIN VERB   TENSES OF THE SUBJUNCTIVE

	Incomplete Action (during or after that of main verb)	Completed Action (prior to that of main verb)
PRIMARY SEQUENCE Present Future ⎬ Future perfect	Present	Perfect
SECONDARY SEQUENCE Imperfect Perfect ⎬ Pluperfect	Imperfect	Pluperfect

Examples of Sequence of Tenses

Timeō,   *I fear,*
Timēbō,   *I shall fear,*   } nē veniat,   *that he is coming.*
Timuerō, *I shall have feared,*   nē vēnerit,   *that he has come.*

Timēbam,   *I was fearing,*   nē venīret,   *that he was coming,*
Timuī,   *I feared,*   }   *that he would come.*
Timueram,   *I had feared,*   nē vēnisset,   *that he had come.*

—— Vocabulary ——

aedifi′cium, aedifi′cī, n., *building*
au′ris, au′ris, f., *ear*
fi′dēs, -eī, f., *faith, loyalty, confidence; pledge*
fo′rum, -ī, n., *market place, forum*
nē′mō, nē′minī, m. (dat.), *no one*
o′culus, -ī, m., *eye*

spe′ciēs, -ē′ī, f., *sight, appearance*
ves′tis, ves′tis, f., *clothing*
vigi′lia, -ae, f., *wakefulness, watchfulness; watch*
vīs, vīs, f., *force, violence*
  vī′rēs, vī′rium (pl.), *strength*

Vīs is declined as follows:

	SINGULAR	PLURAL
NOMINATIVE:	vīs	vī′rēs
GENITIVE:	vīs	vī′rium
DATIVE:	vī	vī′ribus
ACCUSATIVE:	vim	vī′rēs
ABLATIVE:	vī	vī′ribus

—— Word Study ——

Fidēs. From the meaning *pledge* have developed the idioms **in fidē, in fidem,** *under protection.*

Forum. Originally a market place, the forum at Rome gradually acquired many other functions. The law courts and stock market were there; meetings were held and political speeches delivered there. It was the scene of gladiatorial shows and dramatic performances, and a favorite loitering place for idlers.

Nēmō is derived from **nē + homō.** Its genitive and dative are seldom used; **nūllīus** and **nūllī** (from **nūllus, -a, -um**) are used instead. There is no plural. The accusative is **neminem.**

Vigilia. In military language, a *watch* was one-fourth of the night.

—— Exercises ——

A. Translate.

1. He feared that I would run.   2. We fear that they are not fleeing.   3. I feared that they would not yield.   4. They feared that he was not present.   5. You fear that I will remain.   6. He feared that you were being dismissed.   7. She feared that he had been killed.   8. They fear that it has not been accomplished. 9. Who feared that he had not departed?   10. They fear that he is sleeping.

B. Read the Latin and translate.

1. Crēdāmus nūllī; nēmō enim fidēlis nōbīs est.   2. Bellum nōn gerent quod timent nē frūmenta sua et vīllae aedificiaque omnia capiantur.   3. Ambulēmus ad forum ut illum nōtum cōnsulem ōrātiōnem habentem audiāmus.   4. Illa animālia et speciē et magnitūdine corporis dissimillima erant eīs quae paulō post vīdimus. 5. Nēmō est quī nōbīs cibum aut vīnum det; quid ergō factūrī sumus?   6. Ab hostibus victīs postulābunt ut omnia arma sibi trādant.   7. Dīcēbat difficillimum esse hunc puerum cursū superāre. 8. Det Fortūna huic proeliō exitum fēlīcem! 9. Nōsne senātus populusque Rōmānus rogābunt ut amīcī et sociī sīmus, an gerent bellum contrā nōs?   10. Tertiā vigiliā ignēs in hostium castrīs vīsī sunt; imperātor noster ergō timuit nē illī fugere incēpissent.

C. Translate.

1. I say that I myself have seen that ancient building with my (own) eyes. 2. This work is very difficult, but we hope that our desire for glory will give us strength. 3. As soon as he arrived in the city he came to see his friend who was about to depart. 4. Fearing that his men would not be able to defend the town, he sent cavalry to guard (be a guard for) the bridge. 5. He tried to persuade the consul not to deliver (**habeō**) a speech in the senate that day. 6. Let's run to the forum as quickly as possible to watch the games. 7. If you hold this same course you will arrive at the island at sundown. 8. He said that that animal was very like a horse in appearance, but that its ears were much larger. 9. There was no one to defend us; therefore I feared that our town would be taken. 10. In the fourth watch Caesar ordered that all the soldiers should take arms.

—— *Reading* ——

THE SACRED GEESE

Gallī urbem Rōmam oppugnābant. Eōrum ducēs mīlitibus imperāvērunt ut acerrimē pugnārent. Rōmānī timēbant nē tōta urbs dēlerētur. Sed Gallī eam expugnāre nōn poterant, quod mōns Capitōlīnus erat altus et moenia valida erant.

Circum Capitōlium Gallī statiōnēs disposuerant nē Rōmānī in monte cibum et aquam acciperent. Rōmānī autem Gallōs dērīsērunt; pānem etiam ad Gallōs dēiēcērunt.

Ūnā nocte tertiā vigiliā ūnus ex custōdibus Gallicīs vīdit nūntium Rōmānum nūdīs pedibus discēdere dē Capitōliō in forum. Statim custōs ad ducem Gallicum properāvit ut id nūntiāret.

Proximā nocte quartā vigiliā dum lūna obscūra est Gallī suīs mīlitibus imperāvērunt ut montem ascenderent magnō silentiō, nē Rōmānī eōs audīrent. Ānserēs autem sacrī excitātī sunt ubi Gallī ad summum montem appropinquāvērunt, et magnum strepitum ēmisērunt. Mīles Rōmānus, Mānlius nōmine, ē somnō excitātus, prīmum Gallum in summum mūrum ascendentem petīvit et eum dē mūrō dēiēcit. Hic Gallus recidēns in Gallōs aliōs incidit, et eī cēterōs omnēs Gallōs ad īmum montem reiēcērunt.

Tālī modō Capitōlium ā Mānliō, virō fortī, et strepitū ānserum sacrōrum servātum est. Posteā Mānlius ''Capitōlīnus'' appellātus est.

The elegant tresses and complicated coiffures of Pompeian women required careful arranging, done here by a slave hairdresser. Wall painting from Herculaneum, 1st century, A.D. National Museum, Naples

47

Indirect Questions

Portrait of a young woman, 2nd century, A.D., Archeological Museum, Florence

Saepe ne utile quidem est scire quid futurum sit.

Often it is not even advantageous to know what will be.—CICERO

—Syntax—

INDIRECT QUESTIONS

Indirect questions in Latin are introduced by an interrogative pronoun, adjective, or adverb and have their verbs in the subjunctive, following sequence of tenses.

> Rogat quid faciāmus.   *He asks what we are doing.*
> Rogat quid fēcerīmus.   *He asks what we have done.*
> Rogāvit quid facerēmus.   *He asked what we were doing.*
> Rogāvit quid fēcissēmus.   *He asked what we had done.*

A reflexive pronoun in an indirect question (just as in an indirect command) has as its antecedent the verb governing the indirect question.

> Mihi "Dabisne," inquit, "mihi dōnum?"
> *"Will you give me a gift?" she said to me.*
> Mē rogāvit num sibi dōnum datūrus essem.
> *She asked me if I would give her a gift.*

Besides verbs of asking, indirect questions may follow verbs of saying, perceiving, knowing, etc.

> Scitne ubi sītis?   *Does he know where you are?*

—Vocabulary—

tre′decim, (indecl. adj.) *thirteen,* (XIII)
quattuor′decim, (indecl. adj.) *fourteen,* (XIV or XIIII)
quīn′decim, (indecl. adj.) *fifteen,* (XV)
sē′decim, (indecl. adj.) *sixteen* (XVI)
septen′decim, (indecl. adj.) *seventeen* (XVII)
duodēvīgin′tī, (indecl. adj.) *eighteen* (XVIII)
ūndēvīgin′tī, (indecl. adj.) *nineteen* (XIX or XVIIII)

commū'nis, -e, *common, general*

immortā'lis, -e, *immortal*

prīvā'tus, -a, -um, *private*

quan'tus, -a, -um, *how great?, how much?*

quot, (indecl. adj.) *how many?*

num, (conj.) *if, whether*

utrum . . . an . . . , (correl. conj.) *whether . . . or . . .*

utrum . . . necne, *whether . . . or not*

— Exercises —

A. Translate.

1. Tē rogābit ubi fuerīs. 2. Rogāvit quid facerem. 3. Scit quī sītis. 4. Scīvī cūr vēnīssēs. 5. Quaerit cuius equus currat. 6. Rogāvistīne ā quō vulnerātus esset? 7. Scīverās quid factūrī essent. 8. Sciam cui id dēs. 9. Cupīvit scīre num eōs vīdissēmus. 10. Rogābat quī mittī dēbērent.

B. Translate.

1. He asked who had been fighting. 2. Do you know to whom she gave it? 3. We shall learn whether he did this. 4. They do not know who is being sent. 5. They had learned why she was going to depart. 6. He will ask whose friends saw her. 7. I knew what she was saying. 8. He wants to find out whether they came or not. 9. Did you see what he was doing? 10. I do not know where he will find it.

C. Read the Latin and translate.

1. Rogāvī utrum agricolīs an mercātōribus pecūnia darētur. 2. Magnā cum dīligentiā temptābāmus cognōscere ubi līberī essent. 3. Quaeram ā Caesare num lapidēs in fossam iēcerint. 4. Nautae nostrī scīvērunt quot nāvēs in portum pervēnissent. 5. Tertiā vigiliā lēgātus cognōvit quī ē castrīs fūgissent. 6. Omnēs timuērunt oppidum relinquere, nēmō enim scīvit quid factum esset. 7. Rogāvī meum patrem quō in locō vestem posuisset. 8. Deī immortālēs sciunt quid hominēs fēcerint et faciant et factūrī sint. 9. Cōnsul timēns nē urbs caperētur rogābat quantae essent hostium cōpiae. 10. Nūntiī missī sunt quī ā rēge quaererent cūr in Graeciam exercitum trādūxisset.

D. Translate.

1. The centurion ordered the captured messenger to say where the buildings were.   2. Do you know whether that ship is equal in size to our ships?   3. My friends asked me why the children had remained in the forum for five hours.   4. Will you ask the captive to what place the barbarian chief will lead his army?   5. The consuls knew that the enemy were in the city, but they did not know how many there were.   6. He sent a boy to find out who had led the animals from the field.   7. I know that you are all asking whether he did it or not.   8. She hesitated to ask the men if they would lead her to the city.   9. Let them not ask what we have given to the wounded foot soldiers.   10. The small boy asked his father what the name was of the man who had stood on the moon.

— Reading —

HANNIBAL AT CANNAE

Pessima calamitās armōrum Rōmānōrum erat in proeliō quod Varrō et Paulus, cōnsulēs Rōmānī, contrā Hannibalem fēcērunt. Pugnātum est apud oppidum quod appellātur Cannae. In hōc proeliō tōtus paene exercitus Rōmānus captus aut interfectus est. Paulus occīsus est.

Ante eam pugnam cōnsilia bellī duōrum cōnsulum erant vērō inter sē dissimillima. Varrō dīxit sē longum bellum cum Hannibale ūnō proeliō statim perfectūrum esse. Sed Paulus crēdēbat malam esse audāciam Varrōnis et meliōra cōnsilia Fabiī Maximī. Timēbat nē cōnsilia Varrōnis Rōmam opprimerent. Ille scīvit quot proeliīs Fabius bellum cum Hannibale gessisset. Itaque ad Fabium accessit et ab eō quaesīvit quid ipse facere dēbēret. Fabius respondit: "Tua rēs, Paule, difficillima est; et cum Varrōne et cum Hannibale pugnāre cōgeris."

Sed cōnsilium Varrōnis, nōn Paulī, vīcit. Exercitus Rōmānus superātus est et multī Rōmānī timēbant nē Hannibal brevī tempore ipsam Rōmam oppugnāret.

48

Result Clauses

Etruscan breastplate, Etruscan Museum, Vatican, Rome

Nullus est liber tam malus ut non aliqua parte prosit.
There is no book so bad that it is not profitable in some part.
—PLINY THE YOUNGER

—Syntax—

RESULT CLAUSES

A clause describing an action which results from the action of the main verb is called a clause of result. The verb in the result clause is put into the subjunctive, and it is always introduced by **ut;** in the negative, **ut . . . nōn, ut . . . nūllus,** etc., are used. The tense of the verb in the subjunctive is normally determined by the rule for sequence of tenses, with the present and imperfect only used, as in purpose clauses (see Lesson 44). Usually there is a word meaning *so* or *such* in the main clause: **sīc, ita, tam, tālis, tantus,** or **tot.**

> Erant tot aedificia ut omnia vidēre nōn possem.
> *There were so many buildings that I could not see them all.*
> Hoc opus tantum est ut numquam id confectūrī sīmus.
> *This work is so great that we shall never finish it.*

Substantive Clauses of Result. Result clauses are also used as the subject or object of certain verbs. A substantive clause may be the object of a verb of causing or bringing about.

Effēcit ut tribūnus discēderet. *He made the tribune leave. He brought it about that the tribune left.*

It may also be used as the subject of such a verb in the passive, of a verb of happening, or of **necesse est,** *it is necessary.*

Accidit ut cōnsul adesset. *It happened that the consul was present. The consul happened to be present.*

—Vocabulary—

sa'tis, n., (defective noun) *enough*

neces'se, (defective adj.) *necessary*
tā'lis, -e, *such, of such a kind*
tan'tus, -a, -um, *so much, so great, so large (such a great, such a large)*
tot, (indecl. adj.) *so many*

ac'cidō, acci'dere, ac'cidī, ——, *fall upon; happen*
effi'ciō, effi'cere, effē'cī, effec'tum, *bring about; complete*

i'ta, (adv.) *so, in such a way, thus*
tam, (adv.) *so*
sīc, (adv.) *so, in this way*

——Word Study——

Satis. This word appears only in the nominative and accusative singular. It is frequently used with a partitive genitive.

> Satis cibī habēmus. *We have enough food (enough of food).*

The accusative is often used adverbially.

> Satis labōrāvimus; opus confectum est.
> *We have worked enough; the task is finished.*

Necesse has only a nominative and accusative neuter singular. It is used only as subjective complement with **esse, est, erat,** etc.
Ita, sīc, tam. Sīc modifies only verbs, **tam** only adjectives and adverbs; **ita** may do either.

——Exercises——

A. Translate.

1. Efficit ut discessūrī sīmus. 2. Tantus est ut nēmō eum superet. 3. Necesse est ut nihil faciāmus. 4. Accidit ut absit. 5. Tot hominēs aderant ut nōn omnēs mē audīrent. 6. Urbs erat tālis ut omnēs dēlectāret. 7. Necesse erat ut ambulārēmus. 8. Tam longē abest ut id nōn videant. 9. Ita territus erat ut fugeret. 10. Factum est ut multī vēnīrent.

B. Read the Latin and translate.

1. Tēla tantā vī coniēcērunt ut duodēvīgintī ex hostibus interficerentur. 2. Necesse erat ut iter maximum illō diē facerent ut ad castra ante sōlis occāsum pervenīrent. 3. Tantus timor mortis omnēs captīvōs occupāverat ut ex castrīs excēderent. 4. Tālēs sunt condiciōnēs pācis ut hostēs nōbīs quīndecim annōs pecūniam datūrī

sint.   5. Cōnsul efficiet ut ille senātor malus ab urbe discēdat.
6. Virtūs peditum nostrōrum tanta erat ut vincī nōn possent.
7. Accidit ut nēmō mitterētur quī nōbīs auxiliō esset.   8. Meus
frāter tam validus est ut tuum gladium frangere possit.   9. Erant
in hostium castrīs tot mīlitēs ut satis cibī et aquae nōn esset.
10. Tantam multitūdinem equitum habēmus ut omnēs hostēs nōs
oppugnāre dubitent.

C. Translate.

1. Our city is so beautiful that many people come to see it.
2. Marcus was so strong that he was able to defeat the rest of the
boys.   3. The Romans had such a large army that they were able
to conquer the Gauls.   4. It is necessary that we find enough food
to give to this crowd.   5. She was so terrified that she asked her
father to guard her.   6. He reads in such a loud voice that the
rest of the children can hear every word very easily.   7. The
consuls brought it about that all enemies were driven out of the
city.   8. The dangers were so great that they did not want to leave
the town.   9. It happened that the merchants, who were nineteen
in number, were sailing to Britain at that time.   10. That river is
so wide that we cannot see the enemy's camp.

——Reading——

ROMAN SUCCESSES

Annō quartō postquam Hannibal in Ītaliam vēnit, M. Claudius Mārcellus, cōnsul, contrā Hannibalem bene pugnāvit. Hic tantam īnsulae
Siciliae partem cēpit ut Poenī auxilium dē insulā in Ītaliam mittere
nōn possent. Syrācūsās, nōbilissimam urbem, expugnāvit. Et dē hāc
urbe tot signa (*statues*) ad urbem Rōmam mīsit ut haec in Forō posita
eum locum pulcherrimum facerent.

Interim in Hispāniam missus est P. Cornēlius Scīpiō. Hic, puer
duodēvīgintī annōrum, in pugnā ad Tīcīnum tantā cum virtūte pugnāverat ut omnēs scīrent hunc futūrum maximum imperātōrem.
Atque ita accidit. Nam in Hispāniā tam bene rēs gessit ut omnēs ferē
Hispāniae cīvitātēs in fidem Populī Rōmānī venīrent.

> Difficile est tenere quae acceperis nisi exerceas.
> *It is difficult to retain what you may have learned unless you should*
> *practise it.*—PLINY THE YOUNGER

REVIEW 12 (LESSONS 45–48)

—Vocabulary Drill—

A. Give the genitive, gender, and meaning of the following nouns.

aedificium	fidēs	oculus	vestis
auris	forum	speciēs	vigilia
	nēmō		vīs

B. Give the other nominative singular forms, and the meanings, of the following adjectives.

commūnis	prīvātus	quot	tālis	tot
immortālis	quantus	necesse	tantus	

C. Give the principal parts and meanings of the following verbs.

accidō	mandō	persuādeō	quaerō
efficiō	ōrō	postulō	rogō
imperō			

D. Give the meaning of:

an	ita	praetereā	num
annōn	necne	procul	tam
ergō	sīc		utrum

E. Give the cardinal numerals from one to twenty.

—Drill on Syntax—

A. Copy the following sentences and fill in the blanks.

1. Affirmative purpose clauses are introduced by ——.
2. Affirmative result clauses are introduced by ——.

3. Negative purpose clauses are introduced by ——.
4. Negative result clauses are introduced by ——.
5. Both purpose and result clauses normally use only the —— or —— tenses of the subjunctive.
6. If the verb in the main clause is present or future tense, the —— tense must be used in the subjunctive in both purpose and result clauses.
7. If the verb in the main clause is in any past tense, the —— tense must be used in the subjunctive in both purpose and result clauses.
8. The hortatory subjunctive uses only the —— tense.
9. A negative hortatory subjunctive in Latin is introduced by ——.
10. The hortatory subjunctive is translated in English by ——.

B. Translate.

1. huic similis speciē
2. postulāvit ā suō amīcō
3. persuāsit patrī suō
4. rogāvit suam mātrem
5. imperāvit servō
6. multa milia passuum
7. rogātūra erat
8. mīlitēs in campō pugnantēs
9. perterritī hīs rēbus
10. Nē pugnēmus.

A vanity case from Pompeii containing an ivory-handled bronze mirror, hairpins, comb, earrings, and cosmetic case

C. Translate.

1. Let them come.
2. enough grain
3. equal to me in strength
4. of the running slaves
5. as an aid to the general

6. We can persuade him.
7. They hesitated to ask me.
8. on top of the mountain
9. for fourteen miles
10. for seventeen days

— *Exercises* —

A. Translate.

1. Centuriō opus tam celeriter confēcit ut castra relinquere merīdiē posset. 2. Fac ut veniās ad mē quam prīmum. 3. Onera erant tam gravia ut equī ea ad nostram vīllam portāre nōn possent. 4. Timuērunt pugnāre aliī; aliī autem timēbant nē urbs ab hostibus caperētur. 5. Nostrī cīvēs postulant ut lēgēs patriae nostrae sint aequae. 6. Ōrātiō tam longa erat ut manēre nōn possem ut fīnem audīrem. 7. Necesse est ut satis pecūniae mittāmus ad illōs mercātōrēs. 8. Virī tam cupidī glōriae erant ut maximā cum virtūte pugnārent. 9. Mē rogābat num ad urbem venīre cuperem ut lūdōs spectārem. 10. Lēgātus suīs imperāvit ut in castrīs eō diē manērent.

B. Translate.

1. We do not know whether the senate has ordered the consuls to defend the city. 2. Her sorrow was so great that she did not wish to see her friends. 3. They feared that the general had heard nothing about the danger; nevertheless they hoped that he would come. 4. The ditch was so wide and so deep that we were not able to fill it. 5. I asked the poet to send me a book about the stars. 6. The power of that king was so great that he could kill even the citizens. 7. It happens that there is not enough grain in this valley; we fear therefore that we cannot remain here (any) longer. 8. The general asked the barbarians to come under the protection of the Roman people. 9. The centurion ran so fast that he arrived at the camp before all others. 10. See to it (**faciō**) that no one leaves this town before sundown.

49

Cum Clauses

Roman glass perfume bottle, jug, ointment jar and vase

> Struit insidias lacrimis cum femina plorat.
> *When a woman weeps, she is setting traps with her tears.*
> —DIONYSIUS CATO

—Syntax—

CUM CLAUSES

The conjunction **cum** is used to introduce four kinds of clauses.

Cum Temporal Clauses (**cum** is translated *when*). If a **cum** clause merely establishes the time when the action of the main verb took place, its verb is in the indicative.

> Cum Caesar in Galliam vēnit, prīncipēs erant Aeduī.
> *When Caesar came into Gaul, the Aedui were the leaders.*

Cum prīmum, *when first, as soon as,* is followed by the perfect indicative, even when the pluperfect would seem more natural in English.

> Cum prīmum in urbem pervēnit, turrim vīdit.
> *As soon as he had arrived in the city he saw the tower.*

The same is true of **postquam** clauses.

> Postquam turrim vīdit, discessit.
> *After he had seen the tower, he left.*

Cameo—victory in a chariot

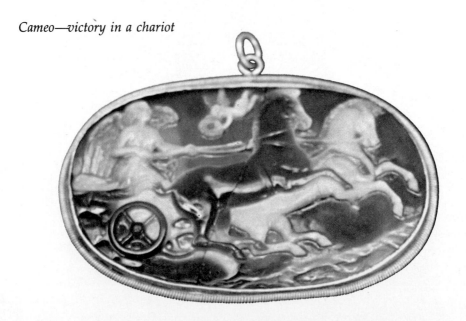

Cum Circumstantial Clauses (**cum** is translated *when*). If a **cum** clause establishes the circumstances under which the action of the main verb takes place, and not merely the time, the verb is in the subjunctive for past events, in the indicative for present or future events.

> Cum Caesar in Galliam vēnisset, Aeduī permōtī sunt.
> *When Caesar had come into Gaul, the Aedui were alarmed.*
> Cum tālia vidēmus, terrēmur.
> *When we see such things, we are frightened.*

Cum Causal (*since*) and **Cum Concessive** (*although*) **Clauses.** When **cum** means *since* or *although* the verb of its clause is in the subjunctive, following sequence of tenses.

> Cum tū nōn adessēs, pecūniam Mārcō dedī.
> *Since you weren't there, I gave the money to Marcus.*

When **cum** means *although,* **tamen** (*nevertheless, yet, still*) or some similar word will often be found in the main clause.

> Cum oppidum incendissēmus, hostēs tamen fortiter pugnābant.
> *Although we had set fire to the town, nevertheless the enemy*
> *kept fighting bravely.*

When the subject of a **cum** clause is the same as that of the main verb, it precedes the **cum** clause.

> Mārcus cum fidēlis amīcus sit mē nōn relinquet.
> *Since Marcus is a faithful friend, he will not abandon me.*

—Vocabulary—

sagit'ta, -ae, f., *arrow*
spa'tium, spa'tī, n., *distance, interval* (of time or space)
stu'dium, stu'dī, n., *eagerness, enthusiasm, zeal*
tempes'tās, tempestā'tis, f., *weather; storm*

dēfes'sus, -a, -um, *tired*
impedī'tus, -a, -um, *hindered, handicapped, in difficulty*
mī'rus, -a, -um, *strange, wonderful*

cōnser'vō, -ā're, -ā'vī, -ā'tum, *save, keep*
incen'dō, -ere, incen'dī, incēn'sum, *set on fire; arouse*
pel'lō, -ere, pe'pulī, pul'sum, *push; rout, defeat*
permo'veō, -ē're, permō'vī, permō'tum, *move deeply, alarm*

prōdū'cō, -ere, prōdūx'ī, prōduc'tum, *lead forward, bring forth*
prōpō'nō, -ere, prōpo'suī, prōpo'situm, *set forth, put forth, propose*
renūn'tiō, -ā're, ā'vī, -ā'tum, *report, bring back word (of)*
vās'tō, -ā're, -ā'vī, -ā'tum, *lay waste, devastate*

cum, (conj.) *when, since, although*

Helps and Hints. Do not confuse the conjunction **cum,** meaning
when, since, or *although,* with the preposition **cum,** meaning *with.*
They are totally different words.

—— Exercises ——

A. Turn the causal or temporal clauses in the following sentences into
cum clauses.

1. Ut ad vīllam ambulābāmus, parvum animal ex silvā cucurrit.
2. Quod Mārcus pecūniam āmīserat, patris īram timuit.
3. Postquam pervēnit in Galliam, Caesar cum Gallīs saepe pugnābat.   4. Ut equitēs suōs pulsōs esse vīdit, ex proeliō excessit.
5. Ubi in Ītaliā sum, in urbe Rōmā maneō.   6. Simul atque mē
valēre iussit, discessit.

B. Read the Latin and translate.

1. Cum animal vulnerātum invenīre nōn possēmus coāctī sumus
id relinquere in silvā.   2. Mārcus tum cum hostium īnsidiās cōnsulibus renūntiāvit parvus puer erat.   3. Cum ad illam īnsulam
pulcherrimam pervēnissent, ibi manēre cōnstituērunt.   4. Cum
sōlus sciās quis vīllam incenderit, id tuō patrī nūntiāre dēbēs.
5. Cum multum frūmentum nōn habeāmus, eīs tamen magnam
partem dabimus.   6. Cum ab hīs quaereret quae cīvitātēs in armīs
essent, causam bellī cognōvit.   7. Cum prīmum Caesar proelium
commīsit, eī renūntiātum est hostium mīlitēs in ūnum locum coāc-
tōs fortiter pugnāre.   8. Cum calamitātis timor magnus sit, Gallī

tamen maximā cum audāciā impetum faciunt. 9. Cum sagittās suās āmīsisset, Gallōrum ducem petere nōn potuit. 10. Cum Caesar esset in Galliā, multa cōnsilia eī prōposita sunt ā lēgātīs.

C. Translate.

1. When all of the infantry had assembled, Caesar gave the signal for battle and led the troops forward. 2. Although we have found out many things about the stars, yet we do not know how far away they are. 3. When I see (shall have seen) the senator I shall report to him everything which you said to me. 4. Since the enemy saw that they could not take our city, they were devastating our fields with fire and sword (**ferrō et igne**). 5. Since he thinks that the enemy are unable to withstand our attacks, he will draw up a line of battle. 6. Although reports of a disaster had been brought to us, yet we did not cease to hope. 7. When the legions had been left in camp, the general led the rest of the soldiers through the territory of the enemy. 8. As soon as we arrived at the town, we came immediately to find our friends. 9. At that time when I saw Caesar himself, I was living in the city. 10. Although they have received many serious wounds, nevertheless they are fighting very bravely.

—— *Reading* ——

THE BATTLE OF ZAMA

Annō decimō tertiō postquam Hannibal in Ītaliam vēnit, Scīpiō cōnsul creātus est. Hic cum posterō annō in Āfricam missus esset exercitum Hannōnis, ducis Carthāginiēnsium, pepulit. Cum prīmum haec victōria renūntiāta est, Hannibal omnēs ferē suōs amīcōs sociōsque in Ītaliā āmīsit. Tot annīs bellī tam dēfessae erant cīvitātēs Ītaliae ut in fidem Rōmānōrum venīrent.

Carthāginiēnsēs permōtī Hannibalem cum exercitū ab Ītaliā in Āfricam discēdere iussērunt. Scīpiō etiam exercitum mare trādūxit in Africam. Cum Hannibal optimē pugnāret, Scīpiō tamen eius exercitum maximō proeliō quod apud Zamam commissum est vīcit. Post hoc proelium pāx cum Carthāginiēnsibus facta est. Cum multae partēs Ītaliae vastātae incēnsaeque essent, Rōmānī tamen Scīpiōnem maximō cum studiō in patriam recēpērunt.

50

Deponent Verbs
Locative Case
Special
Place Constructions

Women's hair styles

Praeceptores suos adulescens veneratur et suspicit.
A young man respects and looks up to his teachers—SENECA

—Forms—

DEPONENT VERBS

Many verbs in Latin have passive forms but active meanings; they are called deponent (from **dēpōnō,** *lay aside*) because they have laid aside their passive meanings.

morātur, *he delays*   cōnātī erant, *they had tried*

Deponent verbs, however, retain a few active forms:

    a. The present active participle: loquēns,   *speaking*
    b. The future active participle: locutūrus,   *about to speak*
    c. The future active infinitive: locutūrus esse,   *to be about to speak*

LOCATIVE CASE

With names of cities, towns, small islands, **domus,** and **rūs,** the preposition is not used in expressions of place. These words express place where by a case called the locative. Its form is like the genitive in the singular of nouns of the first and second declensions, otherwise like the ablative. **Rūs** always, and other third declension nouns occasionally, have a locative in **-ī: rūrī,** *in the country,* **Carthāginī,** *at Carthage.*

Gold jewelry: earrings, fibula (safety pin), and necklaces

—Syntax—

SPECIAL PLACE CONSTRUCTIONS

In nouns which have a locative case there is no need to use a preposition to indicate place from which. On the same principle the accusative of place to which is also used without a preposition.

	ORDINARY NOUNS	NOUNS WITH LOCATIVE CASE
PLACE WHERE	Ablative + **in, sub, super** In urbe est. *He is in the city.*	Locative Case Romae est. *He is in Rome.*
PLACE FROM WHICH	Ablative + **ab, dē, ex** Ab urbe venit. *He comes from the city.*	Ablative without a preposition Rōmā venit. *He comes from Rome.*
PLACE TO WHICH	Accusative + **ad, in, sub, super** Ad urbem venit. *He comes to the city.*	Accusative without a preposition Rōmam venit. *He comes to Rome.*

—Vocabulary—

Athē'nae, -ā'rum, f., *Athens*
Carthā'gō, Carthā'ginis, f., *Carthage*
Corin'thus, -ī, f., *Corinth*
rūs, rū'ris, n., *country, countryside*

ar'bitror, -ā'rī, -ā'tus sum, *think*
cō'nor, -ā'rī, -ā'tus sum, *try, attempt*
hor'tor, -ā'rī, -ā'tus sum, *encourage, urge*
lo'quor, lo'quī, locū'tus sum, *speak, talk*
mo'ror, -ā'rī, -ā'tus sum, *delay*
pa'tior, pa'tī, pas'sus sum, *suffer; permit, allow*
permit'tō, -ere, permī'sī, permis'sum, *entrust; permit*
polli'ceor, -ērī, polli'citus sum, *promise*

proficīs'cor, proficīs'cī, profec'tus sum, *set out, depart*
vi'deor, -ē'rī, vī'sus sum, *seem*

Because there is no perfect active stem, deponent verbs have only three principal parts.

——Word Study——

Rūs means *country* only as opposed to *city*. In the locative case it sometimes means *at one's country place*.

> Estne domī an rūrī?
> *Is he at his town house or his country place?*

Cōnor is followed by a complementary infinitive.

> Venīre cōnātur.   *He tries to come.*

Hortor, like **moneō,** is followed by an accusative and an indirect command.

> Mīlitēs hortātus est ut fortiter pugnārent.
> *He urged the soldiers to fight bravely.*

Patior, permittō. Patior, *permit, allow,* is followed by an infinitive phrase (infinitive with accusative subject); **permittō,** *permit,* is followed by an indirect object and a purpose clause.
Polliceor. Like verbs of hoping, verbs of promising must be followed by an indirect statement. The indirect statement will normally have a future infinitive.

> Pollicitus est sē haec factūrum esse.
> *He promised to do these things.*

——Exercises——

A. Translate.

1. arbitrābimur, hortābātur, patī, cōnāris   2. patiēbar, cōnātus eram, proficīscar, morāta est   3. profectus erat, loquēbātur, arbitrābuntur, videntur   4. passus sum, pollicēre, patientur, cōnātī estis   5. hortābar, loquere, passī sunt, morāta erit

B. Translate.

1. we are delaying, they will think, he has promised, she has tried   2. you will attempt, I was suffering, they delayed, try!   3. he will have talked, he seems, they were setting out, I shall urge   4. you have delayed, you will promise, she will encourage, I shall promise   5. will you try? he has spoken, I had permitted, let him suffer

C. Translate.

1. to Rome, from Carthage, at Corinth, (to) home   2. from the country, in our country, to Italy, from the city   3. In Sardis,* to Veii,** in Greece, to the city   4. from Europe, in Sicily (a large island), from our country, to the country   5. in Troy, from Corinth, to Carthage, at Veii   6. from Rome, in Carthage, to Troy, from home   7. in the country, to Sicily, from Sardis, in the city   8. to Greece, from Veii, to Europe, in Italy   9. from Greece, from Sicily, to our country, at home   10. from Troy, to Corinth, at Rome, to Sardis

D. Read the Latin and translate.

1. Nūntium mittere cōnābimur quī cum cīvibus loquātur.   2. Mē rūs cum amīcīs ambulātūrum pollicitus, nōn arbitrātus sum mē domī dēbēre morārī.   3. Proficīscentur ex urbe nē inimīcī cōnsulibus videantur.   4. Agricolae Rōmam rūre veniēbant ut deīs immortālibus sacra facerent.   5. Imperātor pollicitus est sē ante proelium peditēs hortātūrum esse.   6. Illōs servōs quī linguā Graecā loquuntur rogābō num Corinthō vēnerint.   7. Cōnstituere cōnāmur num ad illum ducem nūntium mittere dēbeāmus.   8. Lēgātī Rōmae quam diūtissimē morābuntur ut cum senātōribus dē pācis condiciōnibus loquantur.   9. Crās proficīscar sī mihi prīmum permīseris ut cum meā mātre loquar.   10. Centūriō cum prīmum īnsidiās hostium in silvā vīdit Corinthum cucurrit ut perīculum lēgātō renūntiāret.

E. Translate.

1. Having tried to devastate our fields, the enemy set out towards the next town.   2. Having set out from home at daybreak, they all tried to walk the twenty miles to Rome.   3. Caesar, having urged his men not to fear the enemy, led the troops forth to

*Sardēs, Sardium, f.   **Veiī, Veiōrum, m.

war.   4. The consuls will urge the citizens who live in the country not to come to Rome.   5. The consuls did not permit the ambassadors who had spoken against the war to set out for **(ad)** Greece.   6. The Greeks, having delayed at Troy for ten years, finally captured and burnt the city.   7. Few of the farmers in this valley seem to have tried to keep their grain.   8. I shall try to persuade the consul to permit you to leave Rome, for you will be much happier in the country.   9. Having thought that you had set out for the city, I spoke with your sister.   10. The enemy seem to think that we will not try to march to Carthage.

Roman jewelry

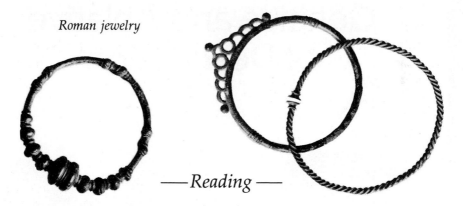

———*Reading*———

A DISASTER REUNITES BROTHERS

Mārcus et Lūcius frātrēs erant. Multōs annōs hī frātrēs, quī in eōdem oppidō fīnitimās domōs habēbant, inimīcissimī inter sē erant. Calamitāte tamen gravissimā ad amīcitiam reductī sunt. Sī scīre cupitis quō modō hoc factum sit, omnia quae ipse audīvī vōbīs nārrābō.

Erat oppidum antīquum, sub monte Vesuviō positum, Pompeiī nōmine, cuius aedificia pulcherrima erant. Mārcus ut negōtium quoddam gereret, ōlim prīmā lūce domō excessit, et Pompeiōs contendit.

Cum suum negōtium cōnfēcisset, domum redīre cōnstituit.

Paulum ex oppidō prōgressus, subitō terram movērī sēnsit. Simul nec sōl nec caelum ipsum cōnspicī poterat; ignēs autem summae magnitūdinis in monte Vesuviō vidēbantur. Hīs rēbus Mārcus ita perterritus est ut longius prōcēdere nōn posset. Eum dubitantem quīdam ex oppidō fugiēns ita monuit, "Nē dubitēmus! Nisi mors tibi grātior est quam vīta, mēcum venī!"

Mārcus vōce magis quam verbīs mōtus, "Frāter," inquit, "tēcum veniam et nunc et semper." Cognōverat enim deōs Lūcium sibi auxiliō mīsisse.

51

Ablative Absolute
Genitive and Ablative
of Description

Sandals from Roman Britain, one with hobnails

Amoto quaeramus seria ludo.

Joking aside, let us turn to serious matters. —HORACE

— *Syntax* —

THE ABLATIVE ABSOLUTE

The ablative absolute consists of two words in the ablative case loosely connected grammatically with the rest of the sentence. It may consist of: 1. a noun and a participle: **signō datō.** 2. two nouns: **Caesare imperātōre.** 3. a noun and an adjective: **perīculō magnō.** (rare)

The first construction (using the participle) is by far the most common of the three mentioned here.

The participle or adjective must agree with the noun in gender, number, and case.

The ablative absolute is usually best translated by a clause. It generally denotes time, cause, condition, or concession. The noun in the ablative absolute *never denotes the same person or thing as the subject or object of the main verb.*

1. Signō datō, oppidum oppugnāvērunt.
   (The signal having been given) When the signal had been given, they attacked the town.
2. Caesare imperātōre, ad victōriam exercitus dūcētur.
   (Caesar [being] general) If Caesar is general, the army will be led to victory.
3. Perīculō magnō, Caesar signum dedit.
   (The danger [being] great) Since the danger was great, Caesar gave the signal.
4. Multīs mīlitibus āmissīs, oppidum expugnāvimus.
   (Many soldiers having been lost) Although many soldiers had been lost, we took the town by storm.

Helps and Hints. The verb **sum** has no present participle. Consequently the connecting word *being* cannot be expressed in Latin, but must be supplied in the English translation. Study sentences 2 and 3.

PERFECT PARTICIPLES

There is no *perfect active* participle in Latin. We cannot put literally into Latin: *The leader, having given the signal, fought bravely.* There is no Latin word meaning *having given*, but the same idea may be expressed by changing the participle to the passive and making it agree with *signal* in the ablative instead of with *leader* in the nominative.

Signō datō, dux fortiter pugnāvit.
 (The signal having been given) Having given the signal, the leader fought bravely.

Such an ablative absolute may be rendered as an independent coordinate clause: *The leader gave the signal and fought bravely.*

GENITIVE AND ABLATIVE OF DESCRIPTION

The genitive or ablative modified by an adjective is used to describe the quality of a noun.

> vir magnae virtūtis *a man of great courage*
> vir magnā virtūte *a man with (of) great courage*

These constructions may not be used without the adjective; for "a man of courage" we can say only *a brave man*, **vir fortis.**

The genitive of description and the ablative of description have essentially the same meaning and are practically interchangeable, except that the genitive must be used for definite measurements. This use is called the genitive of measure.

> mūrus magnā altitūdine *a wall of great height*
> mūrus octō pedum *an eight-foot wall (a wall of eight feet)*

—— Vocabulary ——

collo'quium, collo'quī, n., *conference, conversation*
ini'tium, ini'tī, n., *beginning*
Rhē'nus, -ī, m., *the Rhine*

tū'tus, -a, -um, *safe*

quī'dam, quae'dam, quod'dam (quid'dam), (indef. adj. and pron.) *a certain, one, certain, some*

rūr'sus, (adv.) *back, again*

aggre'dior, -ī, aggres'sus sum, *approach, attack*
congre'dior, -ī, congres'sus sum, *meet, come together*
cōnse'quor, cōnse'quī, cōnse'cūtus sum, *pursue, overtake; obtain, gain*
ēgre'dior, -ī, ēgres'sus sum, *go out, disembark*
prōgre'dior, -ī, prōgres'sus sum, *advance, go forward*
se'quor, se'quī, secū'tus sum, *follow*
ve'reor, -ē'rī, ve'ritus sum, *fear*

—— Word Study ——

Quīdam is declined like **quī, quae, quod (quid)** + **dam,** except that an **m** before the **-dam** becomes **n: quendam, quandam, quōrundam, quārundam.** The partitive idea with **quīdam** (as with **paucī** and cardinal numerals) is expressed by the ablative of place from which (see Lesson 29).

> Quīdam ex nautīs ēgressī sunt.
> *Certain of the sailors have disembarked.*
> Quaedam dē puellīs proficīscitur.
> *One (a certain one) of the girls is setting out.*

—— Exercises ——

A. Translate.

1. Hostibus pulsīs . . . 2. Pāce factā . . . 3. Aedificiīs omnibus incēnsis . . . 4. Sagittīs frāctīs . . . 5. Forō complētō . . . 6. Mīlitibus dēfessīs . . . 7. Victōriā renūntiātā . . . 8. Caesare dūce . . . 9. Cursū cōnfectō . . . 10. Caesare Bibulōque cōnsulibus . . .

B. Translate.

1. These things having been finished . . . 2. After the terms of peace were proposed . . . 3. After seeing the storm . . . 4. Having announced the calamity . . . 5. The enemy's cavalry having been routed . . . 6. Under the leadership of Lentulus . . . 7. In Caesar's consulship. . . . 8. After reading the book . . . 9. Our march having been hindered . . . 10. The javelins having been thrown . . .

~~~~~~

Helps and Hints. Whenever you see a noun and a perfect passive participle in the ablative absolute construction in Latin, translate it first in the following way: After *blank* had been *blank(ed)*. Examples: **hostibus vīsīs,** after *the enemy* had been *seen;* **mīlite vulnerātō,** after the *soldier* had been *wounded*. This will give you a rough translation and you can then make a more exact one, if you need to.

~~~~~~

C. Read the Latin and translate.

1. Hīs rēbus gestīs Belgae statim lēgātōs ad Caesarem dē pāce mīsērunt.   2. Cum prīmum ē nāve ēgressus est vīdit quandam turrim centum pedum altitūdine.   3. Hīs cōpiīs coāctīs Brūtus castra in mediō monte posuit.   4. Lūcius cum puer magnā audāciā esset rēgem malum sagittā petīvit.   5. Omnibus fēminīs līberīsque ab urbe remōtīs adventum hostium exspectābant.   6. Itinere vīgintī mīlium passuum factō exercitus aggressus est magna hostium castra.   7. Litterīs acceptīs imperātor alterum oppidum hostium oppugnāre cōnstituit.   8. Quōdam diē ut domō excēdēbam ut cum amīcō meō congrederer parvum canem nigrum vīdī. 9. Colle occupātō nostrī ad flūmen maximā cum celeritāte cucurrērunt.   10. Quīdam ex senātōribus postulābant ut exercitus Athēnās mitterētur quī illam urbem aggrederētur.

D. Translate.

1. The soldiers, having pitched camp, were ordered to fill up the ditch.   2. (After) having marched nineteen miles from Corinth, the soldiers were ordered to make a six-foot ditch and a twelve-foot rampart.   3. Having done all of these things, the boys thought that their work was finished.   4. The Roman citizens who were living at Athens thought that our army would sail to Greece and disembark from the ships on the eighth day.   5. Having marched eighteen miles that day, all the soldiers were tired. 6. Since the Rhine is a river of great depth, I fear that we cannot lead our army across to attack the enemy.   7. Having seized this farmer's farmhouse, those evil men set fire to it.   8. Although they were about to approach the city at night, the women feared

nothing; but certain of the men wished to remain at home. 9. Having obtained suitable terms of peace, the Germans promised to surrender their weapons. 10. The consul, a man of great authority, talked with my friends for many hours, but could not persuade them to set out.

Male hair style of the first century

——*Reading*——

CAESAR SAILS TO BRITAIN

Caesar in īnsulam Britanniam proficīscī cōnstituerat. Ut cognōsceret quae rēs in īnsulā essent, lēgātum cum nāve longā praemīsit. Huic mandāvit ut, omnibus rēbus explōrātīs, ad sē venīret. Ipse cum omnibus cōpiīs in Morīnōs profectus est, quod inde erat brevissimus in Britanniam cursus. Hūc nāvēs undique ex fīnitimīs regiōnibus iussit convenīre.

Interim cōnsiliō eius cognitō ā multīs īnsulae cīvitātibus ad eum lēgātī vēnērunt quī pollicerentur sē futūrōs Populī Rōmānī amīcōs. Quibus audītīs, eōs hortātus ut in eā sententiā manērent in cīvitātēs rēmīsit.

Lēgātīs Britannōrum domum remissīs, Volusēnus, lēgātus ā Caesare ad Britanniam praemissus, Caesarī quae ibi vīdisset renūntiāvit. Sed ille, vir minimae virtūtis, nāve nōn ēgressus erat; nōn multa ergō imperātōrī renūntiāvit.

Itaque Caesar in nāvibus coāctis exercitum imposuit. Equitēs in ulteriōrem portum prōgredī et nāvēs ibi cōnscendere iussit. Ille cum quibusdam ex mīlitibus ad īnsulam accēdēbat. Ibi in omnibus collibus expositās hostium cōpiās cōnspexit. Hunc locum nōn tūtum arbitrātus nāve nōn ēgressus est.

52

Ferō and Eō

Shrine of the household gods from The House of the Vetti in Pompeii

Potest ex casa magnus vir exire.
A great man can come from a cabin.—SENECA

——Forms——

FERŌ AND EŌ

These verbs, used very frequently in Latin, are both irregular. Learn
the complete conjugations of these verbs on pages 463–464. Transitive
compounds of **eō,** like **adeō,** have passive forms, **adeor, adīris, adītur,**
etc. The present active participle of **eō** is **iēns, euntis.**

——Vocabulary——

e'ō, ī're, i'ī (ī'vī), i'tum, *go*
  a'deō, adī're, a'diī (adī'vī), a'ditum, *go toward, approach*
  ex'eō, exī're, ex'iī (exī'vī), ex'itum, *go out*
  re'deō, redī're, re'diī (redī'vī), re'ditum, *go back, return*
  trāns'eō, trānsī're, trāns'iī, (trānsī'vī), trāns'itum, *cross*
fe'rō, fer're, tu'lī, lātum, *bear, carry; bring; take; relate*
  ad'ferō, adfer're, at'tulī, allā'tum, *bring up, bring to; report*
  cōn'ferō, cōnfer're, con'tulī, collā'tum, *bring together, collect; compare*
  īn'ferō, īnfer're, in'tulī, illā'tum, *carry onward; bring upon, inflict*
  re'ferō, refer're, ret'tulī, relā'tum, *bring back, report*
  tol'lō, tol'lere, sus'tulī, sublā'tum, *raise, lift up; remove*

——Word Study——

Cōnferō, used reflexively, means *betake oneself, proceed, go.*
Īnferō. Bellum īnferre with the dative means *make war upon.*
Signum īnferre (*carry the standard onward*) is a military term meaning
to advance.
Referō. The reflexive **sē referre** and the idiom **pedem referre** mean *go
back, return.* In military terminology **pedem referre** means *give ground,
retreat.*

—— Exercises ——

A. Translate.

1. fers, fertur, vōs contuleritis 2. intulit, adībit, tollēbant
3. tulistis, trānsībunt, vōbīs bellum īnferunt 4. rettulerant, adiē-
runt, pedem rettulērunt 5. rediistī, adeunt, signum intulerint
6. lātus erit, exībant, mē referam 7. redeunt, intulerat, contulerit

B. Translate.

1. we shall go, he was crossing, they have removed 2. he is
approaching, they will bear, you have made war on us 3. he is
going back, I shall go out, we were giving ground 4. they had
inflicted, we approached, you will advance 5. he bears, they
bring, I betake myself 6. they have brought back, we were crossing, they were proceeding 7. you have collected, you will cross,
I go

C. Read the Latin and translate.

1. Rōmānī sē virtūte reliquās gentēs superāre arbitrātī sunt. 2. Mē
cōnferam rūs paucīs diēbus; tum domum rūrsus redībō. 3. Domō
omnia sustulerant et Rōmam sē cōnferēbant. 4. Quīdam mercātor
ad Britanniam ōlim nāvigāvit ut servōs referret. 5. Flūmen
trānsībunt ut hostēs fugientēs sequantur in omnēs partēs.
6. Cōnsul domī manēbit nec Gallīs bellum īnferet. 7. Sī Rōmae
manēbimus, necesse erit iniūriās cuiusdam dē nōbilibus ferre.
8. Cum decima legiō signa īnfert, hostēs pedem referunt.
9. Caesarem Germānīs bellum audācter intulisse scīmus.
10. Domum trāns Rhēnum sē cōnferent nē ab exercitū Rōmānō
vincantur.

D. Translate.

1. They brought together all their weapons from home into the
towns across the Rhine. 2. The lieutenant will go back home to
see his children, since he cannot remain at Rome. 3. The king
said that his town had been captured and his people carried back
to Rome. 4. We marched home to make war on the evil chiefs.
5. They could not bring help to their men from Rome. 6. Certain
of the messengers reported to the centurion that they had seen an
ambush behind the camp. 7. The army will cross the river much

more quickly in large ships.   8. The Roman army then proceeded to the farthest lands of the Germans, and returned home in the same summer.   9. When help had been brought, the wounded soldier was carried back to the town.   10. We tried to cross the river, although it was very wide and very deep.

—— *Reading* ——

THE DAUGHTER OF CREON

Iāson et Mēdēa, ob ea mala quae ibi fēcerant patriam relinquere coāctī, ē Thessaliā exiērunt et Corinthum sē cōntulērunt. Creōn, rēx Corinthī, ūnam fīliam habēbat. Iāsonī relātum est fīliam Creontis pulcherrimam esse atque ille eam in mātrimōnium dūcere cupiēbat. At Mēdēa, cum intellegeret quae ille in animō habēret, haec aegrē ferēbat. Hoc igitur cōnsilium cēpit. Vestem parāvit in quā erat venēnum cuius vīs tanta erat ut vestem gerentem statim interficeret.

Hanc vestem ferēns Mēdēa domum Creontis iit et fīliae rēgis dōnum dedit. Illa dōnum libenter accēpit. Cum vestis in manibus eius esset, tantum dolōrem sēnsit ut ē vītā excēderet. Cīvēs Corinthī, magnō clāmōre sublātō, Mēdēam Corinthō expulērunt.

The Atrium Vestae, type of convent where the six Vestal Virgins lived

Perfer et obdura; dolor hic tibi proderit olim.

Be patient and tough; some day this pain will be useful to you. — OVID

REVIEW **13** (LESSONS 49–52)

— Vocabulary Drill —

A. Give the genitive, gender, and meaning of the following nouns.

colloquium	rūs	spatium	tempestās
initium	sagitta	studium	

B. Give the other nominative singular forms, and the meanings, of the following adjectives.

dēfessus	impedītus	mīrus	quīdam	tūtus

C. Give the principal parts and meanings of the following verbs.

adeō	ēgredior	patior	redeō
adferō	eō	pellō	referō
aggredior	exeō	permittō	renūntiō
arbitror	ferō	permoveō	sequor
cōnferō	hortor	polliceor	tollō
congredior	incendō	prōdūcō	trānseō
cōnor	īnferō	proficīscor	vāstō
cōnsequor	loquor	prōgredior	vereor
cōnservō	moror	prōpōnō	videor

D. Give the meanings of **cum** *and* **rūrsus**.

— Drill on Forms —

A. Give synopses in the indicative, subjunctive, and (where applicable) imperative of the following verbs.

1. vereor *in the 1st person singular*
2. sequor *in the 2d person singular*
3. adferō *in the 2d person singular passive*

4. cōnferō *in the 3d person singular active*
5. patior *in the 1st person plural*
6. exeō *in the 2d person plural*
7. cōnor *in the 2d person plural*
8. trānseō *in the 3d person plural passive*

B. Give, name, and translate the five infinitives of **referō.**

C. Give, name, and translate the three participles of **adeō.**

D. Translate.

1. proficīscētur
2. patī
3. morātus
4. colloquēbantur
5. cōnāns

6. arbitrātī erant
7. exībunt
8. īnfers
9. rettulistis
10. trānsiēns

E. Translate.

1. she promised
2. having tried
3. having been produced
4. they follow
5. while attacking

6. to seem
7. to speak
8. we shall suffer
9. you (*sing.*) bear
10. he had crossed

— *Drill on Syntax* —

A. Translate.

1. domō
2. urbe captā
3. mīles magnīs vīribus
4. Rōmae
5. multōs diēs

6. trānseant!
7. quartā vigiliā
8. nē prōgrediāmur
9. paulō ante
10. Rōmā

B. Translate.

1. having burned the town
2. queen in name
3. at home
4. after seizing the bridge
5. from Corinth

6. for sixteen miles
7. within eight hours
8. much more quickly
9. let him not delay
10. a hundred-foot tower

The Temple of Vesta in the Forum at Rome. (top) The temple, partly reconstructed from fragments, is shown as it looked in antiquity. (bottom) The round shape was derived from primitive round thatched huts.

—— Exercises ——

A. Translate.

1. Cum rogātūrus essem cūr omnia animālia in nostrum agrum contulissēs, subitō discessistī. 2. Tertiā vigiliā quīdam dē mīlitibus quī in īnsidiīs manēbant cōnsulem interfēcit. 3. Tria mīlia passuum circum montem prōgressus, domum ante noctem redīre cōnātus est. 4. Rōmae tredecim diēs morātī sumus ut tōtam urbem pulcherrimam vidērēmus. 5. Captīvī ex castrīs ēgredī et fugere cōnātī ab equitibus, quī eīs celeriōrēs erant, interfectī sunt. 6. Multī Rōmānī arbitrābantur Caesarem omnium imperātōrum maximum esse et virtūte et auctōritāte. 7. Puellae pollicitae sunt sē cum suīs mātribus quam celerrimē reditūrās. 8. Decima legiō, flūmen multa mīlia passuum secūta, castra sub monte posuit quae praesidiō itinerī essent. 9. Nāvibus tempestātis timōre remōtīs, exercitus flūmen quīndecim pedum altitūdine trānsīre nōn potuit. 10. Imperātor lēgātum, virum magnae auctoritātis, hortātus est nē cum reliquīs mīlitibus proficīscerētur.

B. Translate

1. After finishing the work, bring me a few of the books which you are reading. 2. It happens that the general has not arrived, for which reason I fear that we cannot keep the enemy from our walls. 3. Marcus, I urge you not to ask the men what they have seen. 4. He said that he would follow us for five miles, and then go back home. 5. As soon as he had reported the calamity to the people, the man who had been chosen king urged everyone to flee from the city. 6. Since in the farthest lands of the Germans there were no towns nor cities, the barbarians lived in the forests and fields. 7. So great a number of ships was seen in the river that we thought that the enemy had arrived. 8. Although the messenger is tired, he has been sent by the chief to take a letter back to the consul and make him more certain about the danger. 9. We attacked the enemy's winter camp with fire and javelins and arrows, and other weapons suitable for the attack. 10. After delaying at home for a few days, I decided to go back to Rome with great speed.

53

Volō, Nōlō, Mālō
Dative of Possession
Negative Commands

A mosaic charm meant to protect the household against the evil eye

Libenter homines id quod volunt credunt.

Men gladly believe that which they wish for.—CAESAR

—— Forms ——

VOLŌ, NŌLŌ, AND MĀLŌ

These verbs are irregular in the present indicative and the present subjunctive. Learn the following:

vo'lō, vel'le, vo'luī,   *wish, be willing*
nō'lō, nōl'le, nō'luī,   *be unwilling, not wish*
mā'lō, māl'le, mā'luī,   *prefer*

PRESENT INDICATIVE

volō	volumus	nōlō	nōlumus	mālō	mālumus
vīs	vultis	nōn vīs	nōn vultis	māvīs	māvultis
vult	volunt	nōn vult	nōlunt	māvult	mālunt

PRESENT SUBJUNCTIVE

velim	velimus	nōlim	nōlīmus	mālim	mālīmus
velīs	velītis	nōlīs	nōlītis	mālīs	mālītis
velit	velint	nōlit	nōlint	mālit	mālint

All other forms are regular.

—— Syntax ——

The infinitive with subject accusative is used with **volō, nōlō, mālō** when the subject of the infinitive is not the same as that of the governing verb. When the subject of both verbs is the same, the objective infinitive is used.

Volō tē īre.   *I wish you to go.*
Volō īre.   *I wish to go.*

There is no imperative form of **volō** or **mālō. Nōlō,** however, has present imperative forms: *sing.,* **nōlī;** *pl.,* **nōlīte.** These are regularly used with the infinitive of other verbs to form the negative imperative.

Nōlī currere.   *Do not run. (be unwilling to run)*
Nōlite loquī.   *Do not speak. (be unwilling to speak)*

DATIVE OF POSSESSION

Possession may be expressed by the dative of the possessor with **sum**, the subject being the thing possessed.

Puerō canis erat.   *The boy had a dog (a dog was to the boy).*

—— Vocabulary ——

ae'tās, aetā'tis, f., *age*
clas'sis, clas'sis, f., *fleet*
facul'tās, facultā'tis, f., *opportunity, chance, ability*
hos'pes, hos'pitis, m., *stranger; guest, host*
mēn'sis, mēn'sis, m., *month*
or'dō, or'dinis, m., *order*

appropin'quō, -ā're, -ā'vī, -ā'tum, *approach, draw near*
com'parō, -ā're, -ā'vī, -ā'tum, *prepare; compare; get*
cōnscrī'bō, -ere, cōnscrīp'sī, cōnscrīp'tum, *enroll, enlist*
dis'cō, -ere, di'dicī, ——, *learn*
exer'ceō, -ē're, exer'cuī, exercitum, *train, exercise, practice*
īnsti'tuō, -ere, īnsti'tuī, īnstitū'tum, *build, establish, set up*
mālō, māl'le, mā'luī, ——, *wish more, prefer*
nō'lō, nōl'le, nō'luī, ——, *not wish, be unwilling*
osten'dō, -ere, osten'dī, osten'tum, *show, display*
ve'hō, -ere, vex'ī, vec'tum, *carry, transport*
vo'lō, vel'le, vo'luī, ——, *wish, be willing*

inte'reā, (adv.) *meanwhile*
qui'dem, (adv.) *at least, at any rate; as a matter of fact, to be sure, indeed*
nē . . . qui'dem, (adv.) *not even*
quo'que, (adv.) *also, too*

—— Word Study ——

Appropinquō may take either the dative of the indirect object or the accusative of place to which with **ad.**

Oppidō (ad oppidum) appropinquāmus.
We are approaching the town.

Nē . . . quidem. The word modified goes between the two words.

> Nē Mārcus quidem hoc didicit.
> *Not even Marcus has learned this.*

Quoque comes after the word it modifies.
Vehō in the passive may mean *travel, ride* or *sail;* the vehicle is in the ablative of means.

> Illā nāve vectus sum.   *I sailed in that ship.*
> Equō vehitur.   *He is riding a horse.*

—— *Exercises* ——

A. Translate.

1. volunt, vīs, nōn vult   2. mālēs, nōn vīs, nē mālīmus   3. mālunt, vultis, voluerās   4. nōn vultis, nōluistī, māvīs   5. volent, māluī, nōluērunt   6. volumus, mālēbas, nōlīte   7. Nōlī mihi appropinquāre.

B. Translate.

1. we shall prefer, you (*sing.*) wish   2. they were unwilling, he had wished   3. he was unwilling, they will prefer   4. you (*pl.*) will wish, we do not wish   5. to prefer, let them wish   6. you (*pl.*) wish, he prefers   7. Do not speak!

C. Read the Latin and translate.

1. Equō vehī vult Rōmā ut collēs trānseat.   2. Multī mīlitēs, quī subsidiō legiōnī missī erant, paucīs mēnsibus domum redīre mālēbant.   3. Nē Caesar quidem decimam legiōnem praesidiō urbī mittere volēbat.   4. Imperātor rogāvit cūr maiōrēs cōpiās in Galliā hōc mēnse nōn cōnscrīpsissēmus.   5. Dux victus per viās Rōmānās carrō vectus est.   6. Volet esse auxiliō cōnsulibus sed Rōmae manēre nōlet.   7. Māvīsne ad urbem mēcum īre quam domī manēre?   8. Virī octō mēnsēs Rōmae exercitī ad Galliam missī sunt.   9. Est nōbīs classis maxima quā frūmentum et arma ad Āfricam ferāmus.   10. Sciuntne cūr exercitus noster illīs castrīs sine impedīmentīs appropinquāverit?

D. Translate.

1. He wishes to go to Rome with the lieutenant to see the seven hills.   2. Since they were approaching the lands of the enemy, they did not want the cavalry to cross the hills.   3. He will command the wounded messenger to go to Rome and remain at home.   4. The Romans wished to train their sailors in the fleet, rather than in schools.   5. We approached the town to speak with the messenger who had been caught in ambush.   6. They are urging him to set out from the town and follow the captives. 7. He persuaded the citizens not to go out of their boundaries with all their forces.   8. They were not willing that the soldiers who had been enrolled in the farthest territory of Germany go to Rome.   9. I do not want you to think that I have ever sailed on that ship.   10. Not even Caesar wanted the entire army to be transported to Britain.

—— Reading ——

CROESUS AND SOLON

Croesus, rēx Lȳdiae, maximam fāmam propter suam potestātem et pecūniam cōnsecūtus est. Nē rēgnum Persārum quidem erat maius. Multī ex omnibus partibus Graeciae ut tantum rēgem vidērent Sardēs veniēbant.

Athēnīs habitābat Solōn, omnium suōrum cīvium sapientissimus. Hic quoque audīverat quam prōsperum rēgnum Croesus īnstituisset atque id vidēre voluit. Itaque nāve vectus orīs Lȳdiae appropinquāvit. Hunc hospitem Croesus benignē accēpit et eī omnia ostendit. Omnibus vīsīs, "Solōn," Croesus inquit, "quem omnium hominum fēlīcissimum putās?" Rēx vērō crēdēbat Solōnem sē fēlīcissimum esse dictūrum. "Tellum Athēniēnsem," respondit Solōn. "Num alium fēlīciōrem quam mē putās?" clāmāvit Croesus. "Nōlī crēdere, Croese," respondit Solōn, "pecūniam hominēs fēlīcēs facere. Meā aetāte didicī virōs scīre nōn posse quid ante mortem accidat. Post mortem vir 'fēlīx' appellārī potest."

54

Fīō
Subordinate Clauses
in Indirect Discourse

Arch of Constantine, Rome—relief panel with sacrificial scene

Cito fit quod dii volunt.

What the gods want happens soon. —PETRONIUS

— *Forms* —

Fīō. The verb **fīō** is used as the passive of **faciō,** which has no passive forms in the tenses formed from the present stem. For the perfect tenses of **fīō** we use the perfect passive of **faciō. Fīō** takes a predicate nominative, like **sum.** Learn the complete conjugation of **fīō.**

Tē rēgem faciēmus. *We shall make you king.*
Rēx fīēs. *You will be made king.*

| INDICATIVE | | SUBJUNCTIVE | |
SINGULAR	PLURAL	SINGULAR	PLURAL
PRESENT			
fi'ō	fī'mus	fi'am	fīā'mus
fīs	fī'tis	fi'ās	fīā'tis
fit	fī'unt	fi'at	fi'ant
IMPERFECT			
fīē'bam	fīēbā'mus	fi'erem	fierē'mus
fīē'bās	fīēbā'tis	fi'erēs	fierē'tis
fīē'bat	fīē'bant	fi'eret	fi'erent
FUTURE			
fi'am	fīē'mus		
fi'ēs	fīē'tis		
fi'et	fi'ent		

— *Syntax* —

SUBORDINATE CLAUSES IN INDIRECT DISCOURSE

A subordinate clause within an indirect statement, command, or question has its verb in the subjunctive. The subjunctive is used because the action of the verb, being merely reported, is not seen as real.

Subordinate clauses in indirect discourse usually follow sequence of tenses, depending on the tense of the verb introducing the indirect discourse.

> Dīxit virōs quī Rōmam vēnissent posterō diē discessisse.
> *He said that the men who had come to Rome left the next day.*

—— Vocabulary ——

ae′dēs, ae′dis, f., *temple*; pl., *house*
cae′dēs, cae′dis, f., *slaughter, murder*
mūnī′tiō, mūnītiō′nis, f., *fortification*
ob′ses, ob′sidis, m., *hostage*
ra′tiō, ratiō′nis, f., *account; plan; manner; reason*
rī′pa, -ae, f., *bank (of a stream)*

ae′ger, ae′gra, ae′grum, *sick*
aper′tus, -a, -um, *open, exposed*
ēgre′gius, -a, -um, *outstanding*
in′teger, in′tegra, in′tegrum, *untouched, undiminished; whole, entire*
le′vis, -e, *light* (in weight or importance)
mari′timus, -a, -um, *of the sea*
mīlitā′ris, -re, *military*
necessā′rius, -a, -um, *necessary;* (as a noun), *relative*
prū′dēns, prūden′tis, *foresighted; wise, prudent*
re′cēns, recen′tis, *fresh, new, recent*
ve′tus, ve′teris, *old*

fī′ō, fi′erī, factus sum, *be made, become; happen*
vēn′dō, -ere, ven′didī, ven′ditum, *sell*

—— Word Study ——

Aeger. The adverb of this adjective, **aegrē,** means *with difficulty, scarcely.*
Vetus is a consonant-stem (not an **i**-stem): its ablative singular is **vetere** and its genitive plural **veterum.** It is much more general in its meaning than either **antiquus** or **senex,** and means *old* in all three senses: not young, not new, and not modern.

—— Exercises ——

A. Translate.

1. Mārcum cōnsulem faciāmus.   2. Cōnsul factus est.
3. Imperātor fīet.   4. Fīat lūx!   5. Mīlitēs fīēbant.

B. Translate.

1. What happened?   2. He was made a lieutenant.   3. They will become citizens.   4. Caesar was made a dictator.   5. It cannot happen here.

C. Read the Latin and translate.

1. Per clāmōrēs certiōrēs fīēbāmus* hostēs sē recēpisse ad montem quī nōn longē abesset.   2. Dīxit veterem nautam quī ex oppidō exīret obsidem esse.   3. Amīcōs hortātus est ut sē sequerentur Corinthum, quae centum mīlia passuum abesset.   4. Dīxērunt sē proficīscī mālle ad urbem quam trāns campōs vidēre possent.
5. Imperātor, recentī classis victōriā adductus, ad Hispāniam proficīscī voluit.   6. Mīlitēs quī in alterā rīpā stārent hostium esse scīvimus.   7. Intereā certior factus est obsidēs per apertam portam post mūnītiōnem fūgisse.   8. Ex urbe proficīscentur nē iniūria ā mīlitibus fīat.   9. Spērō omnēs puerōs quī ad Eurōpam itūrī sint Rōmae paucōs diēs morātūrōs.   10. Multōs profectōs esse ut cum rēge colloquerentur mē certiōrem fēcit.

D. Translate.

1. I know that if you wish to persuade him you will try to learn his opinion.   2. The messenger informed the lieutenant that the hills, which were three in number, had been surrounded with a fortification.   3. When the centurion had been informed of the danger, the hostages were led to the other bank of the river.   4. He knew that the men who were with him were outstanding senators.   5. The infantry were unwilling to carry light swords, since they preferred heavier weapons.   6. I have heard that he cannot

---

* *To make more certain,* **certiōrem facere,** *and to be made more certain,* **certior fierī,** *are idioms meaning to inform and to be informed. They may be followed by indirect discourse or by the ablative with* **dē** *(about, or concerning).*

be enlisted because he has been wounded before. 7. The wise father did not ask his son what was happening in the camp where he was. 8. Did he ask when the hostages who were being brought from Britain would come to Rome? 9. They will be informed that the old general who has been wounded in battle will not come home. 10. The slaughter of all the sick animals was done the same day.

—— *Reading* ——

HORACE, A ROMAN POET

Q. Horātius Flaccus puer Rōmam adductus est ā patre, quī scīvit fīlium suum in eā urbe disciplīnam meliōrem acceptūrum quam sī domī Venusiae manēret. Mōs erat ut puer Rōmānus servum semper habēret quī cum puerō ad lūdum īret, ut eum ā malīs dēfenderet. Pater ipse Horātī hoc servī officium accipere māluit.

Posteā Horātius Athēnās profectus est. Ibi quōsdam clārōs virōs et Graecōs et Rōmānōs nōvit, inter quōs erat M. Brūtus, quī bellum cum Octāviānō gerere parābat. Horātius sē cum Brūtī cōpiīs iūnxit. Duōbus post annīs, exercitū Brūtī victō, Horātius domum rediit miser et sine pecūniā. Eō tempore carmina scrībere incipiēbat.

Mox autem per Vergilium, alium poētam, auxilium ā potentī amīcō Augustī accēpit. Hic amīcus, Maecēnās nōmine, vir ēgregius, carminibus Horātī audītīs, eī pecūniam atque vīllam in collibus Rōmae propinquīs positam dedit. Horātius, iam imperātōris amīcus, ob sua carmina et levia et gravia nōtissimus in poētīs fīēbat. Carminibus docēbat virum integrum vītam beātiōrem agere quam eum quī potēns esset.

Dē fonte qui erat prope suam vīllam cecinit: "Fīēs nōbilium tū quoque fontium"; atque suam ipsam glōriam hīs verbīs praedīxit: "Nōn omnis moriar." Hoc vērē dictum est, quod etiam hodiē plūrimī sciunt quis fuerit Horātius.

55

Review of
Indirect Statement
Indirect Commands
Indirect Questions

Pantheon, Rome—National Gallery, Washington

Omnia iam fient fieri quae posse negabam.

Everything which I used to say could not happen will happen now.

—OVID

—*Syntax*—

INDIRECT STATEMENT

Review the explanation of indirect statement in Lesson 39. It states that a verb of *saying, thinking, knowing,* etc. in English followed by the word *that* requires the main verb to be in the infinitive form in Latin with the subject in the accusative case. Lesson 54 adds that a subordinate clause in Latin within an indirect statement, command or question has its verb in the subjunctive.

> Sciō puerōs venīre.   *I know that the boys are coming.*
> Sciō puerōs quī sint inimīcī venīre.
> *I know that the boys who are unfriendly are coming.*

The tense of the infinitive depends on the relation of time between the main verb and the infinitive. That is, does it come at the same time, the time before, or the time after the main verb?

INDIRECT COMMANDS

Lesson 45 explains that certain verbs of asking, commanding, advising, etc., require the subjunctive in Latin introduced by **ut** or **nē**. Some of these verbs take the dative case for the person commanded, some the accusative, and some the ablative with **ā** or **ab.** Review the list of these verbs on page 263. Remember that the tense of the subjunctive verb follows the rule for sequence of tenses. (Lesson 46)

> Rogat puerōs nē currant.   *He asks the boys not to run.*
> Rogāvit puerōs nē currerent.   *He asked the boys not to run.*

INDIRECT QUESTIONS

Lesson 47 explains that an indirect question usually following a verb of asking, saying, knowing, etc., and introduced by an interrogative pronoun, adjective, or adverb has its verb in the subjunctive, following sequence of tenses.

Rogat quid faciāmus.　　*He asks what we are doing, will do.*
Rogat quid fēcerimus.　　*He asks what we have done.*
　But
Rogāvit quid facerēmus.　　*He asked what we were doing, would do.*
Rogāvit quid fēcissēmus.　　*He asked what we had done.*

—— *Vocabulary* ——

au'deō, -ēre, au'sus sum, *dare*
ca'dō, -ere, ce'cidī, cā'sum, *fall*
cae'dō, -ere, cecī'dī, cae'sum, *cut, cut down, kill*
e'mō, -ere, ē'mī, emp'tum, *buy*
hi'emō, -ā're, -ā'vī, -ā'tum, *spend the winter*
o'rior, -ī'rī, or'tus sum, *rise, arise*
po'tior, -ī'rī, potī'tus sum, *get possession of* (with abl. of means)
tan'gō, -ere, te'tigī, tāc'tum, *touch*
ū'tor, -ī, ū'sus sum, *use* (with abl. of means)

bis, (adv.) *twice*
cir'citer, (adv.) *about, approximately* (with numbers)
fe'rē, (adv.) *almost, nearly* (with numbers and words of quantity)
frūs'trā, (adv.) *in vain*
i'tem, (adv.) *likewise*
omnī'nō, (adv.) *altogether, in all, at all*
repen'te, (adv.) *suddenly*
su'prā, (adv.) *above*
vix, (adv.) *hardly, scarcely, with difficulty*

—— *Word Study* ——

Audeō has active forms in the present system, but only passive forms in the perfect system. Such a verb is called semideponent. Its meanings are active throughout.

Cadō and **caedō** bear the same relation to each other as "to fall" and "to fell" in English.

Cum arborem caedimus, cadit.　　*When we fell a tree, it falls.*

Each of these two verbs has many compounds, in which **caedō** becomes **-cīdō, -cīdere, -cīdī, -cīsum,** and **cadō** becomes **-cidō, -cidere, -cidī, -cāsum.**

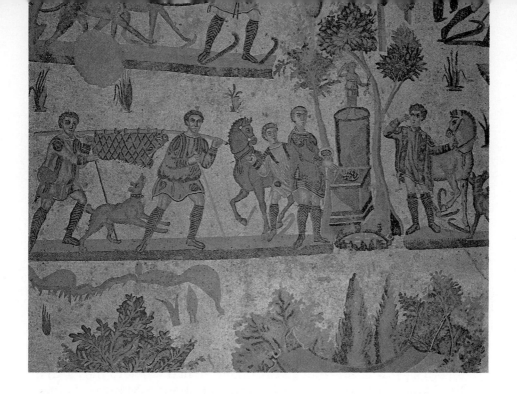

Thank-offering offered to Diana, goddess of the chase, after a successful boar hunt.
Mosaic from Piazza Armerina

—— Exercises ——

A. Translate.

1. Dīcit sōlem orīrī. 2. Putāmus puerōs id discere. 3. Arbitrātī sunt sē exercēre militēs dēbēre. 4. Classem appropinquāre existimāvī. 5. Oppidō nōs potītōs esse dīxerant. 6. Pater suīs fīliīs persuāsit nē equīs veherentur. 7. Obsidēs rogābant ut līberārentur. 8. Tē hortor nē animal tangās. 9. Ā mātre fīliae petīvērunt ut in Hispāniā hiemāre sē paterētur. 10. Puellae puerīs "Nōlīte" inquiunt "nōs sequī!" 11. Scīsne quid acciderit? 12. Rogāvit cui librōs dedissētis. 13. Cognōscēmus ubi amīcī nostrī hiement. 14. Gladiō frūstrā ūsus est. 15. Didicimus cūr mīlitēs nōn exercitī essent.

B. Read the Latin and translate.

1. Fēminae dīxērunt sē vīdisse animālia quae in silvā caesa essent. 2. Mīles item mē monuit nē eam turrim adīrem. 3. Quīdam rēx ōlim mandāvit ut circiter mīlle captīvī ex urbe dūcerentur. 4. Pater fīlium rogāvit cūr parvum animal cecīdis-

set.   5. Didicimus nē imperātōrem quidem fīnibus hostium potīrī potuisse.   6. Senātōris līberī dīxērunt sē nōlle diūtius sē exercēre.   7. Senex aeger ā filiābus petīvit ut cibus sibi darētur.   8. Rogāvit num māllēs Rōmae quam in Graeciā hiemāre.   9. Peditēs ducī respondērunt sē cum equitibus iter facere nōlle.   10. Prūdēns imperātor obsidibus imperāvit ut in praesidiō multōs mēnsēs manērent.

C. Translate

1. Do you know who said that I did not want to buy that book?   2. I heard that a sick animal had fallen from the high tree.   3. That outstanding consul urged the senators not to free the hostages.   4. My mother urged her guests to go with her into the garden.   5. We promised to winter with our friends for five months in Italy and Greece.   6. He thought that we ought not to use those long swords.   7. He saw that a very high tree had fallen to the earth on the bank of the river.   8. We hear that about a hundred soldiers were killed when we took possession of the fortification.   9. He says that he will buy about twenty horses next month.   10. I do not think that he will dare to touch the money.

Funeral chorus of women (5th century B.C. tomb) National Museum, Naples

Funerary relief with chariot—Lateran Museum, Vatican, Rome

—— *Reading* ——

OCTAVIAN

Post Iūlī Caesaris mortem illī quī eum occīderant Rōmā fūgērunt. Imperium exercitūs Rōmānī Marcō Antōniō, virō summae auctōritātis quī Caesarī amīcus fuerat, ā senātū datum est. Octāviānus autem quī posteā Augustus est appellātus, Rōmam ā Graeciā quam celerrimē vēnit, atque imperium sibi petīvit. Tandem Octāviānus pācem et amīcitiam cum Antōniō sociīsque eius cōnfirmāvit. Hī duo prīncipēs, brevī spatiō intermissō, inimīcōs Caesaris oppressērunt.

Paulō posteā Antōnius ad prōvinciam suam profectus apud Cleopātram, rēgīnam Aegyptiōrum, morābātur. Quīdam cīvēs Rōmānī dīxērunt Antōnium Cleopātram populī Rōmānī rēgīnam factūrum esse. Hīs rēbus incitātus Octāviānus bellum Antōniō intulit et victōriam cōnsecūtus est. Omnibus inimīcīs per tōtum orbem terrārum victīs, Octāviānus Rōmam rediit ut sōlus cīvitātem cum pāce regeret.

Id quod Iūlius Caesar facere cōnātus erat cōnfēcit Octāviānus Augustus. Bellī timōre atque perīculō cīvēs Rōmānōs līberāvit. Salūs prōvinciārum Augustō magnae cūrae erat. Itaque postquam cognōvit quantās iniūriās passae essent, aliās prōvnciās regēbat ipse, aliās senātuī commīsit. Ille omnia tam bene gessit ut ā senātū pater patriae appellārētur et post mortem suam in numerō deōrum habērētur.

56

Impersonal Verbs

Diana, Roman Fresco, National Museum, Naples

Mendacem oportet esse memorem.
A liar must be good at remembering. —QUINTILIAN

——*Syntax*——

IMPERSONAL VERBS

An impersonal verb is a verb which either has no subject (e.g. *It is raining*), or has a subject which may be an infinitive, an infinitive phrase, or a clause. **Licet** and **oportet** are two common impersonal verbs in Latin. **Licet** takes the dative for the person, and an infinitive.

> Licet mihi īre.
> *I am permitted to go (It is permitted to me to go).*

Oportet takes the accusative for the person and the infinitive.

> Oportet eōs discēdere.
> *They ought to depart (It is necessary that they depart).*

Accidit, *It happens,* has as its subject a substantive clause of result.

> Accidit ut īre nōn possīmus.   *It happens that we cannot go.*

When a Latin writer wishes to state that an action took place, but without specifying the subject, he uses an intransitive verb impersonally in the passive.

> Perventum est ad montēs.   *The mountains were arrived at.*
> Diū et acriter pugnātum est.   *Fighting went on long and fiercely.*

Do not try to translate such passive intransitives literally; "It was arrived at the mountains" is nonsense in English.

——*Vocabulary*——

ag'men, ag'minis, n., *line of march, army on the march, column*
an'cora, -ae, f., *anchor*
auc'tor, auctō'ris, m., *author, originator, founder, sponsor*
cā'sus, -ūs, m., *fall; chance, accident; fate*
la'tus, la'teris, n., *side, flank*
ōs, ō'ris, n., *mouth, face*
pa'lūs, palū'dis, f., *swamp, marsh*
prae'da, -ae, f., *booty*

cē'terī, -ae, -a, *the rest of, the other*
complū'rēs, complū'ra, *several, quite a few*

au'geō, -ē're, aux'ī, auc'tum, *increase, strengthen*
cōnsī'dō, -ere, cōnsē'dī, cōnses'sum, *sit down; settle, encamp*
con'venit, -ī're, convē'nit, *it is convenient*
do'leō, -ē're, do'luī, do'litum, *grieve, be sorry; grieve for*
explō'rō, -ā're, -ā'vī, -ā'tum, *search out, explore, reconnoiter*
li'cet, -ē're, li'cuit, *it is permitted*
opor'tet, -ē're, opor'tuit, *it is necessary, it is proper*
pertur'bō, -ā're, -ā'vī, -ā'tum, *alarm, upset, throw into confusion*
susci'piō, -ere, suscē'pī, suscep'tum, *undertake*
te'gō, -ere, tēx'ī, tec'tum, *cover*
vī'vō, -ere, vīx'ī, vīc'tum, *live, be alive*

—— Word Study ——

Agmen. In military terminology **prīmum agmen** means *the van*, **novissimum agmen** *the rear*.
Convenit. Convenit is used in the same way as **oportet.**

> Convenit eōs discēdere.
> *It is convenient that they depart (That they depart is convenient.).*

—— Exercises ——

A. Translate.

1. Accidit ut pervenīret.   2. Mihi nōn licuit nāvigāre.   3. Mīlitī exīre nōn licuit.   4. Oportet līberōs ambulāre.   5. Nōs explōrāre palūdem oportuit.

B. Translate.

1. She was not permitted to write a letter.   2. He happened to be away.   3. It was necessary for the column to depart.   4. We were not permitted to go out.   5. It happens that he has been wounded.

C. Read the Latin and translate.

1. Accidit cāsū ut Caesaris lēgātus duōs peditēs trāns flūmen mīsisset quī palūdem explōrārent.   2. Dolēmus cāsum nostrī exer-

citūs, in quem hostēs impetum ab apertō latere fēcērunt. 3. Magistrō mandātum erat ut hostium adventū ancoram tolleret, sed cāsū accidit ut abesset. 4. Oportēbitne Caesarem mūnīre omnia oppida prīmā aestāte? 5. Amīcīs meīs domum cōnsulis vidēre nōn licuit. 6. Ferē tōtus exercitus perturbātus est cum sē circumventum esse repente vīdisset. 7. Nūntiō imperātum est ut īret cum peditibus quī silvās post castra hostium explōrārent. 8. Accidit item ut sciat quis sit huius cōnsuētūdinis auctor. 9. Cum castrīs prīmum agmen appropinquāret novissimum agmen cum hostibus contendēbat. 10. Ferē omnēs fēminās dolēre quod virī in bellō vulnerātī aut interfectī essent dīxit.

D. Translate.

1. The boys were with difficulty persuaded to undertake this work. 2. Having gained possession of the other bank of the Rhine, they progressed about ten miles into Germany. 3. It happens by chance that I have gone to Rome twice already, but I am willing to go again. 4. As soon as the anchors had been thrown from the ship, the sailors disembarked with great speed. 5. On the exposed flank our men were forced to fight with great daring; fighting also went on in (ā) the rear. 6. So much booty was taken from the captured town that the soldiers tried in vain to carry it home. 7. The rest of the citizens were taken to a swamp so that the enemy would not find them. 8. It is necessary for us to remain in this wretched town, since we cannot return home. 9. You will not be permitted to go to the games with your friends. 10. Although the Rhine had been reached, Marcus was not permitted to lead his men into the German territory.

—— *Reading* ——

A NEW CONSTITUTION

Athēniēnsēs, Solōne duce, īnsulā Salamīne potītī sunt. Īnsulā captā, multī tamen cīvēs inopiā omnium rērum et nōbilium iniūriā opprimēbantur. Plūrimī magnopere dolēbant. Itaque complūrēs cīvēs ab Solōne petēbant ut imperium caperet et populum inopiā iniūriāque līberāret. "Tē," inquiunt, "oportet esse rēgem." Sed Solōn sē rēgem appellārī nōn passus est. Tum ille prīnceps cīvitātis appellātus est atque auctor novārum lēgum novam ratiōnem reī pūblicae īnstituit.

Optimīs lēgibus cōnstitūtīs et novīs cīvium ōrdinibus īnstitūtīs, urbs Athēnae potestāte et magnitūdine aucta est.

Tum Solōn Athēnīs diūtius manēre nōluit. Ille enim verēbātur nē cīvēs sē esse dictātōrem māllent. Itaque Athēniēnsibus, "Cīvēs," inquit, "licetne mihi īre in aliās cīvitātēs?" Cīvibus persuāsum est ut Solōnī exīre licēret. Atque pollicitī sunt sē dum ille abesset lēgibus novīs illīus ūsūrōs esse.

Temple of Fortuna Virilis so-called

Leve fit, quod bene fertur, onus.

The burden which is borne well becomes light. —OVID

REVIEW **14** (LESSONS 53–56)

—*Vocabulary Drill*—

A. Give the genitive, gender, and meaning of the following nouns.

aedēs	caedēs	latus	ōs
aetās	cāsus	mēnsis	palūs
agmen	classis	mūnītiō	praeda
ancora	facultās	obses	ratiō
auctor	hospes	ōrdō	rīpa

B. Give the other nominative forms, and the meanings, of the following adjectives (for adjectives of one termination, give the genitive singular).

aeger	ēgregius	maritimus	prūdēns
apertus	integer	mīlitāris	recēns
cēterī	levis	necessārius	vetus
complūrēs			

C. Give the principal parts and meanings of the following verbs.

appropinquō	discō	licet	suscipiō
audeō	doleō	mālō	tangō
augeō	emō	nōlō	tegō
cadō	exerceō	oportet	ūtor
caedō	explōrō	orior	vehō
comparō	fīō	ostendō	vēndō
cōnscrībō	hiemō	perturbō	vīvō
cōnsīdō	īnstituō	potior	volō
convenit			

D. Give the meanings of the following adverbs.

aegrē	frūstrā	nē . . . quidem	quoque
bis	intereā	omnīnō	repente
circiter	item	quidem	suprā
ferē			vix

—Drill on Forms—

A. Give the following forms.

1. *genitive singular:* latus, cāsus, palūs
2. *dative singular:* vetus, obses, ratiō
3. *accusative singular:* agmen, mūnītiō, integer
4. *ablative singular:* recēns, cāsus, mēnsis
5. *vocative plural:* hospes, prūdēns, auctor
6. *genitive plural:* classis, levis, caedēs
7. *dative plural:* complūrēs, vetus, ōrdō
8. *accusative plural:* rīpa, agmen, mīlitāris

B. Give the following synopses, active, indicative, subjunctive, and (where applicable) imperative.

1. volō *in the 2d person singular*
2. ferō *in the 3d person singular*
3. mālō *in the 1st person plural*
4. nōlō *in the 2d person plural*
5. eō *in the 3d person plural*

C. Give the following synopses of deponents, indicative, subjunctive, and (where applicable) imperative.

1. orior *in the 1st person sing.*
2. ūtor *in the 2nd person sing.*
3. potior *in the 3rd person pl.*
4. cōnor *in the 3rd person sing.*
5. moror *in the 1st person pl.*

D. Identify and translate the five infinitives of **caedō** and **tollō**.

E. Identify and translate the three participles of **augeō** and **vehō**.

F. Translate.

1. ausus est
2. oriēns
3. ūtiminī
4. nōn vultis
5. mālētis
6. licēbit
7. fīet
8. cōnscrībent
9. hortātus
10. referrī

G. Translate.

1. to get possession of
2. you (*sing.*) bear
3. they prefer
4. he will be unwilling
5. it happened

6. they will wish
7. she has used
8. it was being made
9. he had touched
10. having delayed

—— *Drill on Syntax* ——

A. Translate.

1. Mihi īre licuit.
2. Gladiō ūtitur.
3. Cūr nōbīs nōn crēditur?
4. Obsidibus caesīs rediit.
5. Cōnsul fīet.

6. Tē venīre oportēbat.
7. Mūnītiōne potītī sunt.
8. Nōlet augēre cīvitātem.
9. In palūdem prōgressus cecidit.
10. Sunt eīs animālia.

B. Translate.

1. He wants to live.
2. I used my shield.
3. He will go within four months.
4. I was persuaded not to go.
5. The city will be reached at noon.

6. They will get possession of the camp.
7. He does not dare to enlist the men.
8. It happens that we have the booty.
9. She says she will go if she can.
10. Will he be allowed to use an anchor?

—— *Exercises* ——

A. Translate.

1. Prīmum agmen flūmen trānsībat cum novissimum agmen ad vallem appropinquābat. 2. Auctōrem illīus librī poētam nōtissimum esse scīvimus. 3. Mūnītiōnibus perfectīs imperātum est mīlitibus ut domum redīrent. 4. Cum castrīs potītī essent praedam carrīs domum vexērunt. 5. Prūdentissimum centuriōnem

mīsimus quī equitēs exercēret. 6. Cum multās hōrās in rīpā morā-
rēmur classem tamen nōn vīdimus. 7. Putāvimus eōs nōn longius prōgredī audēre quod pugnāre nōllent. 8. Nōbīs quidem pecūniam, sī mīlitī vulnerātō auxilium tulissēmus, sē datūrum esse
pollicitus est.   9. Cum equus quō vehēbātur cecidisset eques ferē
septem mīlia passuum ambulāre coāctus est.   10. Postquam ad
īnsulam perventum est, ut oppidum explōrārent profectī sunt.

*Castel Sant'Angelo (Mausoleum of Hadrian), Rome. The huge tomb, in the
Estruscan style, was later converted to a papal fortress and connected to the
Vatican by a fortified passageway.*

Wallpainting showing the Rites of Isis, National Museum, Naples

B. Translate.

1. Although a great slaughter was made, quite a few (**complūrēs**) soldiers were able to save themselves and return to camp. 2. The army was led into an ambush when it was approaching the valley. 3. I have been informed that if he comes he will not stay for many months. 4. He seems to think that we did not dare to explore this place. 5. Caesar likewise asked why the men had not increased the size of the fortification. 6. He said that he did not want to spend the winter on the island because there was not enough water. 7. A star falling into the forest pointed out the way to the hesitating men. 8. Lucius, at any rate, wishes to become a soldier rather than a senator. 9. The fighting went on fiercely for a long time, and about fifteen men were killed when the camp was captured. 10. A new moon was rising when the sun was falling into the sea.

57

Dative with Intransitive Verbs Dative with Compound Verbs

Livia, Augustus' wife, with Tiberius, her son by a previous marriage

Mus uni non fidit antro.

A mouse does not rely on just one hole.—PLAUTUS

—— Syntax ——

DATIVE WITH INTRANSITIVE VERBS

Certain verbs with the following meanings take an indirect object in Latin (instead of a direct object, as in English).

favor	believe	obey	envy	trust
help	persuade	serve	threaten	spare
please	command	resist	pardon	

You have already learned some of these verbs; **crēdō, imperō, licet, mandō, permittō,** and **persuādeō.** Others, in the vocabulary for this lesson, are **cōnfīdō, noceō, parcō, pareō, placeō, resistō,** and **studeō.**

Intransitive verbs that govern the dative are used impersonally in the passive. The dative is retained.

Auctōrī persuāsum est.　*The author was persuaded.*

DATIVE WITH COMPOUND VERBS

Many verbs compounded with the following prefixes may take an indirect object.

ad-	con-	ob-	prō-	circum-	prae-
ante-	in-	post-	sub-	inter-	super-

If the original verb was transitive, the compound will take a direct object as well.

Caesar lēgātum legiōnī praefēcit.
*Caesar placed (**-fēcit**) the lieutenant in command of (**prae-**) the legion.*

—— Vocabulary ——

tur'pis, -e, *base, disgraceful; ugly*
ve'hemēns, vehemen'tis, *violent, forceful*

cōnfī'dō, -ere, cōnfī'sus sum, *trust* (semi-deponent)
cōn'sulō, -ere, cōnsu'luī, cōnsul'tum, *consult; consult the interests of,*
 take counsel for

dē'sum, dēes'se, dē'fuī, dēfutū'rus, *be lacking*

ēri'piō, -ere, ēri'puī, ērep'tum, *rescue*

no'ceō, -ē're, no'cuī, no'citum, *harm, injure*

par'cō, -ere, peper'cī, par'sum, *spare*

pā'reō, -ē're, pā'ruī, pā'ritum, *obey*

pla'ceō, -ē're, pla'cuī, pla'citum, *please*

praefi'ciō, -ere, praefē'cī, praefec'tum, *place over, place in command of*

prae'sum, praees'se, prae'fuī, praefutū'rus, *be at the head of, be in command of*

prōvi'deō, -ē're, prōvī'dī, prōvī'sum, *forsee; provide for*

ra'piō, -ere, ra'puī, rap'tum, *seize, snatch*

resis'tō, -ere, re'stitī, ——, *resist*

sol'vō, -ere, sol'vī, solū'tum, *loose, untie, set free; pay*

stu'deō, -ē're, stu'duī, ——, *be eager for, desire*

—— Word Study ——

Cōnsulō takes an accusative of the person consulted, a dative of the person whose interests are consulted or the thing for which counsel is taken.

> Sī mē cōnsulueris, tē monēbō.
> *If you consult me, I shall advise you.*
> Sī tibi cōnsulueris, hoc faciēs.
> *If you consult your own interests, you will do this.*

Dēsum may take a dative of possession.

> Canis eī est.   *He has a dog.*
> Canis eī dēest.   *He does not have a dog (A dog is lacking to him.).*

Prōvideō takes either a direct object of the verb or an indirect object with the prefix (not both at once, like **praeficiō**).

> Hanc calamitātem prōvīdī.   *I foresaw this calamity.*
> Huic calamitātī prōvīdī.   *I have provided for this calamity.*

Rapiō in compounds becomes **-ripiō, -ripere, ripuī, -reptum.**

Solvō. The ablative of separation with **solvō** is used without a preposition except in the idiom **nāvem (nāvēs) solvere,** *set sail* (i.e., untie the ship).

— Exercises —

A. Translate.

1. Līberīs prōvīsum est.   2. Suō patrī pāruit.   3. Exercituī praeest.   4. Pācī studēbant.   5. Captīvīs pepercit.   6. Equitibus Mārcum praefēcimus.   7. Nostrīs cōpiīs acriter resistēbant. 8. Cīvibus placēbat.   9. Servīs nōn cōnfīsus est.   10. Fēminae cōnsuluit.

B. Translate.

1. We resisted the enemy.   2. I do not trust her.   3. He did not obey the teacher.   4. She will please my mother.   5. Lucius was in charge of the fleet.   6. The horse was being harmed.   7. Caesar placed Marcus in command of the town.   8. He will not injure his friend.   9. Who is in command of this camp?   10. They spared the slave.

C. Read the Latin and translate.

1. Cum nāvēs longae* nōbīs dēessent, nōs oportuit ūtī nāvibus quōrundam mercātōrum.   2. Lēgātō nōn licēbat cōnsulere senātōrem, cum cīvēs illī nōn cōnfīderent.   3. Fēminae puerōs rogāvērunt nē animālibus in agrīs nocērent.   4. Imperātor castrīs appropinquāns quis nostrīs cōpiīs praeesset rogāvit.   5. Agricola prūdēns hiemī prōvīderat cum magnam cōpiam frūmentī domum attulisset.   6. Eī cui auctōritās dēest numquam pārēbitur. 7. Mercātor nautae cui pecūniam dederat nōn cōnfīsus est. 8. Cum hostēs magnā cum audāciā nōbīs resisterent, tamen collibus potītī sumus.   9. Imperātor castrīs quae ad rīpam flūminis posita erant Mārcum praefēcit.   10. Centuriō quī peditibus praefuit sē obsidibus pepercisse dīxit.

D. Translate.

1. I cannot trust you any longer, for you have greatly injured my friends.   2. I shall show you that I am in charge of the troops against the enemy.   3. The cavalry, about to set sail for (**ad**) Britain, did not trust the infantry; this did not please the gen-

---

* **Nāvis longa** is an idiom for *warship*.

eral.   4. It was necessary to send troops to bring help to our cavalry, certain of whom had been wounded in battle. 5. Although the Germans chose their wisest leader, nevertheless he could not resist the Roman cavalry.   6. If we consult the interests of the state in this matter, who of the citizens will be harmed?   7. We ought to trust that citizen who returned the money; at any rate (**quidem**) we cannot harm him.   8. They wished to drive the ambassadors from the town, for the conditions of peace were most disgraceful.   9. On account of the arrival of Caesar himself, the Germans did not harm even the slaves of our allies.   10. The general approached the town and put Lucius in command of his forces.

—— *Reading* ——

MARCUS AURELIUS AND THE CHRISTIANS

Mārcus Aurēlius, vir maximā virtūte et ūnus ex quīnque bonīs imperātōribus Rōmānīs, patriam suam iūstissimē vīgintī annōs rēxit. Erat cōnsuētūdō eiusdem per viās Rōmae cum servō ambulāre et cum cīvibus dē eōrum difficultātibus loquī. Omnibus temporibus erat hīs auxiliō. Itaque Rōmānī exīstimāvērunt illum esse omnium imperātōrum optimum.

Necesse erat Aurēlium multīs proeliīs pugnāre ut Rōmānōs fīnēs dēfenderet. Ōlim bellum in barbaram gentem Quādōs appellātam īnferēbat. Hostēs tam acriter undique aggressī sunt ut Rōmānī sē in inīquum locum recipere cōgerentur. Quō factō, ob vim sōlis omnēs inopiam gravissimam aquae patiēbantur. Quādam in legiōne erant tria mīlia Christiānōrum quī simul clāmāvērunt, "Domine, dā nōbīs auxilium; aqua sit."

Statim tonītrus audītur, lūx discēdit, imber pervenit. Omnibus tantum virtūtis redditur ut in hostēs multō ācriōrem impetum faciant. Quādīs ita victīs, omnēs crēdidērunt ab deō Christiānōrum imbrem missum esse.

Christiānī, imperātōrem ad suam fidem dūcere cōnātī, hāc spē dēiectī sunt. Eīs tamen amīcīssimus erat. Aurēlius cuidam rogantī quod nōmen huic legiōnī darētur respondit sē eam Legiōnem Tonitrūs semper appellātūrum esse.

58

Indefinite Pronouns and Adjectives
Relative Clause of Characteristic

Frieze from the Ara Pacis, The Altar of Peace, erected by Augustus in 13. B.C.

Quaedam iura non scripta sed omnibus scriptis certiora sunt.
Some laws are unwritten but they are better established than all
written ones.—SENECA RHETOR

—Forms —

INDEFINITE PRONOUNS AND ADJECTIVES

Quīdam means *some definite person or thing, someone or something I know of.* For the declension of **quīdam** see the Word Study in Lesson 51. The pronoun and the adjective are identical in form except in the neuter nominative and accusative singular, where the pronoun is **quiddam,** the adjective **quoddam.**

Aliquis (pronoun) and **aliquī** (adjective) mean *someone (something, some) or other,* as opposed to *no one (nothing, no).*

SINGULAR

PRONOUN		ADJECTIVE		
MASC. & FEM.	NEUT.	MASC.	FEM.	NEUT.
aliquis	aliquid	aliquī	aliqua	aliquod
alicuius	alicuius	alicuius	alicuius	alicuius
alicui	alicui	alicui	alicui	alicui
aliquem	aliquid	aliquem	aliquam	aliquod
aliquō	aliquō	aliquō	aliquā	aliquō

PLURAL

PRONOUN AND ADJECTIVE

MASC.	FEM.	NEUT.
aliquī	aliquae	aliqua
aliquōrum	aliquārum	aliquōrum
aliquibus	aliquibus	aliquibus
aliquōs	aliquās	aliqua
aliquibus	aliquibus	aliquibus

Quisquam (pronoun) and **ūllus** (adjective) mean *anyone, any.*

Putāsne quemquam hoc scīre?
Do you think anyone knows this?

Quisquam is declined like **quis, quid** + **-quam;** it has no plural.

	MASC. & FEM.	NEUT.
NOMINATIVE:	quisquam	quidquam *or* quicquam
GENITIVE:	cuiusquam	cuiusquam
DATIVE:	cuiquam	cuiquam
ACCUSATIVE:	quemquam	quidquam *or* quicquam
ABLATIVE:	quōquam	quōquam

Ūllus is declined like **ūnus.** (See Lesson 21.)

Quis (pronoun) and **quī** (adjective) are used instead of **quisquam** and **ūllus** after **sī, nisi, nē,** and **num.** They are declined like **aliquis** and **aliquī** without the **ali-.** In other words they resemble the interrogative pronoun and adjective except in the feminine nominative singular and the neuter nominative and accusative plural.

> Sī quis hunc librum lēgerit, multa discet.
> *If anyone reads this book, he will learn much.*

Nē quis and **nē quid** are used for *no one* and *nothing* in negative purpose clauses and indirect commands.

> Fugiet nē quis eum capiat.
> *He will flee so that no one may capture him.*
> Eīs persuāsit nē quid facerent.
> *He persuaded them to do nothing.*

Quisque (pronoun) and **quīque** (adjective), *everyone, every (each),* are declined like **quis, quid,** and **quī, quae, quod** + **-que.**

> Quīque mīles gladium habet.   *Every soldier has a sword.*

〰〰〰〰〰〰〰〰〰〰〰〰〰〰〰〰〰〰〰〰〰〰〰〰〰〰〰〰〰〰

Distinguish between the two words for *some.*

> Quaedam fēminae hīc habitant.
> *Some women (whom I know of) live here.*
> Aliquae fēminae hīc habitant.
> *Some women (or other) live here.*

〰〰〰〰〰〰〰〰〰〰〰〰〰〰〰〰〰〰〰〰〰〰〰〰〰〰〰〰〰〰

—— Syntax ——

Relative Clause of Characteristic. A relative clause with its verb in the subjunctive (following sequence of tenses) is used to define its antecedent as being of a certain character or kind, rather than merely to state a fact about it; hence it is called a relative clause of characteristic. Note the difference in the following:

> Mārcus nōn est is quī hoc fēcit.
>> *Marcus is not the one who did this.*
> Mārcus nōn est is quī hoc fēcerit.
>> *Marcus is not he who is of such a kind that he would have done this.*
>> *Marcus is not the kind (type) of person to have done this.*

—— Vocabulary ——

adulēs'cēns, adulēscen'tis, m., *young man, youth*
grā'tia, -ae, f., *favor, influence; gratitude*
mōs, mō'ris, m., *custom, habit*
qui'ēs, quiē'tis, f., *rest, sleep*
rū'mor, rumō'ris, m., *rumor, murmur*
san'guis, san'guinis, m., *blood*
volun'tās, voluntā'tis, f., *willingness, wish, consent*

aliquis, aliquid, *someone, something*
aliquī, aliqua, aliquod, *some*
quī, qua, quod (after sī, nisi, nē, num) *any*
quis, quid (after sī, nisi, nē, num) *anyone, anything*
quisquam, quidquam, *anyone, anything*
quisque, quidque, *everyone, each*

ape'riō, -ī're, ape'ruī, aper'tum, *open, expose*
coe'pī, coepis'se, coep'tum (defective), *began*
cōnsuēs'cō, -ere, cōnsuē'vī, cōnsuē'tum, *become accustomed*
ia'ceō, -ē're, ia'cuī, ia'citum, *lie*
in'colō, -ere, inco'luī, ——, *inhabit, live in; dwell*
iū'vō, -ā're, iū'vī, iū'tum, *help, aid*
ri'deō, -ē're, rī'sī, rī'sum, *smile, laugh; laugh at*
rum'pō, -ere, rū'pī, rup'tum, *burst, break*
sū'mō, -ere, sūmp'sī, sūmp'tum, *take, assume*

— Word Study —

Grātia, *gratitude,* is used in several idioms.

grātiās agere	*to thank*
grātiam habēre	*to feel gratitude*
grātiam dēbēre	*to be under an obligation*
grātiam referre	*to show gratitude*

All these are used with a dative of the person.

Tibi grātiās agō.   *I thank you.*

Mōs est is used with a substantive clause.

Mōs est ut populus cōnsulēs dēligat.
The custom is that the people choose the consuls.

Sūmō. The Romans thought of punishment as something which was taken out of the person being punished.

Poenam dē hīs puerīs sūmam.   *I shall punish these boys.*

— Exercises —

A. Read the Latin and translate.

1. Quisque mīles habuit aliquod opus quod faceret, sed omnēs tam dēfessī erant ut nihil facerent.   2. Caesar nōn erat imperātor quī suīs imperāret nē quid facerent.   3. Quid dēbēmus facere sī quis in nōs impetum fēcerit?   4. Tū nōn es is quī hoc nesciāt.   5. Hic nōn est liber quī tibi placeat.   6. Grātiās agimus vōbīs quī nōs iūverītis.   7. Poenam sūmēmus dē eīs quī cīvibus nocuerint.   8. Estne aliquis quī hunc puerum fortem nōn laudet?   9. Difficile est invenīre puellam quae Lūciō placeat.   10. Quārum rērum magnam partem impetus hostium impediēbat.

B. Translate.

1. He fled with such great speed that no one tried to follow him.
2. He ran very swiftly so that no one would try to follow him.
3. Will anyone ever dare to harm Caesar himself?   4. There are some who would say that you are beautiful.   5. Some Germans, at least (**quidem**), live in this town.   6. He is not one who would

feel gratitude. 7. The senators were with difficulty persuaded not to do anything. 8. I do not believe that this man has any authority. 9. It is the custom of the barbarians that they drink the blood of their enemies, but some never become accustomed to do this. 10. Does every boy have a book to read?

—— *Reading* ——

THEMISTOCLES AND ARISTIDES

Cum ducēs Graecōrum convēnissent, Themistoclī, prīncipī Athēniēnsium, nūntiātum est aliquem cum eō loquī velle. Ille cum conventū exīsset comperit hunc esse Aristīdem, quī patriā sex ante annīs inīquē expulsus esset et nunc redīsset. Erat mōs enim apud Athēniēnsēs ut eōs quī plūs posse vidērentur expellerent. Arīstidēs autem potestātem non cupiēbat; vir erat quī semper vellet patriae servīre. Ab omnibus iūstus appellēbātur.

Themistoclēs, cum Aristīdem vidēret "Sī quis," inquit, "Aristīdēs, est quī nōs vērē certiōrēs dē cōnsiliīs hostium faciat, is es. Quid factūrī sunt?"

Prīmum Aristīdēs dīxit tōtam classem Graecōrum ā Persīs circumventam esse. Deinde Themistoclēs Aristīdem rogāvit ut quae rēs esset prīncipibus Graecōrum nūntiāret, nam erat vir cui omnēs cōnfiderent.

59

Future Passive Participle
Gerundive
Passive Periphrastic
Dative of Agent

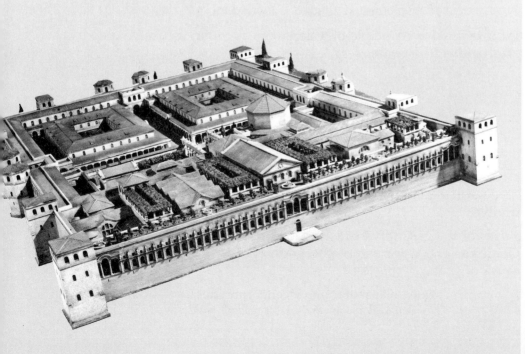

Model of Diocletian's Palace at Spalato in Jugoslavia

> Vitanda est improba siren desidia.
> *One must steer clear of the wicked temptress, Laziness.* —HORACE

—Forms—

THE FUTURE PASSIVE PARTICIPLE

In the first and second conjugations, the future passive participle is formed by adding **-ndus, -nda, -ndum** to the present stem.

> vocandus, vocanda, vocandum   *to be called*
> monendus, monenda, monendum   *to be warned*

In the third and fourth conjugations, the future passive participle is formed by adding **-endus, -enda, -endum** to the present stem.

> regendus, regenda, regendum   *to be ruled*
> capiendus, capienda, capiendum   *to be taken*
> audiendus, audienda, audiendum   *to be heard*

The future passive participles of transitive compounds of **eō** are like that of **adeō:**

> adeundus, adeunda, adeundum

The future passive participle of a deponent verb has a passive meaning: **hortandus,** *to be encouraged.*

—Syntax—

USES OF THE FUTURE PASSIVE PARTICIPLE

The Gerundive Construction. The idea which we express in English by a gerund (the verbal noun in *-ing*) is expressed in Latin by a future passive participle modifying a noun; hence this construction is called gerundive.

The uses of the gerundive construction are as follows.
1. **Genitive.** The chief use of the gerundive in the genitive is with **causā** or **gratiā,** *for the sake of.*

> Domī mānsī librōrum legendōrum causā.
> *I stayed home for the sake of reading books.*

2. **Dative.** The dative of the gerundive is usually the indirect object or the dative with adjectives. (See Lesson 34.)

> Multum tempus librīs legendīs dedit.
> *He gave much time to reading books.*
> Hic locus librīs legendīs idōneus est.
> *This place is suitable for reading books.*

3. **Accusative.** The accusative of the gerundive is confined to the accusative of place to which with **ad** (used to indicate purpose).

> Hūc vēnī ad librōs legendōs.
> *I came here for the purpose of reading books.*
> *I came here to read books.*

4. **Ablative.** The most common ablative of the gerundive is the ablative of means.

> Librīs legendīs multum didicit.
> *He learned much by reading books.*

The gerundive construction is not used in the nominative.

THE PASSIVE PERIPHRASTIC CONSTRUCTION

The use of the future passive participle as a predicate adjective with forms of **sum** is called the passive periphrastic. It denotes necessity or that which ought to be done. The participle agrees with the subject in gender, number, and case.

> Hoc faciendum est.   *This is to be done.*
> *This has to be done.*
> *This must be done.*
> *This ought to be done.*

DATIVE OF AGENT

With the passive periphrastic the agent or doer is not in the ablative of personal agent, but in the dative. This dative is akin to the dative of possession and is known as the dative of agent.

> Hoc mihi faciendum est.   *This must be done by me.*
> *I must do this.*   *I have to do this.*
> *I have this to do.*   *I ought to do this.*

~~~~~~

Helps and Hints. Notice that the English verb *must (ought)* is very irregular. We say, "We must go," for the present time; "We had to go," for past time; and "We shall have to go," for future time. The Latin is regular.

~~~~~~

—— Vocabulary ——

benefi'cium, benefi'cī, n.,
  kindness, favor
co'hors, cohor'tis, f., *cohort*
cus'tōs, custō'dis, m., *guard*
equitā'tus, -ūs, m., *cavalry*
explōrā'tor, explōrātō'ris, m.,
  scout
īn'fāns, īnfan'tis, m. or f., *baby*
la'crima, -ae, f., *tear*
laus, lau'dis, f., *praise*
lī'tus, lī'toris, n., *shore*
magistrā'tus, -ūs, m., *magistracy,*
  public office; magistrate

mu'lier, muli'eris, f., *woman, wife*
opī'niō, opīniō'nis, f., *opinion;*
  expectation; reputation
plēbs, plē'bis, f., *the common*
  people
rē'mus, -ī, m., *oar*
sax'um, -ī, n., *rock, stone*
ux'or, uxō'ris, f., *wife*

in'de, (adv.) *from there, thence*

—— Word Study ——

Cohors. A cohort consisted of six centuries of men, between 420 and 600; there were ten cohorts in a legion.

—— Exercises ——

A. Translate.

1. ad bellum gerendum 2. urbis videndae causā 3. ad portās claudendās 4. ad īnsulam explōrandam 5. flūminis trānseundī grātiā 6. Porta aperienda est. 7. Hoc mihi faciendum erat. 8. Oppidum exercituī nostrō occupandum erit. 9. Signa danda sunt. 10. Grātiae agendae sunt.

B. Translate.

1. for the sake of announcing the victory   2. by burning the town   3. for carrying grain   4. for slaying the enemy   5. for the sake of training the soldiers   6. War must not be waged.   7. War had to be waged.   8. Caesar must send the soldiers.   9. The men will have to carry the water.   10. We must free the slaves.

C. Read the Latin and translate.

1. Uxor ūnīus cōnsulis et complūrēs aliae mulierēs ad senātum iērunt in forum ad rogandōs senātōrēs nē diūtius bellum gererent.   2. Caesarī ūnō tempore omnia agenda erant: aciēs instruenda in apertīs campīs et mīlitēs hortandī erant.   3. Nautae in portum salūtis petendae grātiā nāvigant.   4. Hīs rēbus adductī exīstimāvimus hīberna Gallōrum nōbīs capienda esse.   5. Ad portum prīmā lūce contendērunt quō celerius nāvēs solverent ad Britanniam ad obsidēs referendōs.   6. Arbitrātī sumus auxilia ad hīberna statim mittenda esse.   7. Prīncipēs ad pācem petendam Rōmam venīre contendēbant.   8. Caesar bellī gerendī causā multās legiōnēs parābat.   9. Eī collēs nostrīs peditibus occupandī sunt quō equitēs facilius circumveniant hostēs.   10. Contrā omnium opīniōnem locum invēnimus castrīs ponendīs idōneum.

Plan of the Flavian Palaces on the Palatine (81–96 A.D.).

A. The Lararium
B. Aula Regia or Central Hall ⎤
C. Basilica   ⎬ Domus Flavia
D. Peristyle   ⎪ (Public Palace)
E. Triclinium   ⎦
F. Nymphaeum
   a. Upper Peristyle ⎤ Domus Augustana
   b. Sunken Peristyle ⎦ (Domestic Palace)

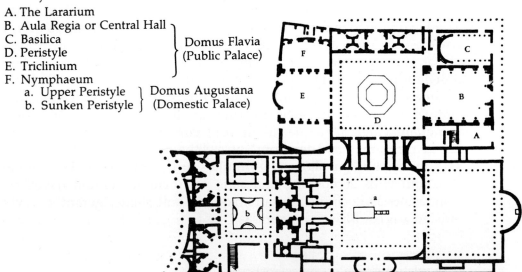

D. Translate.

1. A very wide river must be crossed by our entire army.   2. We know that the winter camp of our allies must be defended with the greatest boldness.   3. The army advanced about fifteen miles for the sake of crossing the river.   4. You must finish your work and give the books to your teacher.   5. The bodies of the soldiers who have been killed must be carried to the city.   6. The poet returned home to Rome to write a book about the wars.   7. We ought to give great thanks to the gods for having* spared our lives in this disaster.   8. Having advanced several miles into the territory of the Germans, our leader decided that he ought to wait for the rest of the army.   9. He said that he had led the cohort around the wall to find an open gate.   10. We do not know what we ought to do.

—— *Reading* ——

CIMON THE WISE

Cīmon ducum Athēniēnsium prūdentissimus putābātur. Quōdam diē eī ūnus ex amīcīs, "Omnibus," inquit, "bene nōtum est, Ō Cīmon, tē cōnsiliīs tuīs cīvitātem nostram maximē iūvisse. Mihi dīc quid tuā opīniōne Athēniēnsibus ūtilissimum fēceris."

   Respondit Cīmon rīdēns, "Ōlim ego et sociī, in Āsiam bellī gerendī causā profectī, quōsdam senēs nōbilēs cēpimus. Ego igitur cui potestās praedae dīvidendae data erat in alterō locō virōs ipsōs, in alterō omnia ornāmenta eōrum aurea posuī. Deinde sociōs hortātus sum ut dēligerent utram partem vellent, cōnfirmāvīque mē partem ab eīs relictam cum gaudiō acceptūrum esse. Quibus verbīs audītīs illī sine ūllā morā ornāmenta cupidē cēpērunt. Athēnās postquam rediī, cīvēs meīs captīvīs Āsiāticīs cōnspectīs rīsērunt quod hominēs hīs miseriōrēs numquam vīderant, atque mīrātī sunt cūr tam stultus fuissem; ego autem tacēbam. Brevī tempore, ut exīstimāveram, quīdam lēgātī ex Āsiā missī sunt quī illōs senēs multō aurō redimerent. Hōc modō mihi, quī virōs accēperam, erat satis pecūniae ad centum nāvēs armandās novās; sociīs nostrīs autem quī ornāmenta dēlēgerant, erat vix satis ad uxōrēs fīliāsque ornandās."

*Use relative clause of characteristic.

60

Passive Periphrastic
Gerund
Supine

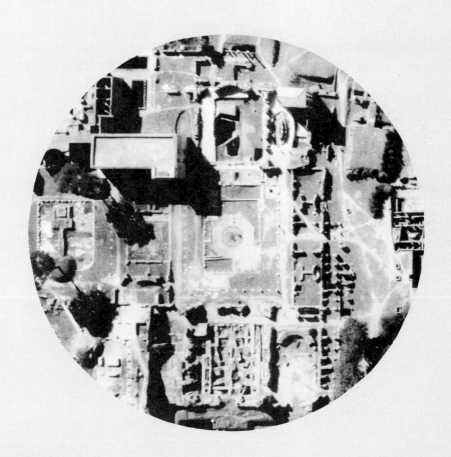

Air view of the Flavian Palaces on the Palatine (81–96 A.D.)

Timendi causa est nescire.
Ignorance is the cause of fear.—SENECA

—*Syntax*—

PASSIVE PERIPHRASTIC (INTRANSITIVE VERBS)

Since intransitive verbs can be used only impersonally in the passive, the passive periphrastic of intransitive verbs uses the future passive participle impersonally, in the neuter nominative singular only.

> Fortiter nōbīs pugnandum est.　*We must fight bravely.*
> Senātōribus persuādendum erit.
>   *The senators will have to be persuaded.*

When verbs which take an indirect object are used in the passive periphrastic construction, agency is usually expressed by the ablative of personal agent rather than the dative of agent, to avoid the ambiguity of two datives.

> Patrī ā tē pārendum est.　*You must obey your father.*

THE GERUND

Since an intransitive verb can have no passive meanings, its future passive participle obviously cannot modify any noun, but must be used impersonally in the neuter singular. The future passive participle in this use is called a gerund because it resembles a neuter singular noun. It has precisely the same uses as the normal gerundive construction.

> Hoc dīxī tibi persuādendī causā.
>   *I said this for the sake of persuading you.*
> Haec vallēs hiemandō idōnea est.
>   *This valley is suitable for spending the winter.*
> Tēla comparāvit ad pugnandum.
>   *He got together weapons for fighting.*
> Quid efficiēmus loquendō?
>   *What will we accomplish by talking?*

The gerunds of the four conjugations and of **eō** are as follows:

NOMINATIVE:	—	—	—
GENITIVE:	pugnandī	nocendī	crēdendī
DATIVE:	pugnandō	nocendō	crēdendō
ACCUSATIVE:	pugnandum	nocendum	crēdendum
ABLATIVE:	pugnandō	nocendō	crēdendō

NOMINATIVE:	—	—	—
GENITIVE:	fugiendī	veniendī	eundi
DATIVE:	fugiendō	veniendō	eundo
ACCUSATIVE:	fugiendum	veniendum	eundum
ABLATIVE:	fugiendō	veniendō	eundo

Helps and Hints. An easy way to distinguish gerund and gerundive is to think that "the gerund*ive* is an adjec*tive*."

SUPINE

The supine is a verbal noun, the fourth principal part of the verb, declined in the fourth declension in only two cases, the accusative and the ablative:

vocātum	monitum	rēctum	captum	audītum
vocātū	monitū	rēctū	captū	audītū

The supine has only two uses, each of which may be translated by an infinitive: the accusative to express purpose (with verbs of motion) and the ablative of specification.

Vēnī pugnātum.   *I have come to fight.*
Hoc est vīsū turpe.   *This is ugly to see.*

—— Vocabulary ——

ascen'dō, -ere, ascen'dī, ascēn'sum, *climb up*
coniun'gō, -ere, coniūnx'ī, coniūnc'tum, *join together, unite*
cōnscen'dō, -ere, cōnscen'dī, cōnscēn'sum, *climb; board, go aboard*

dēdū'cō, -ere, dēdūx'ī, dēduc'tum, *lead down, lead away; launch*
dē'ferō, dēfer're, dē'tulī, dēlā'tum, *carry, bring; report*
dēscen'dō, -ere, dēscen'dī, dēscēn'sum, *descend*
in'eō, inī're, in'iī, in'itum, *enter, begin;* consilium inīre, *to adopt a plan*
me'reor, -ē'rī, me'ritus sum, *deserve, earn*
mī'ror, -ā'rī, -ā'tus sum, *wonder at, be surprised*
mo'rior, -ī, mor'tuus sum (fut. act. part. moritū'rus), *die*
nās'cor, -ī, nā'tus sum, *be born; be found*
refi'ciō, -ere, refē'cī, refec'tum, *repair, restore*
rei'ciō, -ere, reiē'cī, reiec'tum, *throw back, repulse*
repel'lō, -ere, rep'pulī, repul'sum, *drive back*
repe'riō, -ī're, rep'perī, reper'tum, *find, discover*
rever'tor, -ī, rever'sus sum, *go back, return*
ta'ceō, -ēre, ta'cuī, ta'citum, *be silent*
tri'buō, -ere, tri'buī, tribū'tum, *assign, grant*
ver'tō, -ere, ver'tī, ver'sum, *turn*

— Word Study —

Mīror may be followed by an indirect question.

> Mīrātus est quae eius reī causa esset.
> *He wondered what the reason for this fact was.*

Morior. Mortuus is not actually the participle of this verb, but a separate adjective.

> Mortuus erat.   *He was dead = He had died.*

— Exercises —

A. Translate.

1. Obsidibus parcendum erit.   2. Nōbīs in pāce vīvendum est.
3. Huic reī cōnsulendum erat.   4. Hostibus ā nōbīs resistendum est.   5. Fortiter   pugnandum   erit.   6. ad   nāvigandum
7. pugnandō fortiter   8. resistendī grātiā   9. Hoc rōgātum vēnit.
10. Pācem petītum ībit.

B. Translate.

1. You must not fight.   2. Fathers must be obeyed.   3. This must be provided for.   4. We shall have to sail.   5. You must spare the captives.   6. for wintering in Gaul   7. by providing carefully   8. They made an end of fighting.   9. for the sake of pleasing me   10. They came to find her.

C. Read the Latin and translate.

1. Propter tempestātēs difficultās nāvigandī maxima est. 2. Imperātōrēs sē vēnisse colloquendī causā cum nostrīs ducibus dīxērunt.   3. Statim dē captīvīs nōbīs constituendum est.   4. Sibi Rhēnum vadō esse trānseundum putāvit.   5. Cōnsul dīcit grātiās deīs immortālibus ā nōbīs agendās esse prō tantīs beneficiīs. 6. Mīlitēs, postquam hostēs pulsōs vīdērunt, fīnem pugnandī fēcērunt.   7. Impetibus hostium acerrimīs audacter pugnandō resistere poterant.   8. Explōrātōrēs in urbem nocte vēnērunt domum cōnsulis incēnsum.   9. Ā nōbīs nūntiandum cōnsulī est hostēs ab apertīs agrīs statim repellendōs esse.   10. Nāvēs nōbīs dēdūcendae et cōnscendendae sunt ut quam prīmum domum deferāmur.

D. Translate.

1. Although they had been born at Rome, they were nevertheless living in Spain.   2. The messenger reported that the warships had been repaired and launched, and we went into winter quarters to

View of the model of ancient Rome showing the Capitoline Hill (Forum of Trajan in the background).

356

seek safety. 3. They closed the gates; and, a garrison having been left near the harbor, they sent men to find grain. 4. The sailors disembarked at noon for the sake of exploring the shores. 5. One Roman commander conquered the enemy by delaying, another by fighting in line of battle. 6. The nobles were unwilling to allow the magistrates to assign fields to the common people. 7. A scout was sent by the magistrates of the town to descend the hill and carry a letter to Caesar. 8. The chiefs adopted the plan of joining the two armies together in order to repulse the enemy more easily. 9. "If we must die," said the centurion, "let us at any rate die fighting bravely." 10. Do not be surprised at my work; I like repairing wagons.

—— Reading ——

THE FATTEST LION

Erat ōlim Rōmae servus Christiānus, nōmine Geta, quī, omnium puerōrum celerrimus, cotīdiē in Campō Martiō suī exercendī causā currēbat.

Cum Rōma igne vastāta esset, populus dolōre perturbātus dīxit Nerōnem imperātōrem urbem incendisse quō carmen dē Trōiae cāsū melius scrīberet. Ad hunc rūmōrem opprimendum, Nerō dīxit Christiānōs urbī ignem intulisse, atque cīvibus persuāsit ut ab illīs poenam mortis sūmerent. "Licet," inquit, "eōs leōnibus darī." Plēbs, sanguinis semper cupida, "Christiānōs ad leōnem!" clāmāvit.

Geta, captus, ante iūdicēs trāctus est, quī imperāvērunt ut ad leōnem iacerētur. Leō erat quīdam, maximus, fortissimus, crassissimus, cui Geta edendus erat.

Diē constitutā, in arēnam vēnit Geta quī sōlus, sine pīlo, sine scūtō, cum animālī pugnāret. Mox, rugītū mīrō audītō, in arēnam cucurrit leō crassissimus, quī statim Getae appropinquāvit. Fūgit Geta quam celerrimē, leōne celeriter quoque sequente. Bis circum arēnam currunt anhēlantēs et Geta et leō. Tum Geta ante imperātōrem ipsum lapsus cadit. Omnī spē āmissā, iam moritūrus leōnis impetum exspectat. Sed leō, iam appropinquāns, subitō cecidit, corde crassō cursū longō ruptō, atque moriēns ante pedēs Getae iacēbat.

Populus, hōc spectāculō laetissimus, "Deī iūdicāvērunt," clāmāvit. "Parce eī! Līber sit!" Nerō, recūsāre nōn ausus, "Liber es" inquit; "iam abīre licet."

Nil actum reputa si quid superest agendum.
*Don't consider that anything has been done if anything is left
to be done.* —LUCAN

REVIEW **15** (LESSONS 57–60)

—*Vocabulary Drill*—

A. Give the genitive, gender, and meaning of the following nouns.

adulēscēns	grātia	mōs	rūmor
beneficium	īnfāns	mulier	sanguis
cohors	lacrima	opīniō	saxum
custōs	laus	plēbs	uxor
equitātus	lītus	quiēs	voluntās
explōrātor	magistrātus	rēmus	

B. Give the other nominative forms, and the meanings, of the following pronouns and adjectives (for adjectives of one termination, give the genitive singular).

aliquī	quisquam
aliquis	turpis
quī (*after* sī, nisi, nē, num)	vehemēns
quis (*after* sī, nisi, nē, num)	

C. Give the principal parts and meanings of the following verbs.

aperiō	dēsum	parcō	resistō
ascendō	ēripiō	pāreō	revertor
coepī	iaceō	placeō	rideō
cōnfīdō	incolō	praeficiō	rumpō
coniungō	ineō	praesum	solvō
cōnscendō	iūvō	prōvideō	studeō
cōnsuēscō	mereor	rapiō	sūmō
cōnsulō	mīror	reficiō	taceō
dēdūcō	morior	reiciō	tribuō
dēferō	nāscor	repellō	vertō
dēscendō	noceō	reperiō	

—Drill on Forms —

A. Give the following forms.

1. *genitive singular:* aliquis, vehemēns, magistrātus
2. *dative singular:* mōs, quisquam, sanguis
3. *accusative singular:* laus, lītus, rēmus
4. *ablative singular:* equitātus, plēbs, turpis
5. *nominative plural:* vehemēns, rūmor, saxum
6. *genitive plural:* mulier, turpis, lītus
7. *dative plural:* explōrātor, mōs, cohors
8. *accusative plural:* lacrima, rēmus, magistrātus

B. Give a synopsis of **rumpō,** active and passive, indicative and subjunctive, with meanings of the indicative, in the third person plural.

C. Give the following forms.

1. *the present passive infinitive of* dēferō, rapiō, prōvideō
2. *the perfect active infinitive of* aperiō, parcō, vīvō, praesum
3. *the future active infinitive of* vertō, tribuō, ascendō
4. *the pres. active part. of* incolō, rapiō, pāreō, morior, mīror
5. *the future passive participle of* cōnscendō, mereor, reiciō, solvō

D. Give all forms of the gerund of **cōnsulō, resistō, studeō.**

E. Give the complete declension of the comparative of **turpis.**

—Drill on Syntax —

A. Translate.

1. Nē moriāmur.
2. Diū pugnātum est.
3. Cōnsulī placēbant.
4. Mūnītiōnī praefuit.
5. Vēnit urbem vīsum.
6. Audācissimē pugnandō hostēs vincet.
7. Mātrī ā tē pārendum est.
8. Prīnceps capiendus erit.
9. Hoc resistendī causā fēcit.
10. Mē castrīs praeficiet.

B. Translate.

1. He will be born.
2. They have died.
3. We shall obey them.
4. Do not trust him.
5. The horse must be killed.

6. We shall win by resisting bravely.
7. He will be in charge of the camp.
8. We have come to watch the games.
9. He eats for the sake of living.
10. They harmed themselves.

——Exercises——

A. Translate.

1. Accidit ut Mārcus classī praeesset itaque nāvēs longās hostium repellere posset.   2. Bellum cum illīs gentibus quae nōbīs nōn noceant crēdimus nōbīs nōn gerendum esse.   3. Hodiē repperimus quis mīlitibus morantibus imperāvisset nē impetum facerent.   4. Nōn licet nautīs nāvēs Corinthō solūtūrīs praedam portāre sēcum.   5. Omnēs mīlitēs quī in proeliō mortuī nōn sint paucīs mēnsibus domum reversūrōs scīmus.   6. Maxima multitūdō cīvium in viīs urbis convēnerat imperātōris captī videndī causā quī ad forum carrō vehēbātur.   7. Peditēs in castrīs tot diēs morātī interficī quam diūtius manēre māluērunt.   8. Plēbs Rōmāna captīvōs quī Rōmam ā Britanniā relātī erant mīrāta est; erant autem quīdam quī eōrum cāsum dolērent.   9. Imperātor rogāvit cūr lēgātus victōriam equitum ā dextrō cornū sibi nōn nūntiāvisset.   10. Custōdēs nocte castra hostium spectābant nē quis in campum dēscendere cōnārētur.

B. Translate.

1. Does anyone know why the enemy wished to remain in camp rather than fight with our infantry?   2. Four of the scouts were accustomed to go out at night from the camp and try to set fire to the enemy's fortifications.   3. Since you do not know the enemy's plans, you must try to find out what they are intending to do

now. 4. Is there anyone who would say that he has seen a wiser or a braver general than Caesar?   5. I hope that all the citizens who are staying in this town will go with Lucius to the walls to resist the enemy.   6. Having advanced about twenty miles from the river that day, the tired army decided to halt near the hill. 7. Thousands of Romans were accustomed to assemble in the summer of each year to choose new consuls.   8. The army which was surrounded in the valley fought so fiercely that it was able to rout the enemy and arrive at its camp.   9. The centurion who had been put in command of the third cohort was unwilling to obey the lieutenant.   10. You must persuade your brother not to say anything to the consuls about this serious matter.

"Nātāte aut Submergiminī"
A reconstruction of the Naumachia Augusti, a special amphitheatre built by Augustus for mock naval battles

Summary of Case Uses

The following uses of the various cases can now be added to the list that precedes Review Lesson 8.

Genitive

4. Of description and (5.) of measure (Lesson 51)
   Est vir magnae auctōritātis. *He is a man of great authority.*
   Vīdī turrim centum pedum. *I saw a hundred-foot tower.*

Dative

2. Of reference (Lesson 40)
   Vōbīs hoc fēcī. *I did this for you.*
3. Of purpose (Lesson 40)
   Hae rēs ūsuī sunt ad bellum. *These things are useful for war.*
4. Double dative (Lesson 40)
   Tū cūrae mihi es. *You are a worry to me.*
5. With adjectives (Lesson 34)
   Utrum oppidum propius marī est? *Which town is nearer to the sea?*
6. Of possession (Lesson 53)
   Mārcō erat gladius. *Marcus had a sword.*
7. With intransitives (Lesson 57)
   Placetne tibi? *Does it please you?*
8. With compounds (Lesson 57)
   Castrīs praeest. *He is in charge of the camp.*
9. Of agent (Lesson 59)
   Nōbīs currendum est. *We must run.*

Accusative

8. Accusative as adverb (Lesson 36)
   Vos multum amat. *He loves you much.*
   Multa errat. *He makes many mistakes.*
9. Of place to which without a preposition (Lessons 50 and 60)
   Domum it. *He goes home.*
   Vēnērunt urbem vīsum. *They came to see the city.*

Ablative

Showing Separation

5. Of place from which without a preposition (Lesson 50)
   Rūre venit. *He comes from the country.*
6. Of cause (Lesson 39)
   Timōre fugit. *He fled because of fear.*

7. Of comparison (Lesson 33)
   Fortiōrem Mārcō numquam vīdī.
   I never saw a braver man than Marcus.

Showing Instrument or Circumstances

4. Of description (Lesson 51)
   Mūrum magnā altitūdine adībat.
   He was approaching a wall of great height.
5. Of specification (Lesson 37)
   Flūmen est vīgintī pedum altitūdine.   *The river is twenty feet in depth.*
6. Of degree of difference (Lesson 36)
   Multō maior est quam tū.   *He is much bigger than you.*
7. Ablative absolute (Lesson 51)
   Litterīs acceptīs profectī sunt.
   Having received the letter, they set out.

Locative

1. To show place where (Lesson 50)
   Domī manēbunt.   *They will stay at home.*

Relief tondo of comic masks, the Clever Slave and the Irascible Old Man

Summary of Constructions with Verbs

Complementary Infinitive. The following verbs may require an infinitive to complete their meaning:

cōnor, *try*	dēbeō, *ought*	possum, *be able*
cōnstituō, *decide*	dubitō, *hesitate*	temptō, *try*
contendō, *hasten*	parō, *prepare*	videor, *seem*

Infinitive with Subject Accusative. An infinitive phrase is used with the following verbs:

cōgō, *compel*	polliceor, *promise*	verbs of saying, think-
iubeō, *order*	prohibeō, *prevent*	ing, knowing, perceiving
patior, *allow*	spērō, *hope*	(indirect statement)

(In the passive such verbs require a complementary infinitive.)

An Indirect Command (substantive clause of purpose) is used with the following verbs:

WITH ACCUSATIVE OF THE PERSON	WITH DATIVE OF THE PERSON	WITH ABLATIVE OF THE PERSON WITH **ā** *or* **ab**
hortor, *urge*	imperō, *command*	petō, *ask*
moneō, *warn, advise*	mandō, *command*	postulō, *demand*
ōrō, *beg*	permittō, *allow*	quaerō, *ask*
rogō, *ask*	persuādeō, *persuade*	

A Substantive Clause of Result is used with the following:

accidit, *it happens*	faciō, *see to it*	necesse est, *it is*
mōs est, *it is the custom*	efficiō, *bring about*	*necessary*

Tomb marker dedicated by Justus and Nigrinus to their deceased parents and brother

Supplementary Readings

—The Story of Perseus—

(This supplementary selection is designed to be read after Review Lesson 8.)

PERSEUS AND POLYDECTES

Haec fābula ā poētīs dē Perseī rēbus gestīs nārrātur. Perseus fīlius erat Iovis, rēgis deōrum. Avus Perseī propter ōrāculum eum timēbat et cōnsilium cēpit quō poterat eum adhūc īnfantem cum mātre interficere. Itaque eōs inclūsit in arcam ligneam quam iussit in mare conicī. Tempestās magna mare turbābat et timor mortis et mātrem et īnfantem occupāvit.

Iuppiter tamen omnia haec vīdit et fīlium servāre cōnstituit. Itaque perdūxit arcam in īnsulam quae longē aberat, ubi Perseus cum mātre multōs annōs habitāvit in pāce. Sed Polydectēs, rēx huius īnsulae, mātrem Perseī miserē amāvit et Perseō "Tuam mātrem," inquit, "in mātrimōnium dūcam." Hoc tamen cōnsilium Perseum nōn delectāvit. Itaque Polydectēs Perseum dīmittere cōnstituit. Eum vocāvit ad rēgiam et "Iam dūdum," inquit, "tū adulēscēns es. Itaque nunc dēbēs arma capere et virtūtem ostendere. Hinc nāvigā et caput Medūsae ad mē reportā."

PERSEUS LEAVES THE ISLAND

Perseus ab īnsulā discessit et diū Medūsam frūstrā quaesīvit. Tandem per deōrum auxilium ad Medūsae sorōrēs pervēnit, ā quibus tālāria galeamque magicam cēpit. Atque Apollo et Minerva eī falcem et speculum dedērunt. Tum, ubi tālāria induerat, volāre potuit et hōc modō ad eum locum pervēnit ubi Medūsa cum reliquīs Gorgonibus habitābat. Mōnstra horribilia erant hae Gorgonēs, quārum capita serpentibus multīs contēcta erant, et manūs ex aere factae.

THE FIGHT WITH THE GORGON

Iam Perseus Medūsam invēnerat—sed quō modō appropinquāre poterat ad hoc mōnstrum, cuius cōnspectū hominēs in saxum vertēbantur? Propter hanc causam speculum Perseō Minerva dederat. Itaque ille tergum vertit et in speculum īnspiciēbat. Hōc modō caput eius ūnō ictū abscīdit. Reliquae Gorgonēs, quae ē somnō excitātae et īrā commōtae sunt, Perseum interficere studēbant, sed Perseus galeam magicam induit. Ubi hoc fēcit, statim ē cōnspectū eārum excessit.

Post haec Perseus in fīnēs Aethiopiae vēnit, in quibus Cēpheus rēx erat. Cēpheus et Neptūnus, maris deus, inimīcī erant; itaque Neptūnus mōnstrum ferum ē marī cotīdiē mīsit quod hominēs dēvorābat. Cēpheus ōrāculum cōnsuluit et ā deō iussus est filiam mōnstrō trādere. Haec puella, quae Andromeda appellāta est, et pulchra et bona erat et ā patre amābātur; rēx tamen coāctus est facere illa quae deus iusserat.

PERSEUS RESCUES ANDROMEDA

Ubi Andromeda ad lītus dēducta est et ad rūpem adligāta (nam ita ōrāculum iusserat), Perseus subitō advolāvit. Tōtam rem audit et puellam videt. Simul mōnstrum procul cōnspicitur. Iam magnā celeritāte ad locum ubi puella est mōnstrum appropinquat.

At Perseus, ubi haec vīdit, gladium strīnxit et in caelum altum volāvit. Diū et acriter cum mōnstrō pugnat. Tandem Perseus mōnstrum interfēcit et Andromeda salva erat. Prō hōc magnō beneficiō Cēpheus Perseō Andromedam in mātrimōnium dedit. In finibus Aethiopiae Perseus et Andromeda paucōs annōs habitāvērunt in magnō honōre. Sed tandem Perseus cum Andromedā mātrem quaesīvit, quam salvam invēnit in Polydectis īnsulā. Posteā Polydectēs et avus Perseī, quod malī fuerant, ā Perseō interfectī sunt: ille in saxum cōnspectū Medūsae capitis conversus est; hic interfectus est discō quem Perseus in lūdīs iēcerat.

Roman students with teacher

—— *The Story of Ulysses* ——

(To be read after Review Lesson 15)

1. ULYSSES STARTS FOR HOME.

Urbem Trōiam ā Graecīs decem annōs obsessam esse satis cōnstat; dē hōc enim bellō Homērus, maximus poētārum Graecōrum, Īliada opus nōtissimum scrīpsit. Trōiā tandem per īnsidiās captā, Graecī bellō fessī domum redīre mātūrāvērunt. Omnibus rēbus ad profectiōnem parātīs nāvēs dēdūxērunt, et tempestātem idōneam nactī magnō cum gaudiō solvērunt. Erat inter Graecōs Ulixēs quīdam, vir summae virtūtis ac prūdentiae, quem nōn nūllī dīcunt dolum istum excōgitāsse quō Trōiam captam esse cōnstet. Hic rēgnum īnsulae Ithacae obtinuerat, et paulō priusquam ad bellum cum reliquīs Graecīs profectus est, puellam fōrmōsissimam, nōmine Pēnelopēn, in mātrimōnium dūxerat. Nunc igitur cum iam decem annōs quasi in exsiliō cōnsūmpsisset, magnā cupiditāte patriae uxōrisque videndae ārdēbat.

5

10

2. THE LAND OF THE LOTUS-EATERS.

Postquam Graecī pauca mīlia passuum ā lītore Trōiae prōgressī sunt, tanta tempestās subitō coorta est ut nūlla nāvium cursum tenēre posset, sed aliae aliam in partem disicerentur. Nāvis autem quā ipse Ulixēs vehēbātur vī tempestātis ad merīdiem dēlāta decimō diē ad lītus Āfricae appulsa est. Ancorīs iactīs Ulixēs cōnstituit nōn nūllōs ē sociīs in terram expōnere, quī aquam ad nāvem referrent, et quālis esset nātūra eius regiōnis cognōscerent. Hī ē nāve ēgressī imperāta facere parābant. Sed dum fontem quaerunt, quōsdam ex incolīs invēnērunt atque ab eīs hospitiō acceptī sunt. Accidit autem ut maior pars victūs eōrum hominum in mīrō quōdam frūctū, quem lōtum appellābant, cōnsisteret. Quem cum Graecī gustāssent, patriae et sociōrum statim oblītī cōnfirmāvērunt sē semper in illā terrā mānsūrōs, ut dulcī illō cibō in perpetuum vescerentur.

5

10

1. 1. **cōnstat** takes indirect statement, **urbem . . . esse.** 3. **īnsidiās** refers to the wooden horse. 7. **quem,** acc. subj. of **excōgitāsse (excōgitāvisse)** in indirect statement after **dīcunt,** *who some* (**nōn nūllī**) *say had devised . . .*

2. 3. **aliae aliam in partem,** *some in one direction, others in another.* 11. **gustāssent = gustāvissent.** 12. **oblītī (oblīvīscor)** governs objective gen. of **patriae, sociōrum.**

3. FORCIBLE RETURN TO THE SHIP.

Ulixēs cum ab hōrā septimā ad vesperum exspectāsset, veritus nē sociī suī in perīculō versārentur, nōn nūllōs ē reliquīs mīsit, ut quae causa esset morae cognōscerent. Itaque hī in terram expositī ad vīcum quī nōn longē aberat sē contulērunt; quō cum vēnissent, sociōs suōs quasi
5 ēbriōs reppererunt. Tum causam veniendī docuērunt, atque eīs persuādēre cōnātī sunt ut sēcum ad nāvem redīrent. Illī autem resistere ac sē manū dēfendere coepērunt, saepe clāmitantēs sē numquam ex illō locō abitūrōs. Quae cum ita essent, nūntiī rē īnfectā ad Ulixem rediērunt. Hīs rēbus cognitīs ipse cum reliquīs quī in nāve relictī erant
10 ad eum locum vēnit; sociōs suōs frūstrā hortātus ut suā sponte redīrent, manibus vīnctīs invītōs ad nāvem trāxit. Tum quam celerrimē ex portū solvit.

4. THE CYCLOPS'S CAVE.

Tōtam noctem rēmīs contendērunt, et postrīdiē ad ignōtam terram nāvem appulērunt. Tum, quod nātūram eius regiōnis ignōrābat, ipse Ulixēs cum duodecim sociīs in terram ēgressus locum explōrāre cōnstituit. Explōrātōrēs paulum ā lītore prōgressī ad spēluncam ingentem
5 pervēnērunt, quam incolī sēnsērunt; eius enim introitum et nātūrā locī et manū mūnītum esse animadvertērunt. Etsī intellegēbant sē nōn sine perīculō hoc factūrōs, tamen spēluncam intrāvērunt; quod cum fēcissent, magnam cōpiam lactis in vāsīs ingentibus conditam invēnērunt. Dum mīrantur quis in eā sēde habitāret, sonitum terribilem
10 audīvērunt, et oculīs ad ōstium tortīs mōnstrum horribile vīdērunt, hūmānā quidem speciē et figūrā, sed ingentī magnitūdine corporis. Cum autem animadvertissent mōnstrum ūnum modo oculum habēre in mediā fronte positum, intellēxērunt hunc esse ūnum ex Cyclōpibus, dē quibus iam audīverant.

5. TWO COMPANIONS ARE EATEN.

Cyclōpēs autem pāstōrēs erant, quī īnsulam Siciliam praecipuēque montem Aetnam incolēbant; ibi enim Volcānus, praeses fabrōrum ignisque inventor, cuius servī Cyclōpēs erant, officīnam suam habēbat. Graecī igitur simul ac mōnstrum vīdērunt, terrōre paene
5 exanimātī in interiōrem spēluncae partem refūgērunt, et sē abdere

3. 7. **manū,** *by force.*
4. 10. **tortīs (torqueō).**
5. 4. **simul ac,** *as soon as.*

cōnābantur. Polyphēmus autem (sīc enim Cyclōps appellābātur) pecus suum in spēluncam compulit; deinde, cum saxō ingentī ōstium obstrūxisset, ignem in mediā spēluncā fēcit. Hōc factō omnia oculō perlūstrābat. Cum sēnsisset hominēs in interiōre spēluncae parte esse abditōs, magnā vōce exclāmāvit: "Quī hominēs estis? Mercātōrēs an latrōnēs?" Tum Ulixēs respondit sē neque mercātōrēs esse neque praedandī causā vēnisse, sed Trōiā captā domum redeuntēs vī tempestātum ā cursū dēlātōs esse. Ōrāvit etiam ut sibi sine iniūriā abīre licēret. Tum Polyphēmus quaesīvit ubi esset nāvis quā vectī essent. Ulixēs cum magnopere sibi praecavendum exīstimāret, respondit nāvem suam in saxa coniectam omnīnō frāctam esse. Ille autem nūllō respōnsō datō duo ē sociīs eius manū corripuit, et membrīs eōrum dīvulsīs carne vescī coepit.

6. THE GREEKS BEGIN TO DESPAIR.

Dum haec geruntur, Graecōrum animōs tantus terror occupāvit ut nē vōcem quidem ēdere possent, sed omnī spē salūtis dēpositā praesentem mortem exspectārent. At Polyphēmus, postquam famēs hāc tam horribilī cēnā dēpulsa est, humī prōstrātus somnō sē dedit. Quod cum vīdisset Ulixēs, tantam occāsiōnem reī bene gerendae nōn omittendam arbitrātus, pectus mōnstrī gladiō trānsfigere voluit. Cum tamen nihil temere agendum exīstimāret, cōnstituit explōrāre, priusquam hoc faceret, quā ratiōne ex spēluncā ēvādere posset. Cum saxum animadvertisset quō introitus obstrūctus erat, nihil sibi prōfutūrum intellēxit Polyphēmum interficere. Tanta enim erat eius saxī magnitūdō ut nē ā decem quidem hominibus āmovērī posset. Quae cum ita essent, Ulixēs hōc cōnātū dēstitit et ad sociōs rediit; quī cum intellēxissent quō in locō rēs esset, nūllā spē salūtis oblātā dē fortūnīs suīs dēspērāre coepērunt. Ille tamen vehementer eōs hortātus est nē animōs dēmitterent; dēmōnstrāvit sē iam anteā ē multīs et magnīs perīculīs ēvāsisse, neque dubium esse quīn in tantō discrīmine dī auxilium lātūrī essent.

7. ULYSSES FORMS A PLAN.

Ortā lūce Polyphēmus iam ē somnō excitātus idem quod prīdiē fēcit; nam correptīs duōbus virīs carne eōrum sine morā vescī coepit.

15. **sibi praecavendum (esse),** *that he ought to take precautions.*
6. 4. **prōstrātus (prōsternere).** 7. **priusquam hoc faceret,** *before he should do this.* 16. **neque dubium esse quīn,** *nor was there any doubt that.* Neg. expressions of doubt take **quīn** and subjunc.

Deinde, cum saxum āmōvisset, ipse cum pecore suō ex spēluncā
prōgressus est; quod cum Graecī vidērent, magnam in spem vēnērunt
5   sē paulō post ēvāsūrōs. Statim ab hāc spē repulsī sunt; nam Polyphēmus, postquam omnēs ovēs exiērunt, saxum reposuit. Reliquī omnī
spē salūtis dēpositā sē lāmentīs lacrimīsque dēdidērunt; Ulixēs vērō,
quī, ut suprā dēmōnstrāvimus, magnī fuit cōnsilī, etsī intellegēbat rem
in discrīmine esse, tamen nōndum omnīnō dēspērābat. Tandem, cum
10   diū haec tōtō animō cōgitāvisset, hoc cōnsilium cēpit. Ē lignīs quae in
spēluncā reposita erant magnam clāvam dēlēgit. Hanc summā cum
dīligentiā praeacūtam fēcit; tum, postquam sociīs quid fierī vellet ostendit, reditum Polyphēmī exspectābat.

8. NO MAN.

Sub vesperum Polyphēmus in spēluncam rediit, et eōdem modō quō
anteā cēnāvit. Tum Ulixēs ūtrem vīnī prōmpsit, quem forte (id quod
eī erat salūtī) sēcum attulerat; et postquam magnum pōculum vīnō
complēvit, mōnstrum ad bibendum prōvocāvit. Polyphēmus, quī
5   numquam anteā vīnum gustāverat, pōculum statim exhausit; quod
cum fēcisset, tantam voluptātem percēpit ut iterum ac tertium pōculum complērī iubēret. Cum quaesīvisset quō nōmine Ulixēs appellārētur, ille respondit sē Nēminem appellārī; quod cum audīvisset, Polyphēmus ita locūtus est: "Hanc tibi grātiam prō tantō beneficiō
10   referam; tē postrēmum omnium dēvorābō." Hoc cum dīxisset, cibī
vīnīque plēnus humī recubuit, et brevī tempore somnō oppressus est.
Tum Ulixēs sociīs convocātīs, "Habēmus," inquit, "quam petīvimus
facultātem; nē tantam occāsiōnem reī bene gerendae omittāmus."

9. POLYPHEMUS IS BLINDED.

Hāc ōrātiōne habitā extrēmam clāvam ignī calefēcit, atque hāc oculum
Polyphēmī dormientis perfōdit; quō factō omnēs in dīversās spēluncae
partēs sē abdidērunt. At ille hōc dolōre oculī ē somnō excitātus clāmōrem terribilem sustulit, et dum in spēluncā errat, Ulixem manū
5   prehendere cōnābātur; cum tamen iam omnīnō caecus esset, nūllō
modō id efficere potuit. Intereā reliquī Cyclōpēs clāmōre audītō undique ad spēluncam convēnerant; et ad introitum adstantēs quid Polyphēmus ageret quaesīvērunt, et quam ob causam tantum clāmōrem
sustulisset. Ille respondit sē graviter vulnerātum esse, ac magnō do-

8. 3. **eī . . . salūtī,** double dat., *for safety to him.*
9. 5. **cum,** *since.*

lōre adficī. Cum posteā quaesīvissent quis eī vim intulisset, respondit   10
Nēminem id fēcisse; quibus rēbus audītīs ūnus ē Cyclōpibus, "At sī
nēmō," inquit, "tē vulnerāvit, nōn dubium est quīn cōnsiliō deōrum,
quibus resistere nec possumus nec volumus, hōc suppliciō adfectus
sīs." Hoc cum dīxisset, abiērunt Cyclōpēs eum in īnsāniam incidisse
arbitrātī.   15

Archaic Greek Vase
painting showing the
blinding of Polyphemus by
followers of Ulysses

10. ESCAPE FROM THE CAVE.

Polyphēmus ubi sociōs suōs abīsse sēnsit, furōre atque āmentiā im-
pulsus Ulixem iterum quaerere coepit; tandem, cum ōstium invēnis-
set, saxum quō obstrūctum erat āmōvit, ut pecus in agrōs exīret. Tum
ipse in introitū cōnsēdit; et ut quaeque ovis ad hunc locum vēnerat,
eius tergum manibus tractābat, nē hominēs inter ovēs exīre possent.   5
Quod cum animadvertisset Ulixēs, omnem spem salūtis in dolō magis
quam in virtūte positam esse intellēxit. Itaque hoc cōnsilium iniit.
Prīmum ex ovibus trēs pinguissimās dēlēgit, quās cum inter sē
vīminibus coniūnxisset, ūnum ex sociīs suīs ventribus eārum ita sub-
iēcit ut omnīnō latēret; deinde ovēs hominem ferentēs ad ōstium   10
ēgit. Id accidit quod fore suspicātus erat. Polyphēmus enim postquam

10. 4. **ut,** *as.* **Ut** followed by indic. means *as.*   9. **ventribus, dat.** with com-
    pound verb, **subiēcit.**   11. **Id . . . erat,** *That happened which he suspected*
    would happen. **fore = futurum esse.**

terga ovium manibus tractāvit, eās praeterīre passus est. Ulixēs ubi
rem tam fēlīciter ēvēnisse vīdit, omnēs sociōs suōs ex ōrdine eōdem
modō ēmīsit; quō factō ipse novissimus ēvāsit.

11. A PERILOUS DEPARTURE.

Hīs rēbus ita cōnfectīs Ulixēs, veritus nē Polyphēmus dolum cognōsceret, cum sociīs quam celerrimē ad lītus contendit; quō cum vēnissent, ab eīs quī nāvī praesidiō relictī erant magnā cum laetitiā exceptī
sunt. Hī cum iam diēs trēs continuōs reditum eōrum ānxiō animō
5   exspectāvissent, suspicātī (id quidem quod erat) eōs in aliquod grave
perīculum incidisse, ipsī auxiliandī causā ēgredī parābant. Tum Ulixēs
nōn satis tūtum esse arbitrātus in eō locō manēre, quam celerrimē
proficīscī cōnstituit. Itaque omnēs nāvem cōnscendere iussit, et
sublātīs ancorīs paulum ā lītore in altum prōvectus est. Tum magnā
10 vōce exclāmāvit: "Tū, Polyphēme, quī iūra hospitī violās, iūstam et
dēbitam poenam immānitātis tuae solvistī." Hāc vōce audītā Polyphēmus vehementer commōtus ad mare sē contulit. Ubi nāvem paulum
ā lītore remōtam esse intellēxit, saxum ingēns sublātum in eam partem
coniēcit unde vōcem vēnisse sēnsit. Graecī autem, etsī nōn multum
15 āfuit quīn nāvis eōrum mergerētur, tamen nūllō damnō acceptō cursum tenuērunt.

12. AEOLUS'S GIFT OF THE WINDS.

Pauca mīlia passuum ab eō locō prōgressus Ulixēs ad īnsulam Aeoliam
nāvem appulit. Haec patria erat ventōrum.
    Hīc rēx Aeolus vāstō antrō luctantēs ventōs tempestātēsque sonōrās
imperiō premit ac vinclīs et carcere frēnat. Ibi rēx ipse Graecōs hospitiō
5   accēpit, atque eīs persuāsit ut ad reficiendās virēs paucōs diēs com-
morārentur. Septimō diē, cum sē ex labōribus refēcissent, Ulixēs, nē
annī tempore ā nāvigātiōne exclūderētur, sibi proficīscendum statuit.
Tum Aeolus, quī sciēbat Ulixem cupidissimum esse patriae videndae,
eī magnum ūtrem dedit, in quō omnēs ventōs praeter ūnum inclū-
10 serat. Favōnium modo solverat, quod ille ventus nāvigantī ab īnsulā
Aeoliā Ithacam est secundus. Ulixēs hoc dōnum libenter accēpit, et
grātiīs prō tantō beneficiō āctīs ūtrem ad mālum adligāvit. Omnibus
rēbus ad profectiōnem parātīs merīdiānō ferē tempore ex portū solvit.

11. 3. **nāvī praesidiō,** double dat.   14. **etsī . . . mergerētur,** *although their
    ship was almost sunk.*
12. 3. **vāstō antrō,** understand **in** before **vāstō.**   4. **vinclīs = vinculīs.**

Ulysses and companions, Roman mosaic from Bardo Museum, Tunis

13. THE WINDS UNLEASHED.

Novem diēs Graecī secundissimō ventō cursum tenuērunt; iamque in cōnspectum patriae suae vēnerant, cum Ulixēs lassitūdine cōnfectus (ipse enim gubernābat) ad quiētem capiendam recubuit. At sociī, quī iam diū mīrābantur quid in illō ūtre inclūsum esset, cum ducem somnō oppressum vidērent, tantam occāsiōnem nōn omittendam arbitrātī sunt; crēdēbant enim aurum et argentum ibi latēre. Itaque spē praedae adductī ūtrem sine morā solvērunt; quō factō ventī, velut agmine factō, quā data porta, ruunt et terrās turbine perflant. Hīc tanta tempestās subitō coorta est ut illī cursum tenēre nōn possent, sed in eandem partem unde erant profectī referrentur. Ulixēs ē somnō excitātus quō in locō rēs esset statim intellēxit; ūtrem solūtum, Ithacam post tergum relictam vīdit. Tum vērō vehementer exārsit sociōsque obiūrgāvit, quod cupiditāte pecūniae adductī spem patriae videndae abiēcissent.

5

10

13. 8. **quā,** *where.* **ruunt, perflant,** understand **ventī** as subj.
   14. **abiēcissent,** subjunc., implied indirect statement.

14. CIRCE'S ISLE.

Brevī spatiō intermissō Graecī īnsulae cuidam appropinquāvērunt, in quā Circē, fīlia Sōlis, habitābat. Quō cum Ulixēs nāvem appulisset, in terram frūmentandī causā ēgrediendum esse statuit; nam cognōverat frūmentum quod in nāve habēret iam dēficere. Itaque sociīs ad sē
5 convocātīs, quō in locō rēs esset et quid fierī vellet ostendit. Cum tamen omnēs memoriā tenērent quam crūdēlī morte adfectī essent eī quī nūper ē nāve ēgressī essent, nēmō repertus est quī hoc negōtium suscipere vellet. Quae cum ita essent, rēs in contrōversiam dēducta est. Tandem Ulixēs omnium cōnsēnsū sociōs in duās partēs dīvīsit,
10 quārum alterī Eurylochus, vir summae virtūtis, alterī ipse praeesset. Tum hī duo inter sē sortītī sunt uter in terram ēgrederētur. Eurylochō sorte ēvēnit ut cum duōbus et vīgintī sociīs rem susciperet.

*The transformation of
the companions of Ulysses by Circe*

15. CIRCE'S PALACE.

Hīs rēbus ita cōnstitūtīs eī quī sorte ductī erant in interiōrem partem īnsulae profectī sunt. Tantus tamen timor animōs eōrum occupāverat ut nōn dubitārent quīn ad mortem īrent. Vix quidem poterant eī quī in nāve relictī erant lacrimās tenēre; crēdēbant enim sē sociōs suōs
5 numquam posteā vīsūrōs. Illī autem aliquantum itineris prōgressī ad vīllam magnificam pervēnērunt, cuius ad ōstium cum adīssent, cantum dulcissimum audīvērunt. Tanta autem fuit eius vōcis dulcēdō ut nūllō modō retinērī possent quīn iānuam pulsārent. Hōc factō ipsa Circē forās exiit, et summā cum benignitāte omnēs in hospitium

---

14. 6. **quam,** *how*   8. **vellet,** clause of characteristic.   10. **praeesset,** *was to command,* rel. clause of purpose.

15. 8. **retinērī possent quīn,** *could not be restrained from.* **Quīn** introduces subjunc. after neg. expressions of hindering.

invītāvit. Eurylochus īnsidiās sibi comparārī suspicātus forīs exspec- 10
tāre cōnstituit; at reliquī reī novitāte adductī vīllam intrāvērunt. Cēnam
omnibus rēbus īnstrūctam invēnērunt, et iussū dominae libentissimē
accubuērunt. At Circē vīnum quod servī apposuērunt medicāmentō
quōdam miscuerat; quod cum Graecī bibissent, somnō oppressī sunt.

16. ULYSSES DECIDES TO GO TO THE PALACE.

Tum Circē, quae artis magicae summam scientiam habēbat, virgā
aureā quam gerēbat capita eōrum tetigit; quō factō omnēs in porcōs
subitō conversī sunt. Intereā Eurylochus ignārus quid in aedibus ager-
ētur ad ōstium sedēbat. Postquam ad sōlis occāsum ānxiō animō et
sollicitō exspectāvit, sōlus ad nāvem regredī cōnstituit. Eō cum vē- 5
nisset, sollicitūdine ac timōre ita perturbātus fuit ut quae vīdisset vix
nārrāre posset. At Ulixēs satis intellēxit sociōs suōs in perīculō versārī,
et gladiō arreptō Eurylochō imperāvit ut sine morā viam ad istam
domum dēmōnstrāret. Ille tamen multīs cum lacrimīs Ulixem com-
plexus obsecrāre coepit nē in tantum perīculum sē committeret; sī 10
quid gravius eī accidisset, omnium salūtem in summō discrīmine fu-
tūram. Ulixēs respondit sē nēminem invītum adductūrum; illī licēre,
sī māllet, in nāve manēre; sē ipsum sine ūllō praesidiō rem suscep-
tūrum. Hoc cum magnā vōce dīxisset, ē nāve dēsiluit et nūllō sequente
sōlus in viam sē dedit. 15

17. MERCURY TO THE RESCUE.

Aliquantum itineris prōgressus ad vīllam magnificam pervēnit; quam
cum oculīs perlūstrāsset, statim intrāre statuit; intellēxit enim hanc
esse eandem domum dē quā Eurylochus mentiōnem fēcisset. At cum
līmen intrāret, subitō sē ostendit adulēscēns fōrmā pulcherrimā au-
ream virgam gerēns. Hic Ulixem iam domum intrantem manū pre- 5
hendit. "Quō," inquit, "ruis? Nōnne scīs hanc esse Circēs domum?
Hīc inclūsī sunt amīcī tuī ex hūmānā speciē in porcōs conversī. Num
vīs ipse in eandem calamitātem venīre?" Ulixēs simul atque vōcem
audīvit, deum Mercurium agnōvit; nūllīs tamen precibus ab īnstitūtō
cōnsiliō dēterrērī potuit. Quod cum Mercurius sēnsisset, herbam 10
quandam eī dedit, quam contrā carmina multum valēre dīcēbat. "Hanc
cape" inquit, "et cum Circē tē virgā tetigerit, tū gladiō dēstrictō im-

---

16. 10. **sī quid . . . accidisset,** *if anything serious should happen to him.* **Accidisset,** subjunc. in indirect statement.
17. 6. **Circēs,** gen.   11. **multum valēre,** *was very strong.*

petum in eam vidē ut faciās." Priusquam finem loquendī fēcit, mor-
tālēs vīsūs mediō sermōne relīquit, et procul in tenuem ex oculīs
15 ēvānuit auram.

18. ULYSSES TURNS THE TABLES.

Brevī intermissō spatiō Ulixēs ad omnia perīcula subeunda parātus
iānuam pulsāvit, et foribus apertīs ab ipsā Circē benignē exceptus est.
Omnia eōdem modō atque anteā facta sunt. Cēnam magnificē
īnstrūctam vīdit, et accumbere iussus est. Ubi famēs cibō dēpulsa est,
5   Circē pōculum aureum vīnī plēnum Ulixī dedit. Ille etsī suspicābātur
venēnum sibi parātum esse, tamen pōculum exhausit; quō factō Circē
caput eius virgā tetigit, atque ea verba dīxit quibus sociōs eius anteā
in porcōs converterat. Rēs tamen omnīnō aliter ēvēnit atque illa spē-
rāverat. Tanta enim vīs erat eius herbae quam Ulixī Mercurius dederat
10 ut neque venēnum neque verba quicquam efficere possent. Ulixēs
autem, ut erat eī praeceptum, gladiō dēstrictō impetum in eam fēcit
mortemque minitābātur. Circē cum artem suam nihil valēre sēnsisset,
multīs cum lacrimīs eum obsecrāre coepit nē sibi vītam adimeret.

19. ALL TURNS OUT WELL.

Ulixēs ubi sēnsit eam timōre perterritam esse, postulāvit ut sociōs
suōs sine morā in hūmānam speciem restitueret (certior enim factus
erat ā deō Mercuriō eōs in porcōs conversōs esse); nisi id factum esset,
sē dēbita supplicia sūmptūrum ostendit. Circē hīs rēbus graviter com-
5   mōta sēsē eī ad pedēs prōiēcit, et multīs cum lacrimīs iūre iūrandō
cōnfirmāvit omnia quae ille imperāsset sē factūram. Tum porcōs in
ātrium immittī iussit. Illī datō signō inruērunt. Cum ducem suum
agnōvissent, magnō dolōre affectī sunt, quod nūllō modō eum dē
rēbus suīs certiōrem facere poterant. Circē tamen unguentō quōdam
10 corpora eōrum ūnxit; quō factō sunt omnēs statim in hūmānam speciem restitūtī. Magnō cum gaudiō Ulixēs amīcōs suōs agnōvit, et
nūntium ad lītus mīsit, quī reliquīs Graecīs sociōs receptōs esse
dīceret. Illī autem hīs rēbus cognitīs celeriter in domum Circēs sē
contulērunt; quō cum vēnissent, ūniversī laetitiae sē dēdidērunt.

13. **vidē ut faciās,** *see that you make* (subjunc. in substantive clause).
18. 3. **eōdem modō atque,** *in the same way as.*   8. **aliter . . . atque,** *otherwise
than.*
19. 5. **eī,** dat. of reference, used rather than gen. **eius.**

20. ULYSSES'S DEPARTURE.

Postrīdiē eius diēī Ulixēs ex hāc īnsulā quam celerrimē discēdere in animō habēbat. Circē tamen cum id cognōvisset, ab odiō ad amōrem conversa omnibus precibus eum ōrāre et obtestārī coepit ut paucōs diēs apud sē morārētur; quā rē impetrātā tanta beneficia in eum contulit ut facile eī persuādērētur ut diūtius manēret. Postquam tōtum   5
annum apud Circēn cōnsūmpsit, Ulixēs magnō dēsīderiō patriae suae mōtus est. Itaque sociīs ad sē convocātīs quid in animō habēret ostendit. Sed ubi ad lītus dēscendit, nāvem suam tempestātibus ita afflīctam invēnit ut ad nāvigandum paene inūtilis esset. Quō cognitō omnia quae ad nāvēs reficiendās ūsuī erant comparārī iussit; quā in rē tantam   10
dīligentiam omnēs adhibēbant ut tertiō diē opus perficerent. At Circē ubi omnia ad profectiōnem parāta vīdit, rem aegrē tulit, atque Ulixem vehementer obsecrāvit ut cōnsiliō dēsisteret. Ille tamen, nē annī tempore ā nāvigātiōne exclūderētur, mātūrandum sibi exīstimāvit, et idōneam tempestātem nactus nāvem solvit. Multa quidem perīcula Ulixī   15
subeunda erant priusquam in patriam suam pervenīret, quae tamen hōc locō perscrībere longum est.

---

20. 6. Circēn, Greek acc. form.   **patriae,** obj. gen., *for his country.*
16. **priusquam . . . pervenīret,** *before he would arrive.*

At left: Roman remains in Greece

Roman Civilization through Art

The following section contains background material about the special art categories and additional information about many of the photos in the text.

HOUSES, GARDENS AND FURNISHINGS

The basic characteristic of ancient Italian* houses is the *ātrium*, a reception hall which normally has a funnel-shaped roof with a central opening (*compluvium*) to collect rainwater and direct it to a shallow pool (*impluvium*) below, whence it was drained into a cistern with a wellhead. The placement of other units, *tablīnum, ālae, cubicula, trīclīnia, peristÿlum*, etc., so canonical in Pompeii, is much less standardized in other sites such as Herculaneum, Ostia, and Rome itself. The origin and derivation of the *ātrium* is in doubt. The primitive Roman dwelling, plentiful traces of which have been found on the Palatine and in the Forum, was a horseshoe-shaped hut, presumably of wattle and daub with a thatched roof, a ridgepole, central hearth, and shallow porch. These are not unlike primitive Greek buildings, but the contemporary funerary urns in the shape of huts show that the smoke-hole was in the gable at the front of the building, not in the roof above the hearth. For this reason, and also because of the difference in function, it is probably not correct to derive the *compluvium/impluvium* arrangement from the primitive hearth and smoke-hole. Since (if we may judge from their tombs) the Etruscans had houses with central reception halls, it may be that the Italians borrowed the atrium from them, their own ingenuity adding the water-collecting arrangements.

   The most likely theory is that the atrium house developed from an enclosed yard, around which buildings were gradually added until they surrounded it completely. The next step was the addition of a portico around the courtyard, roofing it except for the center, as in the peristyle of Pompeii; then reducing the size of the central opening produced the true *ātrium*. The fact that the typical Italian town house turns in upon itself, with few windows to the outside, supports this theory of its origin.

Illustrations in the Text

p. xii. Much of what we know of Roman gardens comes from paintings like this, which were intended to extend visually the space of cramped town houses. Recent work done with plaster casts of root systems and with fossilized pollen at Pompeii confirm what we learn from such paintings.

* It is a misnomer to call such houses Roman, since at Pompeii, for example, the type appears long before the Roman period.

p. 3. Many Campanian houses have outdoor dining places. In this one the table foot is also a fountain jet. Once the meal was over, the mattresses were removed and the water turned on, making an attractive fountain and at the same time, washing away any crumbs and spills.

p. 4. This is not the plan of any particular house, but an attempt to derive a canonical plan for an early Campanian house from observations of the older houses at Pompeii. The rooms opening from the *ātrium* are usually bedchambers (*cubicula*). The *ālae*, in many houses, appear to have served as waiting rooms for clients, or office space for clerks. The rooms flanking the *tablīnum* were dining rooms; in later houses one, at least, would be open to the garden for summer use.

p. 8. This view is through the two peristyles, the first a flower garden with a fountain and the second a vegetable garden. Beyond the columns there is a reception room for social purposes with a view of both peristyles. The long vista from the entrance of the house through the garden was one of the most charming features of Pompeian architecture.

p. 10. The small door just inside the front door of the house leads to one of the shops which flank the entrance. The three doors in the *ātrium* lead to a stairway and two bedrooms (*cubicula*); the large paintings of the *ātrium* were illustrations of the *Iliad*. The double doors in the *tablīnum* belong to a large store cupboard. The mosaic on p. 150 is from the floor of this *tablīnum*. A study/bedroom and a pantry open from the peristyle (which has a colonnade around three sides only). At the rear is a back door opening on a side street. In the garden of the peristyle is a little shrine of the household gods.

p. 11. In the *faucēs* ("throat"—the name given to the narrow entrance hall) another door on this side leads to the shop next door. The presence of these doors suggests that the shops were run by slaves or freemen of the family, who also served as doorkeepers to the house. The entrance must also have been guarded by a dog, for just inside the front door is a mosaic pavement showing a dog with the inscription *Cavē canem*. The door in the *ātrium* on this side leads to a bedroom with the single *āla* to its left. From the garden a passage runs alongside the *tablīnum* to the *ātrium*; next to it is the entrance to a small dining room overlooking the colonnade. Off the colonnade on this side are a latrine and, far left, a large dining-room facing the garden.

p. 14. The Bay of Naples was a resort area for wealthy Romans. Seaside property was at such a premium that many people sank foundations into the sea and built their villas over the water.

p. 17 (*above*). Many of the older apartment houses in Italy today were built on a similar plan. Second-story apartments facing the street have stairways directly to the street. The other apartments are reached from galleries surrounding the central courtyard, which usually has in it a fountain for the use of tenants whose apartments do not have running water.

p. 17 (*below*). Trajan's market served for general trading and possibly for the distribution of grain to the populace. There were 150 shops, each with small living-quarters in the loft above it, a great two-storied hall, rooms with tanks for the sale of fish and liquids, and offices of administration. The market rose in tiers on the steep south slope of the Quirinal hill. This illustration has been placed in the section on housing primarily to show the arrangement of living-quarters above the shops, a plan found in most Roman cities, but it may be that in this case these quarters were for the overnight accommodation of merchants who had come to Rome to show their wares or samples to buyers from overseas. We know, for example, from a graffito at Pompeii, that the blacksmiths of Campania displayed their wares at Rome regularly.

p. 19. The funnel top in this elaborate bronze is covered by a lid with a figurine. The olive oil reservoir in the lamp is covered over to prevent spills, but the top is made funnel-shaped with a hole in the center for ease in filling. The wicks in the three spouts could be pulled up when they had burnt too low, by means of the hook on the chain. The large shield on the handle protected one's hand from the flames when the lamp was picked up.

p. 21. The one- and two-handled cups are from the house of the Poppaeus family at Pompeii, where a large silver service was found locked away in the cellar. The one-handled cup (*skyphos*) was for individual drinking; the two-handled *cantharus* was passed from person to person at the drinking bout following a banquet. The porringer and large silver serving dish are from Roman villas in Britain.

p. 25. Such small folding altars were used for domestic sacrifices of incense, libations of wine, etc. Folding tables of similar design have also been found in Pompeii.

In the brazier below, hot coals were raked into the curved hollow water-heater at the right; boiling water was drawn from the mask, while steam escaped through the swans at the top. Lukewarm water could be drawn from the tank at the left.

FAMILY LIFE AND EDUCATION

The head of the household (*familia*) was the father (*paterfamiliās*). In law he had the power of life and death over all the members of the *familia*, both *servī* and *līberī*. Religious sanctions also bound the family together; the *pietās* which meant so much to the Romans involved primarily the mutual duties of parents and children toward each other.

Because artificial lighting was poor, the Roman family rose at dawn. The father, if he was a person of any importance, began the day by receiving his clients in the *tablīnum* and *ātrium;* this was called the *salūtātiō*, and was followed by the *dēductiō*, as the clients escorted him down to the Forum, the center for both business and politics. His wife, having laid out the day's work for the slaves (and even poor households had at least one slave), was free to spend the rest of the day in visits.

The children's day was spent in schooling and play. Roman children played with many of the same kinds of toys children use today, stick horses, jacks (using knucklebones), dolls, tops, hoops, marbles. The older children played house or shops; the boys might pretend to be gladiators or soldiers, perhaps with miniature weapons and armor. The evidence of the plastic arts seems to show that they might have miniature dog- or goat-drawn chariots for racing. Simple games included "Odd or Even?" and "How Many Fingers Do I Hold Up?" (*Bucca, bucca, quot sunt hīc?*). The more sophisticated games resembled backgammon (*duodecim scrīpta*) and chess or checkers (*lātrunculī*). There were also ball games played rather like our field hockey, football, and lacrosse (but without sticks), and a three-cornered catch called *trigōn*, in which as many balls as possible were kept going at one time.

Elementary education, which was given to both boys and girls, began with reading, writing, and arithmetic. Roman history was taught through literature, and the study of Greek language and literature was also begun early. Children of wealthy families might be tutored at home. Some of the great houses of Pompeii have schoolrooms where we can see scratched on the walls alphabets, tags from Vergil, geometric figures, and insults directed at the tutor. There were also elementary schools, public and private, located in or near the Forum. When the boys came of age, at 12–15 years, they were sent to schools run by Greek rhetors to learn rhetoric in Greek. Girls pursued the study of Greek and Roman literature with tutors at home. Boys finished their education by attaching themselves to some well-known orator (i.e. lawyer-politician) to learn oratory, history, and law. They might also be sent to Athens for a time to learn philosophy. Music and athletics, the core of Greek education, were considered unnecessary, even unsuitable, for good Romans.

The Romans had different kinds of marriage ceremonies, corresponding to different legal states of matrimony. The most elaborate was *cōnfarreātiō*, "spelt-cake-sharing" (the spelt cake was the Roman's most primitive form of bread). The bride dedicated her girlish clothes and her childhood toys to the *Lār* or *Larēs* of her household. A spear-point was then used to part her hair into three tresses which were wound around her head and fastened with woolen fillets. She was dressed in a white seamless tunic, saffron-colored hair net, veil and shoes (saffron was the Roman wedding color). As soon as the evening star appeared she was escorted to the groom's house in solemn procession, accompanied by boys and girls singing, and by matrons of honor (*prōnubae*) and by men carrying torches, as well as by her unmarried female friends carrying a distaff and spindle, symbols of her new duties as a wife. Nuts, cakes, and coins, symbols of wealth and fertility, were scattered among the bystanders. At the groom's door the torches were extinguished and thrown to the spectators, who scrambled to get them as lucky charms. The bride then anointed the door with oil and wreathed the doorposts with woolen fillets. She was then lifted over the threshold by the young men, to keep her from stumbling, an inauspicious omen. Inside, the priest called *Flāmen Diālis*, surrounded by ten witnesses, sacrificed a sow and read the auspices from its entrails. The groom offered the bride fire and water, and she spoke the words *"Ubi tū Gāius, ego Gāia."* The couple then sat on two seats covered with a single sheepskin, broke and ate a spelt-cake, and joined hands while the marriage contract was read and witnessed. There followed the marriage feast, and the singing of songs making fun of or insulting the bride and groom (to ward off the evil eye).

When a baby was born, it was placed on the floor at its father's feet, who recognized its legitimacy by picking it up. For the first week of its life it was thought to be vulnerable to evil spirits or the evil eye. Juno and Hercules were invoked to protect it. A couch for Juno and a table of food for Hercules were set up in the *ātrium*. At the end of this period, on the *diēs lustricus*, a male child was given a name, and a locket containing charms against the evil eye was hung around his neck.

When a Roman of good family died, the body was washed, dressed in the dead man's robes of office, and laid out on a bed in the *ātrium* with its feet toward the door. A branch of cypress was hung outside the door. During the mourning period the bereaved family did not wash, comb their hair, or change their clothes. On the day of the funeral, the body was carried to the forum, where a near relative pronounced a eulogy on the dead man, naming his chief accomplishments; these might also be written or depicted on signs carried in the funeral procession. The corpse was escorted outside the city walls by a band of musicians, hired female mourners singing dirges, and clients or hired actors wearing the wax masks of the dead man's ancestors (normally kept in the *tablīnum* of the house) and dressed in their official garments. The heir carried a torch to light the funeral pyre, which was piled with offerings and anointed with perfumed oil. When the fire had burnt out, the bones were collected, washed in wine, and placed in an urn. The urn (or coffin, if the body was to be inhumed rather than cremated—both customs were used) was then placed in the tomb. Some days later the heir swept death out of the house with a special broom.

Illustrations in the Text

p. 27. Altar showing a wedding scene. The children are carrying the implements for the sacrifice with the incense and salted meal cakes used in elaborate Roman wedding ceremonies. The round dish carried by the boy is the *patera*, a special vessel used for pouring wine-offerings.

p. 29. The second scene on this relief may represent the moment when the father legitimizes the child by picking him up from the floor.

p. 32. This portrait comes from one of the largest bakeries in Pompeii, part of which is also a dwelling. The man in the picture is probably T. Terentius Neo, brother of T. Terentius Proculus, the baker. If so, he refers to himself in an election poster as *stūdiōsus* (in this context probably "law student"). This may be why he had his portrait painted holding a book, or the inclusion of a scroll and tablet may indicate that the subjects of the portrait were proud of their literacy.

p. 35. Note the living effect of Roman portraiture, in spite of the mutilations. This *paterfamiliās* seems well-endowed with the Roman ideal of *gravitās*. The fact that the child appears as a portrait bust indicates that he had predeceased his parents. The funeral scene below shows the procession of musicians, bier, family, and hired female mourners. Tearing the hair and beating the breast were Roman signs of mourning.

FOOD AND EATING

The Romans ate three meals a day: a very light breakfast (*ientāculum*), bread moistened with olive oil or wine, sometimes accompanied by fruit or cheese; a lunch (*prandium*), also light, usually cold, often composed of leftovers from the evening before; and dinner (*cēna*), the substantial meal of the day. The *cēna*, because artificial light was so poor, was eaten early by our standards: it might begin at 2:00 or 3:00 P.M. It consisted of three parts: the *gustātiō* (appetizers) of eggs, shellfish, salad, and the like, accompanied by *mulsum*, wine flavored with honey; the *fercula*, the main part of the meal, made up of an odd number of courses of fish, poultry, and meat (the chief dish was the middle one of the series); and the *secunda mēnsa or secundae mēnsae* (dessert) of fruits and sometimes pastry. Wine was drunk during the *fercula* and *secunda mēnsa*. If the host was serving some especially prized wine it accompanied the dessert. Between the *fercula* and *secunda mēnsa* there was a pause during which offerings were made to the household gods. The meal was often followed by a drinking bout (*commissātiō*) during which a large wine cup was passed around and toasts were drunk.

Kitchens were very simple. If we may judge by Pompeii, many houses had no kitchen, using braziers to warm food bought already cooked. Only the larger houses had kitchens, and only the very wealthy had their own ovens. The ordinary kitchen was small, open to the sky, with a raised hearth to serve as a stove; the pots and pans sat on tripods and hot coals were raked under them. The number of coals determined the heat; a high heat was obtained by fanning them. Most people bought their bread from the bakery or made it at home and sent it to the bakery to be baked, first stamping it with the family monogram to be sure of getting the same loaves back.

The Romans reclined at meals, resting on the left elbow. Each diner might have a small couch to himself, but the normal arrangement was that of three large sloping couches on three of the four sides of the table, the *triclinium*, with three diners on each couch. The slaves served from the open fourth side. There were places of greater and lesser honor, as follows:

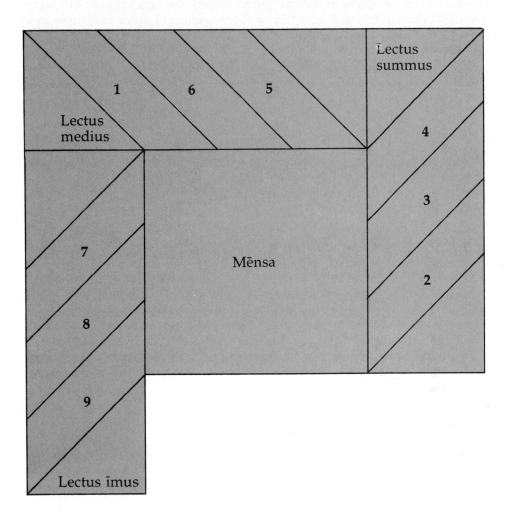

1. Locus cōnsulāris—guest of honor
2. Locus summus in lectō summō
3. Locus medius in lectō summō
4. Locus īmus in lectō summō
5. Locus summus in lectō mediō
6. Locus medius in lectō mediō
7. Locus summus in lectō īmō—host
8. Locus medius in lectō īmō—member of host's family
9. Locus īmus in lectō īmō—member of host's family

Roman tableware was made of pottery of all grades from coarse to fine, glass, bronze, silver, and gold. The finer pottery and metalware were often beautifully decorated. Besides the various wine cups, there were plates and bowls of different sizes, as well as special dishes like eggcups. Spoons were used for soup and boiled eggs. Since there were no knives and forks in a place setting, a special slave carved the various dishes into bite-sized pieces, which were eaten with the fingers.

The staple food of the early Romans was a kind of pulse or spelt porridge. Later this was baked into a cake or wafer on a griddle. Eventually these were replaced by bread, which remained the staple food. A Roman proverb says: *"Pānis rādix vīnum cēna pauperōrum"* (the *rādix* was probably a turnip), and bread, wine and vegetables were the basic diet of the Romans throughout most of their history. By the late Republic and during the Empire some fish and poultry had been added for special occasions. The wealthy also had meat fairly often, along with more expensive fish and poultry (including such unlikely birds as parrots, flamingos, and ostriches). Fish were particularly important; the Romans knew 150 varieties, most of them edible, in all price ranges. Ubiquitous in Roman cuisine was the highly prized fish sauce called *garum* or *liquāmen*, which came at different prices depending on how long it had matured. It has been made in modern times by the ancient recipes, and is hardly distinguishable from anchovy paste. Roman cuisine was essentially one of sauces, added to dishes cooked simply by baking, broiling, frying, or boiling. To the modern western palate these sauces have odd combinations of sweet and salty or sweet and sour elements. Olive oil was mostly used where we would use butter, and honey for sugar, which was not known to the Romans. They had no rice, noodles, potatoes, tomatoes, corn, oranges, bananas, strawberries, raspberries, chocolate, coffee, tea, or distilled spirits. They drank a great variety of wines, however, from all over the Roman world. They seem to have had some concept of good and bad vintage years but believed in the fallacy that wines go on improving with age.

One curious feature of the more elaborate dinners was the attempt on the part of the cooks to show their skill by making one food resemble another, e.g. suckling pig disguised as a chicken, cakes made to look like boiled eggs, etc. In general the presentation of the food was as important as its taste.

Illustrations in the Text

p. 39. In most cities, fish, meat, and fresh fruits and vegetables were all sold at a central market called a *macellum*, rather than in shops scattered through the town. Such markets usually included a chapel, since the animals to be slaughtered were actually sacrificed to the gods.

p. 41. The relief shows a market stall. The dealer is using her cages of poultry and rabbits as a counter. Notice also the hamper in which the vegetables were carried.

pp. 44–45. In the northern provinces, the more old-fashioned custom was preserved of having only the men recline at table, while the women sat in chairs. At a Roman banquet the food and wines to be consumed might be set out on display for the guests to see (some of the great houses of Pompeii have a special room for this purpose). Here we see the wines set out on a table, while the dishes are displayed on a sideboard.

p. 48. The simplest kind of *thermopōlium* or cookshop, found in great numbers in any excavated Roman town, was a small open-fronted shop with a counter in which were sunk large pots to keep the food warm. Families too poor to maintain kitchens would buy their food here ready-cooked and carry it home. Some of the larger *thermopōlia* have tables inside or in a garden behind, where customers could eat their food; some also functioned as wine shops and gambling houses. This *thermopōlium* is one of the most elaborate: note the buffet counters with niches and stepped marble shelves for displaying food and drink, and the sign showing that one could buy vegetables, wine, and cheese. The counter to the left, at the wide opening to the street, has the food-warming pots sunk inside, a kind of ancient steam table. The garden for outdoor dining is to the right.

p. 52. Since bread and wine were staples in the diet, bakeries and wine shops were not centrally located, but scattered throughout the city. Wealthy families bought their wine in *amphorae* (i.e., by the barrel); poorer people bought a pitcherful at a time, like the boy in the picture.

p. 55. The popularity of seafood is shown by the widespread use of mosaics showing sea life in the decoration of dining rooms.

p. 57. The Romans knew a very large variety of edible fish and other seafood. In their decorations they were fond of scenes showing cupids at various occupations. This mosaic comes from the Basilica (public hall and courthouse) of Aquileia.

p. 59. Since there seems to be no place for this kind of wood-built counter in any of the numerous bakeries found in Pompeii, this picture probably represents a distribution of free bread to the populace, perhaps at the large opening from the Comitium into the Colonnade at the southeast corner of the Forum of Pompeii. The distributor in his white wool tunic is (by Roman standards) better dressed than the dark-wool clad people receiving the bread. The loaves are of a shape known from both Pompeii and Herculaneum, and possibly one of two kinds common in Campania today.

BUSINESS AND INDUSTRY

Roman industry, crafts, and trades were as multifarious as ours. All the necessities of daily life had of course to be supplied, and as the great fortunes were more and more derived, not slowly from the land, but rapidly from speculation, the principle of conspicuous waste created a growing demand for luxuries as well. Almost any kind of modern industry, craft, or trade can, *mūtātīs mūtandīs,* be matched in antiquity. The chief difference lies in the failure of the Romans to develop a machine-based technology, for they had no industrial revolution. The ingenuity of scientists produced inventions which could have revolutionized industry. For example, the principle of the steam-engine was widely understood, and numerous hydraulic devices had been developed, but these were thought of essentially as amusing toys, and were never applied to production methods. The institution which inhibited and replaced machine technology was that of slavery. In the long run the machine would no doubt have been more economical than the slave, whose upkeep was expensive, having to be maintained through the unproductive periods of extreme youth and old age—even when a faithful slave was rewarded with manumission, his former master had some obligation to support him—but the abundant supply of slaves, who could be bought or bred at home, meant that there was no immediate pressure to develop more efficient methods.

Consequently the Romans had nothing we would recognize as a factory. Some of the principles of mass production were understood and applied— for example, cheap terra cotta lamps of the same design and identical decoration are found in every part of the empire—but the place of the factory was held by the large slave workshops (*ergastēria*), or more often by the guilds of free proprietors of small slave-run workshops, who banded together to standardize their output, fix prices, and market their wares. Like our labor unions, these guilds functioned also as political factions, supporting particular candidates for public office. This is known from the election posters of Pompeii.

In the Roman world, with its good roads and harbors and its lack of trade barriers, the market for manufactured goods was very wide. The fine red pottery of Arretium, the bronzes of Campania, Italian glassware, Egyptian papyrus, the dyed woolen cloth of the Levant, etc., were sent to the furthest corners of the empire. A small ironmonger of Pompeii includes Rome on his list of eight market towns (the others are all near Pompeii). Presumably the guild of ironmongers there sent samples to Rome for exporters and foreign buyers to inspect. Rome was certainly not the only center of this kind. Wholesale buyers of processed woolen cloth must have flocked to Pompeii to view samples in the great cloth-processors' hall there, a colonnaded courtyard surrounded by dozens of large show windows, and offices for representatives of the various houses. The Square of the Corporations at Ostia was a similar construction, a park surrounded by many small offices in which various guilds and large trading corporations could install their representatives.

In the late republic and early empire great fortunes could be made in the import-export business. This trading could be engaged in by individuals with capital, by the great commercial families, or by joint stock companies with capital invested by shareholders. The Knights (*Equitēs*) of Rome amassed huge fortunes safely by diversifying their investments. Investors with less capital who were willing to gamble (particularly freedmen) went in for more risky speculations, with even more dramatic returns and losses. A quick response on the part of an importer to the changing fads and fashions in fabrics for clothing, or in wines and foodstuffs, could make a fortune, particularly if he was able to be the first to meet the demand, before the market was flooded, prices fell, and the fickle wealthy turned to some new craze. The large businesses, family-run or shareholder-controlled, had branch offices in every part of the empire, and indeed well beyond its borders. The 80,000 Roman citizens massacred in Asia Minor at the orders of Mithridates of Pontus must have been there mostly to engage in trade, as also the Italian residents of Numidia slaughtered by Jugurtha. Spices were imported from Arabia, silk from China—this last at such a rate as to cause a serious gold drain in the early empire.

Banking practices kept pace with the expansion of big business. Ancient equivalents of checking accounts and bank loans can be identified.

Illustrations in the Text

p. 61. The tails and animal-skin garments show these vintners to be satyrs and the relief Dionysiac. However, ordinary humans pressed grapes in the same way, using a staff to support themselves and keep their balance.

p. 63. A dish to match one of these molds may be seen on p. 21. Silver utensils were probably sold by weight.

p. 65. The merchant appears to be showing the customer a book of samples. Notice the display of cushions and belts.

p. 72. Cutlery was probably made, sold and reconditioned in this shop. The display board contains pruning-hooks and knives.

p. 75. (*upper*) Each of these offices, lined up behind a portico, had its own sign in the form of a mosaic in the portico pavement. Many of the offices were maintained by shipowners from the provinces. (*lower*) The inscription reads *Nāvicul (āriī) Karthāg (iniēnsēs) dē suō.* "Independent Ship-Owners of Carthage" (*dē suō = suā sponte* or *per sē*).

p. 77. Notice the worker treading the cloth in a washtub. A good example of the Roman use of slaves where we would use machinery: the washtub has a human agitator. The handrails were to keep him from losing his balance as he jumped on the cloth. Such tubs with rails are found in the *fullōnicae* of Pompeii. The complete process seems to have been as follows: when it came from the weavers, the cloth was first soaked in an ammonia solution to remove the oil; then it was stretched on a frame over burning sulphur to bleach it; when it had dried it was hung up and teased with a comb to raise the nap which was then shaved off; finally it was washed and pressed in a mangle.

p. 79. (l.) An assistant blows on the bellows. (r.) Various implements of the trade and a lock. Note the shield protecting the bellows man from the heat of the forge.

p. 81. This table of linear measures from the market at Leptis Magna in North Africa was used by the market commissioners to insure the honesty of vendors by providing a check for their measures. In the Forum at Pompeii there was a large stone table marked with linear measures. It had hollows carved out in its thick top corresponding to the various measures of volume. There was also a place for a set of standard weights.

p. 83. Scales with two pans were used, as well as steelyards, for weighing merchandise. Our word *balance* comes from the two-pan (*bilanx*) scales.

p. 86. These two coins issued in the reign of Hadrian (A.D. 117–138) are representative of two of the main denominations, the denarius in silver and the sestertius in bronze. The sestertius was worth one-quarter of a denarius (the ratio of a twenty-five cent piece to a dollar). The *ās* from earliest times was the basic unit, a denarius containing ten of them. In the denarius shown *S C* stands for *Senātūs cōnsultō*, "by decree of the Senate"; the inscription reads *Pont(ifex) Max(imus) Tr(ibūniciā) Pot(estāte), Cō(n)s(ul) III (tertium)*, "High Priest, with the power of a Tribune, Consul for the third time" (titles of Hadrian). Frequently the reverse of coins commemorates the acts of the emperors. Here the Emperor is shown enthroned; before him stands a woman with three children. *Lībertās restitūta*, "freedom restored," may refer to Hadrian's approval of the principle that children born to a couple of whom one was a citizen and the other a slave would be classed as Roman citizens. The sestertius here shown has the same inscription as the denarius, with the addition of a warship, a common type on Roman coins. The obverse of imperial coins usually bears a portrait head of the emperor.

p. 87. The tablet contains a contract. The part containing the agreement is sealed with string and the seals of the eight witnesses; the unsealed part contains a summary of the contents.

p. 90. Consumption of olive oil was great. Perfumed oil was widely used both by men and women. At the baths one was rubbed with it before exercising, and at dinner parties guests were given bottles of it to pour on their hair. In cookery olive oil was used where we would use any kind of oil, fat, or butter; and in most of the empire olive oil was the only lamp oil. The third pressing oil tends to be rather watery. There must have been a good deal of trouble with lamps sputtering and going out, and at best the flame from olive oil is smoky and yellow.

p. 93. The *L* in the fourth line of the inscription is for *lībertae*, so the meaning is "Publius Nonius Zethus, (Priest) of Augustus, had (this sarcophagus) made for himself, for Nonia Hilara his fellow-freedwoman, (and) for his wife Nonia Pelagia, freedwoman of Publius (Nonius); Publius Nonius Heraclio." The inscription is incomplete in that there is no predicate for this last subject. The terminology tells us a good deal about these people. When a slave was manumitted he took the praenomen and nomen of his former master, keeping his own name as a cognomen. His son would keep the same praenomen and nomen but have a new cognomen, whereas in a family not of servile origin the son would keep the same nomen and cognomen but have a new praenomen. Therefore we can see that Zethus, Hilara, and Pelagia were all originally slaves of one Publius Nonius and were later manumitted (though Zethus is not called *libertus*, Hilara could not be his *conliberta* if he had not been a slave as well). Zethus then married Pelagia. Heraclio, since he is not said to be a freedman, was probably their son, born after they had been freed.

A grain mill consisted of an hour-glass-shaped stone turning on a conical stone. Grain was put into the funnel-shaped top of the upper stone and the meal which came out below was caught in a circular trough. The coarseness of the meal could be regulated by raising or lowering the upper stone on its pivot.

MEDICINE

The science of medicine has always been empirical, a matter of making an educated guess as to what treatment will be efficacious and then trying it out. Methods of treatment have been refined over the centuries; principles of research remain unchanged. Part of the progress has been the isolation of diseases, the distinguishing of different diseases which have the same symptoms. For example, the cough (*tussis*) and the fever (*febris*) to the Romans were names of diseases, just as for us pneumonia, a disease a generation ago, is now a symptom.

We may, however, distinguish between folk medicine, in which the accumulated experience of a people is passed down informally by tradition, and scientific medicine, practiced by people specially trained and following some particular set of theories. For example, Hippocrates (460–359 B.C.) considered diseases to result from an imbalance in the four main fluids of the body, while Asclepiades (Ist Century B.C.) blamed a slowing down of the movement of the atoms of the body; each treated his patients accordingly.

Until the third century B.C. Roman medicine was essentially folk medicine. An example of its methods can be found in the *Dē Agrī Cultūrā* of the elder Cato, especially his long passage on cabbage. A typical treatment: "The wild cabbage has very great powers. You should dry it and grind it up quite small. If you want to purge anyone, he shouldn't eat the day before; the next morning before he eats anything, give him the ground cabbage and four *cyathī* of water. Nothing else purges so well, neither hellebore nor scammony, and without danger, and let me tell you it's good for the body. You'll cure people you had no hope of curing. This is how you treat someone who's going to be purged with this purge: give him this in water for seven days. When he wants to eat, give him roast meat. If he doesn't want to eat, give him cooked cabbage and bread, and let him drink a mild wine, diluted; he should bathe seldom, but be rubbed with oil. Anyone who has been purged this way will enjoy good health for a long time, and he won't catch any disease unless it's his own fault."

In 293 B.C. there was a plague in Rome so serious that the books of the Cumaean Sybil (originally sold by her to Tarquin the Proud) were consulted. The response was that the cult of the Greek god of healing, Asclepius, should be brought to Rome. The Romans sent an embassy to his greatest cult center at Epidaurus, and were given a snake embodying the god, which they brought back to Rome. As the barge was being brought up the Tiber, the snake slipped from it and swam to the Tiber Island. The temple of Aesculapius (as the Romans called him) was thus built on a spot which the god himself had chosen. A smaller shrine of the god was later placed in the Forum near the healing spring of Juturna.

With the arrival of Aesculapius, the Romans accepted Greek medical science more readily. Soon there were many Greek doctors at Rome, attached as private physicians to the great families or running their own hospitals and clinics. Later they received government support, and free medical treatment was made available to the people.

Medicine has also its religious side. In the temples of many of the gods are found votive offerings in the form of replicas of parts of the human body, testimonials to prayers for healing answered. The votive offerings demanded by Aesculapius are more informative. They were inscriptions describing the cure in some detail. To be healed by Aesculapius one had to make appropriate sacrifices and then spend the night sleeping in his temple (*incubātiō*); the god appeared in a dream and gave his advice. The quality of his advice naturally depended upon the intuitions of the dreamer. Some cures are quite sensible—an obese man is told to eat less—some are magical, and must be classed as faith healing of psychosomatic disorders. The most interesting testimonials come from the long series at Epidaurus, but there are extant quite a number from Rome itself.

Illustrations in the Text

p. 94. The oculist may be applying a salve to the eyes. This relief from the sarcophagus of the Sossi at Ravenna may record the family's gratitude for a cure.

p. 98. Note the careful workmanship and the non-slip grips. These instruments are only a part of the collection found in the House of the Surgeon at Pompeii. There were also trepanning tools (rather like modern Italian lever corkscrews), clamps for holding wounds or incisions open, and large hypo-dermic needles for injecting medicines into wounds or sores which had closed up.

BATHS AND WATER SUPPLIES

The development of good municipal water supplies was one of Rome's greatest contributions to the ancient world. Before the emergence of the Romans as a world power, most cities and towns relied upon natural springs and streams, wells or rainwater collected in cisterns. Most people had to fetch their water from some central source, and contaminated water must have caused much disease. With the coming of the Romans there was hardly any place of importance which did not have its aqueducts. These covered stone channels brought water often from great distances, tunneling straight through hills and crossing valleys on great arches of brick, masonry, or (from the first century B.C.) poured concrete. Another way of getting the water across valleys was by the inverted siphon, an achievement less spectacular, but hardly less impressive when we remember that the water-tight pipe required had to be made by rolling and fusing sheets of lead. Water was plentiful: only four of Rome's many waters are still in use today, but they adequately supply the present city.

An aqueduct carried water from some upland lake or river (*caput aquārum*) to a reservoir (*castellum*) from which it was distributed to its various desti-nations. The *castella* at Nîmes (in France) and Thuburbo Maius (North Africa) were simple, regulated by gravity and size of pipe bores. Water for the public fountains was drawn off from the bottom, for the public baths above that, and for private use from the top of the tower. Hence in time of drought or in case of damage to the aqueduct, private users would be the first, and public fountains the last, to lose water. At Pompeii, where the important wool-finishing trade required a large supply of water, a more sophisticated system was used. The public fountains were supplied constantly, but the flow to baths, private houses, and the wool-factories could be regulated by adjusting gates so that the amount of water supplied depended on the time of day. More water went to the factories during working hours, to the baths in the afternoon, etc.

From the *castella* the water was brought by inverted siphons to various water-towers; these were often disguised as triumphal arches, built into city gates, etc. The towers provided the water pressure for adjacent buildings. Within the house the flow of water was regulated by stopcocks and faucets much like ours.

The great public baths were also a uniquely Roman institution. They began to appear early in the second century B.C., and reached their full development in the early empire. After that, more and bigger baths were built (there were 952 in the city of Rome by the fourth century of our era), but the plan remained essentially the same. The term "baths" is a little misleading; they were more like very elegant versions of what today we would call community centers. There were warm and hot rooms (heated by hypocausts, hot air channels beneath the floors and in the hollow walls), and cold and hot baths and pools; but there were also many arrangements which we would not associate with baths. There were rooms for massage, rooms and open court-yards for exercises and games, often with trainers or coaches provided by the establishment; there were often tracks for running. There were large gardens, laid out with pleasant walks among trees and shrubs. There were lecture halls for lectures on philosophy, cooking, and other subjects, and for poetry-readings; there were public libraries of Greek and Latin books. Finally, there were often eating-houses and wineshops in or near the complexes. In other words, though the baths were luxurious, they did not necessarily make their patrons decadent or effete; the standard cinema image of fat old men lolling in steaming water might be replaced by that of large numbers of people earnestly improving their bodies and their minds. The variety of activities offered also explains why the Romans could spend so much time in the baths; the usual hour for the actual bathing was between two and three, but the establishments remained open until sunset.

There was no fixed routine for using the baths—one could use whatever facilities he liked—but a popular order was: warm room (*tepidārium*), hot room (*lacōnicum*), hot bath (in the *caldārium*), oil massage, physical exercise, cold plunge (in the *frīgidārium*), the skin scraped with a special scraper (*strigilis*), a rub-down with a linen towel.

Illustrations in the Text

p. 106. The central building is 750′ × 380′; the grounds cover 33 acres; the entire complex, grounds and all, is raised 20′ above ground level on huge vaults, making room for service passages and for storage. (*left*) The Hot Room (*Caldārium*) of the baths contained a basin of cool water so that bathers who were oppressed by the heat might refresh themselves.

p. 110. The Pons Aemilius, built under the supervision of members of the Gens Aemilia from 174 to 142 B.C., replaced the original wooden bridge below the Tiber Island, the Pons Sublicius.

p. 113. On this plan the **a**'s along the NE side mark the arcade which made a covered sidewalk for this side of the street. Behind it the foundation vaults are left open to form a long row of two-storied shops, each about 14′ wide. The main entrance is up steps at **N,** though there are smaller access stairs flanking the lateral apses of the enclosure (also marked **a**).

The main block of the baths has four entrances (**b**); the two central ones lead through large vestibules to the disrobing rooms (**L**) or to the large central hall (**JBJ**). The three great cross-vaults of **B** are buttressed by three barrel vaults on each side. Under the ones at the four corners are pools; under the central one to the NE a round basin. The large room marked **A** is an open air pool. The NE wall is covered with applied architectural decoration surrounding niches in which were numerous statues. This room is usually called the *frīgidārium*. Through **C**, the *tepidārium*, one could reach the *caldārium* (**D**) with its central round hot pool. The two niches flanking the entrance had smaller hot pools. The outer entrances (**b**) led through antechambers (**H**) flanked by anointing rooms to the *palaestrae* (**G**), open-air exercising areas. These were surrounded on three sides by a portico, on the fourth by a series of alcoves (*exedrae*, marked **F** on the plan) for spectators and trainers. The service passages, running under not only the main block but the enclosed grounds as well, were reached from the open courtyards (on the plan **M** and the areas on each side of **M**). To the SW of the main block was a large garden, onto which opened a series of rooms (**c** and **E**) for lectures, recitations, etc. This garden was surrounded on the other three sides by a portico (**U**). At **P** there were large *exedrae*, sheltered spots overlooking the garden between their own columns and those of the portico. In chilly weather one could sit in room **R**, heated by hypocausts; if the weather was hot, in **Q**, which had fountains. Reached from **R** and **Q** were curved ambulatories, each half open, half covered by an arcade. The rooms marked **T** were libraries, one Greek, one Latin. **S** was a running track, with seats for spectators to the SW. The reservoirs (**V**), were 64 vaulted chambers in two stories, fed by a branch of the Aqua Marcia (**Z**).

THE ARMY

For an account of the army in Caesar's day, see Book II of this series, Jenney, Scudder and Baade, *Second Year Latin*, Allyn and Bacon, Inc.

Illustrations in the Text

p. 117. Constantine's triumphal arch is decorated mostly with sculpture taken from earlier monuments. The rectangular reliefs inside the arch and the figures over the columns came from the Basilica Ulpia in the Forum of Trajan. The circular reliefs are from an arch of Hadrian and the upper panels and sculptures are from an Arch of Marcus Aurelius. In reliefs showing an emperor, the emperor's head has been recut as a portrait of Constantine. Actually, only the decorative details and the small friezes date from Constantine's time.

p. 122. During the Republic it was usual for a general to have one cohort of elite troops as a bodyguard; this was called *cohors praetōriāna* (just as the general's headquarters was the *praetōrium*). It was made up of men chosen for their valor and loyalty from the general's army, though the governor of a peaceful province might appoint to his *cohors praetōriāna* impoverished friends. In 27 B.C. Augustus established a bodyguard of nine praetorian cohorts under the command of two Praetorian Prefects appointed by him from the class of Equites. Augustus merely kept these troops on hand in case of trouble. Under Tiberius, however, the Praetorians were all concentrated in one camp at Rome, and became a very powerful force in maintaining the imperial regime. Frequently there was only one Praetorian Prefect, and he served as a kind of Prime Minister to the Emperor. To be chosen for the Praetorian Cohorts was a great honor for a soldier, and the choice was long restricted to soldiers from Italy and the home provinces. The Praetorians' pay was three times that of the ordinary soldier. When an Emperor died without having made arrangements for the succession, the Senate theoretically chose his successor, the choice being ratified by the people; but since there was no nearby military force to match theirs, it was actually the Praetorians and their Prefect who made the choice. After the death of Commodus, the Praetorians actually sold the Empire at a formal auction to the highest bidder, Didius Julianus. Didius had not intended to attend the auction, but was talked into it by his wife and daughter. Arriving at the Praetorian camp after the gates were closed and the auction begun, he was hoisted up and did his bidding from the top of the wall. When Septimius Severus seized the throne, he replaced the Italians of the Cohorts with men from his own army, at the same time increasing the number in each cohort to 1000. By this time there were ten Praetorian Cohorts. The Praetorians were finally disbanded by Constantine.

p. 127. This triumphal procession shows captives, sacrificial bulls and triumphator. The *triumphus* was a religious rite celebrating the return of a victorious general. The general remained outside the gates until the Senate made arrangements for him to retain his *imperium* as he entered. If he entered the city before such arrangements were made, he automatically lost his *imperium* as he crossed the city's magical boundary, and could not triumph. The procession, which went through the Forum along the Sacra Via to the Capitolium, consisted of the magistrates and the Senate, trumpeters, paintings of battles and allegorical figures representing the cities, rivers, mountains, etc. of the enemy, the more impressive spoils of the war, the principal captives in chains, white bulls for sacrifice, the lictors, and then the Triumphator in a chariot drawn by four white horses, followed by his army. The Triumphator wore royal purple-dyed garments embroidered in gold, and carried a branch of laurel and an ivory sceptre. Behind him a public slave held a golden crown over his head and whispered to him "Remember that you are a human being!" (*Hominem tē mementō*). If to these facts we add that the general's face was painted red it seems obvious that he was for this one day Jupiter incarnate, since the garments, crown and sceptre were those of Jupiter, and since the earliest statue of Jupiter at Rome was of terra-cotta. The army sang coarse songs, insulting their general, to protect him from the envy of the gods. At the Capitolium the Triumphator laid his laurel branch in the lap of the god's statue and then offered a sacrifice of thanksgiving.

pps. 131–132. The artillery pieces were grouped under the general name of *tormenta* because they worked by torsion power. Women's hair was considered the best material for making the tightly-twisted bundles which powered these machines.

p. 139. Hadrian's Wall, built in A.D. 122, fifteen feet high by eight feet wide, was 73 miles long, protected by a series of fortresses, mile-castles, and turrets. North of it was a ditch twenty feet wide and ten feet deep. The photographs show a portion of the wall and the remains of a granary attached to one of the fortresses.

p. 143. In this scene Roman soldiers in Egypt prepare to celebrate a victory. The Romans loved "Egyptian" decorations, which seemed to them remote and exotic, in much the same way as the English did Chippendale's vision of China, neither being at all authentic. This is a detail from a very large semicircular mosaic which filled one of the apses of Sulla's Temple of Fortuna Primigenia at Praeneste (modern Palestrina).

ENTERTAINMENT

Theatre. Dramatic performances formed part of the religious festivals (*lūdī*) of Rome. By and large, the Roman taste was for farce rather than comedy, melodrama rather than tragedy; above all, a Roman audience liked a spectacular effect. The native Italian drama consisted of extempore exchanges of slapstick and rude repartee among comically masked actors, interspersed with dances; the characters were probably stock types, the "theatre" a booth at the fair. In the third century B.C. both comedy and tragedy were introduced in translations from the Greek; later historical plays (on Roman themes) were invented, as well as comedies with Roman (not Greek) characters. It was not until 145 B.C. that theatres with fixed seats were built. These were temporary theatres of wood, and were taken down after the performance. Before this time spectators presumably had to bring their own seats, or stand. The first permanent theatre was built by Pompey in 55 B.C., and was followed by the theatres of Balbus and Marcellus in 13 B.C. These were the only permanent theatres at Rome; temporary wooden ones were still erected as the need arose.

Late republican and early imperial productions were lavish. At the opening of Pompey's theatre, in a tragedy about Agamemnon's return from Troy, the booty of Troy was brought on stage loaded on 600 mules. Under Nero, in a play called *The Fire*, a house was erected on stage, furnished, and then actually burnt down. To add realism to the acting the actors were allowed to keep anything they rescued from the blaze. Occasionally condemned criminals might take part in dramatic performances and actually be killed on the stage. In spite of these spectacular effects the Romans soon lost interest in the drama and turned more and more to comic opera (*mīmī*) and ballet (*pantomīmī*).

All of these forms of entertainment produced their popular stars; we know the names of many actors, singers, and dancers. There may even have been fan clubs—on the wall of an inn in Pompeii we find scribbled a notice of a meeting of men calling themselves *fanāticī Actiānī Anicētiānī*, fans of Actius Anicetus (an actor very popular at Pompeii).

Illustrations in the Text

p. 145. From tomb frescoes it appears that the dance played an important part in Etruscan culture. Except for certain primitive ritual dances in honor of the Gods, performed by priests, the Romans did not dance. They did, however, enjoy watching Etruscan and Greek dancers perform.

p. 150. There is little literary evidence for any popularity of satyr-plays among the Romans, though they may have been performed in the more Hellenic atmosphere of Campania. In Athens a satyr-play accompanied each set of three tragedies. The basic plots are taken from mythology, but the chief interest lies in the amusing dances and antics of the impudent but cowardly chorus of satyrs. The Roman architect Vitruvius does give a brief description of appropriate scenery for satyr-plays, so perhaps they were performed in some parts of the Roman world. The mosaic of a backstage scene (from the floor of the tablinum of the House of the "Tragic Poet" in Pompeii) shows actors dressing for a satyr-play. Two actors wear goatskin loin-cloths, while another dons a goatskin tunic. The producer (possibly also the author) of the play sits with his hand resting on a tragic mask of a heroine. Behind him on the table is the mask of a tragic hero. The other mask in the box is that of an irascible old man from comedy. The figure in the long tunic is a flute player who accompanied songs on the stage; a piece of leather strapped across his mouth allows him to play the two flutes (actually shawms) simultaneously. The house of the "Tragic Poet" is so nicknamed because of the fact that its walls are frescoed with scenes from epic and tragedy.

p. 152. Two musical instruments which remained popular throughout antiquity appear in this tomb painting, the lyre (with a tortoise shell as a sounding board) and the double "flute" (in reality not a flute but a pair of shawms). In this painting two of the men wear himatia, the third, a toga. The Etruscans may be credited with the invention of the toga, which differs from the Greek himation in being trapezoidal and semicircular rather than rectangular. The himation was too bulky to be used as a military garment, on horseback or in battle, and the Etruscans solved this problem by removing two of the corners, keeping the essential width and length, which eliminated much of the weight. The Romans must have originally thought of the toga as a military uniform: hence it could be worn only by male citzens and was forbidden to respectable women. Hence also, the fact that the client had to wear the toga when he reported each morning to his patron's house (originally a military muster).

p. 155. The built-up hairdos were meant to increase the height of the actors. They also wore platform shoes.

p. 162. The Clever Slave taking sanctuary on an altar is a favorite theme of sculpture. The scene must have occurred in more than one comedy. At the end of Plautus' *Mōstellāria*, when the old master, Theopropides, discovers that he has been duped by his slave Tranio, he attempts to seize him and have him punished, but Tranio sits on the altar and refuses to leave it until the old man's wrath has been mollified. In the figure on the right the mouth of the actor can be seen through the mouth of the mask.

p. 167. The stock masks made it easy for the audience to follow the play, since they could tell at a glance the nature of any of the characters. The clever slave who saves his master from his father's wrath and helps him get the girl was a favorite character. He has direct lineal descendants in Harlequin and Mr. Punch.

p. 168. This theatre was built by Augustus in 13 B.C. and was dedicated to his nephew. It could hold 20,000. It is now the Palazzo Sermoneta near the Roman Forum. The exterior facade anticipates the Colosseum in the superposition of the three orders, Doric, Ionic, and Corinthian, one above the other. At the dedication of this theatre, Augustus' throne tipped over when he took his seat, so that he fell over on his back.

Gladiators. The Circus was the scene of the gladiatorial games. Unlike the plays and the races (*lūdī scaenicī* and *lūdī circēnsēs*), these were not called *lūdī* but *mūnera* (i.e. "funeral offerings"). The *mūnera gladiātōrum* appear to have originated among the Etruscans as funeral games, human sacrifices to provide the dead man with brave companions in the other world, or perhaps to give him some kind of vitality beyond the grave by offering him the lives of others. The *mūnera* were brought to Rome for the funeral of Marcus Brutus in 264 B.C. The games kept their funeral significance for a century and a half; important men left money in their wills for funeral games or later memorial games. But at the same time the gladiatorial games also became an immensely popular entertainment. At Brutus' funeral only three pairs of gladiators had fought; at the funeral of Titus Flamininus in 174 B.C. there were 37 pairs, and shortly after that 100 pairs became standard. In 105 B.C. the giving of games passed for the most part into the hands of the Aediles; they were not at first required by law to put on games, but a lavish spectacle became in effect a bribe to the electorate for further political advancement. Politicians vied with each other in their attempts to please the urban mob; Julius Caesar in his Aedileship sponsored games in which 320 pairs of gladiators fought. The expense of such games was ruinous; but advancement to the Praetorship and Consulship guaranteed appointment to the lucrative governorship of a province. The expense of the gladiatorial games explains to a great degree the corruption and dishonesty of provincial government: the Propraetor or

Proconsul had to recoup his losses somehow, and he did it by fleecing the provincials.

Under the Empire this incentive for giving games disappeared, but the mob still demanded them. One cannot but deplore the waste of human life in these spectacles, but it is perhaps unfair to accuse the citizenry of blood-lust pure and simple. It was the spectacle of human bravery, not of slaughter, which they came to see; they complained vehemently if the gladiators were not well-trained. The rationalization of the philosophers, that the games taught one not to fear death when even slaves despised it, may have been perfectly sincere. At any rate the games continued under the Empire; lavish games not only insured an Emperor's popularity, but became a kind of sounding board to test the attitude of the people towards the government. The urban mob was not afraid to hiss when the Emperor appeared, if he had done something unpopular. He could tell from his reception just how he stood with the people of Rome. The gladiatorial games grew in scope under the emperors. Trajan celebrated his victories in Dacia by exhibiting 5000 pairs of gladiators on one occasion.

The first gladiators were probably prisoners of war, Samnites, Gauls, Thracians, Britons, etc.; much of the interest of the spectacle was for the Romans to observe the styles of fighting of the different nationalities. Slaves were then trained to fight in these styles, and other methods of fighting were developed. It was also possible for a free man to volunteer to be a gladiator, but in doing so he lost his citizenship and to some degree even his freedom, since he took an oath to obey orders like the slaves. Gladiators were trained by *lanistae* (trainers) in special schools run by the city or municipal government or by private individuals. The gladiators were given a special diet and kept on strict training. Suicides and attempts at escape were not uncommon, but many of the trainees developed great pride in their specialties.

Gladiators were trained in many different styles of fighting. The earliest kind of gladiator was probably the Samnite (*Samnīs*). At first they would have been actual Samnite prisoners, but later native gladiators were taught to fight by their methods. The *Samnīs* wore a visored helmet with a plume, a broad belt, a greave on the left leg only (the left leg would be exposed when he knelt behind his shield), and on his left shoulder the *galērus*, a piece of armor extending upward to protect his neck from side blows of a sword. His sword was the *spatha*, a broad two-edged sword without a point; his shield, the *scūtum*. Other types derived from foreign methods of fighting were the *Thrāx* (Thracian), the *Essedārius* (Charioteer), and the *Myrmillō* (armed in Gallic fashion). The *Thrāx* wore a helmet and two greaves; he carried a small round shield (*parma*) and a curved sword (*sīca*). The lightly-armed *Essedārius* fought from the *essedum*, a light two-wheeled British war chariot drawn by two horses. The *Myrmillō* was armed as a Gaul with sword and shield; his name comes from that of a fish which was represented on his helmet.

The Romans preferred to pit one style of fighting against another; one of the favorite combinations was a *Thrāx* against a *Myrmillō*. At some point some *lanista* hit upon the idea of having the *Myrmillō* opposed by a fisherman, and so gladiators were trained to fight with a net and a three-pronged fish-spear. They were called *Rētiāriī* (Netmen), and had no defensive armor except occasionally the *galērus*. The *Rētiārius* proved so popular that soon a special opponent for him began to be trained, the *Secūtor* (Follower; apparently the *Rētiārius'* tactic was to keep withdrawing until he saw a chance to throw his net to good effect). The *Secūtor* was armed like the *Samnīs*, but with a different sort of helmet, and without the *galērus*, since he had no need to protect his neck from sword blows. This contest of a more heavily against a more lightly armed man was varied further by the introduction of the *Laqueārius* (Noose-man), armed only with a lasso and a curved piece of wood with which to disarm the *Secūtor* by twitching his sword from his grasp. Other specialty fighters were the *Dimachaerus* (Two-dagger-man) who fought with a dagger in each hand, the *Hoplomachus* (Armor-fighter) who wore a breastplate as well as greaves and a visored helmet, and the *Andābata* who was heavily armed but had a helmet-visor with no eye-holes, so that he fought blind and had to find his opponent by the sounds he made.

Some of the wealthier private citizens had gladiatorial schools of their own to supply such games as they might give, and some towns ran their own schools. The *ēditor* (giver of the games) might hire gladiators from a *lanista* who was in business for himself, keeping a troup of gladiators to rent out. The *ēditor* might get a consignment of prisoners who had been condemned to death (he had to make sure that each was either killed or returned to prison), but this was unpopular with the crowd, since the prisoners would not be trained fighters.

When there were to be games, advertisements (*programmata*) would be circulated and painted on walls. One such, from Pompeii, reads:

A(ulī) Suettī Certī Aedīlis familia gladiātōria pugnāb(it) Pompe(i)īs pr(īdiē) k(alendās) Iūniās; vēnatiō et vēla erunt.

"The gladiatorial troup of the Aedile Aulus Suettius Certus will fight at Pompeii on the day before the Kalends of June (30 May); there will be an animal show and awnings."

The *vēla,* for which the *ēditor* had to pay extra, were stretched over the seating part of the amphitheatre to shield spectators from the sun.

On the evening before the games, the gladiators were given an especially lavish meal, at which time connoisseurs who planned to bet on the games could come and inspect the gladiators.

The games were held in the Forum, the Circus, or in an amphitheatre. The first amphitheatre at Rome was that of Caesar's friend Curio, who for his games had two theatres built back to back. When the theatrical performances were over, the two theatres revolved, carrying the audiences with them, until they joined into one amphitheatre for the gladiatorial games. Rome went on using wooden amphitheatres until the reign of the Flavians, although other cities had had stone buildings for some time (Pompeii's stone amphitheatre, for example, was built in 80 B.C.). Vespasian, Titus and Domitian built the Amphitheatrum Flavium (which we usually call the Colosseum) on the site of the great lake of Nero's Golden House.

On the day of the games, very early while the spectators were still arriving, criminals who had been sentenced *ad bestiās* were exposed to wild animals. This spectacle was not considered very entertaining, and was probably performed to raise the blood-lust of the animals and make them fiercer for the next show, the *vēnātiō* (hunt), in which specially trained gladiators (*bestiāriī*) hunted or fought with wild animals, or the wild animals fought with each other. These shows had some of the fascination of the zoo, since every effort was made to import exotic animals which had not been seen before. The Romans especially liked to pit animals from different parts of the world against each other, lions against tigers, elephants against wild oxen, etc. The search for novelty led to some strange contests: for example, a man with his foot tied to the leg of a bull, fights a lion whose leg is tied to the foot of a man who is fighting the bull.

The spectacle was not always bloody. Animals might merely be shown in carefully constructed natural habitats, or trained animals might do tricks, as in our circuses. We hear of panthers trained to pull a chariot, and stranger still, of elephants trained to walk a tightrope. A favorite spectacle was one in which a concert artist in the guise of Orpheus (the legendary poet whose songs charmed wild animals) played and sang while trained wild animals crept out of their dens to lie down around him and listen to the music. During the games celebrating the opening of the Colosseum, an insufficiently trained bear spoiled the effect by killing and eating the singer.

At noon many of the spectators left for lunch. To give those who had brought their lunch something to look at, the *gladiātōrēs merīdiānī*, condemned criminals, were brought in. One was armed and made to kill another who was not; then the arms were taken from him and given to a third, who killed him, and so on. This was not considered very interesting.

The afternoon began with a great parade (*pompa*) of gladiators wearing special parade armor. They were accompanied by musicians, who continued to play during the fighting. First came a *prōlūsiō*, a preliminary skirmish with wooden swords. Amateurs among the spectators who wished to try their skill could duel with the experts using these harmless weapons. Then followed what everyone had been waiting for, the actual combats of the gladiators themselves.

If a gladiator found himself at the mercy of his opponent, he raised a finger to show he surrendered. It was then up to the *ēditor* to decide whether or not he was to be killed. The killing of a gladiator cost the *ēditor* money, so his impulse must usually have been to spare him. Since his aim was popularity however, he usually let himself be guided by the wishes of the people, who waved handkerchiefs if they wanted the fallen gladiator spared. If they wanted him killed they displayed upturned thumbs, the symbol of the *coup de grâce,* a sword-thrust through the throat. A man who had fought bravely would usually be spared. After a number of victories a gladiator might be set free at the demand of the audience. He was then presented with a wooden sword, which signified that though still a slave, he no longer had to fight in the arena unless he wished. He might end his days teaching other gladiators; if he was willing to fight, he might be able to buy his freedom or be set free by popular acclamation.

The smaller towns appear to have supported loyally their own gladiators. On one occasion, games between the gladiators of Pompeii and of Nuceria caused such a riot in the amphitheatre at Pompeii that the Emperor closed the amphitheatre for ten years.

Though gladiators were at the bottom of the social scale, they were often popular heroes, particularly with the ladies. The gladiators must have teased each other about what ladies' men they were. We find scratched on the walls of one of the gladiators' schools at Pompeii:

Crēscē(n)s rētiā(rius), pūpārum nocturnārum, matūtīnārum, aliārum mēdicus.
    "Crescens the Net-man, doctor for nighttime dolls, daytime dolls, and others."
Suspīrium puellārum Celadus T(h)r(āx).
    "Celadus the Thracian, the sigh of the girls."

Illustrations in the Text

p. 158. This picture shows a combat between two *Samnītēs* (or *Secutōrēs,*) since they do not wear the *galērus.*

p. 172. (*left*), a *Secūtor* has killed a *Rētiārius;* (*above*), a *Samnīs* delivers the *coup de grâce.*

p. 178. The armor in this picture is parade armor, not the armor used in actual fighting.

p. 188. Outer view of the Colosseum. An enormous awning drawn by ropes fixed to beams in the top outside cornice provided shade. The substructure contained arrangements for elevators to raise the animals to the arena. Sixty-six of the seventy ground-floor archways on the outside are numbered with Roman numerals. A spectator entered the arch corresponding to the number on his ticket and was led by an ingenious system of stairways to the section where his seat was. The masts which held the awning were put through holes in the cornice and supported by the projecting consoles. A special detachment of the navy was stationed at Rome to rig this awning.

p. 193. The tiers of seats for spectators rose to four stories, and accommodated 45–50,000 people. The basement was used for stage properties and cages for wild beasts.

p. 202. In this picture the artist has relied solely on literary descriptions since at that time there had been no archeological evidence. Some of the things shown in the picture are mounted and unmounted gladiators, boxing and wrestling, and in the center a representation of the *Lūdus Trōiānus,* a close-order horseback drill.

Chariot Races. Another class of *lūdī* were the chariot races, *lūdī circēnsēs.* Like the theatrical performances, they had a primarily religious significance. They were held in honor of various gods, but they also provided entertainment immensely popular with all classes of Romans.

The races were held in the various *circī* of Rome, the largest of which was the Circus Maximus, lying in the valley between the Palatine and Aventine Hills. This racecourse was thought to have been laid out by King Tarquinius Priscus (616–579 B.C.). It was continually enlarged and remodeled (notably by Julius Caesar) until by the fourth century it could seat 385,000. In the photograph of the model on p. 215, at the near end of the Circus are the *carcerēs* flanking the entrance gate with the box for the giver of the games above it. On either side of the *carcerēs* was a tower (*oppidum*) where the musicians were placed. The two-storied imperial box on the far side of the Circus was connected with the imperial palace on the Palatine Hill behind it. The monumental gate in the curved end of the Circus was called the *porta triumphālis.* It was used only when the triumphal procession of a victorious general passed through the Circus on its way to the Forum. The columns on curved bases were the *mētae,* the markers for the turns. These were joined by the *spīna,* a wall 4′ high and 12′ wide. In the center of the *spīna* was the underground altar of Consus, the god of the stream whose course had been put underground to make room for the racecourse. It was uncovered on his festivals in August and December. Near it was an obelisk of Ramses II brought from Egypt. Also on the *spīna* were numerous small temples, fountains, and statues (notable among them one of Victory). The lap markers were seven large wooden eggs, one of which was removed after each lap; and seven bronze dolphins, one of which was turned over after each lap (the egg was the symbol of Castor and Pollux, the horse-taming gods; the dolphin, of Neptune, creator of the horse). The Circus was 1800′ × 350′.

A day of races began with a parade (*pompa*) which proceeded from the Capitolium through the Forum to the Circus and once around the track. The *pompa* was led by the magistrate giving the games, riding in a triumphal chariot and wearing triumphal costume, scarlet tunic, wide-bordered toga, golden crown, and ivory sceptre. He was followed by the images of the gods on carts or litters, each accompanied by his own priests. There were also musicians.

After the procession the presiding magistrate took his place in his box above the starting gates (*carcerēs*). When he signaled the start by dropping a handkerchief, the gates were opened and the race began. These starting gates, twelve in number, were arranged across the end of the Circus on a slant so as to equalize the distance. The chariots, usually four in number, and with four horses each, made seven laps (about four and a half miles) around the central barrier. The two center horses were harnessed to the chariot pole, the outside ones tied directly to the chariot. The left-hand horse, the one on the inside at the turns, was considered to be the most important. Because of the difficulty of controlling four horses at once, the driver had the reins tied around his waist. He carried a knife to cut them so as not to be dragged if the chariot should smash into the barriers or be overturned. The chariots were light and tipped easily, and there was great danger of their going over at the turns; the driver had to keep them balanced with movements of his body. To facilitate this, his short tunic was strapped close to his body. To provide some protection from the other chariots if there should be an accident, the charioteer wore boots and a helmet-like cap.

As the chariots began their last lap, a chalk line was drawn across the end of the course, and the first chariot to cross it was the winner. Spirits ran high during the races, bets were laid (both form sheets and programs were published), and charioteers and horses were cheered enthusiastically. An additional dimension was added to the interest by the curious fact that the factions or teams of charioteers became associated with specific political views, so that the races became a place for the demonstration of partisan feelings.

In Greece, chariot racing had been essentially a rich man's sport, since each team was owned, and its charioteer hired, by an individual; but at Rome chariot racing was engaged in by companies, each of which had its own distinctive color, worn by its charioteers. Teams and charioteers were hired from these companies (*factiōnēs*) by the government or the giver of the games. The two original factions were the Red and the White. At the beginning of the imperial period the Blue and the Green were added. The Greens were backed by the emperors and the mob, the Blues by the senatorial aristocracy. The other two factions may at first have been backed by opponents of the imperial system. Toward the end of the third century the Whites joined the Greens, and the Reds joined the Blues, leaving only the Blue and the Green.

Illustrations in the Text

p. 158. Many mosaics show children pretending they are taking part in chariot races or gladiatorial fights. These may be merely fanciful scenes, but there is some evidence, both literary and archeological, that children did entertain themselves in this way.

p. 198. The crude but vivacious relief shows the chariots circling the *spīna*. The *mētae* show up clearly in the picture, as well as some of the decorations of the *spīna*. The row of *carcerēs* may be seen at the left, with the giver of the games in his box above; the columned structure to the right may represent the imperial box.

p. 215. Besides the Colosseum and the Circus, two sets of imperial baths can be seen, the Baths of Trajan behind the Colosseum and the Baths of Caracalla in the upper right-hand corner. In the foreground are the wharves and warehouses to receive freight brought up the Tiber on barges.

LAW AND GOVERNMENT

For an account of Roman political institutions, see Book III of this series, Jenney, Scudder, and Coffin, *Third Year Latin*, Allyn and Bacon, Inc., 1984, pp. 1–19.

Illustrations in the Text

p. 210. The provincial capitals copied the facilities of Rome with baths, basilicas, etc. In this model of the remains of the Severan Forum at Leptis, one sees the temple with its high podium in the foreground; here orators could address the people. In the background are seen the remains of the great basilica, faced on this side with a row of shops.

p. 216. An actual view of the basilica which appears at the far end of the model on p. 210. This basilica has a tribunal at each end of its central hall.

p. 221. This basilica was begun by Julius Caesar in 54 B.C. and dedicated by Augustus in A.D. 12. The illustration shows the basilica as rebuilt by Diocletian. This type of building was developed by the Romans to provide a sheltered place near a forum for various types of business, including court trials.

p. 222. Like the Basilica Julia, the Basilica at Pompeii had a central hall surrounded by aisles; unlike it, it had a tribunal at one end but no upper gallery. The archives of legal documents were found under the raised tribunal at the far end. In the floor of the tribunal there were two holes. When the presiding officer called for a document, a clerk from the archives could find it and hand it up through one of the holes.

p. 232. The Forum at Rome was a low-lying area between the Palatine and Capitoline Hills, utilized from early times as a market-place and as a meeting place for the Comitia and Senate. Over the centuries it became crowded with temples, basilicas, shops and monuments, all erected with no general plan in mind, so that by the late Republic the Forum Romanum, seat of the government of most of the Mediterranean world, presented a cluttered and haphazard appearance. Julius Caesar did a good deal of remodeling, building the Basilica Julia opposite the Basilica Aemilia so that the Forum was bordered by the colonnades of the two buildings along both its long sides; and moving the platform where speakers stood to address the Comitia from in front of the Curia to one end of the Forum, thus marking a third side of a long rectangle. Insofar as religious sanctions allowed, the space in the midst was cleared of the monuments of earlier ages. This refurbished Forum was still too small for all the business which it had to accommodate; thus Caesar built a new small forum, the Forum Julium, at the rear of the Curia. It consisted of a rectangular area surrounded by a colonnade with shops behind it, and at one end the temple of Venus Genetrix. The design may have been meant to echo the newly rearranged Forum Romanum with the porticoed basilicas along both sides and the Temple of Concord and the Temple of Vesta at the ends. At any rate, this design became canonical for future Fora. Augustus completed Caesar's remodeling of the Forum Romanum by completing the Basilica Julia and by closing the fourth side of the rectangle with the Temple of the Deified Julius Caesar. He also built the Forum Augusti, on much the same plan, with the temple of Mars Ultor at one end. It had no shops, but it did improve on Caesar's plan by the addition of two large apses behind its colonnade; these had some of the amenities of a basilica, providing sheltered areas for the carrying on of various sorts of business. The Emperors Vespasian and Nerva opened up more space in the center of the city by building small forums of similar design. In this picture the columns in the foreground are those of the Temple of Saturn. Through them can be seen the Arch of Septimius Severus, the Senate House, and the remains of the Basilica Aemilia. On the right the Temple of Vesta is seen beyond the remains of the Basilica Julia.

p. 228. This statue, saved from the melting pot because it was erroneously thought to be a portrait of Constantine, now dominates Michelangelo's beautiful piazza on the Capitoline Hill. It was originally gilt. The gilding had disappeared, but is now reappearing through some odd chemical process. It is a superstition among modern Romans that when the gilding is again complete, the strange upright tuft between the horse's ears will sing and this will be the end of the world. (The mistaken portrait of Constantine was preserved because Constantine was the emperor who legalized and favored Christianity.)

p. 226. Trajan built the largest of the imperial Fora, a very long rectangle, one of whose short sides was contiguous to a long side of the Forum Augusti. Like the other Fora, it had a temple at one end, and colonnades around it; it also had larger versions of the two apses of the Forum Augusti. Trajan departed from the plan of the other Fora by adding a large basilica. To accommodate the trying of court cases, this basilica had an apsidal tribunal at each end. In this illustration, we are looking through the columns of the basilica toward the temple area. In front of the remains of the temple stands the Column of Trajan, covered with a sculptured account of the Emperor's

Dacian campaigns spiraling around it. It was flanked on each side by libraries, one Greek, one Latin. The series of imperial Fora was probably built to realize a project of Caesar's city planning to open up a new civic center in the Campus Martius and to connect it to the old one by a line of open piazzas. Trajan's Forum completed this plan but at great expense, since a spur of the Capitoline Hill had to be removed to make room for it. The top of Trajan's Column marks the height of this spur.

p. 237. This strange city carved from living rock gives free reign to architectural flights of fancy. In Italy this type of architecture appears only in villas and tombs as it was considered too frivolous for official civic architecture or for dignified town houses.

p. 244. This Curia was built by the Emperor Diocletian on the plan and site of that built by Julius Caesar as part of his design for remodeling the Forum Romanum. The earlier Curia was on a site dating back to King Tullus Hostilius, occupying one corner of the Forum with the Comitia in front of it. Caesar built the new Curia further back and moved the Comitia speakers' platform (Rostra) to one end of the Forum. If the voting was close, an actual count was taken by having the senators file out through the two doors at the far end, the "aye's" through one door, and the "no's" through the other.

TRANSPORTATION

Not the least of Rome's contributions to western civilization was the paved road. She began her road building in response to military exigencies, but the roads, once built, served the purposes of trade, communication, and even pleasure trips. Under the Pax Romana, movement from one part of the Empire to another was unrestricted, and travel was relatively easy over a vast network of roads which stretched eventually from Mesopotamia to Lisbon, from upper Egypt to the north of England, altogether nearly 100,000 of our miles. This elaborate network began with Rome's need for military communications within Italy itself, starting with the Via Appia (312 B.C.), connecting Rome with Capua, and continuing until, by the end of the Republic, almost any part of Italy could be reached by one of the great roads, the routes (and in some cases even the pavement) of which are still in use today. The Empire saw the extension of the network to the provinces. These roads were marked every thousand paces with milestones; measurements were from a golden milestone set up in the Forum Romanum by Augustus. Roman road-building took little account of the actual terrain; the roads were for the most part quite straight, crossing valleys on arched bridges, cutting through hills by man-made terraces or cuts. When the cuts and bridges had been made, the route of the road was marked by parallel ditches 15 to 20 feet apart. The earth was then dug out from between the ditches (road-building was done by soldiers as part of their basic training) and the excavation leveled. A *pavīmentum* of sand and lime, forming a kind of mortar, was then laid. On top of this went the *statūmen*, a layer of large flagstones, then the *rūdus*, a layer of gravel and lime rammed down into a kind of concrete. The next layer, the *nucleus*, was also a concrete, this time of dirt, lime and pieces of brick. On top went the *summum dorsum* or *summa crusta*, the final pavement, made of polygonal blocks of flint or basalt, of concrete, or of rammed flint gravel. The center of the road was made a little higher than the edges, to facilitate drainage. The depth of all these strata was 5 to 10 feet. On marshy ground the road was laid on rafts. The Romans had many kinds of vehicles for travel or transport over these roads. For freight there were at least three kinds of wagons: the *carrus*, with sloping sides like an ox cart, and two spoked wheels; the *plaustrum*, a heavier version of the *carrus*, with solid wheels, used for the transport of somewhat heavier items, particularly farm produce; and the *sarrācum*, a much more solidly built vehicle, with smaller wheels (perhaps 4 instead of 2), used to carry amphorae of wine, blocks of stone, etc. These freight wagons were drawn by oxen, or sometimes by donkeys. The army truck of the Romans, used to transport troops, was the *clabulāre*, an open four-wheeled wagon with wickerwork sides. Another specialized vehicle of the Romans was the *arcera*, a closed-in, padded four-wheeled cart used as an ambulance for the transport of sick or aged people. For ordinary passengers there were four vehicles. Two which could be hired outside city gates and at various points along the major roads were the *essedum* and the *cisium*; these were both two-passenger, mule-drawn two-wheeled gigs. The *cisium* was lighter and faster, the *essedum* more solid and steady; a driver would be hired with the *cisium*, but the *essedum* could be driven by anyone. Slower, but more comfortable, were the *raeda* and the *carrūca*. The *carrūca* was a four-wheeled mule-drawn cart with a cover; there was room in it to recline or even to sleep; the *raeda* was a much larger cart, also four-wheeled and mule-drawn, which had several seats and could take a large party with their luggage. Especially adapted to the use of ladies were the two-wheeled *carpentum*, for use in the city, and the four-wheeled *pīlentum*, used for driving short distances. Except for the *carpentum*, whose use was restricted to matrons and Vestal Virgins (and later to women of the imperial family), no wheeled traffic was allowed in the cities between sunrise and the tenth hour (about 4:00 P.M.). This ruling was to insure the safety of pedestrians; deliveries would be made during the evening or at night. For through traffic, some towns provided a kind of ringroad in the form of a street that followed the city wall from gate to gate on the inside. This was the long way around, and at Pompeii the manure-truck drivers must have been in the habit of taking a short cut, for we find a notice on one of the houses near the north gate: *Stercorārī, ad mūrum prōgredere. Sī prē(n)sus fueris, (ut) poena(m) patiāre neces(s)e est. Cavē.* "Manure-truck driver, go along by the wall. If you get caught, you will have to pay the penalty. So look out." Because no wheeled vehicles could be used in the towns and cities, the wealthier people used litters (*lecticae*) and sedan chairs (*sellae*). The *lectica* whose poles were carried on the shoulders of stalwart slaves, lifting its occupant above the mob, could be closed with a cover and side curtains; the occupant rode in a reclining position, and could even sleep. The poles of the *sella* were slung from the slaves' shoulders by leather straps. There was also a kind of litter called a *basterna* which was carried by two mules.

With the mule-drawn carts the average rate of travel, allowing for stops for changes of mules, would have been about 5 MPH; a government courier might average twice that rate. Travel accommodations were very poor; most country inns were dirty and there was danger of both fire and robbers. Many wealthy people maintained little houses where they could put up for the night, and in the cities the custom of hereditary guest-friendship (*hospitium*) made up for the lack of good hotels. By *hospitium* families in different cities made more or less permanent arrangements for putting each other up (this is why *hospēs* can be translated either "guest" or "host;" it really means "guest-friend," a member of a family with which one's own family has entered into *hospitium*).

Sea travel was much less comfortable and more dangerous than travel by land. The Romans were not by nature or inclination good sailors; their merchant fleet was gradually acquired by their bringing into alliance Italian towns which had fleets of their own. In an early treaty with Carthage, Rome renounced all claim to trade in Africa and Spain. Trade relations did develop with the Greek city of Massilia (Marseilles), and from here Rome's interests were extended a little way along the Spanish coast. After Rome's surprising victory in the First Punic War (the Romans had so little idea of shipbuilding that they had to copy a grounded Carthaginian warship), her ships traveled freely through the western Mediterranean. The east was at first shut off by the activities of the piratical privateers of Illyria; but by the beginning of the second century B.C. there were already many Roman businesses with offices at the free port of Delos, and also at Rhodes. The two chief kinds of ships were the warships (*nāvēs longae*) and the freight and passenger ships (*nāvēs onerāriae*). Speed and maneuverability were the chief requirements for the warships; they relied more on oars than sails, and under battle conditions did not even carry sails. The Romans used both triremes and quinqueremes, with three and five banks of oars respectively. A quinquereme was about 120 feet by 17 feet and carried 300 sailors and rowers, 120 soldiers, and 20 officers; it naturally had to put ashore to allow the men to sleep or to eat any substantial meal.

A *nāvis onerāria* was 70 to 80 feet long by 18 to 20 feet wide. It was decked, with a cabin aft, and carried passengers as well as freight. The Romans rated ships by amphorae, and the ordinary ships carried 3000 to 4000 amphorae; modern estimates rate the average ship at 50 tons. These merchant ships relied primarily on sails, though they also carried sweeps. The masts, unlike those of warships, were permanently fixed: a vertical mainmast amidships, carrying a large square or trapezoidal sail and a small triangular sail above it, and a slanted mast forward carrying a jib. Three-masted vessels were rare. The ships were not really very sea-worthy, and ordinarily made only coasting voyages, and these between mid-March and early October. They made 70 to 90 miles per day. Roman trade routes covered the Mediterranean and Black Seas, the north Atlantic coast of Africa, the English Channel, the Red Sea, the Persian Gulf, and much of the Indian Ocean.

Illustrations in the Text

p. 103. Pont du Gard, Provence, France. This splendid piece of Roman road engineering carried an aqueduct on the upper level and a roadway on the lower level. It is mentioned here because it is a good illustration of the Romans' disregard of the nature of the terrain when building roads.

pp. 249–250. The relief and the model taken from it represents a *carrūca*, a covered wagon for more luxurious travel; the passengers could sleep while traveling.

pp. 250–253. Mosaic and model show a *cisium*, a light fast two-passenger gig which could be hired outside the gates of cities and towns.

p. 254. A *nāvis onerāria*. Note the steering oar. The figure of the god (in this case Bacchus) represents the vessel's patron and also serves to identify it.

p. 258. This represents one of the smaller ships which navigated rivers, particularly the Nile, Danube, Rhone and Rhine. The inscription near the stern is the name of the ship, Isis, and the adjective form of the place she hails from, the area called Ciminia in Etruria.

p. 261. Claudius constructed the harbor to the left but as more protection was needed, Trajan constructed the hexagonal harbor to the right. A canal connected them with the Tiber and is now the Fiumicino mouth of the river. Claudius made his harbor by building two moles into the sea and placing a long artificial island bearing a lighthouse (*left* in the illustration) between them. Trajan's harbor was excavated out of the dry land. Claudius' harbor was about 10 million square feet in area, Trajan's about half that.

FASHION AND CLOTHING

The basic garment of both men and women in ancient Rome was the *tunica*, a plain woolen garment with a neck-hole, either sleeveless or short-sleeved. It reached the ankles, but was normally pulled up through the belt worn around the waist to shorten it; it would be girt up to above the knee for active occupations, otherwise it was calf-length. The *tunica* was worn alone by slaves and workmen, and by men of any class in the privacy of the home; it was the "shirt-sleeves" dress of the Romans. Besides the belt around the waist, women wore another belt girt beneath the bosom, the *strophium;* and over the basic *tunica* matrons wore the *stola,* a long-sleeved tunic with a flounce sewn on the bottom, so that it reached the ankles. The basic outer garment of antiquity was a straight piece of woolen cloth wrapped around the body, the midpoint of its long side being placed under the right arm and the two ends being thrown over the left shoulder and arm. The Greek *himation,* a rectangular garment of this kind, might be as big as two yards by four. The Romans knew the himation under two names, calling it *pallium* when worn by men, *palla* when worn by women; it was essentially an outdoor wrap. The *palla* might be a little more elaborate than the *pallium,* with embroidery, fringe, etc. *Tunica, stola,* and *palla* were the normal street dress of a respectable Roman lady; other women were forbidden the use of the *stola.* Men who were citizens of Rome were permitted (and on some occasions required) to wear a special variant of the himation, the *toga.* The *toga* was an Etruscan invention, an adaptation of the himation for military use, particularly for horseback riding. The himation, with its great weight of cloth on the left arm, was a very inconvenient garment for any kind of active occupation; yet if it were shortened it would be difficult to wear, since it was just this weight of cloth over the left arm, front and back, that kept it from falling off. The Athenians solved the problem of military wear by cutting off all the extra cloth at the ends of the himation and holding it on with a safety pin, thus creating the garment called a *chlamys.* The Etruscans, who also wore the himation, solved the problem in a different way. They cut off only the corners of the himation, leaving enough length of cloth over the left arm to hold the garment on, but reducing considerably the voluminous folds which so hampered the movement of the left arm. The resulting garment, of trapezoidal shape, was what the Romans called the *toga.* The fact that the toga was originally a military uniform explains why its use was restricted to Roman citizens, since originally citizenship depended on service in the army. In time the toga grew in size, still keeping its trapezoidal shape. Eventually a double version was developed, two trapezoids joined along their long sides and folded over on this line before being wrapped around the body. Part of the inner trapezoid was then pulled out over the outer one at the breast, forming the *sinus.* In its largest form the toga was a formal garment, requiring a good deal of time and trouble to drape properly; then its use began to be more and more restricted to special occasions. A citizen had to wear the toga when he paid his morning call on his patron (no doubt a relic of the days when the morning *salūtātiō* represented a military muster of clients in uniform). It also had to be worn at all religious ceremonies, including plays, races, and gladiatorial games, and whenever the citizen was exercising his rights, as at elections, *comitia,* etc. Young boys wore a toga with a broad purple-dyed stripe until they came of age, when they were given plain white togas. The broad stripe was also worn by Senators, and a narrower one by the Equites. When the toga had reached a size which made it inconvenient for less formal occasions, new garments were developed for dinner parties.

This outfit was called the *synthesis* ("ensemble"), and consisted of a *tunica* and smallish *pallium* in the same color or in harmonizing colors. As the toga grew larger, it also became inconvenient as a military uniform, and was replaced by the *sagum*, a cloak like the Greek chlamys, more or less square and pinned on the right shoulder. Generals wore a slightly larger, purple-dyed version called a *palūdāmentum*. Another larger version of the chlamys, the *lacerna*, served as an overcoat or raincoat in cold or wet weather; it might even be worn over the toga, except on formal occasions. For traveling, a large cape (*paenula*) with a hood (*cucullus*) attached was worn. Indoors, men and women wore sandals (*soleae*) with a narrow strap around the ankle and another between the toes; these were removed for meals. Outdoors men wore *calceī*, sandals fastened on with straps so broad that they covered the foot, so that these might really be called shoes or, when the straps were wound also around the leg, boots. The *calceus* varied in style according to the rank of the wearer. Soldiers wore *caligae*, hob-nailed boots, and peasants wore wooden shoes, *sculpōneae*. Except for the developments noted above, styles in dress did not change among the Romans as they do with us; hair styles, however, did vary a good deal, especially women's. Much use was made of hot curling-irons, dyes and bleaches, and false hair-pieces.

Illustrations in the Text

p. 266. A Roman matron in *tunica*, *stola*, and *palla*. The Consul's boots are the senatorial version of the *calceī*.

p. 271. This painting may represent a young bride having her hair parted into the traditional three tresses. The elaborate turning on the leg of the chair was a popular design in the early empire. The box on the table is decorated with ivory.

p. 272. The pearl earrings and necklace (perhaps of emeralds) resemble jewelry found in excavations. Portraits of this kind were often painted on the lids of wooden coffins.

p. 276. Etruscan men, as well as women, wore elaborate brooches and other jewelry. The costumes of Roman men were not adorned with jewelry although they did wear rings.

p. 281. The objects are a mirror, two earrings, a finger ring, four hairpins, a comb, a small rouge box and a coin.

p. 283. Glass vases of this kind were used for cosmetic oils.

p. 288. Ladies' hair styles began to become fantastically elaborate toward the end of the first century of our era. Occasionally a female portrait bust would be made with detachable hair, and the subject would leave a bequest to have new hair carved as the styles changed, so that after her death her portrait would never be out of fashion.

p. 299. During most of the Republican period and in the early Empire men were short-haired and clean-shaven, like this portrait head of Augustus' friend Agrippa, although fashionable young men might cultivate carefully-trimmed beards. A full beard was the mark of a philosopher. The Emperor Hadrian brought beards back into fashion, and hair was worn a little longer.

RELIGION

State Religion and Private Worship. Roman religion was animistic in its origins: that is, the primitive Romans believed that literally everything had will or intention (*nūmen*, originally = "nod"). Not only human beings were capable of purposive action, but also animals, inanimate objects, natural processes, events, and abstract qualities. In a sense, all these were persons, but it would be a mistake to think of them as really having personality— merely intention and the power to carry it out. Yet all these *nūmina* could be communicated with to some degree. If it became necessary for a farmer to cut down a grove of trees, he would address the *nūmen* of the grove politely, expressing his intention and the hope that the *nūmen* would accept, for example, one pig in payment. He would then kill a pig. If all went well, and if the pig appeared from its internal organs to be a healthy one, the price had been accepted, but if something untoward happened during the process (an *ōmen*, i.e. *ausmen*, "something heard") or the pig appeared to be diseased, the process had to be repeated until the *nūmen* was satisfied. In other words, the three chief parts of Roman religion consisted of what we would call prayer, sacrifice, and divination. A Roman was surrounded by countless *nūmina*: there were separate gods of the door, the hinge, and the threshold; of cattle-breeding, horse-breeding, sheep-breeding; of the planted seed, the sprouted seed, the growing plant, of the various diseases of plants; of a normal birth, of a breech birth, of a baby's first cry, of tooth-cutting, of learning to walk—in short, of everything. The names of many of these divinities were known, but countless more were not. As new *nūmina* were identified they were given names, but the Romans in their recorded prayers usually betray a good deal of nervousness on this subject, listing a number of possible names and then adding "or whatever name you would prefer to be called by." In 390 B.C. a citizen heard a voice telling him to inform the consuls that the Gauls were approaching Rome. On the spot where the voice was heard, the city dedicated an altar to Aius Locutius ("Telling Speaker"), a god hitherto unknown and never heard from again.

The system of paying the gods for their services led to a kind of *quid prō quō* religion, an almost contractual concept of the duties of men and gods toward each other. If a god was paid the proper honors, he was expected to do his part. If he did not, there must have been something wrong with the way the honors were paid: a wrong word was said, the god was called by the wrong name, it was the wrong day, etc. Much depended on the exact performance of a fixed ritual arrived at empirically (it worked this way last time; best not change it) and followed in painful detail. Some of the preserved hymns and prayers were in such archaic language that the later Romans no longer knew what they meant, but they went on repeating them because they seemed to work. The observation of omens (*augūrium*) was developed to an exact science. The usual methods were observation of the flight of birds and inspection of the internal organs of sacrificial animals. This contractual aspect in one sense made the performance of religious duties easy. The gods did not require that their worshippers love them or (strangely enough!) even believe in them, only that they do certain things. But this arrangement left the Romans at a loss if, after all honors had been duly paid, things still went wrong. If this happened, they had to turn to their Etruscan neighbors, who had a much more detailed system of inspecting the sky and the organs of victims; or to the Greek Apollo, either at his oracle at Delphi or in the recorded prophecies of his Sybil at Cumae in the south of Italy.

In this religion, so simple in concept, so complex in its ritual, a good deal of technical knowledge must have been needed. A priesthood probably developed fairly early. The priests were not a separate family, but rather the *patrēs*, the heads of families, and it was from this group that the priests of the community were drawn. Those gods whose functions affected the whole community would naturally be worshipped in common. Thus they acquired a higher rank than the gods whose functions affected primarily the individual or the family. These gods were Jupiter (Diou-pater, Sky-father), Juno/Diana, Mars, Vesta, Janus, and Quirinus. Jupiter was the god of the sky and the weather, hence the chief god. Juno and Diana may originally have been the same goddess, a goddess of the sky and of light, the female principle of which Jupiter is the male; but these aspects became separated, and the goddess became two goddesses. Juno is the protectress of women, the goddess of marriage and childbirth, and through her connection with Jupiter, the highest goddess. Diana is a goddess of light, especially of the moon and hence of the night sky, and as bringer of light (under the name Lucina), also a goddess of childbirth. The two goddesses were never totally separated in this last function. The goddess Juno Lucina who assists at births is both Juno and Diana. Mars is a god of harvests, hence the god of war, since the object of primitive warfare was to destroy the enemy's crops and keep him from destroying yours. Insofar as such an abstract concept could be thought of as a person, he was also the ancestor of the Roman race. Vesta was the goddess of the fire on the hearth, essentially a domestic divinity, but in a time when fire-making was difficult, the public hearth, where a fire was kept going at all times, was important. Janus was a god of going (his name contains the same root as *eō, īre*), whose importance arose from the magical practice of surrounding a settlement with a special ditch over which spirits of the dead and supernatural powers in general could not pass. The ditch protected the community, but such magical powers as the community itself possessed could not be taken out against an enemy unless some passages were made through the invisible barrier. Such a passage was called a *Jānus*, a word applied both to bridges over the magical ditch (hence perhaps the word *pontifex*, "bridge maker" for a priest) and gates through the wall which followed it. Quirinus was, so to speak, the Mars of the Sabines, and was brought to Rome when the Romans and Sabines were amalgamated into one nation (eighth century B.C.). Jupiter, Mars, and Quirinus had special priests, called *flāminēs*, and may represent a primitive supreme triad.

These gods were not pictured in human form. Jupiter was represented by a piece of flint (lightning), Mars by a spear, Vesta by the fire on the hearth. The Romans did not have any mythology. They did not even have temples, for their *templa* were simply consecrated areas, sometimes containing an altar. Temples, statues and anthropomorphism seem to have been introduced by the Etruscan lords of Rome, traditionally by the first Tarquin. The Romans recognized the chief triad of the Etruscans as their own Jupiter, Juno, and Minerva (a goddess of wisdom and crafts). For these they built the Capitolium, a temple on the citadel of Rome. These three gods remained the chief official gods of Rome, and are often called the Capitoline Triad. Through the terra cotta sculptures of Vulca of Veii, the Etruscans also taught the Romans to think of their gods in human forms.

The Etruscan pantheon had already been considerably Hellenized; and the Romans also undoubtedly had made contacts with Greek religion and its attendant mythology through the Greeks of South Italy. The second Tarquin had bought books of prophecy from the Sybil of Apollo at Cumae. The Sybilline Books were consulted when Roman or Etruscan methods of divination did not provide sufficiently clear answers. The advice, when interpreted, was often that the Romans should import the worship of some Greek god. The Roman feeling that there were many gods which they did not know made them hospitable to new deities like Apollo, Cybele, and Aesculapius; in other Greek gods they recognized gods whom they already knew under different names. Thus they identified Zeus with Jupiter, Hera with Juno, Artemis with Diana, Ares with Mars, and Hestia with Vesta. They recognized other gods important in the Greek pantheon as minor gods of their own, and this identification added to the importance of some of the gods of farm and household, elevating them to the level of the state cult. Thus Neptune, a god of water, was assimilated to the sea-god Poseidon, Minerva to Athena, Venus to Aphrodite, the fire-god Vulcan to Hephaestus, Mercury, the god of trade, to Hermes, and Ceres to Demeter. Along with Apollo, who had no Roman counterpart, these were the twelve major gods of the Roman state. Janus and Quirinus, having no Greek counterparts, declined somewhat in importance.

To some degree the myths of the Greek gods were transferred to their Roman counterparts, but more as subjects for literary treatment than as any part of the theology. Legend, history, and also folk-tales, were more important to the Romans than myth, but from the myths the Romans did derive some notions of the characters and personalities of the various gods, as well as of their family relationships to each other.

These developments of the state cult seem to have had little or no effect on domestic worship. The family continued to honor all the little *nūmina* of everyday life, and when it did chance to worship the gods of the major pantheon, it was in their more homely guise of gods of the household. For example, a cloth-processer of Pompeii would worship Venus of Pompeii (as the goddess of his city), Minerva (as the goddess of the cloth-trades), Mercury (as the god of profit in business). These three gods were probably this man's *Dī Penātēs* ("gods who dwell in the store-cupboard"). Literary sources tell us of domestic cults of the Penates, the Lar or Lares, Vesta, the Genius of the *paterfamiliās*, and occasionally the Juno of his wife. Every man had his own Genius, perhaps a personification of his power of procreation, viewed as a kind of benevolent guardian spirit; a woman had not a Genius but a Juno. The Lares seem definitely to have been attached to particular locations. When a family changed dwellings it changed Lares, though it took its Penates with it. Hence it may be that the *Genius locī,* who also is mentioned, is the same as the Lar. Vesta, who had no image but was the fire on the hearth, may have been the protectress of the family and particularly of its perpetuation.

A system of vows and votive offerings is typical of the contractual nature of Roman religion: the Romans made use of vows where we would use prayers. A vow (*vōtum*) is the promise of some kind of payment (a sacrifice or a gift) to be made to the god only after he has granted a particular favor. If the god did not grant the wish, the promised payment would not be made. If he did, the vow had to be fulfilled scrupulously or the votary would risk the future enmity of the god he had cheated. Vows, usually made in writing and attached to the statue of the god, were kept on file and periodically checked by the priests. When the vow had been paid, a commemorative tablet was set up at the votary's expense, showing what the vow was and sometimes depicting the favor which the god had granted. Cicero mentions paintings of shipwrecks hanging in temples, presented by people who had been saved from them through a vow; many Roman temples contain replicas of parts of the body healed as the result of a vow.

The domestic gods may have been the objects of more love and devotion than those of the state, but their relationship with their worshippers remained basically legalistic and contractual. For something which we would recognize as a religion, we must look to the mystery cults. The chief of these were the cult of Bacchus or Liber (which seems to have combined elements of the Orphic and Eleusinian Mysteries of Greece), the cult of Isis (a Hellenized version of the Egyptian goddess), that of Mithras (a Persian sun-god), and Christianity. These religions had a number of things in common. They had initiation rituals and levels of initiation, separate priesthoods, a doctrine of personal immortality and beatitude, and a state of grace to be achieved by a sacramental union with a resurrected god. Some of these religions were at first viewed with suspicion by the conservative Romans, who had the same distaste for enthusiasm in religion as did the Church of England in the 18th century. In the end the natural hospitality of the Romans toward foreign gods won out. Even Christianity would probably have been accepted on these terms, had it not been for its intolerance of other gods, its steady refusal to syncretize its god with those of other faiths, and its insistence on virtues which seemed foolish to the pagan mind.

Illustrations in the Text

p. 1. From a room perhaps devoted to the Mysteries of Dionysus (Bacchus). The *cista mystica* (mystic basket) contains the secret objects sacred to Dionysus. The matron unveils the basket and then washes her hands before handling the objects.

p. 300. The central figure, offering incense from a box with a sacrificial plate (*patera*), represents the *genius* of the *paterfamiliās*. Such a figure is often shown carrying a cornucopia. The two dancing figures in boots and girt-up tunics, holding drinking horns from which a stream of wine flows into small buckets, are the Lares. The bearded and crested serpent approaching an altar to eat the offering is another way of depicting a Lar.

p. 303. The statues lining the colonnade are those of the Chief Vestals. The Vestal Virgins' chief task was to keep alight the fire (which was Vesta herself) in the temple of Vesta, the public hearth of Rome. The maintenance of this fire was considered so important to the stability of the empire that Constantine went on supporting this cult long after he had made Christianity the official state religion. The temple was not closed until A.D. 382. There were six Vestals; each served for thirty years, after which she might marry. When vacancies occurred, new Vestals were chosen by lot from a list of twenty girls nominated by the Pontifex Maximus; the girls had to be between six and ten years of age, and anyone might be chosen, there being no exemptions. A Vestal spent ten years learning the duties, ten years performing them, and ten years teaching them to novices. The Vestals had many privileges: they were released from the *potestās* of their fathers (though the Pontifex Maximus might have a Vestal beaten if she allowed the fire to go out, buried alive if she proved unchaste). When they left their convent they were accompanied by a lictor and took precedence even over the Consuls. They had special seats at the games; anyone who harmed them or a person under their protection was put to death. Because they were considered incorruptible, wills were entrusted to their keeping.

p. 306. The temple, partly reconstructed from the fragments found, is shown in the relief as it looked in antiquity. It was burned six times and always rebuilt in the original round shape which, derived from primitive round thatched huts, shows the antiquity of the cult. When the sacred fire did go out it had to be rekindled by friction, which also suggests the antiquity of the worship, as does the fact that water used in the rites had to come from a spring, rather than from the mains. Within the temple was also a separate compartment which no one might enter, containing the Penates of Rome, especially the Palladium, a sacred image connected with Athena, which Aeneas had brought from Troy.

p. 308. A belief in the *fascinum*, the Evil Eye, still persists in many parts of the world, even among educated people. A person possessed of the Evil Eye brings misfortune to whomever he looks at, by malice or even involuntarily. The charms which are used against the Evil Eye today are those used in antiquity: coral, ivory, ox-horns, hunchbacks, the hand with the forefinger and little finger extended, the protruding tongue, as well as sharp objects of all kinds. These are thought of as being able to destroy the spell by a kind of symbolic blinding, but the original associations are almost certainly phallic. This mosaic, which resembles a more elaborate version found in Antioch on the Orontes, shows the eye rendered harmless by a lance and menaced by a variety of horns, fangs, talons, claws, and stings. Similar charms, usually more frankly phallic, are found in Pompeii at the entrances to houses, in dining rooms and latrines, and over the ovens in bakeries.

p. 313. Sacrifices were an important part of the Roman religious rites. The animal victim was decked out and brought to the altar. If it struggled or tried to escape, the sacrifice was considered unsuccessful. With his head veiled to keep him from hearing unpropitious sounds (and usually accompanied by a flute-player for the same reason) the priest read the prayer, being careful not to change any words, even if the antiquity of the prayer made it unintelligible to him. The priest then sprinkled the victim's head with ground spelt mixed with salt, and then with wine. When the beast had been killed its entrails were inspected. If there was something wrong, another animal of the opposite sex was sacrificed, and if its entrails were also not propitious it was a sign that the god had not accepted the sacrifice. All this was done in the morning; in the evening the entrails of the victim (if found satisfactory) were sprinkled with salt, spelt, and wine and burnt on the altar, while the persons making the offering cooked and ate the rest of the victim. This relief represents the *suovetaurīlia*, a special sacrifice of a pig, a sheep, and an ox.

p. 318. The Pantheon at Rome is a temple of the Olympian gods erected by the Emperor Hadrian. The original temple on this spot was erected by Augustus' friend M. Vipsanius Agrippa in 27–25 B.C. as part of the development of a new civic center in the Campus Martius, which included a set of baths behind it. It was completely rebuilt, to his own design, by the Emperor Hadrian, who nevertheless modestly preserved the original inscription *M(ārcus) Agrippa, L(ūcī) f(īlius), Cō(n)s(ul) tertium fēcit*. It is not known precisely to what gods it was dedicated. The present building has seven niches for statues, and the original temple had in it at least three, those of Mars, Venus, and the deified Julius Caesar. Hence it was probably intended to lend a religious sanction to Augustus' regime, since these three gods were all connected with him; Julius Caesar as his adoptive father, Venus as the mother of Aeneas and grandmother of Iulus, and Mars as the Avenger, who aided Augustus in punishing the murderers of his adoptive father. The practice of finding a religious basis for the emperors' rule led to the deification of deceased, and eventually of living, emperors. Considered an architectural masterpiece of ancient Rome, the Pantheon is now a Christian church and a national shrine. It is the burial place of King Victor Emmanuel I, King Humbert I, and the painter Raphael.

p. 321. The emperor sacrificing to Diana from a *patera* is probably paying a vow made for a successful hunt. The ancient countryside was dotted with many small shrines of this kind, dedicated to various gods.

p. 322. The funeral dance was not a Roman custom but may have been practised in the Greek-influenced cities of southern Italy.

p. 323. In this relief from a tomb, the victory of the charioteer may symbolize triumph over death.

p. 324. The goddess is not dressed as a huntress in this picture, despite her bow. This painting may represent her as a goddess of health.

p. 328. The so-called Temple of Fortuna Virilis may actually have been that of Portunus, the god of Rome's original landing place on the Tiber.

p. 332. Like the tomb of Augustus, Hadrian's tomb is a larger version of an old Etruscan tomb style—a cylinder of masonry with a mound of earth on top, which was planted with cypress. In papal times the tomb was made into a fortress. The angel on the top commemorates a vision of one of the popes, who during a plague, dreamt that he saw an angel alight on the building and sheathe his sword. Very shortly after this dream, the plague ended. In thanksgiving, the pope had the angel carved and placed on top of the building.

p. 333. Like the Temple of Isis at Pompeii, the one depicted here has a stage-like area at the top of a high flight of steps. The painting represents the morning service (corresponding to the Christian Matins). Two priests, accompanied by a flute-player, perform a sacrifice, while another sings a hymn or intones a prayer. On the stage two more priests shake the *sistra* (sacred rattles) while a third displays a vase of holy water taken from the Nile (note that he covers his hands with his sleeves to avoid touching the sacred vase with his hands). The connection with Egypt is shown not only by the linen costumes of the priests, but by the sphynxes and the presence of tame ibises. Isis was originally an Egyptian goddess, wife of her brother Osiris and mother of Horus. Osiris was killed by his wicked brother Set who dismembered his body and threw the pieces into the Nile. Isis gathered all the pieces after much searching and reassembled Osiris' body; then, assisted by Horus, she defeated Set, restored Osiris to life, and returned him to power. When the Ptolemies, the Macedonian kings of Egypt, were looking for a state religion which would be acceptable to both their Greek and their Egyptian subjects, they looked to this myth, and with the help of Greek philosophers and Egyptian priests, succeeded in interpreting it in Greek terms. The myth remained essentially the same, and this new cult, in spite of its artificial origins, had great appeal, quickly spreading from Egypt to all parts of the Hellenistic world. At this point it was still a public cult, rather than a true mystery religion, but from it developed a mystery in which Isis gradually assumed the leading position, being now identified with literally all the goddesses known in antiquity. These goddesses were thought of as being merely different names of one goddess, whose true name was Isis. The cult of Isis, brought to Rome after the Second Punic War, was viewed at first with suspicion by the Romans, who found it too emotional or evangelistic. Eventually it gained a solid foothold, and was widespread by the time of the late Republic. Its appeal at first (like that of Christianity) was to the lower classes; during the early Empire it was popular with the numerous nouveaux riches, and later we hear of upper-class devotees. The religion had a separate trained priesthood, who shaved their heads and wore white linen garments. They enjoined on their congregations abstinence, asceticism, purifications and penances, and regular attendance at religious services, promising them a perception of the divine life and personal immortality. There were daily offices and annually recurring feasts. The "Easter" of Isis-worship, celebrated on March 5, marked the opening of the sailing season and honored Isis as patroness of navigation; it was called the Embarkation of Isis (*Isidis nāvigium*) and involved the loading of an Egyptian ship with precious offerings and committing it to the sea. The "Christmas" feast, held at the onset of winter, was some kind of cult drama, re-enacting the grief of Isis at the death of Osiris and her joy at his resurrection. The worshippers hoped for sacramental union with Isis (if they were women) or Osiris (for men).

p. 339. The frieze, from the wall surrounding the altar itself, probably depicts the actual dedication of the altar, which commemorated Augustus' pacification of Spain and Gaul and his restoration of peace to the Roman world.

p. 355. The large temple in the foreground is that of Jupiter Capitolinus. Jupiter Capitolinus, his sister/wife Juno, and his daughter Minerva are the three deities that make up the Capitoline Triad. The worship of triads of gods was a feature of Etruscan religion which the Tarquins brought to Rome. Beyond the temple can be seen the Colonnades of the Forum of Julius Caesar, part of the Forum of Augustus (at the extreme right) and the Forum of Trajan (left of the Forum of Augustus.)

PALACES

The development of the palace as the official residence of the chief of state began late and proceeded gradually among the Romans. In republican times there was no official state residence (except those of the Pontifex Maximus and the Vestal Virgins), though most of the *nōbilēs*, the class from whom the consuls were elected, lived on the fashionable Palatine Hill. Residence here became a kind of symbol of membership in this class (Cicero, when he had arrived politically, bought a house on the Palatine); and Ovid could speak of the Palatine as the residence of the leaders of Rome (*"sub . . . ducibus . . . Palātia fulgent"*). The imperial residence on the Palatine grew larger and larger until at the end of the classical period the name of the hill had become the word for any elaborate official residence; *palātium, palazzo, palais, palace.*

Augustus' own house on the Palatine was an ordinary upper-class residence. The growth of the palace as such went hand in hand with the growth of the Emperor's powers and responsibilities, as reflected in the size of the bureaucracy (slaves and freedmen at first) which was under his direct control. These civil servants, from clerks up to cabinet ministers, were all members of the Emperor's household, and for convenience and efficiency lived in the Emperor's house.

Tiberius enlarged the imperial residence by building vaults over the street to the north of the Palatine. On these foundations rose a complex of buildings surrounding a central courtyard. Caligula extended this complex still further by adding a throne room or reception hall and a basilica or hall of justice in the forum below, these rooms being connected with the upper levels of the palace by a covered ramp. Claudius built still further out to the north, right up to the south wall of the House of the Vestals.

Up to this point, though the grandeur of the architecture may have been meant to impress both citizen and foreigner with the emperor's importance, the palaces had been essentially office buildings, designed to house the huge machinery of the imperial bureaucracy. Nero, however, who was (unfortunately for him, as it turned out) more of an artist than an administrator, conceived a palace as a building of architectural beauty, a luxurious pleasure-house. His first palace, the so-called *Domus Trānsitōria*, was restricted in size by the smallness of the area available, though he used most of the Palatine Hill, demolishing much of his predecessors' construction. A small section of the *Domus Transitoria* has been found in the foundations of the later Flavian palace. A fountain of colored marbles in the shape of a theatre façade shows the elegance of Nero's conception. When the great fire had destroyed a large part of central Rome, Nero found that on the land thus vacated he could give free rein to his imagination. The result was the famous Golden House. The *Domus Aurea,* which covered perhaps 370 acres in the center of the city, consisted primarily of colonnaded buildings surrounding a central park; the buildings were overlaid with semi-precious stone and mother-of-pearl. In the park was a large lake, around which stood a series of pavilions designed to look like villages from the outside, while the surrounding land was landscaped to resemble forests, plowed fields and meadowlands. The whole park was a microcosm of the countryside, a true *rūs in urbe*. One of the buildings overlooking the lake has been excavated and contains many rooms, most of them carefully arranged to provide a view of the lake and the landscape, all of them decorated with a riot of fanciful fresco. There are courtyards within the building, and several fountains, one a huge cascade tumbling down several stories to pass through one of the rooms.

With the accession of the Flavian emperors the Golden House was demolished. Vespasian and Titus, to dramatize their new fiscal policies, used its site for a number of public buildings, one of which, the Colosseum, occupies the position of Nero's great lake. These two emperors apparently lived in a portion of the Golden House which survived. It was Domitian who built the large Flavian palace on the Palatine Hill, the palace which remained, with few changes, throughout the period of Rome's greatness, and the remains of which are to be seen today.

All Roman magnates had several country places, and the Emperors, we may assume, were no exception. Because much of the imperial bureaucracy had to accompany the Emperor wherever he went, the imperial villas had to be very large, including (besides the usual parklands, gardens, and other pleasure-grounds, dining halls, baths, reception rooms, etc.) office space and dwellings for large numbers of civil servants, as well as barracks and parade grounds for the imperial bodyguard. There must have been a great number of these non-urban palaces, but only four are well known from their remains: Tiberius' villa on the island of Capri, Hadrian's villa at Tibur (modern Tivoli) near Rome, the villa of Maximianus at Piazza Armerina in Sicily, and Diocletian's palace at Split (Spalato) in modern Jugoslavia.

Illustrations in the Text

p. 12. An elegant miniature palace of many small rooms, baths and courtyards, this round building is separated from the palace by a circular moat crossed by ingenious folding drawbridges. This artificial island may have been a retreat for the emperor or even a kind of zoo for exotic birds and animals.

p. 345. The difference between Diocletian's retreat at Spalato and Hadrian's at Tivoli reflects the changes in the state of the Empire. In Hadrian's time the Empire was at peace internally; Diocletian's settlement followed a century of civil wars. Note its resemblance to the Roman fort on p. 140. This palace was built as a retreat for his retirement after he had conquered the empire and organized its administration (A.D. 245–313). This extraordinary complex of buildings, a self-contained and easily defendable palace-fortress, formed the basis for the later town. Its architectural devices constitute a transitional style between imperial Roman and Byzantine construction. The hexagonal building (right center) was the Emperor's mausoleum and is now the city cathedral.

pp. 349–351. This complex consists of two sections, the private part of the palace at the bottom, the more public apartments at the top. The public part stands at the top of the *Clīvus Palātīnus,* the street which runs from the upper end of the Forum (near the Arch of Titus) to the top of the Palatine. The central room (**B**) is a large reception hall or *ātrium*—we might also call it the throne room. Its niches held great statues of the gods in basalt. (**C**) is a little basilica with a tribunal to house the emperor's judicial functions. (**A**) was a private chapel. These three rooms open into a colonnaded garden with an elaborate fountain in the center. The almost square room beyond (**E**) was the state dining hall, with a view over the garden and (through the openings at the sides) two smaller open courtyards (**F** is one of them) filled with pools and fountains. The rooms at the left of the bottom complex are in two stories, as the hill slopes down toward the Circus Maximus. The emperor could watch the races (at the left of the plan) from the curved concave colonnade.

Latin Expressions Sometimes Encountered in English

These expressions are from many sources, some known, some not. They come from classical authors, medieval proverbs, legal Latin, terms of logic and scholastic disputation, the liturgy of the Roman Catholic Church. Pronunciation varies: some are pronounced as if they were English, some as Classical Latin, some in the manner of Church Latin.

—— Abbreviations ——

A.D., Anno Domini
A.M., Ante Meridiem
D.V., Deo Volente
et al., et alia
etc., et cetera
e.g., exempli gratia
ibid., ibidem
i.e., id est
I.N.R.I., Iesus Nazarenus Rex
   Iudaeorum
infra dig., infra dignitatem
nem. con., nemine contradicente
N.B., Nota Bene

op. cit., opus citatum
P.M., Post Meridiem
P.S., Post Scriptum
pro and con, pro et contra
pro tem., pro tempore
Q.E.D., Quod Erat Demonstrandum
q.v., quod vide
R.I.P., Requiescat In Pace
SPQR, Senatus Populusque
   Romanus
verb. sat, verbum sat sapienti
vs., versus

a fortiori, *from a stronger position, i.e., all the more so*
ab ovo, *from the egg, i.e., from the very beginning*
ad hoc, *for this (particular purpose)*
ad hominem, *for the man, i.e., by interest or prejudice rather than truth* or *logic*
ad infinitum, *to eternity, i.e., endlessly*
ad nauseam, *to nausea, i.e., to the point of being disgusting*
alias, *otherwise (named)*
alibi, *elsewhere, i.e., evidence of absence from a given place*
Alma Mater, *foster mother, nurse (used of a school or college)*
alumnus, *foster child, nurseling (used of a graduate of an Alma Mater)*
Anno Domini, *in the year of our Lord*
ante bellum, *before the war (used, in the South, especially of the War between the States)*

ante meridiem, *before noon*

argumentum ex silentio, *an argument based on silence,* i.e., *an attempt to prove something by the absence of evidence to the contrary*

Ars gratia artis, *Art for the sake of art (alone)*

Ars longa, vita brevis, *Art is long, life short.*

bona fide, *in good faith,* i.e., *real, without deceit*

Carpe diem, *Seize the day,* i.e., *live in the present.*

casus belli, *an occasion of war,* i.e., *an excuse for making war*

ceteris paribus, *all other things being equal*

Credo, *I believe (the opening of the Christian creed; used generally of any set of firm beliefs)*

Cui bono? *To whose advantage? (Lit., to whom for a good?)*

cum grano salis, *with a grain of salt,* i.e., *with some allowance*

cum laude, *with praise (of academic distinctions)*

data, *things given (as a basis for proof or investigation)*

de facto, *on the basis of fact,* i.e., *in reality*

De gustibus non est disputandum, *One ought not to argue about tastes.*

de jure, *on the basis of right,* i.e., *legally*

De minimis non curat lex, *The law does not care about the smallest things,* i.e., *The Law does not concern itself with trivial matters (a legal maxim).*

De mortuis nil nisi bonum, *(Say) nothing but good of the dead.*

de novo, *anew*

Deo volente, *God willing*

Dies Irae, *Day of wrath (Judgment Day) (the opening words of a hymn by Thomas of Celano)*

Dominus vobiscum, *The Lord be with you.*

Dramatis Personae, *masks of the drama,* i.e., *characters in the play*

E pluribus unum, *one from many (used, in an ancient poem, of the ingredients in a stew)*

Ecce homo, *Behold the man! (Pilate's words, presenting Jesus to the populace)*

emeritus, *discharged,* i.e., *retired*

et alia, *and other things*

et cetera, *and the rest*

ex cathedra, *from the chair,* i.e., *with authority*

Ex nihilo nihil fit, *Nothing is made from nothing.*

ex officio, *on the basis of his office,* i.e., *by virtue of his position*

ex post facto, *on the basis of something done afterwards,* i.e., *retroactive*

ex tempore, *out of the moment,* i.e., *on the spur of the moment, without preparation*

exeat, *let him go out (a permission to leave)*

exeunt, *they go out (a stage direction)*

exit, *he goes out (a stage direction)*

Festina lente, *Make haste slowly.*

fiat, *let it be done (a term for an absolute command)*

genius loci, *the spirit of the place*

Gloria in excelsis, *Glory in the highest (the opening words of the Greater Doxology)*

habeas corpus, *that you may have the body (a common-law writ requiring that a person be brought before a court without delay)*

ibidem, *in that same place (used to refer to a passage already cited)*

id est, *that is*

ignis fatuus, *foolish fire,* i.e., *the will-o'-the-wisp*

in esse, *in being,* i.e., *existing*

in extremis, *among the last things,* i.e., *at the point of death*

in flagrante delicto, *while the crime is blazing,* i.e., *(caught) in the act*

In hoc signo vinces, *In this sign you will conquer (the words heard by the Emperor Constantine when he saw the sign of the cross or the monogram of Christ).*

in loco parentis, *in the place of a parent*

in medias res, *into the midst of things,* i.e., *without preamble*

In Memoriam, *to the memory of*

in posse, *in possibility,* i.e., *potentially*

in propria persona, *in one's own character,* i.e., *without disguise*

in situ, *in place,* i.e., *in its original position*

in toto, *on the whole,* i.e., *generally or entirely*

in vacuo, *in emptiness,* i.e., *without considering other factors*

In vino veritas, *In wine there is truth.*

infra dignitatem, *beneath one's dignity*

inter alia, *among other things*

Ipse dixit, *He himself said so (used of an assertion supported only by someone's authority, without further proof).*

ipso facto, *by that very fact*

lapsus calami, *a slip of the pen*

lapsus linguae, *a slip of the tongue*

litteratim, *letter by letter, literally*

locum tenens, *one holding a place,* i.e., *a substitute*

magna cum laude, *with great praise (of academic distinctions)*

magnum opus, *a great work,* i.e., *a masterpiece*

materfamilias, *mother of the family, matriarch*

mea culpa, *by my fault*

Memento mori, *Remember to die,* i.e., *remember that you are mortal.*

Mens sana in corpore sano, *a sound mind in a sound body*

minutiae, *trifles, minor details*

mirabile dictu, *amazing to say*

modus operandi, *method of working*

Morituri te salutamus, *We, destined to die, salute you (said by gladiators to the sponsor of the games before the fighting began).*

multum in parvo, *much in little*

mutatis mutandis, *having changed the things which must be changed,* i.e., *after making all necessary changes or transpositions*

ne plus ultra, *no more beyond,* i.e., *the summit of achievement* nemine contradicente, *no one contradicting,* i.e., *unanimous*

Nil desperandum, *Nothing is to be despaired of,* i.e., *one must never lose hope.*

nolens volens, *willy-nilly*

non compos mentis, *not sound of mind*

non sequitur, *it does not follow (used of an illogicality)*

nota bene, *note well*

Nunc dimittis, *Now lettest thou (thy servant) depart (in peace) (the opening words of the song of Simeon, used as a hymn).*

O tempora! O mores! *Oh, the times! Oh, the customs!*

obiter dictum, *said by the way,* i.e., *a parenthetical remark, (in law) an incidental opinion, not pertinent to the case at hand*

opus citatum, *the work previously cited*

pace, *by the leave of (used to express polite disagreement)*

pari passu, *at an equal pace,* i.e., *in an equal proportion*

paterfamilias, *father of the family, patriarch*

Paternoster, *Our Father (the opening words of the Lord's Prayer; used as a title for it)*

Pax vobiscum, *Peace be with you.*

peccavi, *I have sinned*

per annum, *by the year, annually*

per capita, *by heads,* i.e., *for each individual*

per diem, *by the day, each day*

per se, *in itself, intrinsically*

pons asinorum, *bridge of donkeys (a name for Euclid's fifth proposition, the diagram for which resembles a bridge, so called because some students could not pass it; used of a difficult stage in any study)*

Post hoc ergo propter hoc, *After this, therefore because of this,* i.e., *the false argument that any event which follows another must be a result of it.*

post meridiem, *after noon*

post mortem, *after death (used as a contraction of post mortem examination)*

post scriptum, *written afterwards*

prima facie, *by first appearance,* i.e., *obvious on the face of it*

pro bono publico, *for the people's good*

pro et contra, *for and against*

pro forma, *for form's sake, as a matter of form*

pro rata, *according to a fixed (share),* i.e., *in proportion*

pro tempore, *for the time being*

quasi, *as if,* i.e., *as it were; in a certain sense*

quid pro quo, *something for something,* i.e., *something in return, tit for tat*

Quod erat demonstrandum, *Which was to be demonstrated (used at the end of a logical proof)*

quod vide, *which see (used to refer to another entry or article in a dictionary or encyclopedia)*

rara avis, *a rare bird,* i.e., *an extraordinary person or thing* reductio ad absurdum, *reduction to absurdity,* i.e., *disproving a proposition by arguing from it to an impossible conclusion*

Requiescat in pace, *May he rest in peace.*

sanctum sanctorum, *holy of holies (used of any very private place)*

Senatus Populusque Romanus, *the Senate and the Roman People (summing up the sovereign power of Rome)*

seriatim, *in series*

Sic transit gloria mundi, *Thus passes the glory of the world.*

sine die, *without a day (appointed for reassembly)*

sine qua non, *without which not,* i.e., *an indispensable condition, a necessity*

status quo ante, *the condition in which (matters were) before*

sub rosa, *under the rose,* i.e., *secretly, privately (the rose being a symbol of secrecy)*

sui generis, *of its own kind (and no other),* i.e., *unique*

summa cum laude, *with highest praise (of academic distinctions)*

summum bonum, *the highest good (a term in ethics)*

Sursum corda, *(Lift) up your hearts (the opening words of a versicle of Christian liturgy).*

tabula rasa, *a smoothed tablet,* i.e., *a blank page (used to refer to the mind before it has received sensory perceptions from the outside world)*

Te Deum, *(We praise) Thee God (the opening words of a famous Christian hymn).*

Tempus fugit, *Time flies.*

terra firma, *solid earth*

terra incognita, *unknown land,* i.e., *undiscovered territory*

ultima Thule, *furthest Thule (a remote northern land of legend); used of any very distant place*

Vade mecum, *Go with me (a name for a handbook to be carried at all times)*

verbatim, *word by word,* i.e., *in the same words*

Verbum sat sapienti, *A word to the wise is sufficient.*

versus, *against*

vice versa, *the order having been changed,* i.e., *conversely*

viva voce, *by the living voice,* i.e., *orally*

vivat, *may he live,* i.e., *long live . . .*

vox populi, *the voice of the people*

Appendix

Part of a bronze breastplate with protective divinities

Agrippina

Inflections

—*Nouns*—

FIRST DECLENSION

Puella, f., *girl*

	SINGULAR	PLURAL
NOM.	puella, *a girl*	puellae, *girls*
GEN.	puellae, *of a girl*	puellārum, *of girls*
DAT.	puellae, *to a girl*	puellīs, *to girls*
ACC.	puellam, *a girl*	puellās, *girls*
ABL.	puellā, *by* or *with a girl*	puellīs, *by* or *with girls*

SECOND DECLENSION

	Amīcus, m., *friend*	Fīlius, m., *son*	Puer, m., *boy*	Ager, m., *field*
		SINGULAR		
NOM.	amīcus	filius	puer	ager
GEN.	amīcī	fīlī	puerī	agrī
DAT.	amīcō	filiō	puerō	agrō
ACC.	amīcum	filium	puerum	agrum
ABL.	amīcō	filiō	puerō	agrō
		PLURAL		
NOM.	amīcī	filiī	puerī	agrī
GEN.	amīcōrum	filiōrum	puerōrum	agrōrum
DAT.	amīcīs	filiīs	puerīs	agrīs
ACC.	amīcōs	filiōs	puerōs	agrōs
ABL.	amīcīs	filiīs	puerīs	agrīs

note: The vocative is always the same as the nominative, except of nouns and adjectives in **-us** of the second declension, which have **-e** in the vocative. Proper nouns ending in **-ius,** and **fīlius,** have the vocative ending in **-i.**

Verbum, N., *word*

	SINGULAR		PLURAL
NOM.	verbum	NOM.	verba
GEN.	verbī	GEN.	verbōrum
DAT.	verbō	DAT.	verbīs
ACC.	verbum	ACC.	verba
ABL.	verbō	ABL.	verbīs

THIRD DECLENSION

	Frāter, m., *brother*	Soror, f., *sister*	Iter, n., *journey*	Tempus, n., *time*
		SINGULAR		
NOM.	frāter	soror	iter	tempus
GEN.	frātris	sorōris	itineris	temporis
DAT.	frātrī	sorōrī	itinerī	temporī
ACC.	frātrem	sorōrem	iter	tempus
ABL.	frātre	sorōre	itinere	tempore
		PLURAL		
NOM.	frātrēs	sorōrēs	itinera	tempora
GEN.	frātrum	sorōrum	itinerum	temporum
DAT.	frātribus	sorōribus	itineribus	temporibus
ACC.	frātrēs	sorōrēs	itinera	tempora
ABL.	frātribus	sorōribus	itineribus	temporibus

THIRD DECLENSION—I-STEMS

	Ignis, m., *fire*	Urbs, f., *city*	Mare, n., *sea*
		SINGULAR	
NOM.	ignis	urbs	mare
GEN.	ignis	urbis	maris
DAT.	ignī	urbī	marī
ACC.	ignem	urbem	mare
ABL.	igne	urbe	marī

	NOM.	ignēs	urbēs	maria
	GEN.	ignium	urbium	marium
	DAT.	ignibus	urbibus	maribus
	ACC.	ignēs	urbēs	maria
	ABL.	ignibus	urbibus	maribus

FOURTH DECLENSION

Passus, m., *pace*   Cornū, n., *horn*

	SINGULAR	PLURAL	SINGULAR	PLURAL
NOM.	passus	passūs	cornū	cornua
GEN.	passūs	passuum	cornūs	cornuum
DAT.	passuī	passibus	cornū	cornibus
ACC.	passum	passūs	cornū	cornua
ABL.	passū	passibus	cornū	cornibus

FIFTH DECLENSION

Dies, m. and f., *day*   Rēs, f., *thing*

	SINGULAR	PLURAL	SINGULAR	PLURAL
NOM.	diēs	diēs	rēs	rēs
GEN.	diēī	diērum	reī	rērum
DAT.	diēī	diēbus	reī	rēbus
ACC.	diem	diēs	rem	rēs
ABL.	diē	diēbus	rē	rēbus

IRREGULAR DECLENSIONS

	Deus, m., *god*	Dea, f., *goddess*	Domus, f., *house*	Vīs, f., *force, strength*
			SINGULAR	
NOM.	deus	dea	domus	vīs
GEN.	deī	deae	domūs, -ī	vīs
DAT.	deō	deae	domuī, -ō	vī
ACC.	deum	deam	domum	vim
ABL.	deō	deā	domō, -ū	vī

PLURAL

NOM.	deī, diī, dī	deae	domūs	vīrēs
GEN.	deōrum, deum	deārum	domuum, -ōrum	vīrium
DAT.	deīs, diīs, dīs	deābus	domibus	vīribus
ACC.	deōs	deās	domōs, -ūs	vīrēs
ABL.	deīs, diīs, dīs	deābus	domibus	vīribus

PARSING

To parse a noun give: (1) declension, (2) nominative and genitive singular, (3) gender, (4) number, (5) case, and (6) rule for the case.

Example: In the sentence **Victōrēs oppidum magnum per virōs occupāvērunt,** the noun **oppidum** would be parsed as follows:

oppidum: second declension; **oppidum, oppidī;** neuter (gender); singular (number); accusative (case), direct object of the verb occupāvērunt.

Lady performing on the cithara—fresco from Pompeii

—Adjectives—

FIRST AND SECOND DECLENSIONS

Malus, *bad*

SINGULAR

	MASC.	FEM.	NEUT.
NOM.	malus	mala	malum
GEN.	malī	malae	malī
DAT.	malō	malae	malō
ACC.	malum	malam	malum
ABL.	malō	malā	malō

PLURAL

	MASC.	FEM.	NEUT.
NOM.	malī	malae	mala
GEN.	malōrum	malārum	malōrum
DAT.	malīs	malīs	malīs
ACC.	malōs	malās	mala
ABL.	malīs	malīs	malīs

Miser, *wretched*   Sacer, *sacred*

SINGULAR

	MASC.	FEM.	NEUT.	MASC.	FEM.	NEUT.
NOM.	miser,	misera,	miserum	sacer,	sacra,	sacrum
GEN.	miserī,	miserae,	miserī	sacrī,	sacrae,	sacrī
etc.	etc.	etc.	etc.	etc.	etc.	etc.

THIRD DECLENSION—THREE ENDINGS

Celer, *swift*

	SINGULAR			PLURAL		
	MASC.	FEM.	NEUT.	MASC.	FEM.	NEUT.
NOM.	celer	celeris	celere	celerēs	celerēs	celeria
GEN.	celeris	celeris	celeris	celerium	celerium	celerium
DAT.	celerī	celerī	celerī	celeribus	celeribus	celeribus
ACC.	celerem	celerem	celere	celerēs	celerēs	celeria
ABL.	celerī	celerī	celerī	celeribus	celeribus	celeribus

THIRD DECLENSION—TWO ENDINGS

Brevis, *short*

	M. AND F.	NEUT.	M. AND F.	NEUT.
NOM.	brevis	breve	brevēs	brevia
GEN.	brevis	brevis	brevium	brevium
DAT.	brevī	brevī	brevibus	brevibus
ACC.	brevem	breve	brevēs	brevia
ABL.	brevī	brevī	brevibus	brevibus

THIRD DECLENSION—ONE ENDING

Audax, *bold*

NOM.	audāx	audāx	audācēs	audācia
GEN.	audācis	audācis	audācium	audācium
DAT.	audācī	audācī	audācibus	audācibus
ACC.	audācem	audāx	audācēs	audācia
ABL.	audācī	audācī	audācibus	audācibus

Vesta

—Declension of Comparatives —

Certior, *more certain*

	SINGULAR		PLURAL	
	M. AND F.	NEUT.	M. AND F.	NEUT.
NOM.	certior	certius	certiōrēs	certiōra
GEN.	certiōris	certiōris	certiōrum	certiōrum
DAT.	certiōrī	certiōrī	certiōribus	certiōribus
ACC.	certiōrem	certius	certiōrēs	certiōra
ABL.	certiōre	certiōre	certiōribus	certiōribus

Plūs, *more*

	SINGULAR		PLURAL	
	M. AND F.	NEUT.	M. AND F.	NEUT.
NOM.	——	plūs	plūrēs	plūra
GEN.	——	plūris	plūrium	plūrium
DAT.	——	——	plūribus	plūribus
ACC.	——	plūs	plūrēs	plūra
ABL.	——	plūre	plūribus	plūribus

DECLENSION OF IRREGULAR ADJECTIVES

Alius, *another*   Ūnus, *one*

	SINGULAR					
	MASC.	FEM.	NEUT.	MASC.	FEM.	NEUT.
NOM.	alius	alia	aliud	ūnus	ūna	ūnum
GEN.	alīus	alīus	alīus	ūnīus	ūnīus	ūnīus
DAT.	aliī	aliī	aliī	ūnī	ūnī	ūnī
ACC.	alium	aliam	aliud	ūnum	ūnam	ūnum
ABL.	aliō	aliā	aliō	ūnō	ūnā	ūnō

The plural of *alius* is regular, of the First and Second Declensions.

<table>
<tr><th></th><th colspan="3" align="center">Duo, two</th><th colspan="3" align="center">Trēs, three</th></tr>
<tr><th></th><th>MASC.</th><th>FEM.</th><th>NEUT.</th><th>MASC.</th><th>FEM.</th><th>NEUT.</th></tr>
<tr><td>NOM.</td><td>duo</td><td>duae</td><td>duo</td><td>trēs</td><td>trēs</td><td>tria</td></tr>
<tr><td>GEN.</td><td>duōrum</td><td>duārum</td><td>duōrum</td><td>trium</td><td>trium</td><td>trium</td></tr>
<tr><td>DAT.</td><td>duōbus</td><td>duābus</td><td>duōbus</td><td>tribus</td><td>tribus</td><td>tribus</td></tr>
<tr><td>ACC.</td><td>duōs, duo</td><td>duās</td><td>duo</td><td>trēs</td><td>trēs</td><td>tria</td></tr>
<tr><td>ABL.</td><td>duōbus</td><td>duābus</td><td>duōbus</td><td>tribus</td><td>tribus</td><td>tribus</td></tr>
</table>

COMPARISON OF ADJECTIVES

POSITIVE	COMPARATIVE	SUPERLATIVE
fortis	fortior	fortissimus
vēlōx	vēlōcior	vēlōcissimus
miser	miserior	miserrimus
ācer	ācrior	ācerrimus

COMPARISON OF IRREGULAR ADJECTIVES

POSITIVE	COMPARATIVE	SUPERLATIVE
bonus, *good*	melior	optimus
malus, *bad*	peior	pessimus
magnus, *great*	maior	maximus
parvus, *small*	minor	minimus
multus, *much*		plūrimus
multum, *much*	plūs	plūrimum
multī, *many*	plūrēs	plūrimī
senex, *old*	senior (maior nātū)	maximus nātū
iuvenis, *young*	iūnior (minor nātū)	minimus nātū
idōneus, *suitable*	magis idōneus	maximē idōneus
exterus, *outer*	exterior	extrēmus (*or*) extimus
īnferus, *below*	īnferior	īnfimus (*or*) īmus
posterus, *following*	posterior	postrēmus (*or*) postumus
superus, *above*	superior	suprēmus (*or*) summus
(cis, citrā)	citerior, *hither*	citimus
(in, intrā)	interior, *inner*	intimus
(prae, prō)	prior, *former*	prīmus
(prope)	propior, *nearer*	proximus
(ultrā)	ulterior, *farther*	ultimus
facilis, *easy*	facilior	facillimus

COMPARISON OF IRREGULAR ADJECTIVES

POSITIVE	COMPARATIVE	SUPERLATIVE
difficilis, *difficult*	difficilior	difficillimus
similis, *like*	similior	simillimus
dissimilis, *unlike*	dissimilior	dissimillimus
humilis, *low*	humilior	humillimus

COMPARISON OF ADVERBS

POSITIVE	COMPARATIVE	SUPERLATIVE
lātē (lātus)	lātius	lātissimē
pulchrē (pulcher)	pulchrius	pulcherrimē
miserē (miser)	miserius	miserrimē
fortiter (fortis)	fortius	fortissimē
ācriter (ācer)	ācrius	ācerrimē
facile (facilis)	facilius	facillimē
bene (bonus)	melius	optimē
male (malus)	peius	pessimē
magnopere (magnus)	magis	maximē
parum (parvus)	minus	minimē
diū	diūtius	diūtissimē

NUMERALS

	CARDINALS	ORDINALS
1.	ūnus, -a, -um	prīmus, -a, -um
2.	duo, duae, duo	secundus, alter
3.	trēs, tria	tertius
4.	quattuor	quārtus
5.	quīnque	quīntus
6.	sex	sextus
7.	septem	septimus
8.	octō	octāvus
9.	novem	nōnus
10.	decem	decimus
11.	ūndecim	ūndecimus
12.	duodecim	duodecimus
13.	tredecim	tertius decimus
14.	quattuordecim	quārtus decimus
15.	quīndecim	quīntus decimus
16.	sēdecim	sextus decimus

NUMERALS

CARDINALS	ORDINALS
17. septendecim	septimus decimus
18. duodēvīgintī	duōdēvīcēsimus
19. ūndēvīgintī	ūndēvīcēsimus
20. vīgintī	vīcēsimus
21. vīgintī ūnus	vīcēsimus prīmus
(ūnus et vīgintī)	
29. ūndētrīgintā	ūndētrīcēsimus
30. trīgintā	trīcēsimus
40. quadrāgintā	quadrāgēsimus
50. quīnquāgintā	quīnquāgēsimus
60. sexāgintā	sexāgēsimus
70. septuāgintā	septuāgēsimus
80. octōgintā	octōgēsimus
90. nōnāgintā	nōnāgēsimus
100. centum	centēsimus
200. ducentī, -ae, -a	ducentēsimus
300. trecentī	trecentēsimus
400. quadringentī	quadringentēsimus
500. quīngentī	quīngentēsimus
600. sescentī	sescentēsimus
700. septingentī	septingentēsimus
800. octingentī	octingentēsimus
900. nōngentī	nōngentēsimus
1000. mīlle	mīllēsimus
2000. duo mīlia	bis mīllēsimus

*Etruscan bronze
of a light
one-horse chariot*

—Pronouns —

PERSONAL

FIRST PERSON	SECOND PERSON	THIRD PERSON
Ego, *I.*	Tū, *you*	Is, *he;* ea, *she* id, *it*

	SINGULAR	PLURAL	SINGULAR	PLURAL	*For declension see p. 444*
NOM.	ego	nōs	tū	vōs	
GEN.	meī	{ nostrum { nostrī	tuī	{ vestrum { vestrī	
DAT.	mihi	nōbīs	tibi	vōbīs	
ACC.	mē	nōs	tē	vōs	
ABL.	mē	nōbīs	tē	vōbīs	

REFLEXIVE

FIRST PERSON
Meī, *of myself*

THIRD PERSON
Suī, *of himself, herself, itself*

SECOND PERSON
Tui, *of yourself*

These are declined like the personal pronoun of the same person, except that they have no nominative.

	SINGULAR	PLURAL
GEN.	suī	suī
DAT.	sibi	sibi
ACC.	sē (*or*) sēsē	sē (*or*) sēsē
ABL.	sē (*or*) sēsē	sē (*or*) sēsē

DEMONSTRATIVE

Hic, *this*

	SINGULAR			PLURAL		
	MASC.	FEM.	NEUT.	MASC.	FEM.	NEUT.
NOM.	hic	haec	hoc	hī	hae	haec
GEN.	huius	huius	huius	hōrum	hārum	hōrum
DAT.	huic	huic	huic	hīs	hīs	hīs
ACC.	hunc	hanc	hoc	hōs	hās	haec
ABL.	hōc	hāc	hōc	hīs	hīs	hīs

Ille, *that*

	SINGULAR			PLURAL		
	MASC.	FEM.	NEUT.	MASC.	FEM.	NEUT.
NOM.	ille	illa	illud	illī	illae	illa
GEN.	illīus	illīus	illīus	illōrum	illārum	illōrum
DAT.	illī	illī	illī	illīs	illīs	illīs
ACC.	illum	illam	illud	illōs	illās	illa
ABL.	illō	illā	illō	illīs	illīs	illīs

Iste, *that, that of yours*   Ipse, *self*

	SINGULAR					
	MASC.	FEM.	NEUT.	MASC.	FEM.	NEUT.
NOM.	iste	ista	istud	ipse	ipsa	ipsum
GEN.	istīus	istīus	istīus	ipsīus	ipsīus	ipsīus
DAT.	istī	istī	istī	ipsī	ipsī	ipsī
ACC.	istum	istam	istud	ipsum	ipsam	ipsum
ABL.	istō	istā	istō	ipsō	ipsā	ipsō

The plural is regular.

Is, *that, he*

	SINGULAR			PLURAL		
	MASC.	FEM.	NEUT.	MASC.	FEM.	NEUT.
NOM.	is	ea	id	eī	eae	ea
GEN.	eius	eius	eius	eōrum	eārum	eōrum
DAT.	eī	eī	eī	eīs	eīs	eīs
ACC.	eum	eam	id	eōs	eās	ea
ABL.	eō	eā	eō	eīs	eīs	eīs

Īdem, *same*

	SINGULAR			PLURAL		
	MASC.	FEM.	NEUT.	MASC.	FEM.	NEUT.
NOM.	īdem	eadem	idem	eīdem	eaedem	eadem
GEN.	eiusdem	eiusdem	eiusdem	eōrundem	eārundem	eōrundem
DAT.	eīdem	eīdem	eīdem	eīsdem	eīsdem	eīsdem
ACC.	eundem	eandem	idem	eōsdem	eāsdem	eadem
ABL.	eōdem	eādem	eōdem	eīsdem	eīsdem	eīsdem

RELATIVE

Quī, *who, which, that*

| | SINGULAR | | | PLURAL | | |
	MASC.	FEM.	NEUT.	MASC.	FEM.	NEUT.
NOM.	quī	quae	quod	quī	quae	quae
GEN.	cuius	cuius	cuius	quōrum	quārum	quōrum
DAT.	cui	cui	cui	quibus	quibus	quibus
ACC.	quem	quam	quod	quōs	quās	quae
ABL.	quō	quā	quō	quibus	quibus	quibus

INTERROGATIVE

Quis, *who? what?*

| | SINGULAR | | PLURAL | | |
	M. AND F.	NEUT.	MASC.	FEM.	NEUT.
NOM.	quis	quid	quī	quae	quae
GEN.	cuius	cuius	quōrum	quārum	quōrum
DAT.	cui	cui	quibus	quibus	quibus
ACC.	quem	quid	quōs	quās	quae
ABL.	quō	quō	quibus	quibus	quibus

The adjective **quī,** *what,* is declined like the relative **quī.**

INDEFINITE

Aliquis, *some one*

| | SINGULAR | | PLURAL | | |
	M. AND F.	NEUT.	MASC.	FEM.	NEUT.
NOM.	aliquis	aliquid	aliquī	aliquae	aliqua
GEN.	alicuius	alicuius	aliquōrum	aliquārum	aliquōrum
DAT.	alicui	alicui	aliquibus	aliquibus	aliquibus
ACC.	aliquem	aliquid	aliquōs	aliquās	aliqua
ABL.	aliquō	aliquō	aliquibus	aliquibus	aliquibus

The adjective is **aliquī, aliqua, aliquod.**
Quis, *any one,* is declined like **aliquis** without **ali-.**
Quī, qua, quod, the adjective *any,* is declined like **aliquī, aliqua, aliquod** without **ali-.**

Quīdam, *a certain* (*one*) (the pronoun)

	SINGULAR		PLURAL		
	M. AND F.	NEUT.	MASC.	FEM.	NEUT.
NOM.	quīdam	quiddam	quīdam	quaedam	quaedam
GEN.	cuiusdam	cuiusdam	quōrundam	quārundam	quōrundam
DAT.	cuidam	cuidam	quibusdam	quibusdam	quibusdam
ACC.	quendam	quiddam	quōsdam	quāsdam	quaedam
ABL.	quōdam	quōdam	quibusdam	quibusdam	quibusdam

Quīdam, quaedam, quoddam, *certain* (the adjective)

SINGULAR

	MASC.	FEM.	NEUT.
NOM.	quīdam	quaedam	quoddam
GEN.	cuiusdam	cuiusdam	cuiusdam
DAT.	cuidam	cuidam	cuidam
ACC.	quendam	quandam	quoddam
ABL.	quōdam	quādam	quōdam

PLURAL

The plural is declined like the plural of the pronoun.

Quisquam, *any one*

SINGULAR

	M. AND F.	NEUT.
NOM.	quisquam	quidquam (quicquam)
GEN.	cuiusquam	cuiusquam
DAT.	cuiquam	cuiquam
ACC.	quemquam	quidquam (quicquam)
ABL.	quōquam	quōquam

(This is substantive only; there is no plural.)

Quisque, *each*

Quisque, quidque is declined like **quis, quid** with **-que** added.
Quīque, quaeque, quodque, the adjective, is declined like **quī, quae, quod** with **-que** added.

—— Verbs ——

FIRST CONJUGATION

PRINCIPAL PARTS: vocō, vocāre, vocāvī, vocātum
STEMS: vocā-, vocāv-, vocāt-

<table>
<tr><td colspan="2">ACTIVE VOICE</td><td colspan="2">PASSIVE VOICE</td></tr>
</table>

INDICATIVE
PRESENT

I call, am calling		*I am called*	
vocō	vocāmus	vocor	vocāmur
vocās	vocātis	vocāris	vocāminī
vocat	vocant	vocātur	vocantur

IMPERFECT

I was calling		*I was being called*	
vocābam	vocābāmus	vocābar	vocābāmur
vocābās	vocābātis	vocābāris	vocābāminī
vocābat	vocābant	vocābātur	vocābantur

FUTURE

I shall call		*I shall be called*	
vocābō	vocābimus	vocābor	vocābimur
vocābis	vocābitis	vocāberis	vocābiminī
vocābit	vocābunt	vocābitur	vocābuntur

PERFECT

I have called, I called		*I have been called, I was called*			
vocāvī	vocāvimus	vocātus	⎰ sum	vocātī	⎰ sumus
vocāvistī	vocāvistis	(-a, -um)	⎨ es	(-ae, -a)	⎨ estis
vocāvit	vocāvērunt		⎱ est		⎱ sunt

PLUPERFECT

I had called		*I had been called*			
vocāveram	vocāverāmus	vocātus	⎰ eram	vocātī	⎰ erāmus
vocāverās	vocāverātis	(-a, -um)	⎨ erās	(-ae, -a)	⎨ erātis
vocāverat	vocāverant		⎱ erat		⎱ erant

FUTURE PERFECT

I shall have called · · · · · · · · · · · · · · · · · · *I shall have been called*

vocāverō	vocāverimus	vocātus (-a, -um) { erō eris erit	vocātī (-ae, -a) { erimus eritis erunt
vocāveris	vocāveritis		
vocāverit	vocāverint		

SUBJUNCTIVE
PRESENT

vocem	vocēmus	vocer	vocēmur
vocēs	vocētis	vocēris	vocēminī
vocet	vocent	vocētur	vocentur

IMPERFECT

vocārem	vocārēmus	vocārer	vocārēmur
vocārēs	vocārētis	vocārēris	vocārēminī
vocāret	vocārent	vocārētur	vocārentur

PERFECT

vocāverim	vocāverīmus	vocātus (-a, -um) { sim sīs sit	vocātī (-ae, -a) { sīmus sītis sint
vocāverīs	vocāverītis		
vocāverit	vocāverint		

PLUPERFECT

vocāvissem	vocāvissēmus	vocātus (-a, -um) { essem essēs esset	vocātī (-ae, -a) { essēmus essētis essent
vocāvissēs	vocāvissētis		
vocāvisset	vocāvissent		

IMPERATIVE
PRESENT

Call · · · · · · · · · · · · · · · · · · *Be called*

vocā	vocāte	vocāre	vocāminī

FUTURE

You, he, they shall call · · · · · · · · · · · · · · · · · · *You, he, they shall be called*

vocātō	vocātōte	vocātor	——
vocātō	vocantō	vocātor	vocantor

INFINITIVES

PRES.	vocāre, *to call*	vocārī, *to be called*
PERF.	vocāvisse, *to have called*	vocātus esse, *to have been called*
FUT.	vocātūrus esse, *to be about to call*	———

PARTICIPLES

PRES.	vocāns, *calling*	———
PERF.	———	vocātus, *having been called*
FUT.	vocātūrus, *about to call*	vocandus, *to be called*

GERUND	GERUNDIVE
GEN. vocandī, *of calling*	(*see Fut. Pass. Part.*)
DAT. vocandō, *for calling*	SUPINE
ACC. vocandum, *calling*	ACC. vocātum, *to call*
ABL. vocandō, *by calling*	ABL. vocātū, *to call*

SECOND CONJUGATION

PRINCIPAL PARTS: moneō, monēre, monuī, monitum
STEMS: monē-, monu-, monit-

ACTIVE VOICE   PASSIVE VOICE

INDICATIVE
PRESENT

I advise, am advising   *I am advised*

moneō	monēmus	moneor	monēmur
monēs	monētis	monēris	monēminī
monet	monent	monētur	monentur

IMPERFECT

I was advising   *I was being advised*

monēbam	monēbāmus	monēbar	monēbāmur
monēbas	monēbātis	monēbāris	monēbāminī
monēbat	monēbant	monēbātur	monēbantur

FUTURE

I shall advise   *I shall be advised*

monēbō	monēbimus	monēbor	monēbimur
monēbis	monēbitis	monēberis	monēbiminī
monēbit	monēbunt	monēbitur	monēbuntur

PERFECT

I have advised, I advised   *I have been advised, I was advised*

monuī	monuimus	monitus	{ sum	monitī	{ sumus
monuistī	monuistis	(-a, -um)	es	(-ae, -a)	estis
monuit	monuērunt		est		sunt

PLUPERFECT

I had advised   *I had been advised*

monueram	monuerāmus	monitus	{ eram	monitī	{ erāmus
monuerās	monuerātis	(-a, -um)	erās	(-ae, -a)	erātis
monuerat	monuerant		erat		erant

FUTURE PERFECT

I shall have advised   *I shall have been advised*

monuerō	monuerimus	monitus	{ erō	monitī	{ erimus
monueris	monueritis	(-a, -um)	eris	(-ae, -a)	eritis
monuerit	monuerint		erit		erunt

SUBJUNCTIVE
PRESENT

moneam	moneāmus	monear	moneāmur
moneās	moneātis	moneāris	moneāminī
moneat	moneant	moneātur	moneantur

IMPERFECT

monērem	monērēmus	monērer	monērēmur
monērēs	monērētis	monērēris	monērēminī
monēret	monērent	monērētur	monērentur

PERFECT

monuerim	monuerīmus	monitus (-a, -um)	sim sīs sit	monitī (-ae, -a)	sīmus sītis sint
monuerīs	monuerītis				
monuerit	monuerint				

PLUPERFECT

monuissem	monuissēmus	monitus (-a, -um)	essem essēs esset	monitī (-ae, -a)	essēmus essētis essent
monuissēs	monuissētis				
monuisset	monuissent				

IMPERATIVE
PRESENT

Advise		*Be advised*	
monē	monēte	monēre	monēminī

FUTURE

You, he, they shall advise		*You, he, they shall be advised*	
monētō	monētōte	monētor	——
monētō	monentō	monētor	monentor

INFINITIVES

PRES.	monēre, *to advise*	monērī, *to be advised*
PERF.	monuisse, *to have advised*	monitus esse, *to have been advised*
FUT.	monitūrus esse, *to be about to advise*	

PARTICIPLES

PRES.	monēns, -entis, *advising*	——
PERF.	——	monitus, -a, -um, *having been advised*
FUT.	monitūrus, -a, -um, *about to advise*	monendus, -a, -um, *to be advised*

	GERUND		GERUNDIVE
GEN.	monendī, *of advising*		*(see Fut. Pass. Part.)*
DAT.	monendō, *for advising*		SUPINE
ACC.	monendum, *advising*	ACC.	monitum, *to advise*
ABL.	monendō, *by advising*	ABL.	monitū, *to advise*

THIRD CONJUGATION

PRINCIPAL PARTS: regō, regere, rēxī, rēctum
STEMS: reg-, rēx-, rēct-

ACTIVE VOICE		PASSIVE VOICE	

INDICATIVE
PRESENT

I rule, am ruling		*I am ruled*	
regō	regimus	regor	regimur
regis	regitis	regeris	regiminī
regit	regunt	regitur	reguntur

IMPERFECT

I was ruling		*I was being ruled*	
regēbam	regēbāmus	regēbar	regēbāmur
regēbās	regēbātis	regēbāris	regēbāminī
regēbat	regēbant	regēbātur	regēbantur

FUTURE

I shall rule		*I shall be ruled*	
regam	regēmus	regar	regēmur
regēs	regētis	regēris	regēminī
reget	regent	regētur	regentur

PERFECT

I have ruled, I ruled		*I have been ruled, I was ruled*			
rēxī	rēximus	rēctus	{ sum	rēctī	{ sumus
rēxistī	rēxistis	(-a, -um)	es	(-ae, -a)	estis
rēxit	rēxērunt		est		sunt

PLUPERFECT

I had ruled		*I had been ruled*			
rēxeram	rēxerāmus	rēctus (-a, -um)	eram / erās / erat	rēctī (-ae, -a)	erāmus / erātis / erant
rēxerās	rēxerātis				
rēxerat	rēxerant				

FUTURE PERFECT

I shall have ruled		*I shall have been ruled*			
rēxerō	rēxerimus	rēctus (-a, -um)	erō / eris / erit	rēctī (-ae, -a)	erimus / eritis / erunt
rēxeris	rēxeritis				
rēxerit	rēxerint				

SUBJUNCTIVE
PRESENT

regam	regāmus	regar	regāmur
regās	regātis	regāris	regāminī
regat	regant	regātur	regantur

IMPERFECT

regerem	regerēmus	regerer	regerēmur
regerēs	regerētis	regerēris	regerēminī
regeret	regerent	regerētur	regerentur

PERFECT

rēxerim	rēxerīmus	rēctus (-a, -um)	sim / sīs / sit	rēctī (-ae, -a)	sīmus / sītis / sint
rēxerīs	rēxeritis				
rēxerit	rēxerint				

PLUPERFECT

rēxissem	rēxissēmus	rēctus (-a, -um)	essem / essēs / esset	rēctī (-ae, -a)	essēmus / essētis / essent
rēxissēs	rēxissēs				
rēxisset	rēxissent				

IMPERATIVE
PRESENT

Rule		*Be ruled*	
rege	regite	regere	regiminī

FUTURE

You, he, they shall rule		*You, he, they shall be ruled*	
regitō	regitōte	regitor	———
regitō	reguntō	regitor	reguntor

INFINITIVES

PRES.	regere, *to rule*	regī, *to be ruled*
PERF.	rēxisse, *to have ruled*	rēctus esse, *to have been ruled*
FUT.	rēctūrus esse, *to be about to rule*	———

PARTICIPLES

PRES.	rēgens, *ruling*	rēctus, *having been ruled*
PERF.	———	regendus, *to be ruled*
FUT.	rēctūrus, *about to rule*	

GERUND   **GERUNDIVE**

GEN.	regendī, *of ruling*	(*see Fut. Pass. Part.*)		
DAT.	regendō, *for ruling*		**SUPINE**	
ACC.	regendum, *ruling*	ACC.	rēctum, *to rule*	
ABL.	regendō, *by ruling*	ABL.	rēctū, *to rule*	

FOURTH CONJUGATION

PRINCIPAL PARTS: audiō, audīre, audīvī, audītum
STEM: audī-, audīv-, audīt-

ACTIVE VOICE   **PASSIVE VOICE**

INDICATIVE
PRESENT

I hear, am hearing, do hear		*I am heard*	
audiō	audīmus	audior	audīmur
audīs	audītis	audīris	audīminī
audit	audiunt	audītur	audiuntur

IMPERFECT

	I was hearing		*I was being heard*
audiēbam	audiēbāmus	audiēbar	audiēbāmur
audiēbās	audiēbātis	audiēbāris	audiēbāminī
audiēbat	audiēbant	audiēbātur	audiēbantur

FUTURE

	I shall hear		*I shall be heard*
audiam	audiēmus	audiar	audiēmur
audiēs	audiētis	audiēris	audiēminī
audiet	audient	audiētur	audientur

PERFECT

	I have heard, I heard				*I have been (was) heard*		
audīvī	audīvimus	audītus	sum	audītī	sumus
audīvistī	audīvistis	(-a, -um)	es	(-ae, -a)	estis
audīvit	audīvērunt		est		sunt

PLUPERFECT

	I had heard				*I had been heard*		
audīveram	audīverāmus	audītus	eram	audītī	erāmus
audīverās	audīverātis	(-a, -um)	erās	(-ae, -a)	erātis
audīverat	audīverant		erat		erant

FUTURE PERFECT

	I shall have heard				*I shall have been heard*		
audīverō	audīverimus	audītus	erō	audītī	erimus
audīveris	audīveritis	(-a, -um)	eris	(-ae, -a)	eritis
audīverit	audīverint		erit		erunt

SUBJUNCTIVE
PRESENT

audiam	audiāmus	audiar	audiāmur
audiās	audiātis	audiāris	audiāminī
audiat	audiant	audiātur	audiantur

IMPERFECT

audīrem	audīrēmus	audīrer	audīrēmur
audīrēs	audīrētis	audīrēris	audīrēminī
audīret	audīrent	audīrētur	audīrentur

PERFECT

audīverim	audīverīmus	audītus (-a, -um) $\begin{cases} sim \\ sīs \\ sit \end{cases}$		audītī (-ae, -a) $\begin{cases} sīmus \\ sītis \\ sint \end{cases}$	
audīverīs	audīverītis				
audīverit	audīverint				

PLUPERFECT

audīvissem	audīvissēmus	audītus (-a, -um) $\begin{cases} essem \\ essēs \\ esset \end{cases}$		audītī (-ae, -a) $\begin{cases} essēmus \\ essētis \\ essent \end{cases}$	
audīvissēs	audīvissētis				
audīvisset	audīvissent				

IMPERATIVE
PRESENT

Hear		*Be heard*	
audī	audīte	audīre	audīminī

FUTURE

You, he, they shall hear		*You, he, they shall be heard*	
audītō	audītōte	audītor	———
audītō	audiuntō	audītor	audiuntor

INFINITIVES

PRES.	audīre, *to hear*	audīrī, *to be heard*
PERF.	audīvisse, *to have heard*	audītus esse, *to have been heard*
FUT.	audītūrus esse, *to be about to hear*	———

PARTICIPLES

PRES.	audiēns, -entis, *hearing*	———
PERF.	———	audītus, -a, -um, *having been heard*
FUT.	audītūrus, -a, -um, *about to hear*	audiendus, -a, -um, *to be heard*

	GERUND		GERUNDIVE
GEN.	audiendī, *of hearing*		(*see Fut. Pass. Part.*)
DAT.	audiendō, *for hearing*		**SUPINE**
ACC.	audiendum, *hearing*	ACC.	audītum, *to hear*
ABL.	audiendō, *by hearing*	ABL.	audītū, *to hear*

THIRD CONJUGATION—VERBS IN -IŌ

PRINCIPLE PARTS: capiō, capere, cēpī, captum
STEMS: capi-, cēp-, capt-

ACTIVE VOICE		**PASSIVE VOICE**	

INDICATIVE

PRESENT

I take, am taking		*I am taken*	
capiō	capimus	capior	capimur
capis	capitis	caperis	capiminī
capit	capiunt	capitur	capiuntur

IMPERFECT

I was taking	*I was being taken*
capiēbam, etc.	capiēbar, etc.

FUTURE

I shall take		*I shall be taken*	
capiam	capiēmus	capiar	capiēmur
capiēs	capiētis	capiēris	capiēminī
capiet	capient	capiētur	capientur

PERFECT

I took, have taken	*I have been (was) taken*
cēpī, etc.	captus sum, etc.

PLUPERFECT

I had taken	*I had been taken*
cēperam, etc.	captus eram, etc.

FUTURE PERFECT

I shall have taken	*I shall have been taken*
cēperō, etc.	captus erō, etc.

SUBJUNCTIVE
PRESENT

capiam	capiāmus	capiar	capiāmur
capiās	capiātis	capiāris	capiāminī
capiat	capiant	capiātur	capiantur

IMPERFECT

caperem, etc.	caperer, etc.

PERFECT

cēperim, etc.	captus sim, etc.

PLUPERFECT

cēpissem, etc.	captus essem, etc.

IMPERATIVE
PRESENT

Take		*Be taken*	
cape	capite	capere	capiminī

FUTURE

You, he, they shall take		*You, he, they shall be taken*	
capitō	capitōte	capitor	———
capitō	capiuntō	capitor	capiuntor

INFINITIVES

PRES.	capere, *to take*	capī, *to be taken*
PERF.	cēpisse, *to have taken*	captus esse, *to have been taken*
FUT.	captūrus esse, *to be about to take*	———

PARTICIPLES

PRES.	capiēns, -ientis, *taking*	———
PERF.	———	captus, -a, -um, *having been taken*
FUT.	captūrus, -a, -um, *about to take*	capiendus, -a, -um, *to be taken*

GERUND	GERUNDIVE

GEN.	capiendī, *of taking*	(*see Fut. Pass. Part.*)	
DAT.	capiendō, *for taking*	**SUPINE**	
ACC.	capiendum, *taking*	ACC.	captum, *to take*
ABL.	capiendō, *by taking*	ABL.	captū, *to take*

IRREGULAR VERBS

PRINCIPAL PARTS:	PRINCIPAL PARTS:
sum, esse, fuī	possum, posse, potuī

INDICATIVE
PRESENT

I am		*I am able, I can*	
sum	sumus	possum	possumus
es	estis	potes	potestis
est	sunt	potest	possunt

IMPERFECT

I was		*I was able, I could*	
eram	erāmus	poteram	poterāmus
erās	erātis	poterās	poterātis
erat	erant	poterat	poterant

FUTURE

I shall be		*I shall be able*	
erō	erimus	poterō	poterimus
eris	eritis	poteris	poteritis
erit	erunt	poterit	poterunt

PERFECT

I was, have been		*I have been able, I could*	
fuī	fuimus	potuī	potuimus
fuistī	fuistis	potuistī	potuistis
fuit	fuērunt	potuit	potuērunt

PLUPERFECT

I had been		*I had been able*	
fueram	fuerāmus	potueram	potuerāmus
fuerās	fuerātis	potuerās	potuerātis
fuerat	fuerant	potuerat	potuerant

FUTURE PERFECT

I shall have been		*I shall have been able*	
fuerō	fuerimus	potuerō	potuerimus
fueris	fueritis	potueris	potueritis
fuerit	fuerint	potuerit	potuerint

SUBJUNCTIVE
PRESENT

sim	sīmus	possim	possīmus
sīs	sītis	possīs	possītis
sit	sint	possit	possint

IMPERFECT

essem	essēmus	possem	possēmus
essēs	essētis	possēs	possētis
esset	essent	posset	possent

PERFECT

fuerim	fuerīmus	potuerim	potuerīmus
fuerīs	fuerītis	potuerīs	potuerītis
fuerit	fuerint	potuerit	potuerint

PLUPERFECT

fuissem	fuissēmus	potuissem	potuissēmus
fuissēs	fuissētis	potuissēs	potuissētis
fuisset	fuissent	potuisset	potuissent

IMPERATIVE
PRESENT

Be		(lacking)
es	este	

FUTURE
You, he, they shall be   (lacking)

estō	estōte
estō	suntō

INFINITIVES

PRES.	esse, *to be*	posse, *to be able*
PERF.	fuisse, *to have been*	potuisse, *to have been able*
FUT.	⎧ futūrus esse, ⎫ ⎨ or ⎬ *to be about to be* ⎩ fore ⎭	(lacking)

PARTICIPLES

PRES.	(lacking)	potēns, -entis (used as an adjective), *powerful*
FUT.	futūrus, -a, -um, *about to be*	(lacking)

PRINCIPAL PARTS: volō, velle, voluī, *be willing, wish*
                       nōlō, nōlle, nōluī, *be unwilling*
                       mālō, mālle, māluī, *be more willing, prefer*

INDICATIVE
PRESENT

volō	volumus	nōlō	nōlumus	mālō	mālumus
vīs	vultis	nōn vīs	nōn vultis	māvīs	māvultis
vult	volunt	nōn vult	nōlunt	māvult	mālunt

IMPERFECT

volēbam	nōlēbam	mālēbam

FUTURE

volam	nōlam	mālam

PERFECT

voluī	nōluī	māluī

PLUPERFECT

volueram	nōlueram	mālueram

FUTURE PERFECT

| voluerō | nōluerō | māluerō |

SUBJUNCTIVE
PRESENT

velim	velīmus	nōlim	nōlīmus	mālim	mālīmus
velīs	velītis	nōlīs	nōlītis	mālīs	mālītis
velit	velint	nōlit	nōlint	mālit	mālint

IMPERFECT

| vellem | nōllem | māllem |

PERFECT

| voluerim | nōluerim | māluerim |

PLUPERFECT

| voluissem | nōluissem | māluissem |

IMPERATIVE
PRESENT

| (lacking) | nōlī | nōlīte | (lacking) |

FUTURE

| (lacking) | nōlītō | nōlītōte | (lacking) |
| | nōlītō | nōluntō | |

INFINITIVES

| PRES. | velle | nōlle | mālle |
| PERF. | voluisse | nōluisse | māluisse |

PARTICIPLES

| PRES. | volēns | nōlēns | (lacking) |

PRINCIPAL PARTS: ferō, ferre, tulī, lātum, *bear, carry.*

PRESENT INDICATIVE

ACTIVE		PASSIVE	
ferō	ferimus	feror	ferimur
fers	fertis	ferris	feriminī
fert	ferunt	fertur	feruntur

INDICATIVE		SUBJUNCTIVE	
ACTIVE	PASSIVE	ACTIVE	PASSIVE
IMPERFECT		PRESENT	
ferēbam	ferēbar	feram	ferar

FUTURE		IMPERFECT	
feram	ferar	ferrem	ferrer

PERFECT		PERFECT	
tulī	lātus sum	tulerim	lātus sim

PLUPERFECT		PLUPERFECT	
tuleram	lātus eram	tulissem	lātus essem

FUTURE PERFECT	
tulerō	lātus erō

IMPERATIVE
PRESENT

fer	ferte	ferre	feriminī

FUTURE

fertō	fertōte	fertor	———
fertō	feruntō	fertor	feruntor

INFINITIVES

PRES.	ferre	ferrī
PERF.	tulisse	lātus esse
FUT.	lātūrus esse	———

PARTICIPLES

PRES.	ferēns	———
PERF.	———	lātus
FUT.	lātūrus	ferendus

GERUND		GERUNDIVE

GEN.	ferendī	(see Fut. Pass. Part.)	
DAT.	ferendō	SUPINE	
ACC.	ferendum	ACC.	lātum
ABL.	ferendō	ABL.	lātū

PRINCIPAL PARTS: eō, īre, iī (īvī), itum, *go*.

INDICATIVE	SUBJUNCTIVE	INFINITIVES

PRESENT

eō	īmus
īs	ītis
it	eunt

PRESENT

eam

PRES.	īre
PERF.	īsse (ivisse)
FUT.	itūrus esse

IMPERFECT
irem

IMPERFECT
ībam

PARTICIPLES

PRES.	iēns, euntis
FUT.	itūrus

PERFECT
ierim (īverim)

FUTURE
ībo

GERUND

GEN.	eundī
DAT.	eundō
ACC.	eundum
ABL.	eundō

PLUPERFECT
īssem (īvissem)

PERFECT
iī (īvī)

IMPERATIVE

PRES.	ī, īte
FUT.	ītō, ītōte
	ītō, euntō

PLUPERFECT
ieram

SUPINE

ACC.	itum
ABL.	itū

FUTURE PERFECT
ierō

PRINCIPAL PARTS: fīō, fierī, factus sum, *be made, become.*

INDICATIVE	SUBJUNCTIVE	INFINITIVES

PRESENT   **PRESENT**   PRES.   fieri
fīō   fīmus   fīam   PERF.   factus esse
fīs   fītis
fit   fīunt

IMPERFECT
fierem

IMPERFECT   **PARTICIPLES**
fīēbam   PRES. ———
       PERF.   factus
       FUT.   faciendus

PERFECT
factus sim

FUTURE   **GERUNDIVE**
fīam   (SEE FUT. PART.)

PLUPERFECT
factus essem

PERFECT
factus sum

PLUPERFECT
factus eram

FUTURE PERFECT
factus erō

PARSING

To parse a verb give: (1) conjugation, (2) principal parts, (3) voice, (4) mood, (5) tense, (6) person, (7) number, and (8) rule.

Example: In the sentence **Pater fīliō praemium mittit, mittit** would be parsed as follows:

mittit: third conjugation; principal parts, **mittō, mittere, mīsī, missum**; active voice; indicative mood; present tense; third person; singular number; agrees with the subject **pater.** Rule: A verb agrees with its subject in person and number.

Bronze of Alexander the Great on his horse Bucephalus

Word Formation

—— Prefixes ——

A. On adjectives

1. in-, *not:* amīcus, *friendly,* inimīcus, *unfriendly*
2. per-, *very:* magnus, *large,* permagnus, *very large*
3. sub-, *somewhat:* albus, *white,* subalbus, *whitish*

B. On verbs

1. ab-, ā-, abs-, *away, off:* sum, *be,* absum, *be away*
2. ad-, *to, towards, near, for:* eō, *go,* adeō, *go to*
3. ante, *before:* cēdō, *move,* antecēdō, *precede*
4. com-, con-, co-, *together, completely, forcibly:* faciō, *make,* cōnficiō, *finish*
5. dē, *down, utterly:* mittō, *send, let go,* dēmittō, *lower*
6. dis-, dī, *apart, in different directions:* teneō, *hold,* distineō, *hold apart*
7. ē-, ex-, *out, completely:* faciō, *do,* efficiō, *accomplish*
8. in-, *in, on, against:* capiō, *take,* incipiō, *take on, begin*
9. inter-, *between, at intervals, to pieces:* eō, *go,* intereō, *go to pieces, perish*
10. ob-, *towards, to meet, in opposition:* pugnō, *fight,* oppugnō, *attack*
11. per-, *through, thoroughly:* moveō, *move,* permoveō, *move deeply*
12. prō-, por-, *forward:* videō, *see,* prōvideō, *foresee*
13. red-, re-, *back, again:* capiō, *take,* recipiō, *take back*
14. sed-, sē-, *apart:* claudō, *shut,* sēclūdō, *shut away*
15. sub-, *up to, under, to the aid:* veniō, *come,* subveniō, *come to the aid*
16. trāns-, trā-, *across, over:* dūcō, *lead,* trādūcō, *lead across*

—— Suffixes ——

A. Making nouns from verbs

1. -tor, -tōris, m., *the agent or doer of the action (-er)*: vincere, *conquer*, victor, *conqueror*
2. -or, -ōris, m., *the abstract noun*: amāre, *love*, amor, *love*
3. -iō, -iōnis, f. ⎫ *the name of the action*: con + dīcere, *agree*, condi-
   -tiō, -tiōnis, f. ⎬ ciō, *agreement*; oppugnāre, *attack*, oppugnātiō, *at-*
   -tus, -tūs, m. ⎭ *tack*; advenīre, *arrive*, adventus, *arrival*
4. -men, -minis, n., *the means* or *result of the action*: flūere, *flow*, flūmen, *a stream*

B. Making nouns from adjectives

-ia, -iae, f. ⎫
-tia, -tiae, f. ⎬ *the abstract noun (-ness)*: audax, *bold*, audācia, *bold-*
-tās, -tātis, f. ⎬ *ness*; amīcus, *friendly*, amīcitia, *friendship*; līber, *free*,
-tūdō, -tūdinis, f. ⎭ lībertās, *liberty*; magnus, *large*, magnitūdō, *great size*

C. Making adjectives from nouns

1. -tus, -ta, -tum, *having (-ed)*: turris, *tower*, turrītus, *turreted*; cornū, *horn*, cornūtus, *horned*
2. -ālis, -āle ⎫
   -āris, -āre ⎬ *pertaining to*: nātūra, *nature*, nātūrālis, *natural*; mīles,
   -īlis, -īle ⎭ mīlitis, *soldier*, mīlitāris, *military*; cīvis, *citizen*, cīvīlis, *civil*
3. -timus, -tima, -timum, *belonging to*: mare, *sea*, maritimus, *of the sea*

D. Making adjectives from verbs

1. -ax, -ācis, *having an aggressive tendency (-ing)*: audeō, *dare*, audāx, *daring*
2. -idus, -ida, -idum, *tending to (-ing)*: cupio, *desire*, cupidus, *desirous*
3. -īvus, -īva, -īvum, *having the passive tendency (-ed)*: capiō, captum, *capture*, captīvus, *captive*
4. -ilis, -ile, *having the passive quality (-ble)*: ūtor, *use*, ūtilis, *usable, useful*

E. Verb suffixes

1. -scō, -scere, ——, ——, *begin*: cognōscō, *begin to know*, cōnsuēscō, *begin to be accustomed*
2. -tō, -tāre, -tāvī, -tātum, *try to do, keep doing*: capiō, *catch*, captō, *try to catch*; sequor, *follow*, sector,,-ārī, *keep following*

Vocabularies

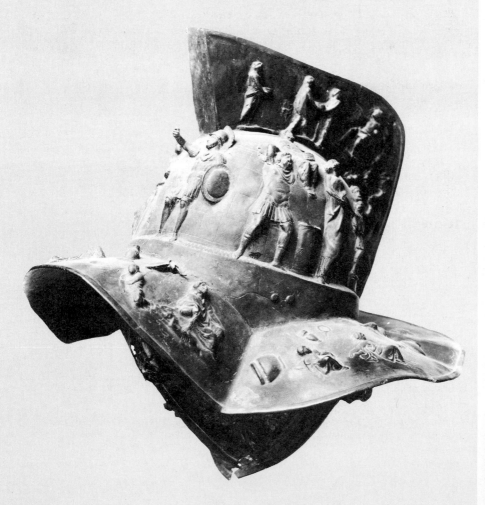

Gladiator's bronze parade helmet from Pompeii

Reconstruction of an ancient lyre

Latin-English

Words which appear in the vocabularies are marked by the number of the Lesson in which each occurs.

A

ā, ab, prep., with abl., *from, away from, by;* **ā tergō,** *in the rear.* 5

abdō, -ere, -didī, -ditum, *put away, hide.*

abdūcō, -ere, -dūxī, -ductum, *lead away.*

abeō, -īre, -iī (-īvī), -itum, *go away.*

abiciō, -ere, -iēcī, -iectum, *throw away.*

abscīdō, -ere, -cīdī, -cīsum, *cut off.*

absum, abesse, āfuī, āfutūrus, *be away, be distant, be absent.* 32.

ac, conj. (same as **atque**), *and, and also, and even;* **simul ac,** *as soon as.* 21, 36

accēdō, -ere, -cessī, -cessum, *go to, approach.* 39

accidō, -ere, accidī, ——, *fall upon, happen.* 48

accipiō, -ere, -cēpī, -ceptum, *receive, accept.* 24

accumbō, -ere, -cubuī, -cubitum, *recline (at table).*

ācer, ācris, ācre, adj., *sharp, fierce.* 18

aciēs, -ēī, f., *straight line, line of battle.* 31

ācriter, adv., *sharply, fiercely.* 31

ad, prep., with acc., *to, near, toward, for, at.* 5

addūcō, -ere, -dūxī, -ductum, *lead to, bring to; influence.* 41

adeō, -īre, -iī (-īvī), -itum, *go toward, approach* (followed by acc.). 52

adferō, -ferre, attulī, allātum, *bring up, bring to, report.* 52

adficiō, -ere, -fēcī, -fectum, *affect, afflict.*

adhaereō, -haerēre, -haesī, -haesum, *cling to.*

adhibeō, -ēre, -uī, -itum, *hold to, apply, employ.*

adhūc, adv., *up to this time, still.*

adimō, -ere, -ēmī, -emptum, *take away.*

adligō, -āre, -āvī, -ātum, *bind to, bind.*

adstō, -stāre, -stitī, *stand by* or *near.*

adsum, -esse, -fuī, -futūrus, *be near, be present.* 32

adulēscēns, -centis, m., *young man, youth.* 58

adventus, -ūs, m., *arrival, approach.* 29

advolō, -āre, -āvī, -ātum, *fly to, fly in.*

aedēs, -is, f., *temple;* pl., *house.* 54

aedificium, -ī, n., *building.* 46

aedificō, -āre, -āvī, -ātum, *build.*

Aeduī, -ōrum, m., *the Aeduans,* a Gallic tribe.

aeger, aegra, aegrum, *sick.* 54

aegrē, adv., *with difficulty, hardly, scarcely.* 54; **aegrē ferre,** *to take it hard.*

Aegyptius, -a, -um *Egyptian.*

Aeneadēs, -ae, m., *follower of Aeneas.*

Aenēās, -ae, m., *Aeneas.*

Aeolia, -ae, f., *Aeolia.*

Aeolus, -ī, m., *Aeolus,* god of the winds.

aequē, *equally.* 33

aequus, -a, -um, *level, equal, fair, just, like.* 33

aes, aeris, n., *bronze.*

aestās, -tātis, f., *summer;* **prīmā aestāte,** *at the beginning of summer.* 20, 36

aestus, -ūs, m., *heat, tide.*

aetās, -tātis, f., *age.* 53

Aethiopa, -ae, f., *Ethiopia.*

Aetna, -ae, f., *Etna,* a volcano in Sicily.

afflīgō, -flīgere, -flīxī, -flictum, *damage.*

Āfrica, -ae, f., *Africa.* 10

Āfricānus, -a, -um, *African, Africanus* (as a cognomen).

ager, agrī, m., *field, territory.* 4

aggredior, -gredī, -gressus sum, *approach, attack.* 51

agmen, -minis, n., *line of march, marching column;* **novissimum agmen,** *rear;* **prīmum agmen,** *van.* 56

agnōscō, -ere, -nōvī, -nitum, *recognize.*

agō, agere, ēgī, āctum, *drive; do;* grātiās agere, *give thanks.* 22, 58

agricola, -ae, m., *farmer.* 1

Alba, -ae, f., *Alba Longa,* a city.

Albānus, -a, -um, *Alban (of Alba).*

albus, -a, -um, adj., *white.* 13

Alexander, -drī, m., *Alexander (the Great).*

aliēnus, -a, -um, *belonging to another, another's; foreign, strange.* 37

aliī . . . aliī, *some . . . others.* 37

aliquantum, -ī, n., *somewhat, some.*

aliquī, aliqua, aliquod, adj., *some.* 58

aliquis, aliquid, pron., *someone, something.* 58

aliter, adv., *otherwise.*

alius, -a, -ud, adj., *another, other.* 37

alius . . . alius, *one . . . another.* 37

Alpēs, -ium, f. pl., *Alps.*

altē, adv., *on high, deeply.*

alter, altera, alterum, *the other* (of two), *one* (of two). 37

alter . . . alter, *the one . . . the other* (of two). 37

altitūdō, -inis, f., *height, depth.* 44

altum, -ī, n., *the deep, the sea.*

altus, -a, -um, adj., *high, tall, deep.* 6

Amāta, -ae, f., *Amata,* wife of Latinus, king of the Latins.

ambulō, -āre, -āvī, -ātum, *stroll, walk.* 10

āmentia, -ae, f., *madness.*

amīcitia, -ae, f., *friendliness, friendship.* 2

amīcus, -a, -um, adj., *friendly; friendly to* (with dat.). 13

amīcus, -ī, m., *friend.* 4

āmittō, -ere, āmīsī, āmissum, *lose.* 28

amō, -āre, -āvī, -ātum, *love; like.* 2

amor, -ōris, m., *love, longing, passion.*

āmoveō, -ēre, -mōvī, -mōtum, *move away, remove.*

amplus, -a, -um, *large, ample, distinguished.* 33

an, conj., *or.* 45

Anchīsēs, -ae, m., *Anchises,* father of Aeneas.

ancora, -ae, f., *anchor.* 56

Ancus, -ī, m., *Ancus.*

Androclus, -ī, m., *Androclus.*

Andromeda, -ae, f., *Andromeda.*

anhēlō, -āre, -āvī, -ātum, *to pant.*

animadvertō, -ere, -tī, -sum, *turn one's mind to, notice.*

animal, -ālis, n., *animal.* 16

animus, -ī, m., *mind, spirit;* pl., *courage.* 11

annōn, *or not.* 45

annus, -ī, m., *year.* 4

ānser, -eris, m., *goose.*

ante, adv., *before, ago.* 8

ante, prep., with acc., *before, in front of.* 8

anteā, adv., *before, formerly.*

antīquus, -a, -um, *old-fashioned, old, of old, ancient, former.* 23

Antōnius, -ī, m., *Antonius.*

antrum, -ī, n., *cave.*

anxius, -a, -um, adj., *troubled, anxious.*

aperiō, -īre, -uī, apertum, *open, expose.*

apertus, -a, -um, *open, exposed.* 54

Apollō, -inis, m., *Apollo,* god of music, medicine, prophecy.

appellō, -āre, -āvī, -ātum, *address, call, name.* 7

appellō, -pellere, -pulī, -pulsum, *drive to,* with or without navem, *put in.*

Appius, -a, -um, adj., *Appian.*
   Appia Via, f., *Appian Way,* a famous road, running from Rome to Southern Italy.

Appius, -ī, m., *Appius,* a praenomen.

appōnō, -ere, apposui, appositum, *put near, set before, serve.*

appropinquō, -āre, -āvī, -ātum, *approach, draw near* (with ad and acc., or with dat.). 53

apud, prep., used with accusative, *among, in the presence of, near, at the house of.* 39

aqua, -ae, f., *water.* 1

aquaeductus, -ūs, m., *aqueduct.*

Arar, Araris, m., *the Arar,* now the *Saone* (a river in France).

arbitror, -ārī, -ātus sum, *think.* 50

arbor, -oris, f., *tree.* 40

arca, -ae, f., *box, chest.* ,

Ardea, -ae, f., *Ardea,* a town in Latium.

ārdeō, -ēre, ārsī, ārsum, *be on fire, burn, blaze.*

arēna, -ae, f., *sand, arena.*

argentum, -ī, n., *silver, money.*

Ariōn, -onis, m., *Arion.*

Aristidēs, -is, m., *Aristides.*

arithmētica, -ae, f., *arithmetic.*

arma, -ōrum, n., *arms, weapons, defensive arms, weapons for close fighting.* 11

armō, -āre, -āvī, -ātum, *arm, equip.* 42

arripiō, -ere, arripui, arreptum, *snatch up.*

ars, artis, f., *art, skill; branch of learning.*

Ascanius, -ī, m., *Ascanius, son of Aeneas.*

ascendō, -ere, -scendī, -scēnsum, *climb up.* 60

Asia, -ae, f., *Asia.* 10

asȳlum, -ī, n., *place of refuge, asylum.*

at, conj., *yet, but yet.*

Atalanta, -ae, f., *Atalanta.*

Athēnae, -ārum, f., *Athens.* 50

Athēniēnsis, -e, m., *Athenian.*

atque, conj. (same as ac), *and, and also, and even; as;* simul atque (ac), *as soon as.* 21, 36

ātrium, -ī, n., *atrium,* the principal apartment of a Roman house.

auctor, -ōris, m., *author, originator, founder, sponsor.* 56

auctōritās, -tātis, f., *authority, influence, prestige.* 26

audācia, -ae, f., *boldness, daring.* 12

audācter, adv., *boldly, rashly.* 31

audāx, -ācis, *bold, daring.* 18

audeō, -ēre, ausus sum, *dare.* 55

audiō, -īre, -īvī, -ītum, *hear, listen to.* 30

augeō, -ēre, auxī, auctum, *increase, strengthen.* 56

Augustus, -ī, m., *Augustus.*

aura, -ae, f., *air, breeze.*

Aurelius, -ī, m., *Aurelius.*

aureus, -a, -um, *golden, of gold.* 34

auris, -is, f., *ear.* 46

aurum, -ī, n., *gold.* 42

aut, conj., *or;* aut . . aut, *either . . or.* 21

autern, conj. (always postpositive), *however, but, moreover, and.* 42

auxilior, -ārī, -ātus sum, *help, bring aid.*

auxilium, -ī, n., *aid, help;* pl., *auxiliary forces, troops, reinforcements.* 11

avis, avis, f., *bird.* 26

avus, -ī, m., *grandfather.*

B

barbarus, -a, -um, *foreign, strange, barbarous, barbarian, uncivilized.* 33

Baucis, -idis, f., *Baucis.*

beātus, -a, -um, adj., *happy, well-off.*

Belgae, -ārum, m., *Belgians.*

bellum, -ī, n., *war;* bellum gerere, *wage war,* bellum īnferre, *make war on, make an attack on* (with dat.). 5, 22, 52

bene, adv., *well, fully.* 9

beneficium, -ī, n., *kindness, favor.* 59

benignē, adv., *kindly, in a kind way.*

benignitās, -tātis, f., *kindness.*

bibō, -ere, bibī, *drink.* 25

bīduum, -ī, n., *period of two days, two days.*

bis, num. adv., *twice.* 55

bonitās, -tātis, f., *kindness, goodness.*

bonum, -ī, n., *good thing;* in pl., *goods.*

bonus, -a, -um (comp., melior; sup., optimus), adj., *good.* 6, 35

brevis, -e, adj., *short, brief;* brevī tempore or brevī, *in a short time, soon.* 18

brevitās, -tātis, f., *shortness, brevity.*

breviter, adv., *briefly.* 31

Britannia, -ae, f., *Britain.* 21

Britannus, -a, -um, *British,* as noun, *Briton.* 18

Brūtus, -ī, m., *Brutus.*

Būcephala, -ae, f., *Bucephala,* a town on the Hydaspes founded by Alexander.

Būcephalus, -ī, m., *Bucephalus,* the name of Alexander's horse.

C

C., abbreviation for Gāius, -ī, m.

cadō, -ere, cecidī, cāsum, *fall.* 55

caecus, -a, -um, *blind.*

caedēs, -is, f., *slaughter, murder.* 54

caedō, -ere, cecīdī, caesum, *cut, cut down, kill.* 55

caelum, -ī, n., *sky, heavens.* 5

Caesar, -aris, m., *Caesar.* 15

calamitās, -tātis, f., *calamity, misfortune, disaster.* 43

calefaciō, -ere, -fēci, -factum, *to make warm, heat.*

calidus, -a, -um, *hot.* 43

campus, -ī, m., *plain, (level) field.* 4

Campus Martius, *The Field of Mars,* originally used for military exercises and athletic sports.

canis, -is, m. or f., *dog.* 26

Cannae, -ārum, f., *Cannae,* village in Apulia.

canō, -ere, cecinī, ——, *sing; prophesy.*

cantus, -ūs, m., *singing.*

capiō, -ere, cēpī, captum, *take, capture;* cōnsilium capere, *form (make) a plan.* 24

Capitōlīnus, -a, -um, adj., *of (on) the Capitoline Hill, Capitoline.*

Capitōlium, -ī, n., *Capitoline Hill.*

captīvus, -a, -um, adj., *captive.*

captīvus, -ī, m., *captive, prisoner.* 11

captō, -āre, -āvī, -ātum, *catch.*

Capua, -ae, f., *Capua.*

caput, -itis, n., *head.* 15

Carbo, -ōnis, m., *Carbo.*

carcer, carceris, m., *prison.*

carmen, -minis, n., *song, poem, incantation.* 15

carō, carnis, f., *flesh.*

carrus, -ī, m., *cart, wagon.* 12

Carthāginiēnsēs, -ium, m., *Carthaginians.*

Carthāgō, -inis, f., *Carthage,* a city in Africa. 50

Cassius, -ī, m., a Roman.

castīgō, -āre, -āvī, -ātum, *rebuke, punish.*

castra, -ōrum, n., *camp.* 11

cāsus, -ūs, m., *fall, chance; accident, fate.* 56

causa, -ae, f., *cause, reason;* quā dē causā *for which reason:* causā, *for the sake of.*

cavus, -a, -um, *hollow.* 13, 39, 59

cēdō, -ere, cessī, cessum, *move, give way, yield, withdraw.* 23

celer, celeris, celere, adj., *quick, swift, speedy.* 18

celeritās, -tātis, f., *swiftness, speed.* 14

celeriter, adv., *quickly, swiftly;* quam celerrimē, *as quickly as possible.* 31, 36

cēna, -ae, f., *dinner.* 21

cēnō, -āre, -āvī, -ātum, *dine, sup.*

centum, num. adj., indecl., *one hundred, a hundred.* 21

centuriō, -ōnis, m., *centurion.* 44

Cēpheus, -ī, m., *Cepheus.*

certāmen, -inis, n., *contest, struggle;* certāmen pedum, *foot race.*

certē, adv., *surely, certainly.* 33

certus, -a, -um, adj., *sure, certain;* certiōrem, (-ēs) facere, *make more certain, inform;* certior (-em) fierī, *be informed.* 33

cēterī, -ae, -a, adj., *the other, the rest (of).* 56

Christiānus, -a, -um *Christian.*

cibus, -ī, m., *food.* 28

Cicerō, -ōnis, m., *Cicero.*

Cimōn, -ōnis, m., *Cimon,* an Athenian general.

Cincinnātus, -ī, m., *Cincinnatus.*

circā, adv., *about;* as prep., with acc., *about, around*

Circē, -ēs, abl. -ē, f., *Circe.*

circiter, adv., *about, approximately.* 55

circum, prep., with acc., *around, about;* adv., *about, around.* 39

circumveniō, -īre, -vēnī, -ventum, *come around, surround.* 41

cīvis, -is, m. and f., *citizen, fellow citizen.* 16

cīvitās, -tātis, f., *citizenship, citizenry, state.* 27

clāmitō, -āre, -āvī, -ātum, *shout repeatedly.*

clāmō, -āre, -āvī, -ātum, *shout.* 10

clāmor, -ōris, m., *shout, noise.* 26

clārus, -a, -um, *bright, clear; famous.* 23

classis, -is, f., *fleet.* 53

Claudius, -ī, m., *Claudius.*

claudō, -ere, clausī, clausum, *shut, close.* 38

clāva, -ae, f., *stick, club.*

Cleopatra, -ae, f., Cleopatra.

coepī, -isse, coeptum began. 58

cōgitō, -āre, -āvī, -ātum, think over.

cognōmen, -inis, n., surname; new (added) name.

cognōscō, -ere, -nōvī, -nitum, find out, learn; (in perf., know). 39

cōgō, -ere, coēgī, coāctum, collect, compel (with inf.). 22

cohors, cohortis, f., cohort. 59

collis, -is, m., hill. 40

colloquium, -ī, n., conversation, conference. 51

committō, -ere, -mīsī, -missum, entrust (to); proelium committere, join (begin) battle, begin an engagement. 28

commoror, -ārī, -ātus sum, delay, stay.

commoveō, -ēre, -mōvī, -mōtum, move thoroughly, upset, alarm. 41

commūnis, -e, adj., common, general. 47

comparō, -āre, -āvī, -ātum, get; prepare; buy; compare. 53

compellō, -ere, -pulī, -pulsum, drive together.

comperiō, -īre, -perī, -pertum, find out, discover.

complector, -plectī, -plexus sum, embrace, grasp.

compleō, -ēre, -ēvī, -ētum, fill, fill up, complete. 41

complūrēs, -a, adj., quite a few, several. 56

cōnātus, -ūs, m., attempt, effort.

concurrō, -ere, -currī, -cursum, run together, run.

condiciō, -ōnis, f., condition, terms, 43

condō, -ere, -didī, -ditum, put away.

condūcō, -ere, -dūxī, -ductum, bring together.

cōnferō, -ferre, -tulī, collātum, bring together, collect; compare, (refl.) proceed. 52

cōnficiō, -ere, -fēcī, -fectum, finish, accomplish; exhaust. 24

cōnfīdō, -ere, -fīsus sum, trust (used with dat. of person, abl. of thing) entrust. 57

cōnfīrmō, -āre, -āvī, -ātum, strengthen; encourage; declare; pācem cōnfīrmāre, arrange (establish) peace. 10

congredior, -gredī, -gressus sum, meet, come together. 51

coniciō, -ere, -iēcī, -iectum, throw together, hurl. 24

coniungō, -ere, -iūnxī, -iūnctum, join together, unite. 60

cōnor, -ārī, -ātus sum, try, attempt (used with infin.). 50

cōnscendō, -ere, -scendī, -scēnsum, climb; board, go aboard. 60

cōnscrībō, -ere, -scrīpsī, -scrīptum, enroll, enlist. 53

cōnsēnsus, -ūs, m., agreement, unanimity.

cōnsequor, -sequī, -secūtus sum, pursue, overtake, obtain, gain. 51

cōnservō, -āre, -āvī, -ātum, save, keep. 49

cōnsīdō, -ere, -sēdī, -sessum, sit down, encamp, settle. 56

cōnsilium, -ī, n., plan, advice, foresight; cōnsilium capere, form a plan; cōnsilium inīre, adopt a plan. 11, 24, 60

cōnsistō, -sistere, -stitī, -stitum, halt, take a stand; cōnsistere in + abl., consist of.

cōnspectus, -ūs, m., sight, view.

cōnspiciō, -ere, -spexī, -spectum, look at attentively, observe closely. 41

cōnstat (impers.), it is well-known, it is evident.

cōnstituō, -ere, -stituī, -stitūtum, set up, determine, decide; establish; diem cōnstituere, appoint a day. 23

cōnsuēscō, -ere, -ēvī, -suētum, become accustomed; in the perfect tenses, be accustomed. 58

cōnsuētūdō, -inis, f., habit, custom. 43

cōnsul, -ulis, m., consul. 14

cōnsulō, -ere, -suluī, -sultum, with acc., consult; with dat., consult the interests of, take counsel for. 57

cōnsūmō, -ere, -sūmpsī, -sūmptum, use up, consume.

contegō, -ere, -tēxī, -tēctum, cover.

contendō, -ere, -dī, -tentum, strive, struggle, hasten. 23

contineō, -ēre, -uī, -tentum, hold together, restrain; bound. 32

continuus, -a, -um, adj., continuous, without interruption.

contrā, adv., *opposite, on the contrary, in reply.*

contrā, prep., with acc., *against, opposite.* 8

contrōversia, -ae, f., *quarrel, argument.*

conveniō, -īre, -vēnī, -ventum, *come together, assemble, meet.* 30. **convenit,** impers. *it is convenient.* 56

conventus, -ūs, m., *meeting, gathering.*

convertō, -ere, -vertī, -versum, *turn, change, transform.*

convocō, -āre, -āvī, -ātum, *call together, assemble, summon.* 7

coorior, -orīrī, -ortus sum, *arise.*

cōpia, -ae, f., *plenty, supply;* pl., *troops, forces.* 11

cor, cordis, n., *heart*

Corinthus, -ī, f., *Corinth.* 50

Coriolānus, -ī, m., *Coriolanus.*

Cornēlius, -ī, m., *Cornelius.*

cornū, -ūs, n., *horn; wing* (of an army); **ā sinistrō cornū,** *on the left wing;* **ā dextrō cornū,** *on the right wing.* 29, 34

corpus, -oris, n., *body.* 15

corripiō, -ere, -ripuī, -reptum, *grasp quickly* or *violently, seize, snatch.*

Cortōna, -ae, f., *a town of Etruria.*

cotīdiē, adv., *daily, every day.* 36

crās, adv., *tomorrow.* 9

crassus, -a, -um, *fat.*

crēdō, -ere, -didī, -ditum, *trust, believe* (used with dat.), 39

creō, -āre, -āvī, -ātum, *appoint, elect.*

Creōn, Creontis, m., *Creon.*

crēscō, -ere, crēvī, crētum, *grow, increase.* 38

Crēta, -ae, f., *Crete.*

Creūsa, -ae, f., *Creusa.*

Croesus, -ī, m., *Croesus.*

crūdēlis, -e, *cruel, unmerciful.*

cum, prep., with abl., *along with, with.* 6

cum, conj., *when, since* (with subjunctive), *although* (with subjunctive).

cum prīmum, *as soon as* (used with indic.), *when first.* 49

cupidē, *eagerly.*

cupiditās, -tātis, f., *desire* (for), *greed* (for) (used with genitive). 40

cupidus, -a, -um, *eager; eager* (for), *desirous* (of) (used with genitive). 34

cupiō, -ere, cupīvī, cupītum, *want, wish, desire.* 24

cūr, adv., *why?* 9

cūra, -ae, f., *care, anxiety.* 12

Curiātius, -ī, m., *Curiatius.*

currō, -ere, cucurrī, cursum, *run.* 25

cursus, -ūs, m., *running, course; quick motion.* 29

custōs, -ōdis, m., *guard, guardian.* 59

Cyclōps, -ōpis, m., *Cyclops;* pl. *Cyclopes.*

D

damnum, -ī, n., *damage, injury.*

Daunus, -ī, m., *Daunus,* king, father of Turnus.

dē, prep., with abl., *down from, from; about, concerning; of;* **quā dē causā,** *for which* (this) *reason, on this account.* 5

dea, -ae, f., *goddess.* 4

dēbeō, -ēre, -uī, -itum, *owe, ought.* **grātiam dēbēre,** *be under an obligation.* 20

decem, num, adj., indecl., *ten.* 21

decimus, -a, -um, num, adj., *tenth.* 21

dēdō, -ere, -didī, -ditum, *give up.*

dēdūcō, -ere, -dūxī, -ductum, *lead down; lead away, bring down; escort; launch* (a ship). 60

dēfendō, -ere, -fendī, -fēnsum, *defend.* 22

dēferō, -ferre, -tulī, -lātum, *carry, bring; report.* 60

dēfessus, -a, -um, adj., *tired.* 49

dēficiō, -ere, -fēcī, -fectum, *revolt, desert* (used with **ā, ab** and abl.); *fail, be deficient.* 41

dēiciō, -icere, -iēcī, -iectum, *throw down; disappoint.*

deinde, adv., *then, next.* 36

dēlectō, -āre, -āvī, -ātum, *please.* 14

dēleō, -ēre, -ēvī, -ētum, *destroy.*

dēligō, -ere, -lēgī, -lēctum, *choose.* 23

Delphī, -ōrum, m., *Delphi,* a town famous for its oracle of Apollo.

delphīnus, -ī, m., *dolphin.*

dēmittō, -ere, mīsī, -missum, *send down, let go down, lower, let fall.*

dēmōnstrō, -āre, -āvī, -ātum, *point out, show.* 10

dēpellō, -ere, -pulī, -pulsum, *drive away.*

dēpōnō, -ere, -posuī, -positum, *put down, put aside, give up, lay aside.*

dērīdeō, -ēre, -rīsī, -rīsum, *mock, laugh at.*

dēscendō, -ere, -dī, -scēnsum, *climb down, descend.* 60

dēsīderium, -ī, n., *desire, longing.*

dēsiliō,-īre, -uī, —, *leap down.*

dēsistō, -ere, -stitī, -stitum, *leave off, stop, desist.* 38

dēspērō, -āre, -āvī, -ātum, *lose hope, despair.*

dēstringō, -ere, -strīnxī, -strictum, *draw.*

dēsum, dēesse, dēfuī, defutūrus, *be lacking.* 57

dēterreō, -ēre, -uī, -itum, *frighten off, deter.*

deus, -ī, m., *god.* 4

dēvorō, -āre, -āvī, -ātum, *eat, devour.*

dexter, -tra, -trum, adj., *right, right-hand;* ā dextrā, *on the right.* 34

dīcō, -ere, dīxī, dictum, *say, tell.* 25

dictātor, -ōris, m., *dictator.*

Dīdō, Dīdōnis, f., *Dido,* queen of Carthage.

diēs, -ēī, m. and f., *day;* diēs cōnstitūta, *the appointed day;* multō diē, *late in the day.* 31

difficilis, -e, adj. (superl., difficillimus), *difficult.* 34

difficultās, -tātis, f., *difficulty.* 43

dīligēns, -gentis, adj., *careful, diligent.* 33

dīligenter, adv., *carefully, diligently.* 33

dīligentia, -ae, f., *diligence, care.* 15

dīmittō, -crc, -mīsī, -missum, *send (let go) in different directions, let go away, send away, dismiss.* 41

discēdō, -ere, -cessī, -cessum, *go away, depart, leave.* 23

disciplīna, -ae, f., *instruction, teaching.*

discipulus, -ī, m., *student.*

discō, -ere, didicī, *learn.* 53

discrīmen, -inis, n., *danger, crisis.*

discus, -ī, m., *discus.*

disiciō, -ere, -iēcī, -iectum, *throw apart, scatter.*

dispōnō, -ere, -posuī, -positum, *distribute, arrange, post.*

dissimilis, -e (superl., dissimillimus), *unlike, unlike to* (with dat.). 34

diū, adv., *for a long time, long;* quam diū, *how long?* 9 diūtius, *for a longer time, any longer;* diutissimē, *for a very long time, for the longest time.* 36

dīvellō, -ere, -vellī, -vulsum, *tear apart.*

dīversus, -a, -um, *turned apart, different.*

dīvidō, -ere, -vīsī, -vīsum, *divide, share.*

dō, dare, dedī, datum, *give, grant;* in fugam dare, *to put to flight;* poenam dare, *to pay the penalty;* sē in viam dare, *to start on one's way;* in compounds, *put, place.*

doceō, -ēre, -uī, doctum, *teach, show, inform* (used with two accusatives). 20

doleō, -ēre, doluī, dolitum, *grieve, be sorry, grieve for.* 56

dolor, -ōris, m., *pain, grief, suffering, sorrow.* 44

dolus, -ī, m., *trick, craft.*

domesticus, -a, -um, *household.*

domina, -ae, f., *mistress (of a house).*

dominus, -ī, m., *master, lord, owner.* 12

domus, -ūs, f. (locative, domī), *house, home;* domī, *at home;* domum (acc.), *homeward, home.* 29, 50

dōnō, -āre, -āvī, -ātum, *to give; to present.*

dōnum, -ī, n., *gift, present.* 5

dormiō, -īre, -īvī, -ītum, *sleep.* 30

dubitō, -āre, -āvī, -ātum, *be in doubt, doubt; hesitate* (used with infin.). 38

dubius, -a, -um, *doubtful, uncertain.*

dūcō, -ere, dūxī, ductum, *lead, bring;* in mātrimōnium dūcere, *marry;* sortēs dūcere, *draw lots.* 22

dūdum, adv., *a while ago;* iam dūdum, *for a long time now.*

dulcēdo, dulcēdinis, f., *sweetness.*

dulcis, -e, adj., *pleasant, sweet.*

dum, conj., *while, as long as; until.*

duo, duae, duo, num. adj., *two.* 21

duodecim, num. adj., indecl., *twelve.* 21

duodēvīgintī, num. adj., indecl., *eighteen.* 47

dūrus, -a, -um, *hard, harsh.* 34

dux, ducis, m., *leader, guide.* 14

E

ē or ex, prep., with abl., *out of, from; of.* 5

ēbrius, -a, -um, *drunk.*

edō, -ere, ēdī, ēsum, *eat.* 25

ēdō, -ere, ēdidī, ēditum, *give forth; produce.*

ēdūcō, -ere, -dūxī, -dūctum, *lead out.*

efficiō, -ere, -fēcī, -fectum, *accomplish, bring about; complete, put into effect.* 48

ego, meī, pers. pron., *l.* 26

ēgredior, -gredī, -gressus sum, *go out, disembark.* 51

ēgregius, -a, -um, *outstanding.* 54

elephantus, -ī, m., *elephant.*

Elissa, -ae, f., *Elissa,* also called Dido, queen of Carthage.

ēmicō, -āre, -āvī, -ātum, *spring out, leap forth.*

ēmittō, -ere, -mīsī, -missum, *send out, let out.*

emō, emere, ēmī, ēmptum, *take; buy.* 55

enim, conj., postpositive, *for.* 42

ēnūntiō, -āre, -āvī, -ātum, *report, announce, declare.* 41

eō, īre, iī (īvī), itum, *go.* 52

eō, adv., *there, thither, to that place.* 36

eōs, *them.*

Epīrus, -ī, f., *Epirus,* a district in northwestern Greece.

epistula, -ae, f., *a letter, an epistle.* 13

eques, -itis, m., *horseman, knight;* pl., *cavalry.* 25 magister equitum, *Master of Horse,* second in command to a dictator.

equester, -tris, -tre, adj., *(of) cavalry.*

equitātus, -ūs, m., *cavalry.* 59

equus, -ī, m., *horse.* 4

erat, *was.*

ergō, adv., *therefore, then.* 45

ēripiō, -ere, -ripuī, -reptum, *rescue.* 57

errō, -āre, -āvī, -ātum, *wander; make a mistake.* 42

est, *is.*

et, conj., *and, also, even;* et . . . et, *both . . . and.* 2, 21

etiam, adv., *also, even;* nōn sōlum . . . sed etiam . . . *not only . . . but also . . .* 30

etsī, conj., *even if, although.*

Eurōpa, -ae, f., *Europe.* 3

Eurylochus, -ī, m., *Eurylochus.*

ēvādō, -ere, -vāsī, -vāsum, *get out, get away, escape.*

ēvānēscō, -ere, ēvānuī, *vanish away.*

ēveniō,-īre, -vēni, -ventum, *come out; turn out, happen.*

ex, *from, out of, on the basis of, of;* ex ordine, *in order.* 5

exanimō, -āre, -āvī, -ātum, *make lifeless; kill.*

exārdescō, -ere, exārsī, -arsum, *blaze up.*

excēdō, -ere, -cessī, -cessum, *go out, leave, depart.* 23

excipiō, -ere, -cēpī, -ceptum, *receive.*

excitō, -āre, -āvī, -ātum, *arouse, awaken.*

exclāmō, -āre, -āvī, -ātum, *shout out.*

exclūdō, -ere, -sī, -sum, *shut out, cut off.*

excōgitō, -āre, -āvī, -ātum, *think out, think up.*

exeō, -īre, -iī (-īvī), -itum, *go out.* 52

exerceō, ēre, -uī, -itum, *train, practice, exercise.* 53

exercitus, -ūs, m., *army.* 29

exhauriō, -īre, -hausī, -haustum, *drain.*

exīstimō, -āre, -āvī, -ātum, *think, suppose, consider.* 39

exitus, -ūs, m., *departure, way out; outcome, end.* 29

expellō, -ere, -pulī, -pulsum, *drive out, drive away.* 28

explōrātor, -ōris, m., *scout.* 59

explōrō, -āre, -āvī, -ātum, *search out, explore, reconnoiter.* 56

expōnō, -ere, -posuī, -positum, *set forth, explain; land; array.* 41

exprimō, -ere, -pressī, -pressum, *squeeze out.*

expugnō, -āre, -āvī, -ātum, *take by storm.*

exspectō, -āre, -āvī, -ātum, *await; wait for.* 7

exspīrō, -āre, -āvī, -ātum, *breathe out; expire, die.*

exterior, -ius, *outer.* 35

extrēmus, -a, -um, *outermost, farthest, last; end of.* 35

exturbō, -āre, -āvī, -ātum, *drive out*

F

faber, fabrī, m., *smith.*

Fabius, -ī, m., a Roman gens.; **L. Fabius Maximus,** Hannibal's enemy.

Fabricius, -ī, m., *Fabricius.*

fābula, -ae, f., *story.* 13

fac: imperative of **faciō.**

facile, adv., *easily;* **minus facile,** *less easily.* 36

facilis, -e, adj., *easy.* 18

faciō, -ere, fēcī, factum, *make, do;* **certiōrem (ēs) facere,** *inform;* **iter facere,** *march;* **fac (facite) ut,** *see to it that.* 24

facultās, -tātis, f., *opportunity, chance; ability.* 53

Faliscus, -a, -um, adj., *of Falerii,* a people north of Rome.

falx, falcis, f., *sickle; curved sword.*

fāma, -ae, f., *report; rumor; reputation.* 11

famēs, -is, abl. -ē, f., *hunger, famine.*

familia, -ae, f., *household.*

familiāris, -e, *belonging to the household, of the family, intimate;* **rēs familiāris, reī familiāris,** f., *family property.*

Favōnius, -ī, m., *the West Wind.*

fēlīcitās, -tātis, f., *good luck.*

fēlīciter, adv., *happily, successfully, fortunately.* 33

fēlīx (gen. fēlīcis), *happy, fortunate, lucky.* 33

fēmina, -ae, f., *woman, wife.* 1

fenestra, -ae, f., *window.* 21

ferē, adv., *almost, nearly.* 55

ferō, ferre, tulī, lātum, *bear, carry, bring, take; relate.* 52

ferrum, -ī, n., *iron, sword, swords, weapons;* **ferrō et igne,** *with fire and sword.* 42

ferus, -a, -um, *wild, fierce, savage.* 6

fessus, -a, -um, adj., *tired, weary.*

fidēlis, -e, adj., *faithful, loyal.* 34

fidēs, -eī, f., *faith, loyalty; pledge; confidence.* **in fidem, in fidē,** *under the protection.* 46

fīdus, -a, -um, *faithful, reliable, loyal.*

figūra, -ae, f., *shape.*

fīlia, -ae, f., *daughter.* 4

fīlius, -ī, m., *son.* 4

fīnis, -is, m., *end; boundary;* pl., *territory.* 16

fīnitimī, -ōrum, m., *neighbors.* 23

fīnitimus, -a, -um, adj., *neighboring.* 23

fīō, fierī, factus sum, *be made; become; happen.* **certior (certiōrēs) fierī,** *be informed.* 54

Flaccus, -ī, m., *Flaccus,* a cognomen.

Flāminius, -ī, m., *C. Flaminius,* defeated and killed at Trasumenus.

flōs, flōris, m., *flower.* 44

fluctus, -ūs, m., *wave.* 29

flūmen, -inis, n., *river, stream.* 15

fōns, fontis, m., *spring.*

forās, adv., *(to) outside, outdoors.*

foris, -is, f., *door.*

forīs, adv., *out of doors, outside.*

fōrma, -ae, f., *appearance, beauty.*

fōrmōsus, -a, -um, adj., *beautiful.*

forte, adv., *by chance, by accident.*

fortis, -e, adj., *brave.* 18

fortiter, adv., *bravely;* **quam fortissimē,** *as bravely as possible.* 31

fortūna, -ae, f., *fortune, chance, luck.* 1

forum, forī, n., *forum, marketplace.* 46

Forum, -ī, n., *the Forum* (in Rome). 46

fossa, -ae, f., *ditch.* 44

frangō, -ere, frēgī, frāctum, *break.* 38

frāter, -tris, m., *brother.* 14

frēnō, -āre, -āvī, -ātum, *bridle; restrain.*

frīgidus, -a, -um, *cold.* 43

frōns, frontis, f., *forehead.*

frūctus, -ūs, m., *fruit; reward.*

frūmentārius, -a, -um, *pertaining to grain, of grain;* **rēs frūmentāria, reī frūmentāriae,** f., *grain supply, forage.* 31

frūmentor, -ārī, -ātus sum, *fetch grain.*
frūmentum, -ī, n., *grain.* 5
frūstrā, adv., *in vain.* 55
fuga, -ae, f., *flight, exile;* in fugam dare,
put to flight. 11
fugiō, -ere, fūgī, fugitum, *flee.* 24
fūr, fūris, m., *thief.*
furor, -ōris, m., *madness, rage.*

G

Gāius, -ī, m., *Gaius.*
galea, -ae, f., *helmet.*
Gallia, -ae, f., *Gaul.* 1
Gallicus, -a, -um, adj., *Gallic, of Gaul.*
Gallus, -a, -um, *Gallic, Gaul* (noun). 18
gaudium, -ī, n., *joy, gladness.* 32
gēns, gentis, f., *nation, family, clan.* 16
genus, -eris, n., *kind, class, sort, race.* 44
Germānia, -ae, f., *Germany.* 3
Germānus, -a, -um, adj., *German.* 15
gerō, -ere, gessī, gestum, *bear, wear; carry
on;* bellum gerere, *wage war;* rēs gestae,
deeds, accomplishments. 22, 31
Geta, -ae, m., *Geta.*
gladius, -ī, m., *sword.* 4
glōria, ae, f., *fame, glory.* 40
Gorgō, -onis, f., *a Gorgon.*
gradior, -i, gressus sum, *walk, go.*
Graecia, -ae, f., *Greece.* 21
Graecus, -ī, m., *a Greek.* 15
Graecus, -a, um, adj., *Greek.* 15
grammatica, -ae, f., *grammar, elementary
study of literature.*
grātē, *gratefully, pleasantly.* 13
grātia, -ae, f., *influence, favor; gratitude,
welcomeness, pleasingness;* grātiās agere,
thank; grātiam habēre, *feel gratitude;*
grātiam dēbēre, *be under an obligation;*
grātiam referre, *show gratitude;* grātiā,
for the sake. 58, 59
grātus, -a, -um, adj., *pleasing, welcome,
grateful.* 13
gravis, -e, adj., *heavy; severe, serious.* 18
gravitās, -tātis, f., *heaviness, seriousness,
weightiness, severity.*

graviter, adv., *weightily, heavily; seriously,
grievously, deeply, severely.* 31
gubernō, -āre, -āvī, -ātum, *steer.*
gustō, -āre, āvī, ātum, *taste.*

H

habeō, -ēre, habuī, -itum, *have, hold,
keep; consider;* ōrātiōnem habēre, *deliver
a speech;* grātiam habēre, *feel gratitude.*
17, 44, 58
habitō, -āre, āvī, -ātum, *live, dwell.* 7
Hannibal, -balis, m., *Hannibal.*
Hannō, Hannōnis, m., *Hanno,* A Carthaginian general.
Helvētia, -ae, f., *Helvetia.* 21
Helvētius, -a, -um, adj., *Helvetian.* 18
herba, -ae, f., *herb, plant, grass.* 37
Herculāneum, -ī, n., *Herculaneum.*
herī, adv., *yesterday.* 9
hīberna, -ōrum, n., *winter quarters, winter
camp.* 44
hīc, adv., *here, at this point.*
hic, haec, hoc, gen. huius, dem. pron.
and adj., *this; this . . . here, the latter;
he, she, it.* 25
hiemō, -āre, -āvī, -ātum, *spend the winter,
winter.* 55
hiems, hiemis, f., *winter.* 20
Hippomenēs, -is, m., *Hippomenes.*
Hispānia, -ae, f., *Spain.* 3
Hispānus, -a, -um, *Spanish.* 15
hodiē, adv., *today.* 9
Homērus, -ī, m., *Homer.*
homō, -inis, m. or f., *human being, man.* 27
hōra, -ae, f., *hour.* 13
Horātius, -ī, m., *Horatius.*
horribilis, -e, adj., *dreadful, horrible.*
hortor, -ārī, -ātus sum, *encourage, urge.* 50
hortus, -ī, m., *garden.* 27
hospes, -itis, *guest; stranger; host.* 53
hospitium, -ī, n., *hospitality.*
Hostīlius, -ī, m., *Hostilius,* a cognomen.
hostis, -is, m., *enemy (of the State);* pl.,
the enemy. 16
hūc, adv., *here, to this place.* 36
hūmānus, -a, -um, adj., *human.*

humī, locative of **humus,** *on the ground.*
humus, -ī, f., *earth, soil; grave.*
Hydaspēs, -is, m., *a river of India.*

I

iaceō, ēre, -uī, -itum, *lie.* 58
iaciō, -ere, iēcī, iactum, *throw.* 24
iam, adv., *now, already;* **nōn iam,** *no longer;* **iam dūdum,** *now for a long time.* 9
iānua, -ae, f., *door.* 31
Iāsōn, Iāsonis, m., *Jason.*
ibi, adv., *there, in that place.* 9
ictus, -ūs, m., *stroke, blow.*
īdem, eadem, idem, dem. pron. and adj., *the same.* 37
idōneus, -a, -um, adj., *suitable.* 34
igitur, conj., postpositive, *therefore, then.*
ignārus, -a, -um, adj., *ignorant, unknowing.*
ignis, -is, m., *fire.* 16
ignōrō, -āre, -āvī, -ātum, *not know, be ignorant of.*
ignōtus, -a, -um, adj., *unknown, strange.*
Īlias, -adis, f., *the Iliad.*
ille, illa, illud, gen., **illīus,** dem. pron. and adj., *that; that . . . there; the former; he, she, it.* 25
illūc, adv., *there, to that place there.* 36
imber, -bris, m., *rain, shower.*
immānitās, immānitātis, f., *inhumanity, cruelty.*
immortālis, -e, adj., *undying, immortal.* 47
imparātus, -a, -um, *unprepared.*
impedīmentum, -ī, n., *hindrance;* pl., *heavy baggage.* 11
impediō, -īre, -īvī, -ītum, *hinder.* 30
impedītus, -a, -um, *hindered, handicapped, in difficulty.* 49
impellō, -ere, -pulī, -pulsum, *drive on.*
imperātor, -ōris, m., *commander, general, emperor.* 14
imperium, -ī, n., *command, sovereignty, military power, empire, government.* 14
imperō, -āre, -āvī, -ātum, *levy* (soldiers); *order, command* (governs dat., followed by **ut** with the subjunctive); *order* (acc.) *from* (dat.) 45
impetrō, -āre, -āvī, -ātum, *obtain by request, gain one's request.*
impetus, -ūs, m., *attack, onrush;* **impetum facere in** (acc.), *attack.* 29
īmus, -a, -um, *lowest; lowest part of; bottom of.* 35
in, prep., with abl., *in, on, upon, over;* with acc., *into, onto, against, towards, for.* 5
incendō, -ere, -cendī, -cēnsum, *set on fire, burn; arouse.* 49
incertus, -a, -um, *uncertain.*
incidō, -ere, -cidī, —, *fall on, fall upon, fall into.*
incipiō, -ere, -cēpī, -ceptum, *begin.* 24
incitō, -āre, -āvī, -ātum, *stir up, arouse.* 41
inclūdō, -ere, -sī, -sum, *shut in.*
incolō, -ere, -uī, — (intrans.), *live, dwell;* (trans.), *inhabit, live in.* 58
incolumis, -e, adj., *unharmed.*
inde, adv., *from here, hence; from there, thence.* 59
Indī, -ōrum, m., *Indians.*
induō, -ere, -duī, -dūtum, *put on.*
ineō, -īre, -iī (īvī), -itum, *enter, begin,* **consilium inīre,** *adopt a plan.* 60
īnfāns, -antis, m. or f., *baby.* 59
īnfectus, -a, -um, adj., *not done.*
īnferior, -ius, *lower.* 35
īnferō, -ferre, intulī, illātum, *bring upon, carry onward, inflict;* **bellum īnferre,** *make* (offensive) *war on,* (with dat.); **signa īnferre,** *advance* (to the attack). 52
īnferus, -a, um, *low.*
īnfimus, -a, -um, *lowest, bottom of.* 35
ingēns, ingentis, adj., *huge.*
ingrātus, -a, -um, *ungrateful, unpleasing, unwelcome.*
inimīcitia, -ae, f., *enmity, unfriendliness.*
inimīcus, -a, -um, adj., *unfriendly, hostile; unfriendly to* (used with dat.); **inimīcus, -ī,** m., (*personal enemy*). 13
inīquus, -a, -um, adj., *uneven, unfavorable; unfair.* 33
initium, -ī, n., *beginning.* 51

iniūria, -ae, f., *injustice, injury, wrong.* 21

inopia, -ae, f., *want, lack, need, poverty.* 12

inquam, inquis, inquit, *say.* 32

inruō, -ere, -ruī, —, *rush in.*

īnsānia, -ae, f., *insanity.*

īnsidiae, -ārum, f., *ambush, trap, plot.* 43

īnstituō, -ere, -stituī, -stitūtum, *establish, build, set up; determine.* 53

īnstruō, -ere, -strūxī, -strūctum, *pile up, arrange, draw up, equip.* 38

īnsula, -ae, f., *island.* 1

integer, -gra, -grum, adj., *untouched, undiminished; whole, entire; upright.* 54

intellegō, -ere, -lēxī, -lēctum, *understand.* 39

inter, prep. with acc., *between, among;* **inter sē, (nōs, vōs)** *each other, one another.*

intereā, adv., *in the meantime, meanwhile.* 53

interficiō, -ere, -fēcī, -fectum, *kill.* 24

interim, adv., *meanwhile.* 9

interior, -ius, adj., *inner.* 35

intermittō, -ere, -mīsī, -missum, *interrupt, stop, pause; lose;* **intermissus, -a, -um,** *interposed; of time, having elapsed.* 41

intimus, -a, -um, *inmost.* 35

intrō, -āre, -āvī, -ātum, *enter.*

introitus, -ūs, m., *entrance.*

inūtilis, -e., adj., *useless.*

inveniō, -īre, -vēnī, -ventum, *come upon, find.* 30

invenīrī, *to be found.*

inventor, -ōris, m., *discoverer.*

invītō, -āre, -āvī, -ātum, *invite.*

invītus, -a, -um, adj., *unwilling.*

ipse, ipsa, ipsum, gen., ipsīus, dem. pron. and adj., *self, himself, etc.;* **ego ipse,** *I myself;* **nōs ipsī,** *we ourselves;* **tū ipse,** *you yourself;* **vōs ipsī,** *you yourselves.* 37

īra, -ae, f., *anger, wrath.* 12

īrāscor, -ī, irātus sum, *become angry.*

is, ea, id, gen., eius, dem. pron. and adj., *this, that; he, she, it, they.* 25

iste, ista, istud, gen., istīus, dem. pron. and adj., *that, that of yours.*

ita, adv., *so* (manner), *in such a way, thus.* 48

Ītalia, -ae, f., *Italy.* 1

itaque, adv., *and so, therefore.* 31

item, adv., *likewise.* 55

iter, itineris, n., *a route; journey, march;* **magnum iter,** *a forced* (unusually long) *march;* **ex itinere,** (from) *on the march;* **iter facere,** *march.* 15, 24

iterum, adv., *a second time, again.*

Ithaca, -ae, f., *Ithaca.*

iubeō, -ēre, iussī, iussum, *order, bid* (used with acc. and inf.). **valēre iubeō,** *bid farewell.* 32

iucundus, -a, -um, *pleasing.*

iūdex, -icis, m., *juror; judge.* 26

iūdicium, -ī, n., *trial; judgment.* 43

iūdicō, -āre, -āvī, -ātum, *judge, consider.* 39

iugum, -ī, n., *ridge; yoke.*

Iūlia, -ae, f., *Julia.* 13

Iūlius, -ī, m., *Julius.* 13

iungō, -ere, iūnxī, iūnctum, *join.* 38

Iuppiter, Iovis, m., *Jupiter.*

iūrō, -āre, -āvī, ātum, *swear;* **iūs iūrandum,** n., *oath.*

iūs, iūris, n., *right, justice, law;* **iūs iūrandum, iūris iūrandī,** n., *oath.* 44

iussus, ūs, m., *order, command.*

iūstus, -a, -um, adj., *right, just.* 33

Iūturna, -ae, f., *Juturna,* a nymph, sister of Turnus.

iuvō, -āre, iūvī, iūtum, *help, aid.* 58

iuvenis, -e, *young.*

L

L. = Lūcius.

lābor, lābī, lapsus sum, *to slip*

labor, -ōris, m., *difficulty, hardship, work.* 27

labōrō, -āre, -āvī, -ātum, *labor, suffer, be hard pressed.* 7

lac, lactis, n., *milk.*

lacrima,- ae, f., *tear.* 59

lacus, -ūs, m., *lake.*

Laelius, -ī, m., a gentile name.
laetitia, -ae, f., gladness.
laetus, -a, -um, adj., happy, joyful, glad. 33
lāmenta, -ōrum, n. pl., lamentations.
lapis, -idis, m., stone. 26
Lārīnās, Lārīnātis, adj., of Larinum.
lassitūdo, -dinis, f., weariness.
lātē, adv., widely; longē lātēque, far and wide. 11
lateō, -ēre, -uī, be hidden, lie hidden.
Latīnī, -ōrum, m., the Latins.
Latīnus, -ī, m., Latinus.
lātitūdō, -inis, f., width. 44
latrō, -ōnis, m., pirate, bandit.
latus, -eris, n., side, flank. 56
lātus, -a, -um, adj., broad, wide. 6
laudō, -āre, -āvī, -ātum, praise. 2
laus, laudis, f., praise. 59
Lāvīnia, -ae, f., Lavinia, daughter of King Latinus and Queen Amata.
lavō, -āre, lāvī, lautum, wash. 38
lectus, -ī, m., dining couch, bed. 31
lēgātus, -ī, m., lieutenant (second in command to a general); ambassador, envoy. 4
legiō, -ōnis, f., legion. 26
legō, -ere, lēgī, lēctum, choose; gather; read. 39
leō, leōnis, m., lion.
levis, -e, adj., light (in weight or importance), slight. 54
leviter, adv., lightly, slightly. 54
lēx, lēgis, f., law. 27
libenter, adv., gladly, willingly.
libentissimē, adv., most willingly, most gladly.
liber, librī, m., book. 12
līber, -era, -erum, adj., free. 8 līberī, -ōrum, m., children. 40
līberālitās, -ātis, f., generosity, liberality.
līberē, adv., freely, frankly. 11
līberō, -āre, -āvī, -ātum, set free, free. 10
lībertās, -ātis, f., freedom, liberty. 26
licet, -ēre, -uit, impers. (with dat.) it is permitted. 56
ligneus, -a, -um, adj., of wood, wooden.
lignum, -ī, n., wood; piece of wood.

līmen, -inis, n., threshold.
lingua, -ae, f., tongue, language. 1
littera, -ae, f., letter of the alphabet; pl., letter, an epistle. 1
lītus, -oris, n., shore (of the sea). 59
locus, -ī, m., pl., loca, n., place; location, situation. 12
longē, adv., by far, far off; longē lātēque, far and wide. 11
longinquuus, -a, -um, adj., far off, distant, remote.
longus, -a, -um, adj., long (usually of space); nāvis longa, warship. 6
loquor, loquī, locūtus sum, speak, talk. 50
lōtus, -ī, f., lotus.
Lūcius, -ī, m., Lucius. 13
luctor, -ārī, -ātus sum, struggle, wrestle.
lūdō, lūdere, lūsī, lūsum, play, mock. 38
lūdus, -ī, m., game, play; school. 4
lūna, -ae, f., moon. 40
lūx, lūcis, f., light; prīmā lūce, at daybreak, at dawn. 20, 36
Lȳdia, -ae, f., a country of Asia Minor.

M

M. = Marcus.
Macedonia, -ae, f., Macedonia, a country in Northern Greece
Macedonicus, -a, -um, Macedonian.
Maecēnās, -ātis, m., Maecenas, a famous Roman patron of letters.
magicus, -a, -um, magical.
magis, adv., comp. of magnopere, more greatly, more. 34
magister, -trī, m., master, teacher, director.
magister equitum, the Master of the Horse (cavalry) was the title of the Dictator's second-in-command.
magistrātus, -ūs, m., magistracy, public office, magistrate. 59
magnificē, adv., splendidly, magnificently.
magnificus, -a, -um, adj., splendid, magnificent.
magnitūdō, -inis, f., size, greatness, great size. 44

magnopere (comp., **magis;** sup., **maxime**), adv., *greatly.* 34

magnus, -a, -um (comp., **maior;** sup., **maximus**), adj., *large, great, loud; much* (of money). 6

maior, -ius, comp. of **magnus,** adj., *greater, larger;* **maior nātū:** see **nātū.** 35

male, adv., *badly, insufficiently.* 9

mālō, mālle, mālui (**magis** and **volō,** *wish more*), *wish rather, prefer.* 53

malus, -a, -um (comp., **peior;** sup., **pessimus**), adj., *bad, evil.* 6

mālus, -ī, m., *mast.*

mandō, -āre, -āvī, -ātum, *entrust to; command, instruct.* 45

maneō, -ēre, mānsī, mānsum, *stay, remain.* 17

Mānlius, -ī, m., *Manlius,* a gentile name.

manus, -ūs, f., *hand; band,* (of men). 29

Mārcellus, -ī, m., *Marcellus.*

Mārcius, -ī, m., *Marcius.*

Mārcus, -ī, m., *Marcus.* 13

Mārcus Antōnius, Mārcī Antōnī, m., *Marc Antony*

mare, -is, n., *sea.* 16

maritimus, -a, -um, adj., *of the sea.* 54

Mārtius, -a, -um, *of Mars,* (god of war).

māter, -tris, f., *mother.* 14

mātrimōnium, -ī, n., *marriage;* **in mātrimōnium dūcere,** *marry.*

mātūrō, -āre, -āvī, -ātum, *hasten.*

maximē adv., *most, most greatly, especially.* 34

maximus, -a, -um, adj., sup. of **magnus;** **maximus nātū:** see **nātū.** 35

Maximus, -ī, m., *Maximus,* a cognomen.

mea, *my.*

Mēdēa, -ae, f., *Medea.*

medicāmentum, -ī, n., *drug.*

medicus, -ī, m., *doctor, physician.*

medius, -a, -um, adj., *middle of;* **mediā nocte,** *at midnight;* (in) **mediō monte,** *halfway up the mountain.* 35

Medūsa, -ae, f., *Medusa,* a Gorgon.

meī, (gen.), reflex. pron., *of myself.* 40

melior, -ōris, comp. of **bonus,** adj., *better.* 35

memoria, -ae, f., *memory.*

memoriā tenēre, *hold by* (in) *the memory, remember.* 1, 23

mēns, mentis, f., *mind.* 44

mēnsa, -ae, f., *table, course;* **secunda mēnsa,** *dessert.* 21

mēnsis, -is, m., *month.* 53

mentiō, -iōnis, f., *mention.*

mercātor, ōris, m., *merchant, trader.* 44

Mercurius, -ī, m., *Mercury.*

mereor, -ērī, meritus sum, *deserve, earn.* 60

merīdiānus, -a, -um, adj., *of midday, noon-day.*

merīdiēs, -ēī, m., *midday, noon, the south.* 31

mēta, -ae, f., *turning-post* (in circus); *goal, end.*

meus, -a, -um, poss. adj., *my, mine.* 6

mīles, -itis, m., *soldier.* 14

mīlia, -ium, n., *thousands;* **mīlia passuum,** *miles.* 30

mīlitāris, -e, *of soldiers, military.* 54

mīlle, adj., indecl., *a thousand; one thousand;* **mille passūs,** *a mile.* 21, 29

Minerva, -ae, f., *Minerva.*

minimus, -a, -um, *smallest, very small;* see **parvus.** 35

minitor, -ārī, -ātus sum, *threaten.*

minor, adj., *smaller;* see **parvus.** 35

Minucius, -ī, m., a gentile name.

mīror, -ārī, -ātus sum, *wonder, wonder at, be surprised.* 60

mīrus, -a, -um, adj., *wonderful, strange.* 49

misceō, -ēre, miscuī, mixtum, *mix.*

miser, -era, -erum, adj., *unhappy, wretched, unfortunate, poor.* 8

miserē, adv., *wretchedly, desperately.* 11

miseria, -ae, f., *misery, wretchedness, unhappiness.*

misericordia, -ae, f., *mercy, pity.*

mittō, -ere, mīsī, missum, *send, let go.* 22

modo, adv., *only; just now, lately.*

modus, -ī, m., *measure, degree; way, manner, method;* **quō mōdō,** *by what way? in what manner? how?;* **quem ad modum,** *to what degree? how?* 28

moenia, -ium, n., *fortifications, walls.*

moneō, -ēre, -uī, -itum, *warn, advise, inform.* 17

mōns, montis, *m., mountain, hill;* **(in) mediō monte,** *halfway up the mountain.* 16, 35

mōnstrum, -ī, *n., portent; monster.*

mora, -ae, *f., delay.* 40

Morinī, -ōrum, *m., the Morini, a Belgic people.*

morior, morī, mortuus sum, (moritūrus), *die.* 60

moror, -ārī, -ātus sum, *delay.* 50

mors, mortis, *f., death.* 16

mortālis, -e, *adj., mortal.*

mortuus, -a, -um, *adj., having died, dead.* 60

mōs, mōris, *m., custom, habit;* pl., *character.* 58

moveō, -ēre, mōvī, mōtum, *move; affect;* with **castra,** *break.* 17

mox, *adv., soon.* 14

Mūcius, -ī, *m., Mucius, a gentile name.*

mulier, -eris, *f., woman, wife.* 59

multitūdō, -inis, *f., great number, crowd.* 27

multō, *by much.* 36

multum, *adv., much.* 36

multus, -a, -um, *adj., much;* pl., *many.* **multā nocte,** *late at night;* **ad multam noctem,** *until late at night;* **multō diē,** *late in the day.* 6, 31

mūniō, -īre, -īvī, -ītum, *fortify, build.* 30

mūnītiō, -ōnis, *f., fortification.* 54

mūrus, -ī, *m., wall.* 28

N

nam, *conj., for.* 30

nancīscor, nancīscī, nactus sum, *get, obtain, find.*

nārrō, -āre, -āvī, -ātum, *relate, tell.* 7

nāscor, nāscī, nātus sum, *be born; be found.* 60

nātū, *m., abl., by birth;* **maior nātū,** *older;* **maximus nātū,** *eldest.* 35

nātūra, -ae, *f., nature.* 1

nauta, -ae, *m., sailor.* 3

nāvigātiō, -iōnis, *f., sailing, voyage.*

nāvigō, -āre, -āvī, -ātum, *sail.* 2

nāvis, -is, *f., ship;* **nāvēs dēdūcere,** *launch ships;* **nāvis longa,** *warship;* **nāvēs solvere,** *cast off, set sail.* 16, 59, 60

nē, *conj., in order that not, that not, lest.*

nē, *adv., not;* **nē . . . quidem,** *not . . . even* (the emphatic word stands between **nē** and **quidem**). 53

-ne, *interrog. particle (enclitic).* 3

nec, *conj.* (same as **neque**), *and not.* 31

necessārius, -a, -um, *adj., necessary;* (as noun) *relative.* 54

necesse, *defective adj., necessary.* 48

necne, *or not.* 47

necō, -āre, -āvī, -ātum, *kill, slay.*

negō, -āre, -āvī, -ātum, *deny, say . . . not.* 39

negōtium, -ī, *n., business, task, trouble.* 40

nēmō, ——, *dat.,* **nēminī,** *abl.,* **nūllō,** *m., no one.* 46

Nēmō, ——, *m., Noman,* Polyphemus's name for Ulysses.

Neptūnus, -ī, *m., Neptune, god of the sea.*

neque, *conj., and . . . not, nor, neither;* **neque . . . neque,** *neither . . . nor.* 31

nesciō, -īre, nescīvī or **nesciī,** *not know.* 39

neuter, -tra, -trum, *pron. and adj., gen.* **neutrīus,** *neither (of two).* 37

niger, -gra, -grum, *adj., black.* 13

nihil, *also* **nīl,** *defective noun, n., nothing;* as adv., *not at all.* 28

nisi, *conj., if . . . not, unless, except.* 34

nō, nāre, nāvī, ——, *swim, float.*

nōbilis, -e, *adj., famous, of high birth, noble, well-bred, well-known.* 34

nōbīs, *to us.*

noceō, -ēre, -uī, -itum, *harm, injure* (with dat.). 57

nōlō, nōlle, nōluī (**nōn** and **volō**), *not wish, be unwilling.* 53

nōmen, -inis, *n., name.* 15

nōn, *adv., not;* **nōn modo** or **sōlum . . . sed etiam,** *not only . . . but also.* 2

nōndum, *adv., not yet.* 36

nōnne, interrog. particle, in questions expecting the answer *yes.* 3

nōnus, -a, -um, num, adj., *ninth.* 21

nōs, nostrum, pron., pl. of **ego,** *we.* 26

noster, -tra, -trum, poss. pron. and adj., *our, ours.* 8

nōtus, -a, -um, adj., *well known, famous.* 33

novem, num. adj., indecl., *nine.* 21

novitās, -tātis, f., *strangeness, newness.*

novus, -a, -um, adj., *new, strange;* **rēs novae,** *revolution;* **novissimus, -a, -um,** *latest, last, rearmost;* **novissimum agmen,** *rear.* 13, 31, 56

nox, noctis, f., *night;* **mediā nocte,** *at midnight;* **multā nocte,** *late at night;* **ad multam noctem,** *until late at night.* 26, 31

nūdus, -a, -um, adj., *bare, naked, unprotected.*

nūllus, -a, -um, adj., gen. **nūllīus,** *not any, none, no.* 37

num, interrog. particle, in questions expecting the answer *no;* 10; *if, whether.* 47

Numa, -ae, m., *Numa.*

numerus, -ī, m., *number, group.* 11

numquam, adv., *never.* 36

nunc, adv., *now.* 9

nūntiō, -āre, -āvī, -ātum, *announce, report.* 7

nūntius, -ī, m., *messenger, message, news.* 4

nūper, adv., *recently.*

O

Ō, interj., *O, Oh!*

ob, prep., with acc., *because of, on account of; for the purpose of.* 8

obiūrgō, -āre, -āvī, -ātum, *reprove, blame.*

oblīvīscor, -līvīscī, -lītus sum, *forget* (used with gen.).

obscūrus, -a, -um, adj., *dark, hidden.*

obsecrō, -āre, -āvī, -ātum, *beseech, plead.*

obses, -idis, m. and f., *hostage.* 54

obsideō, -ēre, -sēdī, -sessum, *besiege.*

obstruō, -ere, -strūxī, -strūctum, *block.*

obtestor, -ārī, -ātus sum, *implore* (in the name of the gods).

obtineō, -ēre, -tinuī, -tentum, *keep hold on, hold* (against opposition); *have; get a hold on, prevail.* 39

occāsiō, -ōnis, f., *opportunity.*

occāsus, -ūs, m., *setting, downfall, a going down;* **sōlis occāsus,** *sunset, sundown, the west.* 29, 40

occīdō, -ere, -cīdī, -cīsum, *kill, cut down.* 41

occupō, -āre, -āvī, -ātum, *seize, capture.* 2

Octāviānus, -ī, m., *Octavian,* a cognomen of the emperor Augustus.

octāvus, -a, -um, num. adj., *eighth.* 21

octō, num. adj., indecl., *eight.* 21

oculus, -ī, m., *eye.* 46

odium, -ī, n., *hatred.*

offerō, -ferre, obtulī, oblātum, *present, offer.*

officīna, -ae, f., *workshop.*

officium, -ī, n., *duty.* 32

ōlim, adv., *once upon a time, formerly, some day.* 25

omittō, -ere, -mīsī, -missum, *pass by, let go.*

omnīnō, adv., *altogether, in all, at all.* 55

omnis, -e, adj., *every, all;* pl., *everyone, everything.* 18

onus, -eris, n., *burden, load.* 44

opīniō, -ōnis, f., *opinion, expectation; reputation.* 59

oportet, -ēre, -uit, impers., *it is proper, it is necessary* (used with acc. of person and inf.). 56

oppidum, -ī, n., *town.* 5

opprimō, -ere, -pressī, -pressum, *crush, overpower, ruin.* 41

oppugnō, -āre, -āvī, -ātum, *attack.* 10

optimē, adv., *best.* 36

optimus, -a, -um, *best, very good, excellent;* see **bonus.** 35

opus, operis, n., *work.* 44

ōra, -ae, f., *coast, shore.*

ōrāculum, -ī, n., *oracle.*

ōrātiō, -ōnis, f., *speech;* **ōrātiōnem habēre,** *deliver a speech.* 44

orbis, -is, m., *circle, wheel;* **orbis terrā- rum,** *the* (inhabited) *world.* 43

ōrdō, -inis, m., *order, rank.* **ex ōrdine,** *in order.* 53

orior, orīrī, ortus sum, *arise, rise.* 55

ornāmentum, -ī, n., *adornment;* pl., *jewelry.*

ōrnō, -āre, -āvī, -ātum, *decorate, bedeck.*

ōrō, -āre, -āvī, -ātum, *beg, ask.* 45

ōs, ōris, n., *mouth; face.* 56

os, ossis, n., *bone.*

ostendō, -ere, -tendī, -tentum, *display, show.* 53

ōstium, -ī, n., *doorway, mouth.*

ovis, -is, f., *sheep.*

P

P. = Pūblius.

paedagōgus, -ī, m., *attendant,* a slave who accompanied children to and from school.

paene, adv., *almost.* 36

Palātium, -ī, n., *Palatine Hill.*

palūs, -ūdis, f., *swamp, marsh.* 56

pānis, -is, m., *bread, loaf.* 16

pār, paris, adj., *equal; equal to* (used with dat.); (as noun) *the equal of* (with gen.). 34

parātus, -a, -um, adj., *ready, prepared.* 13

parcō, -ere, pepercī, parsum, *spare* (used with dat.). 57

pāreō, -ēre, -uī, paritum, *obey* (used with dat.). 57

parō, -āre, -āvī, -ātum, *prepare for, pre- pare.* 2

pars, partis, f., *part, direction;* **magna pars,** *majority, greater part.* 27

parvus, -a, -um (comp., **minor;** sup., **minimus**), adj., *small, little.* 6

passus, -ūs, m., *pace;* **mīlle passūs,** *a mile;* **mīlia passuum,** *miles.* 29, 30

pāstor, -ōris, m., *shepherd, herdsman.*

pater, -tris, m., *father;* in pl., *senators.* 14

patior, patī, passus sum, *suffer, permit, allow* (used with acc. and inf.). 50

patria, -ae, f., *country, native land.* 2

paucī, -ae, -a, adj., *few, a few.* 23

paulum, -ī, n., *a little;* **paulō,** *by a little, a little;* **paulō ante,** *a little while before, a short time ago;* **paulō posteā,** *a little while afterward* (later). 36

Paulus, -ī, m., *Paulus,* a cognomen.

pauper, -eris, adj., *poor, poverty-stricken.*

pāx, pācis, f., *peace.* 20

pectus, -oris, n., *breast.*

pecūnia, -ae, f., *wealth; money.* 13

pecus, -oris, n., *cattle, flock* (of sheep or goats).

pedes, -itis, m., *foot soldier;* pl., *infantry.* 25

peior, peius, adj., *worse;* see **malus.** 35

pellō, -ere, pepulī, pulsum, *push, rout, defeat.* 49

Pēnelopē, -ēs, acc., -ēn, f., *Penelope.*

per, prep., with acc., *through, across; by, by means of.* 8

percipiō, -ere, -cēpī, -ceptum, *feel.*

perdūcō, -ere, -dūxī, -ductum, *lead through, conduct.*

perficiō, -ere, -fēcī, -fectum, *finish, ac- complish, complete.* 42

perflō, -āre, -āvī, -ātum, *blow through or over.*

perfodiō, -ere, -fōdī, -fossum, *dig through, pierce through.*

pergrātus, -a, -um, *very pleasing, welcome, or grateful.*

perīculum, -ī, n., *danger, risk.* 5

perlongus, -a, -um, *very long.*

perlūstrō, -āre, -āvī, -ātum, *survey, examine.*

permagnus, -a, -um, *very big, large, or great.*

permittō, -ere, -mīsī, -missum, *entrust, permit.* 50

permoveō, -ēre, -mōvī, -mōtum, *move deeply, alarm.* 49

permultus, -a, -um, *very much;* pl., *very many.*

perpetuus, -a, -um, adj., *continuous, per- petual;* **in perpetuum,** *forever.*

Persae, -ārum, m. pl., *the Persians.*

perscrībō, -ere, -scrīpsī, -scrīptum, *write in detail, write in full.*

Perseus, -ī, m., *Perseus.*

persuādeō, -ēre, -suāsī, -suāsum, *persuade* (used with the dat., followed by **ut** with the subjunctive). 45

perterreō, -ēre, -uī, -itum, *terrify.* 42

pertineō, -ēre, -uī, —, *extend (to), pertain (to).* 39

perturbō, -āre, -āvī, -ātum, *alarm, upset, throw into confusion.* 56

perveniō, -īre, -vēnī, -ventum, *reach, arrive.* 30

pēs, pedis, m., *foot;* **certāmen pedum,** *foot race.* 27

pessimus, adj., *worst;* see **malus.** 35

petō, -ere, -īvī or **-iī, -ītum,** *attack; aim at, head for, seek; beg, ask* (takes acc. of the thing and **ā** or **ab** with abl. of the person). 25

Philēmon, -ōnis, m., *Philemon.*

Phrygia, -ae, f., *Phrygia.*

pietās, -tātis, f., *family loyalty.*

pīlum, -ī, n., *javelin.* 42

pinguis, pingue, adj., *fat.*

placeō, -ēre, -uī, -itum, *please (with dat.); used impersonally,* **placet** *(with dat.), it seems good (to).* 57

plēbs, plēbis, f., *common people, plebeians.* 59

plēnus, -a, -um, adj., *full.*

plūrēs, -ium, pl. adj., comp. of **multī,** *more, several.* 35

plūrimus, sup. of **multus,** *most.* 35

plūs, plūris, n., *more, a larger amount.* 35

pōculum, -ī, n., *cup.*

poena, -ae, f., *penalty, punishment* (thought of as a debt to be paid); **poenās dare,** *pay the penalty, suffer punishment;* **poenam sūmere,** *inflict punishment.* 12

Poenī, -ōrum, m., *Carthaginians.*

poēta, -ae, m., *poet.* 1

polliceor, -ērī, -itus sum, *promise (usually with* **mē, tē, sē,** *and fut. infin.)* 50

Polydectēs, -ae, acc. **-ēn,** m., *Polydectes.*

Polyphēmus, -ī, m., *Polyphemus.*

polȳpus, -ī, m., *octopus.*

Pompeii, -ōrum, m., *Pompeii, a town of Campania.*

Pompōnius, -ī, m., *Pomponius.*

pōmum, -ī, n., *fruit, apple.*

pōnō, -ere, posuī, positum, *put, set, place, locate; (with* **castra**), *pitch.* 22

pōns, pontis, m., *bridge.* 16

populus, -ī, m., *people, nation, tribe.* 12

porcus, -ī, m., *pig, swine.*

porta, -ae, f., *gate.* 3

portō, -āre, āvī, -ātum, *carry.* 2

portus, -ūs, m., *harbor, port.* 29

Porus, -ī, m., *Porus,* a king of India.

possum, posse, potuī, *can, be able.* 32

post, adv., *after(wards), later.* 8

post, prep., with acc. (of place), *behind; (of time), after;* adv., *afterward.* 8

posteā, adv., *after that time, afterward, thereafter.* 9

posterus, -a, -um (comp., **posterior;** sup., **postrēmus**), adj., *following, next; (as noun, pl.), posterity, descendants.* 34

posthāc, adv., *hereafter, after this.*

postquam, conj., *after.* 36

postrēmus, -a, -um, sup. of **posterus,** adj., *last.*

postrīdiē, adv., *the next day.*

postulō, -āre, -āvī, -ātum, *demand* (used with acc. and **ā** or **ab** with abl.). 45

potēns, potentis, adj., *powerful.* 18

potenter, adv., *powerfully.* 31

potentia, -ae, f., *power, ability.*

potestās, -tātis, f., *power, opportunity.* 43

potior, -īrī, -ītus sum, *get possession of, take possession of* (used with abl.). 55

potis, defective adj., *able.*

prae, prep. with abl., *before.*

praeacūtus, -a, -um, adj., *sharp (at the end), pointed.*

praecaveō, -ēre, -cāvī, -cautum, *beware, be on guard, take precautions.*

praecipiō, -ere, -cēpī, -ceptum, *give instructions.*

praecipuē, adv., *especially.*

praeda, -ae, f., *booty.* 56

praedīcō, -ere, -dīxī, -dictum, *foretell, predict.*

praedor, -ārī, -ātus sum, *plunder, rob.*

praeficiō, -ere, -fēcī, -fectum, *place over or in command of, put in charge of* (used with acc. and dat.). 57

praemittō, -ere, -mīsī, -missum, *send ahead, let go ahead.*

praemium, -ī, n., *reward.* 32

praenōmen, -inis, n., *given name, first name, praenomen.*

praesēns, -sentis, adj., *present; immediate.*

praeses, -idis, m., *guardian, protector.*

praesidium, -ī, n., *protection, guard, garrison.* 32

praesum, -esse, -fuī, -futūrus, *be at the head of, be in command of* (with dat.). 57

praeter, prep., with acc., *beyond, except, besides.* 39

praetereā, adv., *besides, besides that.* 45

praetereō, -īre, -iī (-īvī), -itum, *go by.*

precēs, -um, f., *prayers, pleas.*

prehendō, -ere, -hendī, -hēnsum, *take, grasp.*

premō, -ere, pressī, pressum, *press; crush, overpower, suppress.* 38

prīdiē, adv., *on the day before.*

prīmus, -a, -um, adj., *first, foremost; first part of, early;* **prīmā aestāte,** *at the beginning of summer;* **prīmā lūce,** *at daybreak;* **prīmā nocte,** *early in the night;* **quam prīmum,** *as soon as possible;* **prīmō,** *at first* (in contrasts); **prīmum,** *for the first time, first* (in a series). 21, 35, 36

prīnceps, -cipis, m., *chief.* 26

prior, -ius, adj., *former, earlier; first.* 35

Prīscus, -ī, m., *Priscus.*

prius, adv., *before, previously.* 36

priusquam, adv., *before.*

prīvātus, -a, -um, adj., *private (opposed to* **pūblicus).** 47

prō, prep., with abl., *in front of; in proportion to; for, (= instead of), in place of, in exchange for; in defense of, in behalf of.* 39

probo, -are, -avī, -ātum, *prove; approve of.* 38

prōclāmō, -āre, -āvī, -ātum, *shout forth.*

procul, adv., *at some distance.* 45

procus, -ī, m., *suitor.*

prōdūcō, -ere, -dūxī, -ductum, *lead forward, bring forth.* 49

proelium, -ī, n., *battle.* 11

profectiō, -ōnis, f., *departure.*

proficīscor, proficīscī, profectus sum, *set out; depart.* 50

prōgredior, -ī, -gressus sum, *step (go) forward, advance, go forth.* 51

prohibeō, -ēre, -uī, -itum, *prevent, keep . . . from.* 20

prōiciō, -icere, -iēcī, -iectum, *throw forward;* **sē prōicere,** *prostrate oneself.*

prōmō, -ere, prōmpsī, prōmptum, *bring out.*

prōmoveō, -ēre, -mōvī, -mōtum, *move forward.*

prope, adv., *nearly, almost;* as prep., with acc., *near.* 35

properō, -āre, -āvī, -ātum, *hurry, hasten.*

propinquus, -a, -um, adj., *near, nearby; (as noun), relation, kinsman.* 34

propior, -ius (sup., **proximus**), adj., *nearer; see* **prope.** 34

prōpōnō, -ere, -posuī, -positum, *set forth, put forth, propose.* 49

propter, prep., with acc., *on account of, because of.* 8

prosternō, -ere, prostrāvī, prostrātum, *knock down.*

prostrātus, -a, -um, *lying down.*

prōsum, prōdesse, prōfuī, *be of advantage, profit.*

prōvehō, -ere, -vexī, -vectum, *carry forward;* in pass., with instr., abl., *sail forth.*

prōvideō, -ēre, -vīdī, -vīsum, *foresee, provide for.* 57

prōvincia, -ae, f., *province, esp. the Roman province, a part of southern Gaul, now called Provence.* 1

prōvocō, -āre, -āvī, -ātum, *call forth, challenge, invite.*

proximē, adv., *next, most recently, lately.*

proximus, -a, -um, adj., *nearest, next, last (preceding or following); see* **propior.** 34

prūdēns, -entis, adj., *foresighted, wise, prudent.* 54

prūdenter, adv., *wisely, prudently.* 54

prūdentia, -ae, f., *foresight, wisdom.*

pūblicus, -a, -um, adj., *belonging to the people; public,* (opposed to **prīvātus**); **rēs publica,** *commonwealth, state, republic, government.* 31

Pūblius, -ī, m., *Publius,* a praenomen.
puella, -ae, f., *girl.* 1
puer, puerī, m., *boy.* 4
pugna, -ae, f., *fight.* 21
pugnātum est, *fighting occurred, the fighting occurred.*
pugnō, -āre, -āvī, -ātum, *fight.* 2
pulcher, -chra, -chrum, adj., *beautiful, noble, fine.* 8
pulchrē, adv., *beautifully, nobly.* 11
pulsō, -āre, -āvī, -ātum, *knock at, beat.*
putō, -āre, -āvī, -ātum, *think.* 39
Pyrēnaeus, -a, -um, adj., **montēs Pyrēnaeī,** *the Pyrenees.*
Pyrrhus, -ī, m., *Pyrrhus,* king of Epirus, on the east coast of the Adriatic.

Q

Q. = Quintus.
quā, adv., *where, by which way.*
quā dē causā, *for which reason.* 39
Quādī, -ōrum, m., *Quadi,* the name of a fierce German tribe.
quaerō, -ere, -sīvī, -sītum, *seek, inquire, ask,* (takes the acc. of the thing and the abl. of the person with **ē, ex, ā, ab,** or **dē**). 45
quam, adv. and conj., *how? how! than, as;* with superlatives, *as . . . as possible;* **quam diū,** *how long?* 33
quam ob rem, *why?, for which reason?*
quantus, -a, -um, adj., *how great? how large? how much?* 47
quārtus, -a, -um, numerical adj., *fourth.* 21
quasi, adv., *as if, as it were.*
quattuor, num. adj., indecl., *four.* 21
quattuordecim, num. adj., indecl., *fourteen.* 47
-que (an enclitic), conj., *and.* 3
quī, qua, quod, (after **sī, nisī, num,** and **nē**), *any.* 58
quī, quae, quod, rel. pron., *who, which, that.* 27
quī, quae, quod, interrog. adj., *what? which?* 28

quia, conj., *because.*
quicquid, n., *whatever* (used in affirmative expressions).
quīcumque, quaecumque, quodcumque, indef. pron. and adj., *whoever, whatever.*
quid, *what?*
quīdam, quaedam, quiddam or **quoddam,** indef. pron. and adj., *a certain, one, certain, some.* 51
quidem, adv., postpositive, *to be sure, indeed, at least, at any rate, as a matter of fact;* **nē . . . quidem,** *not even* (see under **nē**). 53
quiēs, -ētis, f., *rest, sleep.* 58
quīn, conj., *how not, that not, but that, from ———ing.*
quīndecim, num. adj., indecl., *fifteen.* 47
quīnque, num. adj., indecl., *five.* 21
quīntus, -a, -um, num. adj., *fifth.* 21
Quīntus, ī, m., *Quintus,* a praenomen.
quis, quid, interrog. pron., *who? what?* 28. indef. pron., *anyone, anything;* **nē, quis, nē quid,** *no one, nothing.* 58
quisquam, quicquam, indef. pron., *any one, anything.* 58
quisque, quaeque, quidque, pron. and adj., *each one, every one, each.* 37, 58
quō, rel. adv., *where, to which place,* interrog. adv., *where? to what place?* 36
quod, conj., *because.* 21
quōmodo, interrog. adv., *how?*
quoque, adv., postpositive, *also, too* (**quoque** adds only the one word — noun or pronoun — which it follows; see **etiam**). 53
quot, adj., indecl., *how many?* 47

R

rapiō, -ere, -uī, raptum, *seize, snatch.* 57
ratiō, -ōnis, f., *account, manner, plan, reason, system.* 54
recēns, recentis, adj., *fresh, new, recent.* 54
recidō, -ere, -cidī, -casum, *fall back.*
recipiō, -ere, -cēpī, receptum, *take back,*

accept, receive; recover; in **fidem recipere,** take under one's protection; **sē recipere,** return, retreat. 38, 40, 46

recumbō, -ere, recubuī, lie back.

recūsō, -āre, -āvī, -ātum, refuse.

reddō, -ere, -didī, -ditum, give back, restore. 28

redeō, -īre, -iī (-īvī), -itum, go back, return, come back. 52

redimō, -ere, -ēmī, -ēmptum, buy back, redeem

reditus, -ūs, m., return.

redūcō, -ere, redūxī, reductum, lead back, bring back. 23

referō, -ferre, rettulī, -lātum, bring back, carry back; report; **pedem referre,** go back, return, give ground, retreat; **gratiam referre,** show gratitude. 52, 58

reficiō, -ere, -fēcī, -fectum, repair, restore. 60

refugiō, -ere, -fūgī, —, flee back.

refulgeō, -ēre, refulsī, —, shine brightly.

rēgia, -ae, f., king's house, palace.

rēgīna, -ae, f., queen. 13

regiō, -ōnis, f., direction, district, region. 43

rēgnum, -ī, n., kingdom; kingship. 5

regō, -ere, rēxī, rēctum, rule. 22

regredior, -ī, -gressus, go back.

Rēgulus, -ī, m., Regulus.

reiciō, -ere, reiēcī, reiectum, throw back, repulse. 60

relinquō, -ere, relīquī, relictum, leave, leave behind. 22

reliquus, -a, -um, adj., remaining, the rest of. 23

remaneō, -ēre, -mānsī, -mānsum, stay behind, stay back, remain.

remittō, -ere, -mīsī, -missum, send back, let go back. 38

removeō, -ēre, -mōvī, -mōtum, move back. 38

rēmus, -ī, m., oar. 59

renūntiō, -āre, -āvī, -ātum, bring back a message, report, bring back word (of). 49

repellō, -ere, reppulī, repulsum, drive back, drive away. 60

repente, adv., suddenly. 55

reperiō, -īre, repperī, repertum, find, discover. 60

repōnō, -ere, -posuī, -positum, store.

reportō, -āre, -āvī, -ātum, carry back, bring back.

repugnō, -āre, -āvī, -ātum, fight against.

requiēscō, -ere, -quiēvī, -quiētum, rest, sleep.

requirō, -ere, -quīsīvī, -quīsītum, search for (again), require.

rēs, reī, f., matter, affair, respect, event, fact, task, exploit; thing, business function, science, property, profit, position; pl. the physical universe, conditions, circumstances, deeds, situation. **rēs frūmentāria,** grain supply, forage; **rēs pūblica,** commonwealth, state, republic, government; **rēs gestae,** deeds, accomplishments; **rēs novae,** revolution; **omnibus rēbus,** in all respects. 31, 57

resistō, -ere, restitī, —, resist. 57

respondeō, -ēre, -dī, respōnsum, answer, reply. 20

respōnsum, -ī, n., answer, reply.

restituō, -ere, -stituī, -stitūtum, restore.

retineō, -ēre, -uī, -tentum, hold back. 20

revertor, -ī, reversus sum, turn back, return. 60

revocō, -āre, -āvī, -ātum, call back.

rēx, rēgis, m., king. 14

Rhēnus, -ī, m., the Rhine (river). 51

rhētorica, -ae, f., rhetoric, oratory.

Rhodanus, -ī, m., the Rhone (river).

rideō, -ēre, rīsī, rīsum, smile, laugh, laugh at. 58

rīpa, -ae, f., bank (of a stream). 54

rogō, -āre, -āvī, -ātum, ask, ask for (used with two accusatives, one of the person, one of the thing; also with **ut** and the subj.). 45

Rōma, -ae f., Rome. 3

Rōmānus, -a, -um, adj., Roman, of Rome. 15

Rōmulus, -ī, m., Romulus.

rugītus, rugītūs, m., roar, roaring.

rūmor, -ōris, m., rumor. 58

rumpō, -ere, rūpī, ruptum, burst, break. 58

ruō, -ere, ruī, ruitum, *rush.*

rūpēs, -is, f., *cliff, reef, rock, crag.*

rūrsus, adv., *back, again, back again.* 51

rūs, rūris, n., *country, countryside;* (loc.) *in the country, at one's country place.* 50

Rutulī, -ōrum, m., *the Rutulians.*

S

Sabīnus, -a, -um, adj., *Sabine.*

sacer, sacra, sacrum, adj., *sacred, holy;* **Via Sacra,** *The Sacred Way,* a street in the Forum in Rome; as neut. pl. noun, *religious ceremonies, rituals.* 8

saepe, adv., *often.* 9

sagitta, -ae, f., *arrow.* 49

Saguntum, -ī, n., *Saguntum.*

Salamīs, Salamīnis, f., *Salamis,* an island off Athens.

saliō, -īre, saluī, saltum, *leap.*

salūs, -ūtis, f., *health; safety, salvation, well-being, welfare.* 20

salūtō, -āre, -āvī, -ātum, *greet.*

salvus, -a, -um, adj., *safe.*

sanguis, sanguinis, m., *blood.* 58

Sardēs, -ium, f., *Sardis.* 49

satis, defective noun, *enough;* (used with gen.); as adv., *enough.* 48

saxum, -ī, n., *stone, rock.* 59

scapha, -ae, f., *skiff, small boat.*

Schoeneus, ī, m., *Schoeneus,* a king of Boeotia.

scientia, -ae, f., *knowledge.*

sciō, -īre, -īvī, -ītum, *know.* 39

Scipiō, -ōnis m., (1) *P. Cornelius Scipio,* defeated at Ticinus. (2) *P. Cornelius Scipio Africanus Maior,* the conqueror of Hannibal.

scrībo, -ere, scrīpsī, scrīptum, *write.* 25

scūtum, -ī, n., *shield.* 42

sē: see **suī;** **inter sē:** see **inter.**

secundus, -a, -um, adj., *following, favorable; second.* 21

sed, conj., *but.* 2

sēdecim, num. adj., indecl., *sixteen.* 47

sedeō, -ēre, sēdī, sessum, *sit.* 17

sēdēs, -is, f., *seat, residence.*

sella, -ae, f., *chair, seat.* 21

semper, adv., *always.* 9

senātor, -ōris, m., *senator.* 40

senātus, -ūs, m., *senate.* 29

senex, -is (comp., **senior;**) adj., *old;* as a subst., *old man.* 35

sententia, -ae, f., *opinion.* 43

sentiō, -īre, sēnsī, sēnsum, *feel, realize.* 39

septem, num. adj., indecl., *seven.* 21

septendecim, num. adj., indecl., *seventeen.* 47

septimus, -a, -um, num., *seventh.* 21

sequor, sequī, secūtus sum, *follow.* 51

sermō, sermōnis, m., *conversation.*

serpēns, -entis, f., *serpent, snake.*

serviō, -īre, -īvī, -ītum, *be slave to, serve* (used with dat.).

Servius, -ī, m., *Servius.*

servō, -āre, -āvī, -ātum, *guard, save, keep.* 10

servus, -ī, m., *slave.* 4

sex, num. adj., indecl., *six.* 21

sextus, -a, -um, num. adj., *sixth.* 21

sī, conj., *if.* 21. **sī quis, sī qua, sī quid,** *if anyone* or *if anything.* 58

Sibylla, -ae, f., *the Sibyl* (a prophetess).

sīc, adv., *so* (manner), *in this way* (used with verbs). 48

Sicilia, -ae, f., *Sicily.* 21

signum, -ī, n., *sign, signal, military standard, statue;* **signa īnferre,** *wage* (offensive) *warfare on, attack.* 11, 52

silentium, -ī, n., *silence.*

silva, -ae, f., *forest.* 1

similis, -e, adj., *like, similar* (used with dat.); superl. **simillimus.** 18

similiter, adv., *in like manner, similarly.* 31

simillimē, adv., *most similarly.* 36

simul, adv., *at the same time;* **simul atque (ac),** *as soon as.* 36

sine, prep., with abl., *without.* 6

sinister, -tra, -trum, adj., *left, left-hand.* 34

socius, -ī, m., *comrade, ally.* 12

sōl, sōlis, m., *sun;* **sōlis occāsus,** *sunset, sundown, the west.* 40

Sōl, Sōlis m., *Sol* or *Helius,* the Sun God.

sollicitūdō, -inis, f., *anxiety, worry.*

sollicitus, -a, -um, adj., *troubled, worried.*

Solōn, Solōnis, m., *Solon,* Athenian lawgiver.

sōlus, -a, -um, adj., gen. sōlīus, *only, alone;* nōn sōlum . . . sed etiam, *not only . . . but also.* 37

solvō, -ere, solvī, solūtum, *loose, untie, set free, pay;* nāvem (nāvēs) solvere, or solvere alone, *cast off, set sail.* 57

somnus, -ī, m., *sleep.*

sonitus, -ūs, m., *sound, noise.*

sonōrus, -a, -um, adj., *sounding, loud.*

Sōracte, -is, n., *Soracte,* a high mountain in Etruria.

soror, -ōris, f., *sister.* 14

sortior, -īrī, -ītus sum, *draw lots.*

spatium, -ī, n., *space; space (period) of time, distance, interval.* 49

speciēs, -ēī, f., *sight, appearance.* 46

spectō, -āre, -āvī, -ātum, *look at.* 2

speculum, -ī, n., *mirror.*

spēlunca, -ae, f., *cave, cavern.*

spērō, -āre, -āvī, -ātum, *hope;* with acc., *hope for.* 39

spēs, speī, f., *hope.* 31

spīna, -ae, f., *thorn.*

sponte, abl. sing., f., *free will;* with suā, *voluntarily, of one's own accord.*

statim, adv., *immediately, at once.* 36

statiō, -ōnis, f., *picket-post, picket.*

statuō, -ere, -uī, -ūtum, *set, decide.*

stella, -ae, f., *star.* 40

stō, -āre, stetī, stātum, *stand.* 10

strepitus, ūs, m., *noise, uproar;* of geese, *cackling.*

stringō, -ere, strīnxī, strīctum, *draw.*

studeō, ēre, studuī, —, *be eager for, desire.* 57

studiōsus, -a, -um, adj., *studious, enthusiastic.*

studium, -ī, n., *eagerness, enthusiasm, zeal.* 49

stultus, -a, -um, adj., *foolish, stupid.*

sub, prep., with acc. after verbs of motion, *close under, under, close to, up to, to the foot of;* with words denoting time, *toward, about;* with abl. of place, *at the foot of, under, close to.* 5

subeō, -īre, -iī, -itum, *undergo.*

subiciō, -ere, -iēcī, -iectum, *put under.*

subitō, adv., *suddenly.* 43

sublātus; see tollō.

subsidium, -ī, n., *aid, support;* in pl., *reinforcements.* 37

suī (gen.), reflex. pron., *of himself, herself, itself, themselves;* inter sē, (*to* or *with*) *each other, one another.* 40, 46

sum, esse, fuī, futūrus, *be, is, am, are, etc.* 3

summus (sup. of superus), adj., *highest, top of.* 35

sūmō, -ere, sūmpsī, sūmptum, *take, assume;* poenam or supplicium sūmere dē (abl.) *punish.* 58

sunt, *are, there are.*

super, prep., with acc., *over, above.*

Superbus, -ī, m., *Superbus, "The Proud."*

superior, -ius, *higher.* 35

superō, -āre, -āvī, -ātum, *surpass, defeat.* 7

supplicium, -ī, n., *punishment* (used with dare and sūmere as poena is).

suprā, adv., *above.* 55

surgō, -ere, surrēxī, surrēctum, *rise, stand up.* 22

suscipiō, -ere, -cēpī, -ceptum, *undertake.* 56

suspicor, -ārī, -ātus sum, *suspect.*

sustineō, -ēre, -uī, -tentum, *hold up, hold in check, withstand.* 32

sustulī: see tollō.

suus, -a, -um, poss. adj., *belonging to the subject, his, her, their, its (own:* not used in the nom. case). 40

Syrācūsae, -ārum, f., *Syracuse.*

T

taceō, -ēre, -uī, -itum, *be silent, become silent.* 60

tālāria, -ium, n. pl., *winged sandals.*

tālis, -e, adj., *of such a kind, such.* 48

tam, adv. of degree, *so* (used with adjectives and adverbs). 48

tamen, conj., *nevertheless, still, yet.* 30

tandem, adv., *at length, at last, finally.* 36

tangō, -ere, tetigī, tāctum, *touch.* 55

tantus, -a, -um, adj., *so much, so great, so big, such a great, such a large.* 48

Tarquinius, -ī, m., *Tarquin.*

tegō, -ere, tēxī, tēctum, *cover.* 56

Tellus, -ī, m., *Tellus,* an Athenian.

tellus, tellūris, f., *the earth* (as a planet). 43

tēlum, -ī, n., *weapon, missile, offensive weapon.* 11

temere, adv., *rashly, thoughtlessly.*

tempestās, -tātis, f., *storm, weather.* 49

templum, -ī, n., *temple, sacred area.*

temptō, -āre, -āvī, -ātum, *try, attempt.* 10

tempus, -oris, n., *time.* 15

teneō, -ēre, -uī, tentum, *hold;* **memoriā tenēre,** *hold by (in) memory, remember.* 17, 23

tenuis, -e, adj., *thin.*

tergum, -ī, n., *back;* **ā tergō,** *in the rear, (from) behind.* 32

terra, -ae, f., *earth, land, country.* 3

terreō, -ēre, -uī, -itum, *frighten.* 20

terribilis, -e, adj., *terrible.*

terror, -ōris, m., *fright, terror.*

tertius, -a, -um, num. adj., *third.* 21

tertium, adv., *a third time.*

Themistocles, -is, m., *Themistocles,* a celebrated Athenian.

Thessalia, -ae, f., *Thessaly.*

Thrācia, -ae, f., *Thrace.*

Tīcīnus, -ī, m., *Ticinus,* a river of Cisalpine Gaul.

timeō, -ēre, -uī, *fear, be afraid.* 17

timor, -ōris, m., *fear.* 26

toga, -ae, f., *toga.* 37

tollō, tollere, sustulī, sublātum, *lift up, raise, remove.* 52

tonitrus, -ūs, m., *thunder.*

torqueō, -ēre, torsī, tortum, *twist, turn.*

tot, adj., indecl., *so many.* 48

tōtus, -a, -um, *whole, entire.* 37

tractō, -āre, -āvī, -ātum, *handle.*

trādō, -ere, -didī, -ditum, *hand over, surrender; hand down.* 22

trādūcō, -ere, -dūxī, -ductum, *lead across.* 41

trahō, -ere, trāxī, trāctum, *draw, drag.* 38

trāns, prep., with acc., *across, over.* 8

trānseō, -īre, -iī (-īvī), -itum, *cross.* 52

trānsfīgō, -ere, -fīxī, -fīxum, *pierce.*

trānsportō, -āre, -āvī, -ātum, *carry across* (with two accusatives); *transport.*

Trasumēnus, -ī, m., *Trasumenus,* a lake of Etruria.

tredecim, num. adj., indecl., *thirteen.* 47

trēs, tria, num. adj., *three.* 21

tribūnus, -ī, m., *tribune.* 42

tribuō, -uere, -uī, tribūtum, *assign, grant.* 60

tristis, -e, *sad, grim.* 33

triumphus, -ī, m., *triumphal procession, triumph.*

Trōia, -ae, f., *Troy.* 21

Trōiānus, -a, -um, adj., *Trojan.* 18

tū, tuī, pers. pron., *you;* pl., **vōs.** 26

tuba, -ae, f., *trumpet.* 3

tuī (gen.), reflex. pron., *of yourself;* see **tū.** 40

Tullius, -ī, m., *Tullius.*

Tullus, -ī, m., *Tullus.*

tum, adv., *then, at that time.* 9

turbō, -āre, -āvī, -ātum, *stir up.*

turbō, turbinis, m., *whirlwind.*

Turnus, -ī, m., *Turnus,* Prince of the Rutuli, an Italic tribe.

turpis, -e, adj., *base, disgraceful; ugly.* 57

turris, -is, f., (**turrim,** acc. sing.) *tower.* 40

tūtus, -a, -um, adj., *safe.* 51

tuus, -a, -um, poss. adj., *your, yours.* 6

U

ubi, interrog. adv., *where?* 3. rel. adv., *where, when.* 9

Ulixēs, -is, m., *Ulysses.*

ūllus, -a, -um, adj., gen. **ūllīus,** *any.* 37

ulterior, -ius adj., *farther.* 35

ultimus, -a, -um, adj., *farthest.* 35

umquam, adv., *ever.* 43

unda, -ae, f., *wave.*

unde, rel. adv., *whence, from which;* interrog. adv., *whence?, where from?* 37

ūndecim, num. adj., indecl., *eleven.* 21

ūndēvīgintī, num. adj., indecl., *nineteen.* 47

undique, adv., *from all sides, from everywhere; on all sides.* 37

ūngō, -ere, ūnxī, ūnctum, *anoint.*

unguentum, -ī, n., *ointment.*

ūniversī, -ōrum, m., *all together, one and all.*

ūnus, -a, -um, adj., gen. ūnīus, *one, a single.* 21

urbānus, -a, -um, *pertaining to a city, urban.*

urbs, urbis, f., *city.* 16

ūsus, -ūs, m., *use; advantage, practice, experience.* 29

ut, utī, conj., *in order that, that* (followed by subjunctive clause of purpose); *so that* (followed by subjunctive clause of result); *just as, as, how, when, since* (followed by indicative). 36, 44, 48

ūter, ūtris, m., *skin,* used as a bag or bottle, *wine-skin.*

uter, utra, utrum, pron. and adj., gen. utrīus, rel. and interrog., *which* (of two). 37

uterque, -traque, -trumque, pron. and adj., *each* (of two). 37

utī: see **ut.**

ūtilis, -e adj., *useful, profitable.* 33

ūtilitās, -tātis, f., *usefulness, utility.*

ūtor, ūtī, ūsus sum, *use* (used with abl.). 55

utrum, conj., not translated in direct questions; in indirect questions, *whether;* **utrum . . . an . . . ,** *whether . . . or . . . ;* **utrum . . . necne,** *whether . . . or not.* 47

uxor, -ōris, f., *wife.* 59

V

vadum, -ī, n., *shallows, ford.* 43

valeō, -ēre, -uī, -itum, *be well, be strong;* **valē,** as greeting, *farewell, goodby;* **iubēre valēre,** *to bid farewell.* 38

validē, adv., *strongly.* 36

validus, -a, -um, adj., *strong.* 34

vallēs, -is, f., *valley.* 42

vāllum, -ī, n., *rampart.* 44

Varrō, -ōnis, m., *Varro.*

vās, vāsis, pl., vāsa, -ōrum, n., *dish, vessel.*

vāstō, -āre, -āvī, -ātum, *lay waste, devastate.* 49

vāstus, -a, -um, adj., *huge, enormous.*

vehemēns (gen. vehementis), adj., *forceful, violent.* 57

vehementer, adv., *violently, extremely, exceedingly, vigorously.* 57

vehō, -ere, vexī, vectum, *carry, transport;* in pass., usually with an instr. abl., **nāve, currū,** etc., *travel, sail, ride.* 53

Veiī, -ōrum, m., *Veii,* an Etruscan city. 49

vel, conj., *or, or even, or if you wish; even;* **vel . . . vel,** *either . . . or.* 42

velut, or velutī, adv., *as if, just as if.*

vēndō, -ere, vēndidī, vēnditum, *sell.* 54

venēnum, -ī, n., *poison.*

veniō, -īre, vēnī, ventum, *come.* 30

venter, -tris, m., *belly.*

ventus, -ī, m., *wind.* 40

Venus, Veneris, f., *Venus,* goddess of love.

Venusia, -ae, f., *Venusia,* a town of Apulia, birthplace of Horace.

verbum, -ī, n., *word.* 5

vērē, adv., *truly.* 13

vereor, -ērī, -itus sum, *fear, dread.* 51

Vergilius, -ī, m., *Vergil.*

vēritās, -tātis, f., *truth, trueness.*

vērō, *in truth, indeed; but, however.* 42

versor, -ārī, -ātus sum, *be busy, be involved.*

vertō, -ere, vertī, versum, *turn.* 60

vērus, -a, -um, adj., *true.* 13

vēscor, vēscī, *feed on* (with abl.).

vesper, -erī, m., *evening.*

vester, -tra, -trum, poss. adj., *your, yours.* 8

vestis, -is, f., *clothing.* 46

Vesuvius, -ī, m., *Vesuvius,* a volcano in Campania.

vetus, gen. veteris, adj., *old.* 54

via, -ae, f., *road, way, street;* **Via Appia:** see under **Appia Via; Via Sacra:** see under **sacer.** 3

victor, -ōris, m., *victor;* (in apposition) *victorious.* 37

victōria, -ae, f., *victory.* 21

vīctus, -ūs, m., *living; food, victuals.*

vīcus, -ī, m., *village, street.*

videō, -ēre, vīdī, vīsum, *see.* 17

videor, -ērī, vīsus sum, *seem, appear.* 50

vigilia, -ae, f., *wakefulness; watchfulness; watch* (i.e., a quarter of the night). 46

vīgintī, num. adj., indecl., *twenty.* 21

vīlla, -ae, f., *farmhouse; country house, villa.* 3

vīmen, -inis, n., *pliant twig, osier.*

vinciō, -īre, vīnxī, vīnctum, *bind.*

vinclum, (vinculum), -ī, n., *bond, chain.*

vincō, -ere, vīcī, victum, *conquer, defeat, be victorious, win.* 22

vīnum, -ī, n., *wine.* 28

violō, -āre, āvī, -ātum, *dishonor, violate.*

vir, -ī, m., *man, husband; hero.* 4

vīrēs, see vīs.

virga, -ae, f., *wand.*

virtūs, -tūtis, f., *manliness, courage, bravery.* 27

vīs, vīs, f., *force, violence;* pl., **vīrēs, vīrium,** *strength, might.* 46

vīsus, -ūs, m., *sight, view, vision.*

vīta, -ae, f., *life.* 1

vīvō, -ere, vīxī, vīctum, *be alive, live.* 56

vīvus, -a, -um, adj., *alive.*

vix, adv., *scarcely, hardly, with difficulty.* 55

vocō, -āre, -āvī, -ātum, *call.* 2

Volcānus, -ī, m., *Vulcan, the god of fire.*

volō, -āre, -āvī, -ātum, *fly.* 7

volō, velle, voluī, —, *be willing, wish.* 53

Volscī, -ōrum, m., pl., *the Volscians, a people in Italy.*

voluntas, -tātis, f., *willingness, wish, consent.* 58

voluptās, -tātis, f., *pleasure.*

Volusēnus, -ī, m., *Volusenus, a lieutenant in Caesar's army.*

vōs: see tū. 26

vōx, vōcis, f., *voice.* 20

vulnerō, -āre, -āvī, -ātum, *wound.* 7

vulnus, -eris, n., *wound.* 15

Z

Zama, -ae, f., *a town in Numidia, scene of Hannibal's defeat.*

English-Latin

A

ability, *facultās*

able: be able, *possum*

aboard: go aboard, *cōnscendō*

about, *circiter, circum, dē;* **about to,** see Participles, Lesson 41; **bring about,** *efficiō*

above, *suprā*

absent: be absent, *absum*

accept, *accipiō, recipiō*

accident, *cāsus*

accomplish, *cōnficiō, perficiō*

accomplishments, *rēs gestae*

account, *ratiō;* **on account of,** *ob, propter*

accustomed: be (or) **become accustomed,** *cōnsuēscō*

across, *trāns;* **lead across,** *trādūcō*

adopt a plan, *cōnsilium ineō*

advance, *prōgredior, signum (signa) īnferō*

advantage, *ūsus*

advice, *cōnsilium*

advise, *moneō*

affair, *rēs*

Africa, *Āfrica*

afraid: be afraid, *timeō*

after, *post, posteā, postquam*

afterward, afterwards, *post, posteā*

again, *rūrsus*

against, *contrā, in*

age, *aetās*

aid, (noun) *auxilium, subsidium;* (verb) *iuvō*

aim at, *petō*

alarm, *commoveō, permoveō, perturbō*

alive, *vīvus;* **be alive,** *vīvō*

all, *omnis;* **in all, at all,** *omnīnō;* **not at all,** *nihil;* **from all sides, on all sides,** *undique*

allow, *patior*

ally, *socius*

almost, *ferē, paene, prope*

alone, *sōlus*

already, *iam*

also, *etiam, quoque;* **and also,** *atque (ac);* **not only . . . but also . . . ,** *nōn sōlum . . . sed etiam . . .*

although, *cum, quamquam*

altogether, *omnīnō*

always, *semper*

am, see **be**

ambassador, *lēgātus*

ambush, *īnsidiae*

among, *apud, inter*

ample, *amplus*

ancient, *antīquus*

anchor, *ancora*

and, *atque (ac), autem, et;* **and also, and besides, and even,** *atque (ac);* **and not,** *neque (nec);* **and so,** *itaque;* **both . . . and . . . ,** *et . . . et . . .*

anger, *īra*

animal, *animal*

announce, *nūntiō, ēnūntiō*

another, *alius;* **another's, belonging to another,** *aliēnus;* **one another, to one another, with one another,** *inter sē (nōs, vōs)*

answer, *respondeō*

anxiety, *cūra*

any, *quī, ūllus;* **not any,** *nūllus;* **any longer,** *diūtius, iam;* **at any rate,** *quidem*

anyone, *quis, quisquam*

anything, *quid, quidquam*

appearance, *speciēs*

appointed day, *diēs cōnstitūta*

approach, (noun) *adventus;* (verb) *accēdō, adeō, aggredior, appropinquō*

approve of, *probō*

approximately, *circiter*

are, see **be**

arise, *orior*

arm, *armō*

arms, defensive arms, *arma*

army, *exercitus;* **army on the march,** *agmen*

around, *circum;* **come around,** *circumveniō*

arouse, *incendō, incitō*

arrival, *adventus*

arrow, *sagitta*

as, *ut*

Asia, *Asia*

ask, ask for, *ōrō, petō, quaerō, rogō*

assemble, *conveniō, convocō*

assign, *tribuō*

assume, *sūmō*

at, see Ablative of Time When, Lesson 25, and Locative Case, Lesson 50

Athens, *Athēnae*

attack, (noun) *impetus;* (verb) *aggredior, impetum faciō, oppugnō, petō*

attempt, *cōnor, temptō*

attentively: look at attentively, *cōnspiciō*

author, *auctor*

authority, *auctōritās*

auxiliary forces, auxiliary troops, *auxilia*

await, *exspectō*

away: be away, *absum;* drive away, *expellō;* go away, *discēdō;* lead away, *dēdūcō;* let go away, send away, *dīmittō;* away from, *ā, ab*

B

baby, *īnfāns*

back, (noun) *tergum*

bad, *malus;* rather bad, too bad, *peior;* very bad, *pessimus;* badly, *male*

baggage, *impedīmenta*

band, *manus*

bank, *rīpa*

barbarian, barbarous, *barbarus*

base, *turpis*

battle, *proelium;* battle signal, *signum proelī;* line of battle, *aciēs;* join battle, *proelium committō*

be, *sum;* be able, *possum;* be absent, be away, be distant, *absum;* be afraid, *timeō;* be alive, *vīvō;* be at the head of, be in command of, *praesum;* be born, be found, *nāscor;* be eager for, *studeō;* be hard pressed, *labōrō;* be in doubt, *dubitō;* be informed, *certior fīō;* be lacking, *dēsum;* be made, *fīō;* be near, be present, *adsum;* be punished, *poenam dō;* be silent, *taceō;* be sorry, *doleō;* be

strong, be well, *valeō;* be surprised, *mīror;* be under an obligation, *grātiam dēbeō;* be unwilling, *nōlō;* be willing, *volō;* be sure, *quidem*

bear, *ferō, gerō*

beautiful, *pulcher*

beautifully, *pulchrē*

because, *quod;* because of, *ob, propter*

become, *fīō;* become accustomed, *cōnsuēscō*

bed, *lectus*

been, see be; having been, see Participles, Lesson 41, and Ablative Absolute, Lesson 51

befall, *accidō*

before, *ante, anteā*

beg, *ōrō, petō*

begin, *incipiō, ineō;* began, *coepī;* begin battle, *proelium committō*

beginning, *initium;* at the beginning of summer, *prīmā aestāte*

behalf: on behalf of, *prō*

behind, *post;* leave behind, *relinquō*

being, see Ablative Absolute, Lesson 51; human being, *homō*

believe, *crēdō*

belonging: belonging to another, *aliēnus;* belonging to the people, *pūblicus*

besides, *praeter, praetereā;* besides that, *praetereā;* and besides, *atque (ac)*

best, (adjective) *optimus,* (adverb) *optimē*

betake oneself, *mē (tē, sē,* etc.) *cōnferō*

better, (adjective) *melior,* (adverb) *melius*

between, *inter*

beyond, *praeter*

bid, *iubeō;* bid farewell, *valēre iubeō*

big, *magnus;* too big, bigger, *maior*

bird, *avis*

birth: by birth, *nātū;* of high birth, *nōbilis*

black, *niger*

blood, *sanguis*

board, *cōnscendō*

body, *corpus*

bold, *audāx*

boldly, *audācter*

boldness, *audācia*

book, *liber*

booty, *praeda*

born: be born, *nāscor*

both, see *uterque;* both . . . and . . . , *et . . . et . . .*

bottom of, *īmus, īnfimus*

bound, *contineō*

boundary, *fīnis*

boy, *puer*

brave, *fortis*

bravely, *fortiter*

bravery, *virtūs*

bread, *pānis*

break, *frangō, rumpō;* break camp, *castra moveō*

bred: well bred, *nōbilis*

bridge, *pōns*

briefly, *breviter*

bright, *clārus*

bring, *dēferō, ferō;* bring about, *efficiō;* bring back, *redūcō, referō;* bring back word of, *renūntiō;* bring forth, *prōdūcō;* bring to, *adferō;* bring together, *cōnferō;* bring up, *adferō;* bring upon, *īnferō*

Britain, *Britannia*

British, *Britannus*

Briton, *Britannus*

broad, *lātus*

brother, *frāter*

build, *aedificō, īnstituō, mūniō*

building, *aedificium*

burden, *onus*

burn, *incendō*

burst, *rumpō*

business, *negōtium*

but, *autem, sed, vērō*

buy, *emō*

by, *ā, ab* (see Ablative of Personal Agent, Lesson 20)

C

Caesar, *Caesar*

calamity, *calamitās*

call, *appellō, vocō;* call together, *convocō*

camp, *castra;* break camp, *castra moveō;* pitch camp, *castra pōnō*

Campus (Martius), *Campus*

can, *possum*

captive, *captīvus*

capture, *capiō, occupō*

care, *cūra, dīligentia*

careful, *dīligēns*

carry, *dēferō, ferō, portō, vehō;* carry back, *referō;* carry on, *gerō;* carry onward, *īnferō*

Carthage, *Carthāgō*

cart, *carrus*

cause, *causa*

cavalry, *equitātus, equitēs* (from *eques*)

centurion, *centūriō*

certain, *certus, quīdam;* a certain one, *quīdam*

certainly, *certē*

chair, *sella*

chance, *cāsus, facultās, fortūna*

character, *mōrēs* (from *mōs*)

check, hold in check, *sustineō*

chief, *prīnceps*

children, *līberī*

choose, *dēligō, legō*

circle, *orbis*

citizen, fellow citizen, *cīvis*

citizenship, citizenry, *cīvitās*

city, *urbs*

clan, *gēns*

class, *genus*

clear, *clārus*

climb, *cōnscendō;* climb down, *dēscendō;* climb up, *ascendō*

close, *claudō*

closely: observe closely, *cōnspiciō*

clothing, *vestis*

cohort, *cohors*

cold, *frīgidus*

collect, *cōgō, cōnferō*

column, marching column, *agmen*

come, *veniō;* come around, *circumveniō;* come together, *congredior, conveniō;* come upon, *inveniō*

command, (noun) *imperium;* be in command of, *praesum;* place or put in command of, *praeficiō;* (verb) *imperō, mandō*

commander, *imperātor*

common, *commūnis;* the common people, *plēbs*

commonwealth, *rēs pūblica*

companion, *socius*
compare, *comparō, conferō*
compel, *cōgō*
complete, *compleō, efficiō, perficiō*
comrade, *socius*
concerning, *dē*
condition, *condiciō*
conference, *colloquium*
confidence, *fidēs*
confusion: throw into confusion, *perturbō*
conquer, *vincō*
conqueror, *victor*
consent, *voluntās*
consider, *exīstimō, iūdicō*
consul, *cōnsul*
consult, consult the interests of, *cōnsulō*
convenient: it is convenient, *convenit*
conversation, *colloquium*
Corinth, *Corinthus*
couch: dining couch, *lectus*
counsel: take counsel for, *cōnsulō*
country, *patria, rūs;* in the country, at one's country place, *rūrī* (from *rūs*); country house, *vīlla*
countryside, *rūs*
courage, *animī, virtūs*
course, *cursus, mēnsa*
cover, *tegō*
cross, *trānseō*
crowd, *multitūdō*
crush, *opprimō, premō*
custom, *cōnsuētūdō, mōs*
cut, cut down, *caedō, occīdō*

D

daily, *cotīdiē*
danger, *perīculum*
dare, *audeō*
daring, (noun) *audācia;* (adjective) *audāx*
daughter, *fīlia*
dawn: at dawn, *prīmā lūce*
day, *diēs;* on the appointed day, *diē cōnstitūtā;* every day, *cotīdiē;* late in the day, *multō diē;* some day, *ōlim*
daybreak: at daybreak, *prīmā lūce*
dead, *mortuus*

death, *mors*
decide, *cōnstituō*
declare, *cōnfirmō*
deeds, *rēs gestae*
deep, *altus*
deeply, *altē, graviter;* **move deeply,** *permoveō*
defeat, *pellō, superō, vincō*
defend, *dēfendō*
defensive arms, *arma*
degree, *modus;* **to what degree,** *quem ad modum*
delay, (noun) *mora;* (verb) *moror*
deliver a speech, *ōrātiōnem habeō*
demand, *postulō*
deny, *negō*
depart, *discēdō, proficīscor*
departure, *exitus*
depth, *altitūdō*
descend, *dēscendō*
descendants, *posterī*
desert, *dēficiō*
deserve, *mereor*
desire, (noun) *cupiditās;* (verb) *cupiō, studeō*
desirous, *cupidus*
desperately, *miserē*
dessert, *secunda mēnsa*
destined, see Participles, Lesson 41
determine, *cōnstituō*
devastate, *vāstō*
die, *morior;* **having died,** *mortuus*
difficult, *difficilis*
difficulty, *difficultās, labor;* **in difficulty,** *impedītus;* **with difficulty,** *aegrē, vix*
diligence, *dīligentia*
diligent, *dīligēns*
diligently, *dīligenter*
dining couch, *lectus*
dinner, *cēna*
direction, *pars, regiō*
director, *magister*
disaster, *calamitās*
discover, *reperiō*
disembark, *ēgredior*
disgraceful, *turpis*
dismiss, *dīmittō*
display, *ostendō*

distance, *spatium*; at some distance, *procul*

distant: be distant, *absum*

district, *regiō*

ditch, *fossa*

do, *agō, faciō*; do not, *nōlī, nōlīte*

dog, *canis*

don't, *nōlī, nōlīte*

door, *iānua*

doubt: be in doubt, *dubitō*

down: down from, *dē*; a going down, *occāsus*; climb down, *dēscendō*; cut down, *caedō, occīdō*; hand down, *trādō*; lead down, *dēdūcō*; sit down, *cōnsīdō*

downfall, *occāsus*

drag, *trahō*

draw, *trahō*; draw near, *appropinquō*; draw up, *īnstruō*

drink, *bibō*

drive, *agō*; drive away, *expellō*; drive back, *repellō*; drive out, *expellō*

duty, *officium*

dwell, *habitō, incolō*; dwell in, *incolō*

E

each, each one, *quisque*; each of two, *uterque*; each other, *inter sē (nōs, vōs)*

eager, *cupidus*; be eager for, *studeō*

eagerly, *cupidē*

eagerness, *studium*

ear, *auris*

early: early in the night, *prīmā nocte*; earlier, *prior*

earn, *mereor*

earth, *terra*

easily, *facile*

easy, *facilis*

eat, *edō*

effect: put into effect, *efficiō*

eight, *octō*

eighteen, *duodēvīgintī*

eighth, *octāvus*

either . . . or . . . , *aut . . . aut . . . , vel . . . vel . . .*

eleven, *ūndecim*

encamp, *cōnsīdō*

encourage, *cōnfīrmō, hortor*

end, *exitus, fīnis*; the end of, *extrēmus*

enemy, *inimīcus, hostis*; the enemy, *hostēs*

enlist, *cōnscrībō*

enough, *satis*

enroll, *cōnscrībō*

enter, *ineō*

enthusiasm, *studium*

entire, *integer, tōtus*

entrust, *committō, cōnfīdō, mandō, permittō*

envoy, *lēgātus*

epistle, *epistula, litterae*

equal, *aequus, pār*

equip, *armō, īnstruō*

especially, *maximē*

establish, *īnstituō*

Europe, *Eurōpa*

even, *etiam*; and even, *atque (ac)*; not even, *nē . . . quidem*; or even, *vel*

ever, *umquam*

every, *omnis, quīque*; every day, *cotīdiē*; everyone, *omnēs, quisque*; everything, *omnia, quidque*; from everywhere, *undique*

except, *nisi, praeter*

exchange: in exchange for, *prō*

exercise, *exerceō*

exhaust, *cōnficiō*

exile, *fuga*

expectation, *opīniō*

experience, *ūsus*

explain, *expōnō*

explore, *explōrō*

expose, *aperiō*

exposed, *apertus*

extend, *pertineō*

eye, *oculus*

F

face, *ōs*

fact: as a matter of fact, *quidem*

fail, *dēficiō*

fair, *aequus*

faith, *fidēs*

faithful, *fidēlis*

fall, (noun) *occāsus*; (verb) *cadō*; fall upon, *accidō*

fame, *glōria*

family, *gēns;* my family, your family, etc., *meī, tuī,* etc.

famous, *clārus, nōbilis, nōtus*

far, far off, by far, *longē;* far and wide, *longē latēque;* farther, *ulterior;* farthest, *extrēmus, ultimus*

farewell, *valē, valēte;* bid farewell, *valēre iubeō*

farmer, *agricola*

farmhouse, *vīlla*

farther, *ulterior*

farthest, *extrēmus, ultimus*

fate, *cāsus*

father, *pater*

favor, *beneficium, grātia*

fear, (noun) *timor;* (verb) *timeō, vereor*

feel, *sentiō;* feel gratitude, *grātiam habeō*

fellow citizen, *cīvis*

few, a few, *paucī;* quite a few, *complūrēs*

field, *ager, campus*

fierce, *ācer, ferus*

fiercely, *ācriter*

fifteen, *quīndecim*

fifth, *quīntus*

fight, (noun) *pugna;* (verb), *pugnō*

fill, fill up, *compleō*

finally, *tandem*

find, *inveniō, reperiō;* be found, *nāscor;* find out, *cognōscō*

fine, *pulcher*

finish, *cōnficiō, perficiō*

fire, *ignis;* with fire and sword, *ferrō et igne;* set on fire, *incendō*

first, *prīmus;* at first, *prīmō;* for the first time, *prīmum;* when first, *cum prīmum*

five, *quīnque*

flank, *latus*

flee, flee from, *fugiō*

fleet, *classis*

flight, *fuga*

flower, *flōs*

fly, *volō*

follow, *sequor*

following, *posterus*

food, *cibus*

foot, *pēs;* at or to the foot of, *sub*

footsoldier, *pedes*

for, (conjunction) *enim, nam;* (preposition) *ad, in, prō;* in exchange for, *prō;* for a long time, *diū;* for the first time, *prīmum;* for the sake of, *causā, grātiā;* for which reason, *quā dē causā;* be eager for, *studeō;* grieve for, *doleō;* prepare for, *parō;* provide for, *prōvideō;* take counsel for, *cōnsulō;* wait for, *exspectō*

forage, *rēs frūmentaria*

force, *vīs;* forces, *cōpiae*

forceful, *vehemēns*

ford, *vadum*

foreign, *aliēnus, barbarus*

foremost, *prīmus*

foresee, *prōvideō*

foresighted, *prūdēns*

forest, *silva*

form a plan, *consilium capiō*

former, *antīquus, prior;* the former, *ille*

formerly, *ōlim*

forth: bring forth, *prōdūcō;* go forth, *prōgredior;* put forth, *prōpōnō;* set forth, *expōnō, prōpōnō*

fortification, *mūnītiō*

fortify, *mūniō*

fortunately, *fēlīciter*

fortune, *fortūna*

forum, *forum*

forward: go forward, *prōgredior;* lead forward, *prōdūcō*

founder, *auctor*

four, *quattuor*

fourteen, *quattuordecim*

fourth, *quārtus*

frankly, *līberē*

free, (adjective) *līber;* (verb) *līberō;* set free, *līberō, solvō*

freedom, *lībertās*

freely, *līberē*

fresh, *recēns*

friend, *amīcus;* my friends, your friends, etc., *meī, tuī,* etc.

friendly, *amīcus*

friendship, *amīcitia*

frighten, *terreō*

from, *ā, ab, dē, ē, ex* away from, *ā, ab;* down from, *dē;* from all sides, from everywhere, *undique;* from here, *inde;*

from where, from which, where from, *unde;* **flee from,** *fugiō;* **keep . . . from . . . ,** *prohibeō;* **order . . . from . . . ,** *imperō*
front: in front of, *ante, prō*

G

gain, *cōnsequor*
Gallic, *Gallus*
game, *lūdus*
garden, *hortus*
garrison, *praesidium*
gate, *porta*
gather, *legō*
Gaul, *Gallia, Gallus*
general, (noun) *imperātor;* (adjective) *commūnis*
German, *Germānus*
Germany, *Germānia*
get, *comparō;* **get possession of,** *potior*
gift, *dōnum*
girl, *puella*
give, *dō;* **give back,** *reddō;* **give ground,** *pedem referō;* **give way,** *cēdō*
glad, *laetus*
gladness, *gaudium*
glory, *glōria*
go, *eō, mē (tē, sē, etc.) cōnferō;* **let go,** *mittō;* **go aboard,** *cōnscendō;* **go away,** *discēdō;* **let go away,** *dīmittō;* **go back,** *redeō, pedem referō, revertor;* **let go back,** *remittō;* **go forth, go forward,** *prōgredior;* **go out,** *ēgredior, excēdō, exeō;* **go to,** *accēdō;* **go toward,** *adeō*
god, *deus*
goddess, *dea*
gold, *aurum;* **of gold,** *aureus*
golden, *aureus*
good, *bonus*
goodbye, *valē, valēte*
government, *imperium*
grain, *frūmentum;* **having to do with grain,** *frūmentārius;* **grain supply,** *rēs frūmentāria*
grant, *tribuō*
grass, *herba*

grateful, *grātus*
gratitude, *grātia;* **feel gratitude,** *grātiam habeō;* **show gratitude,** *grātiam referō*
great, *magnus;* **how great,** *quantus;* **so great, such a great,** *tantus;* **rather great, too great,** *maior;* **very great,** *maximus;* **great number,** *multitūdō*
greater, *maior;* **the greater part,** *magna pārs*
greatest, *maximus*
greatly, *magnopere;* **more greatly,** *magis;* **most greatly,** *maximē*
greatness, *magnitūdō*
Greece, *Graecia*
Greek, *Graecus*
grief, *dolor*
grieve, grieve for, *doleō*
grim, *trīstis*
ground: give ground, *pedem referō*
group, *numerus*
grow, *crēscō*
guard, (noun) *custōs, praesidium;* (verb) *servō, dēfendō*
guest, *hospes*

H

habit, *cōnsuētūdō, mōs*
had, see **have**
halfway up a (the) mountain, *in mediō monte*
halt, *cōnsistō*
hand, *manus;* **hand down, hand over,** *trādō*
handicapped, *impedītus*
happen: it happens, *accidit, fit*
happily, *fēlīciter*
happy, *fēlīx, laetus*
harbor, *portus*
hard, *dūrus;* **be hard pressed,** *labōrō*
hardly, *aegrē, vix*
hardship, *labor*
harm, *noceō*
harsh, *dūrus*
has, see **have**
hasten, *contendō*
have, *habeō* **have to,** *dēbeō*
having, see **have**

he, *hic, ille, is;* he who, *quī*
head, *caput;* be at the head of, *praesum*
hear, *audiō*
heavy, *gravis*
height, *altitūdō*
help, (noun) *auxilium;* (verb) *iūvō*
Helvetia, *Helvētia*
Helvetian, of the Helvetians, *Helvētius*
hence, *inde*
her, see she; for possession, see also *suus*
here, *hīc, hūc;* from here, *inde;* this . . .
  here, *hic*
hero, *vir*
hesitate, *dubitō*
herself, *ipsa, suī (see Lesson 40)*
high, *altus;* on high, *altē;* of high birth,
  nōbilis
higher, *altior, superior*
highest, *altissimus, summus*
hill, *collis, mōns*
him, see he
himself, *ipse, suī (see Lesson 40)*
hinder, *impediō*
hindered, *impedītus*
hindrance, *impedīmentum*
his, see he; for possession, see also *suus*
hold, *habeō, obtineō, teneō;* hold back, *re-*
  tineō; hold in check, hold up, *sustineō;*
  hold together, *contineō*
holy, *sacer*
home, *domus;* at home, go home, etc., see
  Special Place Constructions, Lesson 50
hope, (noun) *spēs;* (verb) *spērō*
horn, *cornū*
horse, *equus*
horseman, *eques*
host, *hospes*
hostage, *obses*
hostile, *inimīcus*
hot, *calidus*
hour, *hōra*
house, *aedēs, domus;* at the house of, *apud;*
  country house, *vīlla*
how, *quam, quemadmodum, quōmodo, ut;*
  how great, how large, how much,
  quantus; how many, *quot*
however, *autem*
human being, *homō*

hundred, one hundred, *centum*
hurl, *coniciō*
husband, *vir*

I

I, *ego*
if, *sī;* if . . . not, *nisi*
immediately, *statim*
immortal, *immortālis*
in, *in;* in all, *omnīnō;* in back, in the rear,
  ā tergō; in difficulty, *impedītus;* in exchange for, *prō;* in front of, *ante, prō;*
  in like manner, *similiter;* in such a way,
  ita; in that place, *ibi;* in the presence
  of, *apud;* in this way, *sīc;* in truth, *vērō;*
  in vain, *frūstrā*
increase, *augeō, crēscō*
indeed, *quidem, vērō*
infantry, *peditēs* (from *pedes*)
inflict, *īnferō*
influence, (noun) *auctōritās, grātia;* (verb)
  addūcō
inform, *certiōrem (certiōrēs) faciō, doceō,*
  moneō; be informed, *certior fīō*
inhabit, *incolō*
injure, *noceō*
injustice, *iniūria*
inmost, *intimus*
inner, *interior*
inquire, *quaerō*
instead of, *prō*
instruct, *mandō*
intend: intending to, see Participles, Lesson 41
interest: consult the interests of, *cōnsulō*
interrupt, *intermittō*
interval, *spatium*
into, *in;* put into effect, *efficiō;* throw into
  confusion, *perturbō*
iron, *ferrum*
is, see be
island, *īnsula*
it, *hoc, id, illud;* it happens, *accidit, fit;* it
  is convenient, *convenit;* it is necessary
  or proper, *oportet;* it is permitted, *licet*

Italy, *Ītalia*
its, *eius, suus*
itself, *ipsum, suī* (see Lesson 40)

J

javelin, *pīlum*
join, *coniungō;* **join battle,** *proelium committō;* **join together,** *coniungō*
journey, *iter*
joy, *gaudium*
joyful, *laetus*
judge, (noun) *iūdex;* (verb) *iūdicō*
judgment, *iūdicium*
Julia, *Iūlia*
Julius, *Iūlius*
juror, *iūdex*
just, *aequus, iūstus*
justice, *iūs*

K

keep, *cōnservō, servō;* **keep . . . from,** *prohibeō*
kill, *caedō, interficiō, occīdō*
kind, *genus;* **of such a kind,** *tālis*
kindness, *beneficium*
king, *rēx*
kingdom, kingship, *rēgnum*
kinsman, *propinquus*
knight, *eques*
know, *sciō, cognōvī* (from *cognōscō*); **not know,** *nesciō*

L

labor, *labōrō*
lack, *inopia*
lacking: **be lacking,** *dēsum*
land, *terra;* **native land,** *patria*
language, *lingua*
large, *amplus, magnus;* **how large,** *quantus;* **rather large, too large,** *maior;* **so large, such a large,** *tantus;* **very large,** *maximus*

larger, *maior;* **a larger amount,** *plūs*
largest, *maximus*
last, *extrēmus, novissimus;* **at last,** *tandem*
late: **late at night,** *multā nocte;* **late in the day,** *multō diē*
latest, *novissimus*
latter: **the latter,** *hic*
laugh, **laugh at,** *rideō*
launch, *dēdūcō*
law, *iūs, lēx*
lay waste, *vāstō*
lead, *dūcō;* **lead across,** *trādūcō;* **lead away,** *dēdūcō;* **lead back,** *redūcō;* **lead down,** *dēdūcō;* **lead forward,** *prōdūcō,* **lead to,** *addūcō*
leader, *dux*
learn, *cognōscō, discō*
least: **at least,** *quidem*
leave, *discēdō, excēdō, relinquō;* **leave behind,** *relinquō;* **leave off,** *dēsistō*
left, *reliquus, sinister;* **left-hand,** *sinister;* **on the left,** *ā sinistrā*
legion, *legiō*
length: **at length,** *tandem*
less, (adjective) *minor;* (adverb) *minus*
lest, *nē*
let, see Hortatory Subjunctive, Lesson 43; **let go,** *mittō;* **let go away,** *dīmittō;* **let go back,** *remittō*
letter, *littera, litterae, epistula*
level, *aequus*
liberty, *lībertās*
lie, *iaceō*
lieutenant, *lēgātus*
life, *vīta*
lift up, *tollō*
light, (noun) *lūx;* (adjective) *levis*
like, (adjective) *aequus, similis;* **in like manner,** *similiter;* (verb) *amō*
likewise, *item*
line: **straight line, line of battle,** *aciēs;* **line of march,** *agmen*
listen to, *audiō*
little, (noun) *paulum;* (adjective) *parvus;* (adverb) *paulō, paulum*
live, *habitō, incolō, vīvō;* **live in,** *incolō*
loaf, *pānis*
long, (adjective) *longus;* **for a long time,**

diū; (adverb) *diū* **longer,** (adverb) *diūtius, iam;* **for a longer time,** *diūtius* **longest: for the longest time,** *diutissimē*

look: look at, *spectō;* **look at attentively,** *cōnspiciō*

loose, *solvō*

lord, *dominus*

lose, *āmittō*

loud, *magnus*

love, *amō*

lower, *īnferior*

lowest, *īmus, īnfimus*

loyal, *fidēlis*

loyalty, *fidēs*

Lucius, *Lūcius*

luck, *fortūna*

lucky, *fēlīx*

M

magistracy, *magistrātus*

magistrate, *magistrātus*

majority, *magna pars*

make, *faciō;* **be made,** *fīō;* **make a mistake,** *errō;* **make a plan,** *cōnsilium capiō;* **make war upon,** *bellum īnferō*

man, *homō, vir;* **our men,** *nostrī;* **young men,** *adulēscēns*

manliness, *virtūs*

manner, *modus, ratiō;* **in like manner,** *similiter*

many, *multī;* **how many,** *quot;* **rather many,** *plūrēs;* **so many,** *tot;* **too many,** *plūrēs;* **very many,** *plūrimī;* **many people,** *multī*

march, (noun) *iter;* **army on the march, line of march,** *agmen;* (verb) *iter faciō*

marketplace, *forum*

marsh, *palūs*

master, *dominus, magister*

matter, *rēs;* **as a matter of fact,** *quidem*

me, see **I**

means: by means of, see Ablative of Means or Instrument, Lesson 9

measure, *modus*

meet, *congredior, conveniō*

memory, *memoria*

merchant, *mercātor*

message, *nūntius*

messenger, *nūntius*

midday, *merīdiēs*

middle of, *medius*

midnight, *media nox*

mile, *mille passūs*

military, *mīlitāris;* **military power,** *imperium;* **military standard,** *signum*

mind, *animus, mēns*

mine, *meus*

misfortune, *calamitās*

missile, *tēlum*

mistake: make a mistake, *errō*

mock, *lūdō*

money, *pecūnia*

month, *mēnsis*

moon, *lūna*

more, (noun) *plūs;* (adjective) *plūrēs;* (adverb) *magis,* and see also Comparison, Lessons 33–36; **more often,** *saepius;* **wish . . . more,** *mālō*

moreover, *autem*

most, (adjective) *plūrimus;* (adverb) *maximē,* and see also Comparison, Lessons 33–36; **most often,** *saepissimē*

mother, *māter*

mountain, *mōns;* **halfway up the mountain,** *in mediō monte*

mouth, *ōs*

move, *cēdō, moveō;* **move back,** *removeō;* **move deeply,** *permoveō;* **move thoroughly,** *commoveō*

much, (adjective) *magnus, multus;* **how much,** *quantus;* **so much,** *tantus;* (adverb) *multō, multum*

murder, *caedēs*

must, see Passive Periphrastic, Lessons 59 and 60

my, *meus*

myself, *ipse, meī* (see Lesson 40)

N

name, (noun) *nōmen;* (verb) *appellō*

nation, *gēns, populus*

native land, *patria*

nature, *nātūra*

near, *ad, prope, propinquus;* **be near,** *adsum;* **draw near,** *appropinquō*

nearby, *propinquus*

nearer, *propior*

nearest, *proximus*

nearly, *ferē, prope*

necessary, *necesse, necessārius;* **it is necessary,** *necesse est, oportet*

neighbor, *fīnitimus*

neighboring, *fīnitimus*

neither, (adjective) *neuter;* (conjunction) *neque (nec);* **neither . . . nor,** *neque (nec) . . . neque (nec)*

never, *numquam, nē . . . umquam*

nevertheless, *tamen*

new, *novus, recēns*

next, (adjective) *posterus, proximus;* (adverb) *deinde*

night, *nox;* **early in the night,** *prīmā nocte;* **late at night,** *multā nocte*

nine, *novem*

nineteen, *ūndēvīgintī*

ninth, *nōnus*

no, *nūllus, nihil;* **no one,** *nēmō, nē quis*

noble, *nōbilis, pulcher*

nobly, *pulchrē*

noise, *clāmor*

noon, *merīdiēs*

nor, *neque (nec)*

not, *nōn;* **and . . . not,** *neque (nec);* **if . . . not,** *nisi;* **or not,** *annōn, necne;* **not any,** *nūllus;* **not at all,** *nihil;* **not even,** *nē . . . quidem;* **not only . . . but also,** *nōn sōlum . . . sed etiam;* **not yet,** *nōndum;* **not know,** *nesciō;* **say . . . not,** *negō;* **not wish,** *nōlō*

nothing, *nihil, nē quid* (see Lesson 58)

now, *iam, nunc*

number, *numerus;* **great number,** *multitūdō*

O

oar, *rēmus*

obey, *pareō*

obligation: be under an obligation, *grātiam dēbeō*

observe closely, *cōnspiciō*

obtain, *cōnsequor*

of, *dē, ē, ex;* see also Genitive of Possession, Lesson 18

off: far off, *longē;* **leave off,** *dēsistō*

offensive weapon, *tēlum*

office: public office, *magistrātus*

often, *saepe;* **more often, rather often,** *saepius;* **most often,** *saepissimē*

old, *antīquus, senex, vetus;* **of old, old fashioned,** *antīquus*

older, *maior nātū, senior*

oldest, *maximus nātū*

on, *in;* see also Ablative of Time When, Lesson 25

once: once upon a time, *ōlim;* **at once,** *statim*

one, *alius, quīdam, ūnus;* **one another, to one another, with one another,** *inter sē (nōs, vōs);* **one hundred,** *centum;* **one thousand,** *mīlle;* **no one,** *nēmō, nē quis* (see Lesson 58); **the one,** *alter*

oneself: betake oneself, *mē (tē, sē, etc.) cōnferō*

only, *sōlus;* **not only . . . but also,** *nōn sōlum . . . sed etiam*

onrush, *impetus*

onto, *in*

onward: carry onward, *īnferō*

open, (adjective) *apertus;* (verb) *aperiō*

opinion, *opīniō, sententia*

opportunity, *facultās*

or, *an, aut, vel;* **or not,** *annōn, necne;* **either . . . or,** *aut . . . aut, vel . . . vel;* **whether . . . or,** *utrum . . . an*

order, (noun) *ordō;* **in order that, in order to,** see Adverbial Clause of Purpose, Lesson 44; (verb) *imperō, iubeō*

originator, *auctor*

other, *alius;* **each other, to each other, with each other,** *inter sē (nōs, vōs);* **the other,** *alter;* **the other(s),** *cēterī*

ought, *dēbeō;* see also Passive Periphastic, Lessons 59 and 60

our, ours, *noster;* **our men,** *nostrī*

ourselves, *ipsī, nostrum* (see Lesson 40)

out: out of, *ē, ex;* **way out,** *exitus;* **drive out,** *expellō;* **find out,** *cognōscō;* **go out,** *ēgredior, excēdō, exeō;* **point out,** *dēmōn-*

strō; **search out,** *explōrō;* **set out,** *prōficīscor*
outcome, *exitus*
outer, *exterior*
outermost, *extrēmus*
outstanding, *ēgregius*
over, *in, trāns;* **hand over,** *trādō;* **place over,** *praeficiō*
overpower, *opprimō, premō*
overtake, *cōnsequor*
owe, *dēbeō*
own: his own, her own, its own, their own, *suus;* **my own,** *meus;* **our own,** *noster;* **your own,** *tuus, vester*
owner, *dominus*

P

pace, *passus*
pain, *dolor*
part, *pars;* **greater part,** *magna pars*
pause, *intermittō*
pay, *solvō;* **pay the penalty,** *poenam dō*
peace, *pāx*
penalty, *poena;* **pay the penalty,** *poenam dō*
people, *populus;* **good people, many people,** etc., *bonī, multī,* etc. (see Adjectives as Substantives, Lesson 6); **the common people,** *plēbs;* **belonging to the people,** *pūblicus*
permit, *patior, permittō;* **it is permitted,** *licet*
persuade, *persuadeō*
pertain, *pertineō*
pile up, *īnstruō*
pitch camp, *castra pōnō*
place, (noun) *locus;* **at one's country place,** *rūrī* (from *rūs*); **in that place,** *ibi;* **to this place,** *hūc;* **to that place,** *eō, illūc;* **to what place,** *quō;* (verb) *pōnō;* **place in command of, place over,** *praeficiō*
plain, *campus*
plan, *cōnsilium, ratiō;* **adopt a plan,** *cōnsilium ineō;* **form or make a plan,** *cōnsilium capiō*

play, *lūdō*
please, *dēlectō, placeō*
pleasing, *grātus*
pledge, *fidēs*
plenty, *cōpia*
plot, *īnsidiae*
poem, *carmen*
poet, *poēta*
point out, *dēmōnstrō*
poor, *miser*
port, *portus*
possession: get or take possession of, *potior*
possible: as . . . as possible, *quam* with superlative, Lesson 36; **as soon as possible,** *quam prīmum*
posterity, *posterī*
power, *potestās;* **military power,** *imperium*
powerful, *potēns*
powerfully, *potenter*
practice, *ūsus*
practise, *exerceō*
praise, (noun) *laus;* (verb) *laudō*
prefer, *mālō*
prepare, *comparō, parō;* **prepare for,** *parō*
prepared, *parātus*
presence: in the presence of, *apud*
present: be present, *adsum*
press, *premō;* **be hard pressed,** *labōrō*
prestige, *auctōritās*
prevent, *prohibeō*
private, *prīvātus*
proceed, *mē (tē, sē,* etc.) *cōnferō*
profitable, *ūtilis*
promise, *polliceor*
proper: it is proper, *oportet*
propose, *prōpōnō*
protection, *praesidium;* **under the protection,** *in fidē, infidem*
prove, *probō*
provide for, *prōvideō*
province, *prōvincia*
prudent, *prūdēns*
public, *pūblicus;* **public office,** *magistrātus*
punish, *poenam sūmō dē;* **be punished,** *poenam dō*
punishment, *poena*
pursue, *cōnsequor*

push, *pellō*

put, *pōnō;* **put forth,** *prōpōnō;* **put in charge of, put in command of,** *praeficiō;* **put into effect,** *efficiō*

Q

quarters: winter quarters, *hīberna*
queen, *rēgīna*
quite a few, *complūrēs*

R

race, *genus*
raise, *tollō*
rampart, *vallum*
rank, *ordō*
rashly, *audācter*
rate: at any rate, *quidem*
rather, see Comparison, Lessons 33–36: **rather large,** *maior;* **rather many,** *plūrēs;* **rather often,** *saepius;* **rather small,** *minor;* **wish . . . rather,** *mālō*
reach, *perveniō*
read, *legō*
ready, *parātus*
realize, *sentiō*
rear, *novissimum agmen;* **in the rear,** *ā tergō*
reason, *causa, ratiō;* **for which reason,** *quā dē causā*
receive, *accipiō, recipiō*
recent, *recēns*
reconnoiter, *explōrō*
region, *regiō*
reinforcements, *auxilia*
relate, *ferō, narrō*
relation, relative, *necessārius, propinquus*
remain, *maneō*
remaining, *reliquus*
remember, *memorā teneō*
remove, *tollō*
repair, *reficiō*
reply, *respondeō*

report, (noun) *fāma;* (verb) *adferō, dēferō, ēnūntiō, nūntiō, referō, renūntiō*
republic, *rēs pūblica*
repulse, *reiciō*
reputation, *fāma, opīniō*
rescue, *ēripiō*
resist, *resistō*
rest, *quiēs;* **the rest of,** *cēterī, reliquus*
restore, *reddō, reficiō*
restrain, *contineō*
retreat, *mē (tē, sē,* etc.) *recipiō, pedem referō*
return, *mē (tē, sē,* etc.) *recipiō, redeō, pedem referō, revertor*
revolt, *dēficiō*
revolution, *rēs novae*
reward, *praemium*
Rhine, *Rhēnus*
ride, *vehor*
right, (noun) *iūs;* (adjective) *dexter, iūstus;* **on the right,** *ā dextrā*
right-hand, *dexter*
rise, *orior, surgō*
risk, *perīculum*
river, *flūmen*
road, *via*
rock, *saxum*
Roman, *Rōmānus*
Rome, *Rōma;* **of Rome,** *Rōmānus*
rout, *pellō*
route, *iter*
rule, *regō*
rumor, *fāma, rūmor*
run, *currō*
running: a running, *cursus*

S

sacred, *sacer*
sad, *trīstis*
safe, *tūtus*
safety, *salūs*
sail, *nāvigō, vehor*
sailor, *nauta*
sake: for the sake, *causā, grātiā*
same, *īdem;* **at the same time,** *simul*
Sardis, *Sardēs*

savage, *ferus*
save, *cōnservō, servō*
say, *dīcō, inquam;* **say . . . not,** *negō*
scarcely, *aegrē, vix*
school, *lūdus*
scout, *explōrātor*
sea, *mare;* **of the sea,** *maritimus*
search out, *explōrō*
seat, *sella*
second, *alter, secundus*
see, *videō*
seek, *petō, quaerō*
seem, *videor*
seize, *occupō, rapiō*
sell, *vēndō*
senate, *senātus*
senator, *senātor*
send, *mittō;* **send away,** *dīmittō;* **send back,** *remittō*
serious, *gravis*
set: **set forth,** *expōnō, prōpōnō;* **set free,** *līberō, solvō;* **set on fire,** *incendō;* **set out,** *prōficīscor;* **set up,** *cōnstituō, īnstituō*
setting, *occāsus*
settle, *cōnsīdō*
seven, *septem*
seventeen, *septendecim*
seventh, *septimus*
several, *complūrēs*
severe, *gravis*
severely, *graviter*
shallows, *vadum*
sharp, *ācer*
sharply, *ācriter*
she, *ea* (from *is*), *haec, illa*
shield, *scūtum*
ship, *nāvis;* **war ship,** *nāvis longa*
shore, *lītus*
short, *brevis*
shout, (noun) *clāmor;* (verb) *clāmō*
show, *dēmōnstrō, doceō, ostendō;* **show gratitude,** *grātiam referō*
shut, *claudō*
Sicily, *Sicilia*
sick, *aeger*
side, *latus;* **from** or **on all sides,** *undique*
sight, *speciēs*
sign, *signum*

signal, *signum*
silent: **be silent,** *taceō*
similar, *similis*
similarly, *similiter*
since, *cum*
sister, *soror*
sit, *sedeō;* **sit down,** *cōnsīdō*
six, *sex*
sixteen, *sēdecim*
sixth, *sextus*
size, *magnitūdō*
sky, *caelum*
slaughter, *caedēs*
slave, *servus*
sleep, (noun) *quiēs;* (verb) *dormiō*
small, *parvus;* **rather small, too small,** *minor;* **very small,** *minimus*
smaller, *minor*
smallest, *minimus*
smile, *rideō*
snatch, *rapiō*
so, *ita, sīc, tam;* **so great, so large, so much,** *tantus;* **so many,** *tot*
soldier, *mīles*
some, *aliquī, quīdam;* **some . . . others,** *aliī . . . aliī;* **some day,** *ōlim;* **at some distance,** *procul*
someone, *aliquis*
something, *aliquid*
son, *fīlius*
song, *carmen*
soon, *mox;* **as soon as,** *cum prīmum, simul atque* (ac); **as soon as possible,** *quam prīmum*
sorrow, *dolor*
sorry: **be sorry,** *doleō*
sort, *genus*
south, *merīdiēs*
space, *spatium*
Spain, *Hispānia*
Spanish, *Hispānus*
spare, *parcō*
speak, *loquor*
speech, *ōrātiō;* **deliver a speech,** *ōrātiōnem habeō*
speed, *celeritās*
spend the winter, *hiemō*
spirit, *animus*

sponsor, *auctor*
stand, *stō;* **stand up,** *surgō;* **take a stand,** *cōnsistō*
standard: military standard, *signum*
star, *stella*
state, *cīvitās, rēs pūblica*
stay, *maneō*
still, *tamen*
stir up, *incitō*
stone, *lapis, saxum*
stop, *dēsistō, intermittō*
storm, *tempestās*
story, *fābula*
straight line, *aciēs*
strange, *barbarus, mīrus*
stranger, *hospes*
street, *via*
strength, *vīrēs* (from *vīs*)
strengthen, *augeō, cōnfirmō*
strive, *contendō*
strong, *validus;* **be strong,** *valeō*
strongly, *validē*
struggle, *contendō*
successfully, *fēlīciter*
such, *tālis;* **such a great, such a large,** *tantus;* **in such a way,** *ita;* **of such a kind,** *tālis*
suddenly, *repente, subitō*
suffer, *labōrō, patior*
suffering, *dolor*
suitable, *idōneus*
summer, *aestās;* **at the beginning of summer,** *prīmā aestāte*
summon, *convocō*
sun, *sōl*
sundown, sunset, *sōlis occāsus*
supply, *cōpia;* **grain supply,** *rēs frūmentāria*
support, *subsidium*
suppose, *exīstimō*
sure, *certus;* **to be sure,** *quidem*
surely, *certē*
surpass, *superō*
surprised: be surprised, *mīror*
surrender, *trādō*
surround, *circumveniō*
swamp, *palūs*
swift, *celer*

swiftly, *celeriter*
swiftness, *celeritās*
sword, *ferrum, gladius;* **with fire and sword,** *ferrō et igne*

T

table, *mēnsa*
take, *capiō;* **take a stand,** *cōnsistō;* **take back,** *recipiō;* **take counsel for,** *cōnsulō;* **take possession of,** *potior*
talk, *loquor*
task, *negōtium*
teach, *doceō*
teacher, *magister*
tear, *lacrima*
tell, *dīcō, narrō*
temple, *aedēs*
ten, *decem*
tenth, *decimus*
terms, *condiciō*
terrify, *perterreō*
territory, *ager, fīnēs*
than, *quam;* see also Ablative of Comparison, Lesson 33
thank, *grātiās agō*
that, (demonstrative pronoun and adjective) *ille, is;* **that . . . there,** *ille;* **that which,** *quod;* **at that time,** *tum;* **in that place,** *ibi;* **to that place,** *eō, illūc*
their, theirs, *eōrum* (from *is*), *hōrum, illōrum, suus*
them, see **they**
themselves, *ipsī, suī* (see Lesson 40)
then, *deinde, ergō, tum*
there, *eō, ibi, illūc;* **there is, there are,** etc., *est, sunt,* etc.; **that . . . there,** *ille*
therefore, *ergō, itaque*
they, *eī* (from *is*), *hī, illī*
thing, *rēs*
think, *arbitror, exīstimō, putō*
third, *tertius*
thirteen, *tredecim*
this, *hic, is;* **this . . . here,** *hic;* **in this way,** *sīc;* **to this place,** *hūc*
thoroughly: move thoroughly, *commoveō*

thousand, *mīlle;* **thousands,** *mīlia*

three, *trēs*

through, *per*

throw, *iaciō;* **throw back,** *reiciō;* **throw into confusion,** *perturbō;* **throw together,** *coniciō*

thus, *ita*

time, *tempus;* **at that time,** *tum;* **at the same time,** *simul;* **for a long time,** *diū;* **for a longer time,** *diūtius;* **for the first time,** *prīmum;* **for the longest time,** *diūtissimē;* **once upon a time,** *ōlim*

tired, *dēfessus*

to, *ad;* **to be sure,** *quidem;* **to each other,** *inter sē;* **to that place,** *eō, illūc;* **to the foot of,** *sub;* **to this place,** *hūc;* **to what place, to which place,** *quō*

today, *hodiē*

toga, *toga*

together: bring together, *cōnferō;* **call together,** *convocō;* **come together,** *congredior, conveniō;* **hold together,** *contineō;* **join together,** *coniungō;* **throw together,** *coniciō*

tomorrow, *crās*

tongue, *lingua*

tonight, *hāc nocte*

too, *nimis, quoque;* **see also Comparison, Lessons 33–36; too big, too great, too large,** *maior;* **too many,** *plūrēs;* **too small,** *minor*

top: on top of, *summus*

touch, *tangō*

toward, towards, *ad, in;* **go toward,** *adeō*

tower, *turris*

town, *oppidum*

trader, *mercātor*

train, *exerceō*

transport, *vehō*

trap, *īnsidiae*

tree, *arbor*

trial, *iūdicium*

tribe, *populus*

tribune, *tribūnus*

Trojan, *Trōiānus*

troops, *cōpiae;* **auxiliary troops,** *auxilia*

trouble, *negōtium*

Troy, *Trōia*

true, *vērus*

trumpet, *tuba*

trust, *cōnfīdō, crēdō*

truth: in truth, *vērō*

try, *cōnor, temptō*

turn, *vertō*

twelve, *duodecim*

twenty, *vīgintī*

twice, *bis*

two, *duo*

U

ugly, *turpis*

unable: be unable, *nōn possum*

under, *sub;* **under the protection,** *in fidem, in fidē;* **be under an obligation,** *grātiās dēbeō*

understand, *intellegō*

undertake, *suscipiō*

undiminished, *integer*

uneven, *inīquus*

unfair, *inīquus*

unfavorable, *inīquus*

unfortunate, *miser*

unfriendly, *inimīcus*

unhappy, *miser*

unite, *coniungō*

unless, *nisi*

unlike, *dissimilis*

untie, *solvō*

untouched, *integer*

unwilling: be unwilling, *nōlō*

up: up to, *sub;* **halfway up the mountain,** *in mediō monte;* **bring up,** *adferō;* **climb up,** *ascendō;* **draw up,** *īnstruō;* **fill up,** *compleō;* **hold up,** *sustineō;* **lift up,** *tollō;* **pile up,** *īnstruō;* **set up,** *cōnstituō, īnstituō;* **stand up,** *surgō;* **stir up,** *incitō*

upon: bring upon, *īnferō;* **come upon,** *inveniō;* **fall upon,** *accidō;* **make war upon,** *bellum īnferō;* **once upon a time,** *ōlim*

upset, *commoveō, perturbō*

urge, *hortor*

us, see **we**

use, (noun) *ūsus;* (verb) *ūtor*

useful, *ūtilis*

V

vain: in vain, *frūstrā*
valley, *vallēs*
van, *prīmum agmen*
Veii, *Veiī*
very, see Comparison, Lessons 33–36;
   very big, very great, very large, *maximus;* **very many,** *plūrimī;* **very small,**
   minimus
victor, *victor*
victory, *victōria*
villa, *vīlla*
violence, *vīs*
violent, *vehemēns*
voice, *vōx*

W

wage, *gerō*
wagon, *carrus*
wait for, *exspectō*
wakefulness, *vigilia*
walk, *ambulō*
wall, *mūrus*
wander, *errō*
want, (noun) *inopia;* (verb) *cupiō*
war, *bellum;* **warship,** *nāvis longa;* **make**
   war (on), *bellum īnferō;* **wage war,** *bellum gerō*
warn, *moneō*
warship, *nāvis longa*
was, see **be**
wash, *lavō*
waste: lay waste, *vāstō*
watch, (noun) *vigilia;* (verb) *spectō*
watchfulness, *vigilia*
water, *aqua*
wave, *fluctus*
way, *modus, via;* **way out,** *exitus;* **in such**
   a way, *ita;* **in this way,** *sīc;* **give way,**
   cēdō
we, *nōs*
weapon, *tēlum;* **weapons,** *arma, ferrum,*
   tēla; **offensive weapon,** *tēlum*
wear, *gerō*
weather, *tempestās*

welcome, *grātus*
welfare, *salūs*
well, *bene;* **well bred,** *nōbilis;* **well known,**
   nōtus; **be well,** *valeō*
were, see **be**
west, *sōlis occāsus*
what, *quī, quid* (from *quis*); **to what degree,** *quem ad modum;* **to what place,**
   quō
wheel, *orbis*
when, *cum, ubi, ut;* **when first,** *cum*
   prīmum
whence, *unde*
where, *quo, ubi;* **from where, where from,**
   unde
whether, *num, utrum*
which, *quī, uter*
who, *quī, quis*
whole, *integer, tōtus*
why, *cūr*
wide, *lātus;* **far and wide,** *longē lātēque*
widely, *lātē*
width, *lātitūdō*
wife, *fēmina, mulier, uxor*
wild, *ferus*
willing: be willing, *volō*
willingness, *voluntās*
win, *vincō*
wind, *ventus*
window, *fenestra*
wine, *vīnum*
wing (of an army) *cornū*
winter, (noun) *hiems;* **winter quarters,**
   hīberna; (verb) *hiemō* **spend the winter,**
   hiemō
wise, *prūdēns*
wish, (noun) *voluntās;* (verb) *cupiō, volō;*
   wish . . . more, wish . . . rather, *mālō;*
   not wish, *nōlō*
with, *cum;* see also Ablative of Means or
   Instrument, Lesson 9, Ablative Absolute, Lesson 51; **with difficulty,** *aegrē,*
   vix; **with each other, with one another,**
   inter sē (nōs, vōs)
within, see Ablative of Time Within
   Which, Lesson 25
without, *sine*
withstand, *sustineō*

woman, *fēmina, mulier*
wonder, wonder at, *mīror*
wonderful, *mīrus*
woods, *silva*
word, *verbum;* **bring back word of,** *renūntiō*
work, (noun) *labor, opus;* (verb) *labōrō*
world, *orbis terrārum, tellus*
worn out, *dēfessus*
worse, (adjective) *peior;* (adverb) *peius*
worst, (adjective) *pessimus;* (adverb) *pessimē*
wound, (noun) *vulnus;* (verb) *vulnerō*
wretched, *miser*
wretchedly, *miserē*
write, *scrībō*
wrong, *iniūria*

Y

year, *annus*
yesterday, *herī*
yet, *tamen;* **not yet,** *nōndum*
yield, *cēdō*
you, *tū, vōs*
young man, *adulēscēns*
your, yours, *tuus, vester*
yourself, *ipse, tuī* (see Lesson 40); **yourselves,** *ipsī, vestrum* (see Lesson 40)
youth, *adulēscēns*

Z

zeal, *studium*

Acknowledgments

i   BBC Copyright Photograph

ii–iii   BBC Copyright Photograph

xii   SCALA/Editorial Photocolor Archives

1   SCALA/Editorial Photocolor Archives

3   SCALA/Editorial Photocolor Archives

4   Fototeca Unione

5   *Pompeii and Herculaneum: The Glory and the Grief* by Marcel Brion. Published by Paul Elek. Merrimack Book Service, Inc.

8   SCALA/Editorial Photocolor Archives

10   Museo della Civiltà Romana

11   Museo della Civiltà Romana

12   Gaetano Barone

13   The Metropolitan Museum of Art, New York

14   SCALA/Editorial Photocolor Archives

17   (*top*)   Alinari/Scala

17   (*bottom*)   Fototeca Unione

19   Alinari/Scala

21   (*two on left*)   Reproduced by Courtesy of the Trustees of the British Museum

21   (*middle*)   Alinari/Scala

21   (*right*)   Alinari/Scala

23   Alinari/Scala

25   (*both*)   Alinari/Scala

27   Deutschen Archaeologischen Instituts

29   Giraudon

31   Deutschen Archaeologischen Instituts

32   Alinari/Scala

35   Alinari/Scala

37   Alinari/Scala

39   Fototeca Unione

41   Fototeca Unione

42   Alinari/Scala

44–45   Alinari/Scala

48   Fototeca Unione

51   SCALA/Editorial Photocolor Archives

52   Alinari/Scala

55   SCALA/Editorial Photocolor Archives

57   SCALA/Editorial Photocolor Archives

59   SCALA/Editorial Photocolor Archives

61   SCALA/Editorial Photocolor Archives

63   Alinari/Scala

65   Alinari/Scala

72   Alinari/Scala

75   (*both*)   Fototeca Unione

77   Alinari/Scala

A Renaissance map of ancient Rome

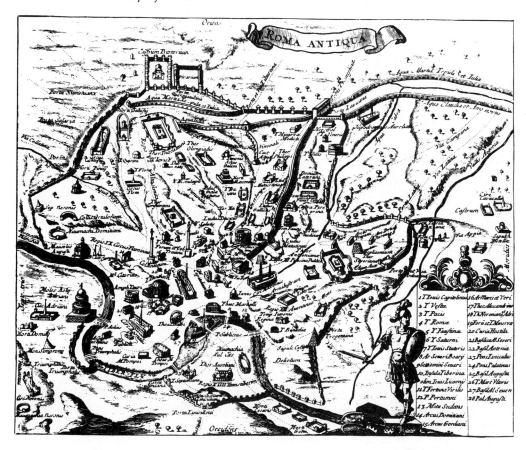

Grammatical Index

"Rident
stolidi verba
Latina."